MANHATTAN
THE BRONX
W 155th St.
W 145th St.
Harlem River Dr.
HARLEM
W 125th St.
7th Avenue
Lenox Avenue
Broadway
Henry Hudson Pkwy.
MANHATTAN
Park Avenue
2nd Avenue
1st Avenue
Amsterdam Ave.
Central Park
E 106th St.
Hudson River
UPPER WEST SIDE
E 96th St.
5th Avenue
W 81st St.
Metropolitan Museum of Art
E 86th St.
E 84th St.
UPPER EAST SIDE
Lincoln Center
Broadway
E 79th St.
E Park Avenue
3rd Avenue
2nd Avenue
1st Avenue
E 66th St.
10th Avenue
9th Avenue
Central Park S.
Lincoln Tunnel
Museum of Modern Art
Rockefeller Center
QUEENS
W 42nd St.
12th Avenue
Avenue of the Americas
5th Avenue
Lexington Avenue
Queensboro Bridge
Times Square
Grand Central Station
W 34th St.
Chrysler Building
High Line
E 42nd St.
MIDTOWN
United Nations
Empire State Building
Queens Midtown Tunnel
NEW JERSEY
9th Avenue
8th Avenue
7th Avenue
Broadway
W 14th St.
E 23rd St.
West Side Highway
Bleecker St.
Greenwich Village
E 14th St.
Holland Tunnel
Hudson St.
Soho
Broadway
Avenue D
LOWER WEST SIDE
Broome St.
Little Italy
E Houston St.
East River
Canal St.
LOWER EAST SIDE
Chinatown
Bowery
Williamsburg Bridge
One World Trade Center
Wall St.
FDR Drive
Brooklyn Bridge
Manhattan Bridge
ELLIS ISLAND
Brooklyn Battery Tunnel
LIBERTY ISLAND
Statue of Liberty
BROOKLYN

NEW YORK CITY
Van Cortlandt Park
THE BRONX
NY Botanical Garden
Long Island Sound
Teterboro Airport
The Cloisters
Bronx Zoo
Yankee Stadium
Hudson River
Harlem
Bronx-Whitestone Bridge
East River
Throgs Neck Bridge
Rikers Island
MANHATTAN
Central Park
La Guardia Airport
Metropolitan Museum of Art
Flushing
Long Island City
Rockefeller Center
Grand Central Station
Louis Armstrong House
Citi Field
Flushing Meadow
New York Hall of Science
Amphitheater
Corona Park
NEWARK
East River
JERSEY CITY
One World Trade Center
Forest Hills Tennis Stadium
Jamaica
Williamsburg
Newark Airport
Ellis Island
Brooklyn Bridge
Forest Park
Golf Course
QUEENS
Statue of Liberty
Governor's Island
Flatbush
East New York
Newark Bay
Brooklyn Museum
Prospect Park
Upper Bay
Spring Creek Park
Children's Museum
Postcards 9/11 Memorial
BROOKLYN
John F. Kennedy International Airport
The Narrows
Clove Lakes Park
Dyker Beach Park
Jamaica Bay
Richmond
Verrazano-Narrows Bridge
Brooklyn Marine Park
US Naval Air Station
Lower Bay
Long Beach
STATEN ISLAND
Coney Island
Rockaway Inlet
Richmondtown
Rockaway Point
Great Kills Park
Crooke's Point
Conference House
Atlantic Ocean
Raritan Bay
NORTH
WEST
EAST
SOUTH
0 1 2 3 4 5 km
0 1 2 3 miles

Blue Line 4

für Klasse 8

Das Lehrbuch versteht sich als Gesamtangebot. Welche Texte und Aufgaben verpflichtend sind, wird durch die schulinternen Curricula festgelegt.

1. Auflage 1 7 6 5 | 23 22 21

Herausgeber: Dr. Frank Haß, Kirchberg
Autorinnen und Autoren: Chris Caridia, London sowie
Jo Cummins, London; Wolfgang Hamm, Marktredwitz; Konstanze Zander, Großenehrich
Beratung: Brunhilde Biek, Leonberg; Karin Braun, Dortmund; Wilma Brings, Bedburg; Amanda Chisnell, Lollar; Sara Conway, Stuttgart; Ulf Degen, Braunschweig; Tanja Frank, Ulm; Sandra Haberland, Recklinghausen; Wolfgang Hamm, Marktredwitz; Ulrike Heringhaus, Altheim; Michael Herrmann, Ludwigsfelde; Christa Kathmann-Fuhrmann, Bonn; Dr. Margitta Kuty, Greifswald-Eldna; Grit Machut, Berlin; Michael Meisenzahl, Karlstadt; Beatrix Pierce, Eppingen; Annegret Preker-Franke, Bielefeld; Dr. Hubert Schwandt, Parchen; Christian Straukamp, Nordhorn; Ines van Hove, Oldenburg; Dieter Vilimek, Helmstadt-Bargen

Redaktion: Ulrike Beutel; Joanne Popp; Dr. Susanne Dyka, Nürnberg; Birgit Piefke-Wagner, Korntal-Münchingen
Herstellung: Ulrike Wursthorn

Umschlaggestaltung und Gestaltungskonzept: know idea, Freiburg; Koma Amok, Stuttgart
Umschlagfoto: Getty Images (Photolibrary/Nick Daly), München; Getty Images (The Image Bank), München
Illustrationen: Marek Blaha, Offenbach; Kirill Chudinskiy, Köln sowie
Friederike Ablang, Berlin; Iris Blanck, Hamburg; Martina Burghardt-Vollhardt, Kamenz; Udo Clormann, Wiesbaden; Christian Dekelver, Weinstadt, Thorsten Droessler, Leipzig; Andreas Florian, Lübeck; Anke Fröhlich, Leipzig; Carolin Görtler, Immenstadt im Allgäu; Josef Hammen, Trierweiler; Christian Hansen, Berlin; Rob Harvey, Cirencester, GB; Carmen Hochmann, Bielefeld; Martin Hoffmann, Stuttgart; Yvonne Hoppe-Engbring, Steinfurt; Steffen Jähde, Sundhagen; Klett Archiv, Stuttgart; Hendrik Kranenberg, Drolshagen; Jeongsook Lee, Köln; Katja Leuschner, Halle; Helga Merkle, Albershausen; Lutz-Erich Müller, Leipzig; Axel Nicolai, Brauweiler; David Norman, Meerbusch; Liliane Oser, Hamburg; Sven Palmowski, Barcelona, Spain; Katja Rau, Fellbach; Anja Rieger, Berlin; Annika Sauerborn, Mainz; Sandra Schmidt, Berlin; Carolin Ina Schröter, Berlin; Friederike Schumann, Berlin; Birgit Tanck, Hamburg; Inge Voets, Berlin; Sylvia Wolf, Wiesbaden; Katrin Wolff, Wiesbaden; Steffen Wolff, Brohl-Lützing; Dorothee Wolters, Köln

Satz: Satzkiste GmbH, Stuttgart
Reproduktion: Schwabenrepro GmbH, Stuttgart
Druck: Mohn Media Mohndruck GmbH, Gütersloh

Printed in Germany
ISBN 978-3-12-547874-9 (fester Einband)
ISBN 978-3-12-548874-8 (flexibler Einband)

9 783125 478749

9 783125 488748

Blue Line 4

Herausgeber: Dr. Frank Haß

Ernst Klett Verlag
Stuttgart • Leipzig

Inhalt

	Kompetenzen / Themen / Ich kann ...	Fertigkeiten	Seite
Zoom in	**The USA** Informationen über die USA	L, S, I	8

Unit 1: Gateway NYC

Way in	**... Informationen über New York verstehen.** *One World Trade Center is the tallest building on the NYC skyline.*	L, S, V, I	12
Station 1	**... interessante Orte einer Stadt präsentieren.** *You can get a very good look at the New York skyline from here.* Sehenswürdigkeiten – revision: simple past	L, R, S, I	14
Station 2	**... einen Artikel über eine Person schreiben.** *My dad had arrived in New York two years before I came.* In ein fremdes Land gehen – past perfect	L, S, I	18
Reading corner	**... einen Text über die Geschichte der Einwanderung verstehen.**	R	22
Mediation	**... Informationen über Einbürgerung weitergeben.**	W, R, I	24
Film corner	**... einen Film über Sehenswürdigkeiten in New York verstehen.**	S, V, I	25
Checkpoint	**... Wissen und Strategien anwenden; den Lernstand überprüfen.**		26
Extra practice	*Wissen wiederholen und festigen*		28
Internet research skills	Tipps und Strategien zur Internetrecherche	R, I	30

Unit 2: Teens in the Midwest

Way in	**... Informationen über den Mittleren Westen verstehen.** *In Tornado Alley there can be terrible storms.*	L, S, V, I	32
Station 1	**... das Schulleben in den USA und in Deutschland vergleichen.** *You weren't allowed to keep things in the classrooms.* Schulen in anderen Ländern – modal auxiliaries and their substitutes	L, S, R, W, I	34
Station 2	**... über Schülerjobs sprechen.** *What will you do if you are late? If you have any questions, I'll help you. Be more responsible.* Schülerjobs – revision: if-clauses I	L, S, R, W, I	38
Reading corner	**... einen Comic über das Highschool-Leben verstehen.**	S, R, W	42
Mediation	**... Informationen über den Führerschein weitergeben.**	S, I	44
Film corner	**... einen Film über den ersten Tag an einer neuen Schule verstehen.**	S, V, I	45
Checkpoint	**... Wissen und Strategien anwenden; den Lernstand überprüfen.**		46
Extra practice	*Wissen wiederholen und festigen*		48
Presentation skills	Tipps und Strategien zur Erstellung einer Präsentation	S	50

L = Listening S = Speaking R = Reading W = Writing V = Viewing I = Intercultural

	Kompetenzen / Themen / Ich kann ...	Fertigkeiten	Seite

Unit 3: In the Northeast

Way in	**... Informationen über den Nordosten der USA verstehen.** *Here you can visit the amazing Niagara Falls.*	L, S, V, I	52
Station 1	**... einen Text ausdrucksstark vorlesen.** *What's up? Thanks so much for inviting me.* Small Talk – revision: questions	L, S, R, W, I	54
Station 2	**... meine Meinung sagen und begründen.** *I really like that. If I had a car, I would drive around town.* Zustimmen und Ablehnen – revision: if-clauses II	L, S, R, I	58
Reading corner	**... eine Geschichte über Freunde verstehen.**	R, I	62
Mediation	**... Informationen über Reisemöglichkeiten weitergeben.**	I	66
Film corner	**... einen Film über Thanksgiving verstehen.**	S, V, I	67
Checkpoint	**... Wissen und Strategien anwenden; den Lernstand überprüfen.**		68
Extra practice	*Wissen wiederholen und festigen*		70
Writing skills	Tipps und Strategien zum Schreiben einer Zusammenfassung	W	72

Unit 4: California dreams

Way in	**... Informationen über Kalifornien und den Westen der USA verstehen.** *People live a relaxed lifestyle here.*	L, S, V, I	74
Station 1	**... eine Werbeanzeige gestalten.** *A surfer is standing next to a small bus. It's always a lot sunnier and warmer here.* Eine Region präsentieren – revision: simple present/present progressive	L, S, W	76
Station 2	**... über Trends sprechen.** *I've had an account since I was 13. But why have they been so successful?* Trends – revision: present perfect	L, S, R, I	80
Reading corner	**... einen Text über den Goldrausch verstehen.**	S, R, I	84
Mediation	**... Informationen über Kinderarbeit weitergeben.**	I	88
Film corner	**... einen Film über Beruf und Karriere verstehen.**	S, V, I	89
Checkpoint	**... Wissen und Strategien anwenden; den Lernstand überprüfen.**		90
Extra practice	*Wissen wiederholen und festigen*		92
Communication skills	Tipps und Strategien zur Gesprächsführung	S	94

L = Listening S = Speaking R = Reading W = Writing V = Viewing I = Intercultural

	Kompetenzen / Themen / Ich kann …	Fertigkeiten	Seite
Unit 5: Southern life			
Way in	**… Informationen über die Südstaaten der USA verstehen.** *The South has its own lifestyle with its own culture and customs.*	L, S, V, I	**96**
Station 1	**… über Einflüsse verschiedener Kulturen im täglichen Leben sprechen.** *The dish is made with chicken. The city was founded by the French.* Multikulturelles Leben – passive voice	S, R, W, I	**98**
Station 2	**… andere über Freizeitaktivitäten informieren.** *He says the jungle trail sounds really interesting too. He wants to know if your dad can take us to the Everglades another time.* Einen Ausflug planen – reported speech	L, S, R	**102**
Reading corner	**… eine Geschichte über Rassismus verstehen.**	R, S, W, I	**106**
Mediation	**… Informationen über Rituale weitergeben.**	I	**108**
Film corner	**… einen Film über die Sommerferien verstehen.**	S, V, I	**109**
Checkpoint	**… Wissen und Strategien anwenden; den Lernstand überprüfen.**		**110**
Extra practice	*Wissen wiederholen und festigen*		**112**

L = Listening S = Speaking R = Reading W = Writing V = Viewing I = Intercultural

	Kompetenzen / Themen / Ich kann ...	Fertigkeiten	Seite
D Diff corner	Parallelaufgaben zu den Units 1–5 auf leichterem Niveau		**114**
	Vertiefung landeskundlicher Aspekte der Units 1–5 (More about ...)		**134**
E Extra	When the earth shakes (Projekt: Geografie)	R	**144**
	Static electricity (Projekt: Physik)	R	**146**
	The Absolutely True Diary of a Part-Time Indian (Romanauszug)	R	**148**
	Deep water (Romanauszug)	R	**152**
G Grammar	Übungen mit Lösungen (Seite 293)		**156**
M Methods	Anleitung für schüleraktivierende Methoden		**172**
V Vocabulary	Vocabulary tips		**178**
	Vocabulary (Unitbegleitendes Vokabular)		**180**
	Instructions (Arbeitsanweisungen mit Operatoren)		**215**
	Classroom phrases		**216**
	List of irregular verbs		**217**
	Dictionary (Wörterbuch Deutsch – Englisch, Englisch – Deutsch)		**220**

So lernst du mit Blue Line

Hier zeige ich dir, wie du dich in deinem Buch gut zurechtfindest. Das Buch hat fünf Units (Kapitel). Jede Unit ist gleich aufgebaut.

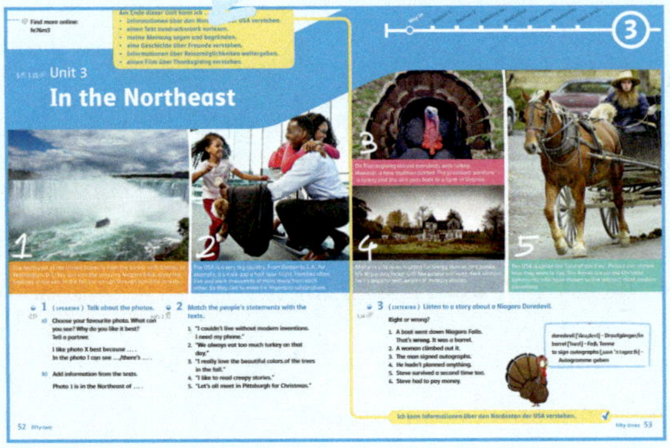

Way in

Hier steigst du in das neue Thema ein. Dazu gibt es auch einen kurzen Film.

Im gelben Kasten siehst du, was du in der *Unit* lernst.

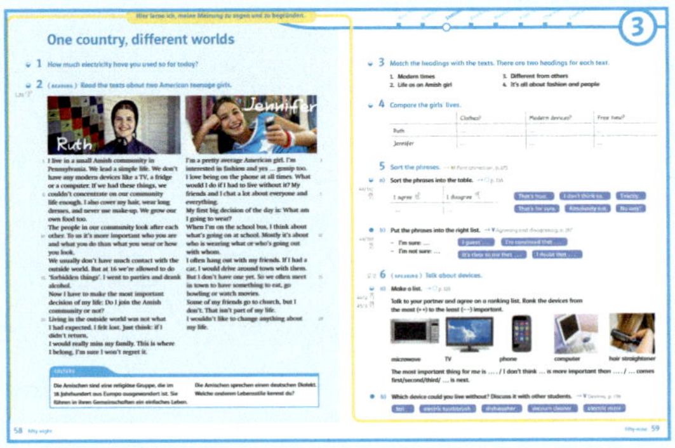

Stations

In jeder *Unit* gibt es zwei *Stations*, in denen du viele neue Dinge lernst. Diese Symbole zeigen dir, wie schwer die Übung ist und ob es im Anhang eine leichtere Variante gibt:

◒ → ○ p. 131, ●

In der *Your turn*-Aufgabe kannst du zeigen, dass du alles verstanden hast, und deine eigenen Ideen einbringen.

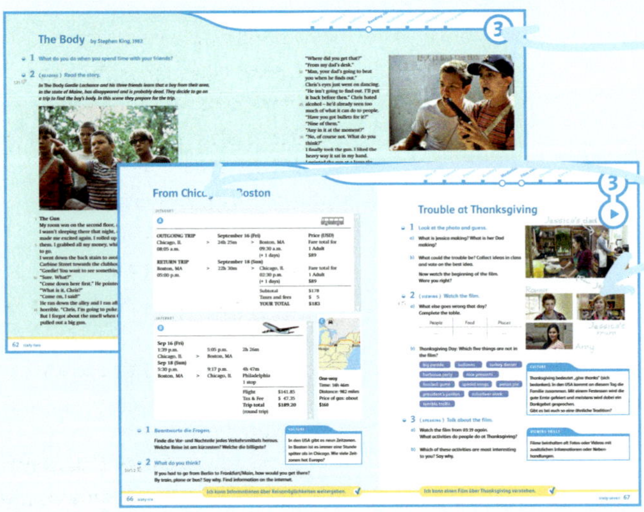

Reading corner

In der *Reading corner* gibt es verschiedene Geschichten und Sachtexte.

Mediation/Film corner

Auf der linken Seite geht es darum, englische Informationen auf Deutsch weiterzugeben oder umgekehrt.

In der *Film corner* geht es um einen englischen Film.

Checkpoint

Auf dieser Seite kannst du überprüfen, ob du in der *Unit* alles verstanden hast. In der *Checklist* sind alle Lernziele noch einmal aufgelistet.

Die Abschluss-Aufgabe (*task*) sollt ihr zu zweit oder in der Gruppe lösen.

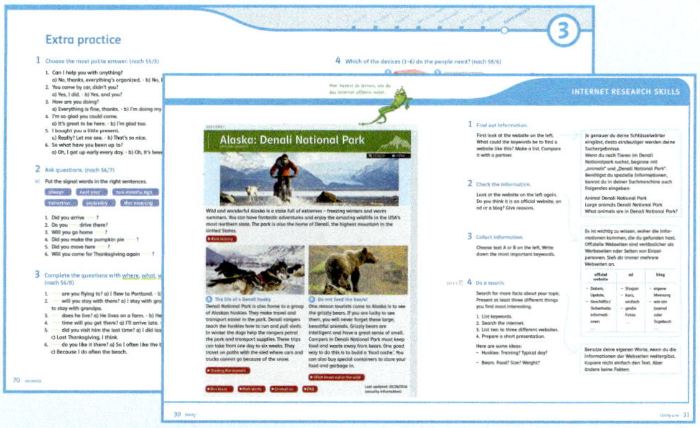

Extra practice

Hier findest du zwei Seiten mit Zusatz-Aufgaben, z. B. zur Vorbereitung auf die Klassenarbeit.

Skills

Auf einige *Units* folgt eine Doppelseite, auf der du eine bestimmte Fertigkeit (*skill*) besonders trainieren kannst, also z. B. das Lesen, Schreiben, Sprechen oder die Wörterbucharbeit.

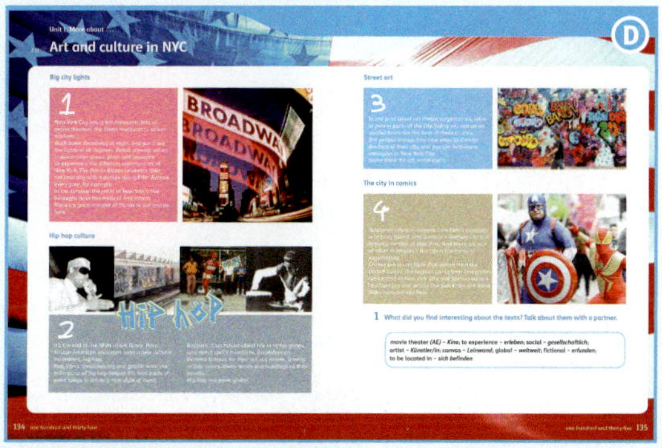

More about

Hier findest du interessante weiterführende Informationen zur Region der Unit.

Im Anschluss an die fünf *Units* gibt es noch weitere nützliche Seiten:

Extra: Hier erwarten dich weitere Lesetexte und vieles mehr.

Grammar: Hier findest du alle Regeln und Erklärungen zur Grammatik sowie weitere Übungen.

Methods: Manche Übungen könnt ihr auf eine bestimmte Art und Weise bearbeiten. Das erkennt ihr an diesem Symbol: → M
Wie es genau funktioniert, kannst du hier nachlesen.

Vocabulary: Im *Vocabulary* findest du alle neuen Wörter in der Reihenfolge, in der sie in der *Unit* auftauchen, und die wichtigsten Arbeitsanweisungen.
Im *Dictionary* sind die Wörter noch einmal alphabetisch aufgelistet: zuerst Englisch-Deutsch und dann Deutsch-Englisch.

Am Schluss des Buches findest du noch
- Sätze, die du im Unterricht sagen kannst, z. B. bei der Gruppenarbeit
- Lösungen zu den Übungen der *Extra practice*-Seiten
- eine Liste mit den unregelmäßigen Verben.

Symbol	Erklärung
○ ◒ ●	leicht/mittel/schwer (Niveaudifferenzierung)
✿	individualisierende Aufgabe (natürliche Differenzierung)
→ ○ p. 131	Verweis auf leichtere Parallelübung auf der *Diff corner*-Seite
OR	Aufgabe zur Auswahl (Wahldifferenzierung)
🔑	Entwicklung von Schlüsselkompetenzen
P	Hier entsteht ein Produkt für das Portfolio.
4/1	Verweis auf eine Übung im *Workbook*
→ G6, p. 163	Verweis auf den Grammatikanhang (*Grammar*)
→ M	Verweis auf die Methodenseite (*Methods*)
→ V	Verweis zum Wortfeld im Vokabular (*Vocabulary*)
	Partnerarbeit
	Gruppenarbeit
	Verweis auf die Lehrer-CD (Audio)
	Verweis auf die Lehrer-DVD (Film)
Find more online:	Code auf www.klett.de eingeben und Zusatzinformationen erhalten

Zoom in – The USA

Every year in fall the New England states shine in bright colors.

1

Denali (Mt. McKinley) is the highest mountain in Alaska and North America (6,190m).

4

flag

rose

bald eagle

Name:	United States of America	**Capital:**	Washington D.C.
Population:	≈ 321,400,000 (July 2015)	**States:**	50
Area (total):	≈ 9,800,000 km² (≈ 3,600,000 sq.mi.) (3rd largest country in the world)	**Time zones:**	9
Currency:	US dollar	**Major rivers:**	Mississippi, Missouri, Colorado
		Mountains:	Rocky Mountains, Appalachian Mountains

The Midwest is a huge open area with lots of corn and soybean fields.

2

Hawaii is a surfer's paradise with perfect waves and white and black beaches.

3

Most parts of the Rocky Mountains are protected. Lots of tourists enjoy the beautiful landscape.

5

In some parts of the American South there are swamps where alligators live.

6

1 Look at the photos and read the texts.

What parts of the USA would you like to visit? Say why.

2 Look at the map at the back of the book. Find the answers.

1. Name the countries that are north and south of the USA.
2. Name the oceans that are east and west of the USA.
3. Name the sea that's south of the states of Louisiana, Mississippi and Alabama.
4. Name the state that's in the Pacific Ocean, southwest of California.
5. Name the state that's to the northwest of Canada.
6. Find out the distances from north to south and east to west.

3 Look at the photos and choose one of the places.

Find out more about it on the internet. Present some interesting facts to the class.

1

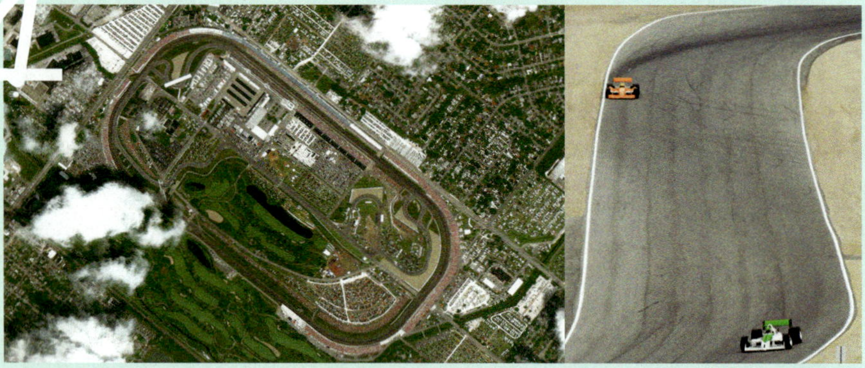

2

4

5

7

8

1. Indiana: Indy 500
2. Kentucky: Fort Knox
3. Pennsylvania: Declaration of Independence
4. Washington: Space Needle, Seattle

3

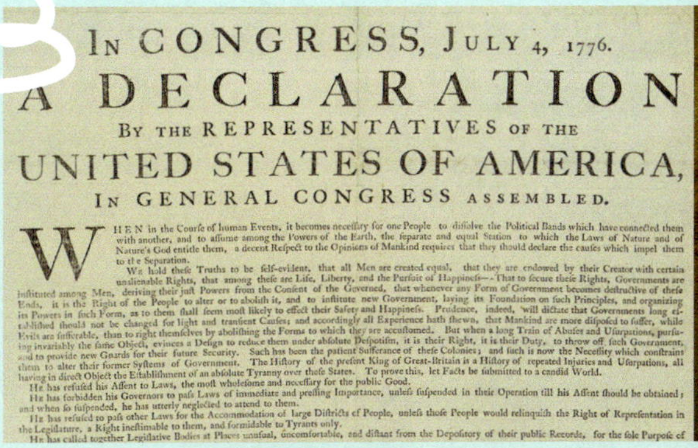

6

9

5. North Dakota: Sitting Bull
6. Alabama: US Space & Rocket Center, Huntsville
7. Colorado: Mesa Verde
8. Nevada: Las Vegas
9. New Mexico: Very Large Array

Find more online:
fe76m3

Am Ende dieser Unit kann ich ...
- Informationen über New York verstehen.
- interessante Orte einer Stadt präsentieren.
- einen Artikel über eine Person schreiben.
- einen Text über die Geschichte der Einwanderung verstehen.
- Informationen über Einbürgerung weitergeben.
- einen Film über Sehenswürdigkeiten in New York verstehen.

1 1,1

Unit 1

Gateway NYC

New York City (NYC) is the biggest city in the United States. Over eight and a half million people live in five boroughs: The Bronx, Brooklyn, Queens, Manhattan and Staten Island.

One World Trade Center (OWTC) is the tallest building on the New York city skyline and in the USA. It replaced the old World Trade Center after the attacks on September 11, 2001.

1 Collect the information.

2/1

a) Before you read: What do you know about New York City? Make a mind map.

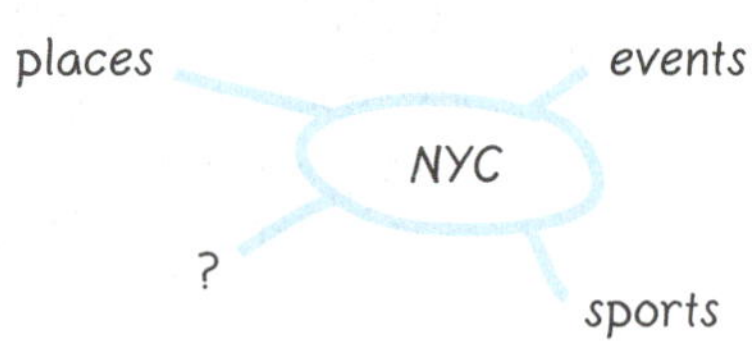

b) Read the texts. Add the information to your mind map.

2 Correct the wrong sentences.

2/2

1. There are eight boroughs in New York City.
2. OWTC is the smallest building in the USA.
3. People in New York like baseball very much.
4. NYC is an important cultural center.
5. The Statue of Liberty was made in the USA.

Baseball is one of the most popular sports in the USA, and New Yorkers love it. Some players are really big stars.

New York is an important center for music, theater, dance and art. It's home to many modern American cultural movements.

The Statue of Liberty was a present from France to celebrate 100 years of American independence. For immigrants it became a symbol of hope.

3 (LISTENING) Listen to a guided tour of One World Trade Center.

1,2

Choose the right answer.

1. On September 11, 2001 a plane hit the building • a train arrived at the building.
2. Two million • Two billion people saw the events on TV.
3. OWTC is 1,735 feet • 1,776 feet tall.
4. A movie shows the visitors the history of the USA • the history of NYC.
5. The elevators produce electricity • light.
6. OWTC is important to remember November 11 • September 11.

billion [ˈbɪliən] – Milliarde
event [ɪˈvent] – Ereignis
feet [fiːt] – Fuß (Maßeinheit)
elevator [ˈelɪveɪtə] – Aufzug; Lift
top [tɒp] – Spitze
grounds [graʊndz] – *hier*: Gelände

Ich kann Informationen über New York verstehen. ✓

A taxi ride in NYC

1 (READING) Read the text.

1,3 3/1

David Singh: A traffic jam! It's always bad during rush hour. Last Monday they started roadwork. It's even worse in winter. Did you know that it gets very cold here? We had so much snow. I didn't get into the city. I live in Queens, but I work in Manhattan because that's where the money is!
Anyway, you can get a very good look at the New York skyline from here.
It's never boring – let me tell you about the landmarks. That's One World Trade Center. Those skyscrapers over there are on Wall Street, the financial center of the world. Can you see the Empire State Building? They built it in the 1930s. With its 102 stories it was the tallest building in the world. The view of Manhattan from the top is really something.
If you only have one day in NYC: buy a sandwich and a drink and go for a walk in Central Park. There are lakes, playgrounds, a zoo and lots more.
Then take the subway at 86th Street and Lexington Avenue to Grand Central Station. When you're in there, look up. The star signs on the ceiling aren't right. I have no idea why. Around the corner there's a hot dog cart. It belongs to my friend Nick. Remember the name – he makes the best hot dogs in New York. Finish the day with a Broadway show. Make sure you walk far enough to get to Times Square too.
At last, the lights are green again.

2 Collect the information. → M Think-pair-share, p. 177

a) Answer the questions.

1. What's David's job?
2. What is he talking about? Give examples.

b) Make a list of the places or buildings from the text. Find them on the map of NYC at the front of your book.

CULTURE

Man kann sich in Manhattan nicht verlaufen, wenn man auf die Straßennamen achtet. Avenues verlaufen von Nord nach Süd; Streets von Ost nach West. Woher haben Straßen bei euch ihre Namen?

David Singh

3 Right or wrong? Find it in the text. → M Peer correction, p. 175

1. The traffic is bad during rush hour.
   That's right. (line 1) "It's always bad during rush hour."
2. David lives in Manhattan.
3. They built the Empire State Building in the 1960s.
4. There's a zoo in Central Park.
5. Nick makes the best hot dogs in New York.
6. The lights are still red at the end.

4 Work with the city words.

a) Find one or more words from the text. → ○ p. 114

1. street • road • …
2. skyscraper • building • …
3. taxi • traffic jam • …
4. park • lake • …
5. take the subway • get into the city • …

b) Match the words with their definitions. → V City words, p. 183

parking lot | commuter | construction site | suburbs

1. a place where they are building something
2. people live here, away from the city center
3. you can leave your car there
4. a person who travels to work every day

3/2
5 (SPEAKING) Act as a guide.

3/3a)
a) Present what is on the map. → ○ p. 114

Over there you can see …

Don't miss …

Right ahead …

Just around this corner we'll come to …

You must visit …

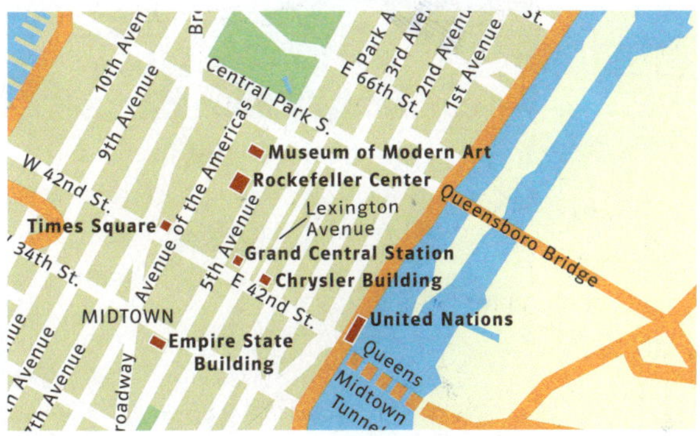

3/3b)
b) Show a visitor places in your town. Bring a map or photos. → V City guide, p. 187

Have a look at … | In the distance you can see … | From here … | Make sure you visit …

CULTURE

Ein paar Wörter unterscheiden sich im britischen und amerikanischen Englisch. Schreibweise und Aussprache sind manchmal auch anders. Viele Sprecher mischen britisches und amerikanisches Englisch.

British	American
car park	parking lot
town centre	downtown
lift	elevator
holidays	vacation

Language → G1, p. 158

Last Monday they started roadwork here.
We had so much snow.
I didn't get into the city.
Did you know that it gets very cold here?

Welche Zeitform ist das?
Wann benutzt du sie?

6 Complete the sentences. → M Bus stop, p. 172

4/4

1. It — eight years to build the OWTC. (take)
2. The Brooklyn Bridge — on May 24, 1883. (open)
3. In 2001 two planes — the World Trade Center. (hit)
4. The Statute of Liberty — a present from France. (be)
5. In the 1980s Central Park — a very safe place. (not be)
6. Two years ago the traffic in New York — because of heavy snow. (not move)

I was in NY.
I wasn't in LA.
Were you there?

7 (WRITING) Tell the taxi driver's story.

a) Make two sentences for each picture. Use the words for help. → ○ p. 114

4/5a)

1. be at the airport • get in

2. be cold • heavy snow

3. talk to • be in a traffic jam

4. not take with her • find it

5. not see her • look for her

6. give back • be happy

1. Last winter I was at the airport. A woman …

b) Write an ending for the story. Here's an idea:

4/5b)

Versuche, einzelne Sätze mit „then“, „later“, „suddenly“ usw. zu verbinden.

4/6
5/7

8 (SPEAKING) What did they do at One World Trade Center yesterday?

a) Ask and answer questions about the people in the picture. → ○ p. 115

drink | eat | look at | phone | take a photo | sit

A: What did Henry eat? – B: He ate a sandwich.
B: Did Susan take a photo? – A: No, she didn't. She …

b) Now Partner B closes his or her book. Partner A asks questions. Then take turns.

5/8

A: Did Lisa eat a sandwich? – B: No, she didn't. Henry ate the sandwich.
A: What did Henry do? – B: Henry …

9 (YOUR TURN) New York City landmarks → V City guide, p. 187

Choose **two** of the five boroughs of New York.
Find out information about the landmarks there in the library or on the internet:

- Where is it?
- What is it?
- What can you do or see there?
- When was it built?
- When did it open?
- …

Imagine you are in NY. Present the landmarks of your boroughs. You can use the phrases from Ex. 15/5. → M Tip top, p. 177

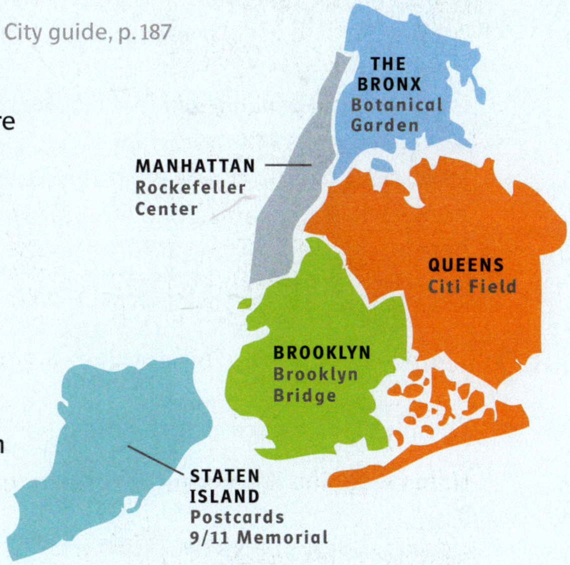

STUDY SKILLS

Oft stehen im Text mehr Information als du brauchst. Konzentriere dich bei deiner Suche auf die Fakten, die du wirklich für deine Präsentation benötigst.

Ich kann interessante Orte einer Stadt präsentieren. ✓

Hier lerne ich, einen Artikel über eine Person zu schreiben.

Living the dream?

1 (READING) Read the interview with José Blanco.

1,4 6/1

Interviewer: Hello José. Can I ask you some questions for our magazine, please?
José: Hi. Sure.
Interviewer: You're new on the baseball team. Are you happy?
José: Yes, I am.
Interviewer: When did you immigrate from Cuba to the USA?
José: I arrived with my mom and sisters when I was ten. My dad had arrived in New York two years before I came.
Interviewer: That was a big decision for your parents. They left their home and moved to a foreign place.
José: Yes, and they were very poor. My father hadn't had a job for a long time. My parents wanted to give my sisters and me the best chances.
Interviewer: What were the first years like?
José: My parents had problems because they hadn't learned English. But there's a strong community. So my parents opened a small shop.
Interviewer: How did you feel? Had you ever seen skyscrapers before?
José: No, I hadn't. It was exciting. Later I was homesick. But I knew I had a better future here.
Interviewer: When did you start your career?
José: I hadn't taken baseball seriously before I was 15. Then I wanted to be successful. I think people who leave their countries are usually motivated. After I had become the star of my team in high school, I had lots of opportunities.
Interviewer: You've been successful!
José: Yes, I have. For most people it's much harder. My story is a perfect example of the American Dream.
Interviewer: So, what about your plans?
José: I have become a US citizen. But I talk to people in Cuba, and I plan to help them.
Interviewer: Thank you. All my best wishes.

CULTURE

Der amerikanische Traum besagt, dass jeder Mensch durch harte Arbeit ein erfolgreiches Leben führen kann. Ist es bei euch möglich, sich vom „Tellerwäscher" zum Millionär hochzuarbeiten?

2 Collect facts about José and his family.

a) Complete the fact card. Take notes. → ○ p. 116 → M Think-pair-share, p. 177

Name: —
From: —
Lives in: —
Family: —
Reasons why they emigrated: —
Career: —

STUDY SKILLS

Halte deine Notizen so kurz wie möglich. Schreibe nur Schlüsselwörter auf.

b) What do you think? How did José feel when he came to NY? How does he feel now?

3 (LISTENING) Listen to the interview with Angela.

1,5

Complete the sentences.

1. When Angela was —— , her mother sent her to live in the USA.
2. Her —— is a good man.
3. It was very hard to make —— .
4. She has a visa now, and a —— . She goes to college too.
5. She would really like to become an American —— .

4 Imagine you want to leave your country.

6/4

a) Complete the sentences with these words. → p. 117

6/2

immigrate · get used to · cross the border · emigrate from · opportunities · feel foreign

1. I will have many —— .

2. I want to —— to the USA.

3. I want to —— by car.

4. I will —— my new life soon.

5. I want to —— Mexico.

6. I will —— .

b) Make your own sentences. You can draw pictures for each sentence too.
→ V Going to a new country, p. 184

6/3

succeed in · fail at · get support from · have the right papers

5 (SONG) Empire State of Mind (Part II) Broken Down

1,6

Listen to the song. What can you find out about New York?

Ooooh, New York!
Ooooh, New York!

Grew up in a town that is famous as a place of movie scenes.
Noise is always loud, there are sirens all around and the streets are mean.
If I can make it here, I can make it anywhere, that's what they say.
Seeing my face in lights or my name in marquees found down on Broadway.
Even if it ain't all it seems, I got a pocketful of dreams.

Language detectives → G2, p. 159

I hadn't taken any sports seriously before I was 15.
After I had become the star of the my team in high school,
I had lots of opportunities.
Had you ever seen skyscrapers before? – No, I hadn't.

Das simple past und past perfect beschreiben Ereignisse in der Vergangenheit.
Was liegt weiter zurück? Welche Zeitform benutzt du dafür?
Welche Wörter zeigen an, welches Ereignis zuerst passiert ist?

6 Choose before or after?

7/5-7

1. We joined my dad	before	he had lived in New York for two years.
2. I had never visited the USA	after	I came to live here.
3. I hadn't spoken English very often		I moved to New York.
4. My dad opened his own shop		he hadn't found a job.
5. I started to play baseball		I had been in school for a year.
6. My grandma had died		I left for the USA.

1. We joined my dad after he had lived in New York for two years.

7 (WRITING) Write about one of Angela's days.

a) Make sentences with the simple past and the past perfect. → ○ p. 117

8/8

After …

buy a present

take the subway home

visit Ellis Island

Before …

order a milkshake

put on their fan T-shirts

invite to party
walk through park
buy tickets
eat pizza
go to stadium

1. After Pablo had invited Angela to his party, she bought a present.
4. Before Angela ate some pizza, she had … .

Die Liste mit den unregelmäßigen Verben findest du auf S. 216.

b) Make more sentences about Angela.

8/9

1. about the party. • Before • she had asked Pablo • she went to work,
2. she had left • and she closed • the windows. • the house, • After • she went back

8 (SPEAKING) Ask and answer questions.

a) What had José done before his first important baseball game? What hadn't he done? Ask questions and answer them. → ○ p. 118

8/10

1. Interviewer: Had you played every day before your first big game?
   José: Yes, I had.
2. Interviewer: Had you …
   José: …

1. play every day ✓
2. buy new sports shoes
3. order tickets for his friends ✓
4. watch the other team ✓
5. phone his dad ✓
6. go to bed early

b) What would you ask Angela? Here are some ideas:

Before you left the Philippines, … ask friends for advice? | plan a party? | be to the USA? | … ?

9 (YOUR TURN) A magazine article

→ V Presenting personal information, p. 188
→ M Writers' conference, p. 177

9/1

Use the information on page 18/Ex. 2 to write an article about José.

A Cuban-American success story

José Blanco is a baseball player with a big future – that's what half of our readers tell us. José immigrated to the USA with his parents when …

His name …
He is from …
He immigrated to … when …
His parents were …
José now lives in …
He started to play … when …

WRITING SKILLS

Sammle zuerst alle Fakten, über die du gerne schreiben würdest.
Strukturiere dann deinen Text.
Schreibe …
- eine kurze Einleitung, mit denen du die Wh-Fragen (Who? What? When? Where? Why?) beantwortest,
- den Hauptteil, in dem du mehr Details zur Person gibst,
- ein interessantes Ende.

Finde dann eine Überschrift.
Überprüfe zum Schluss noch einmal deinen Text.

Ich kann einen Artikel über eine Person schreiben. ✓

Ellis Island – a symbol of immigration

1 Why do people leave their country? → M Think-pair-share, p. 177

2 (READING) Read the text.

1,7

The United States is a country of immigrants. You can learn about them in the museum on Ellis Island. Between 1892 and 1954 Ellis Island was the most important gateway for twelve million immigrants. In the Family History Center visitors can look at millions of lists and find out more about their personal family history.
Families often saved money for the father or oldest son to make the journey. Statistics show that they sent for the rest of the family when they had a home and a job.
The voyage on ship took seven to 21 days. But conditions were very hard on board. Poor immigrants had to stay in a crowded, dirty space. There was bad food and very little fresh air. At the end of the long trip the majority of them were sick.
However, their journey was not over after they had arrived. Before they could leave the ship, doctors came on board to check the passengers. After this, the ship moved into the harbor. The first thing that the people saw was the Statue of Liberty. "Nobody said a word," said one immigrant. "She was the symbol of the big, powerful country which was our future home."
After the ship had arrived in Manhattan, they went to Ellis Island on a small boat. Here there were more checks and personal interviews. If the doctors found any diseases or the immigrants were too weak to work, they sent them back to their home countries. About two percent had to return. A minority of about 20 percent stayed on the island for days or sometimes weeks for more checks, but the rest could leave after a few hours.
The immigrants' journey to the USA, which had started months or years before, was now over. But they still had a long way to go.

3 Answer the questions about Ellis Island.

1. How many immigrants came to Ellis Island between 1892 to 1954?
2. How long was the voyage?
3. What were the conditions on the ships like?
4. Why did doctors come on board?
5. What happened on Ellis Island?
6. How many percent had to return?

CULTURE

Jeder, der in den USA geboren wird, hat automatisch die amerikanische Staatsbürgerschaft und einen amerikanischen Pass.
Wie ist das in deinem Land?

Immigration to the USA

From the 1840s to the 1890s most immigrants came from Britain, Ireland, Scandinavia and Germany.
Between the 1890s and the 1920s the majority of immigrants came from Italy, Greece, Eastern Europe, Russia and Turkey. They came for religious or political freedom, or to find work and escape poverty.

Immigration to the USA today: 2013 (in millions)

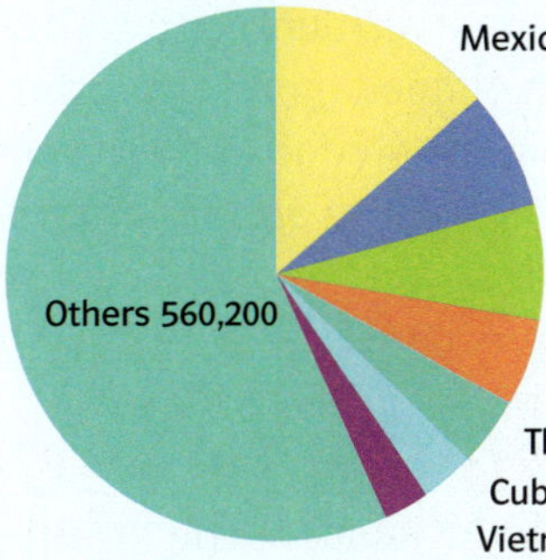

Source: Department of Homeland Security

READING SKILLS

Wenn du ein Kreisdiagramm liest, sieh dir die Beschriftungen genau an. Achte auf die unterschiedlichen Größen der einzelnen Abschnitte innerhalb des Diagramms.

4 Find the facts in the box.

a) Why did people immigrate to the USA?

b) Look at the chart and talk about it. most | the majority | the minority | few

Most people came from … .
The majority came from … .
There is a minority of … came from … .

5 Choose one of these tasks.

10/1
11/2-4

a) Work with a partner. Prepare an interview with an immigrant who has just arrived. Here are some questions:

- Where are you from?
- Why did you choose this country?
- What was the journey like?
- What are your plans for the future?

Present your interview to the class.
→ M Dramatic reading, p. 173

OR

b) What country would you like to immigrate to? What do you like about the country? What don't you like? Give a short presentation to the class.
→ M 1-minute-presentation, p. 172

Ich kann einen Text über die Geschichte der Einwanderung verstehen.

How to become a US citizen

- be age 18 or older
- be a permanent resident for a certain amount of time (usually 5 years or 3 years)
- be a person of good moral character
- have a basic knowledge of US government
- be able to read, write and speak basic English

Sample test questions:

1. What did the Declaration of Independence do?
2. What is the name of the President of the United States now?
3. In what month do we vote for President?
4. What is one reason colonists came to America?
5. What group of people was taken to America and sold as slaves?
6. There were 13 original states. Name three.
7. Name one American Indian tribe in the United States.
8. What ocean is on the West Coast of the United States?
9. Why does the flag have 50 stars?
10. Name two national US holidays.

CULTURE

Um amerikanischer Staatsbürger zu werden, muss man einen Einbürgerungstest machen. Das ist ein mündlicher Test, in dem einem 10 von 100 möglichen Fragen gestellt werden. Von diesen zehn Fragen muss man sechs richtig beantworten. Es gibt auch einen Englischtest. Gibt es so einen Test auch in deinem Land?

Du findest die Lösungen auf S. 292.

1 Fasse die wichtigsten Punkte zusammen.

Was sind die Voraussetzungen, um die amerikanische Staatsbürgerschaft anzunehmen?

- Wie alt muss man sein?
- Was muss man können und wissen? Gib Beispiele.

2 What do you think?

12/1-2

Why do people immigrate to Germany? Give reasons.

Ich kann Informationen über Einbürgerung weitergeben. ✓

New York City, here we come!

1 Talk about New York City.

What do you already know about New York City? Make a mind map of buildings and places.

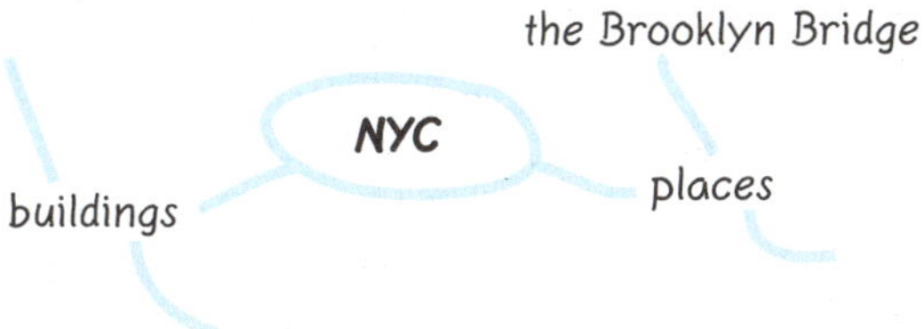

CULTURE

Central Park liegt im Herzen Manhattans. Es gibt dort einen Zoo, sieben Seen, eine Eisbahn, Baseballfelder und vieles mehr. Wusstest du, dass der New York Marathon im Central Park endet?
Wo ist der nächste Park bei dir? Was kannst du dort machen?

2 (VIEWING) Watch the film.

2

a) Name the sights that Wesley and Jessica show to Ronan. Put them in the right order.

b) Match the facts with the photos.

1. It's between Manhattan and Brooklyn. There were once elephants here.
2. It's not far from Little Italy, and there isn't only one of these in NYC.
3. It has names on a 'Wall of Honor'. Maybe Ronan's great-grandparents were here.
4. There are no elevators here. In summer it can get very hot inside.

3 (SPEAKING) Talk about the film.

a) Watch the film again and write four details which you find interesting. Say why.

b) Where would you like to go in New York City? Why? Tell your partner.

VIEWING SKILLS

In einem Film sind nicht nur die Personen und die Geschichte wichtig, sondern auch die Orte und das, was man im Hintergrund sehen kann. Suche dir eine Filmsequenz aus und stelle den Ton ab. Was passiert im Hintergrund?

Ich kann einen Film über Sehenswürdigkeiten in New York verstehen. ✓

Checklist

Ich kann Informationen über New York verstehen. ✓

13

Ich kann interessante Orte einer Stadt präsentieren. ✓

Over there you can see .... • Right ahead ... • You must visit .... • Don't miss .... • Can you see ... ?

13

Ich kann einen Artikel über eine Person schreiben. ✓

It was exciting. • I was homesick. • I missed .... • I had many opportunities.... • ... get used to ...

14

Ich kann einen Text über die Geschichte der Einwanderung verstehen. ✓

14

Ich kann Informationen über Einbürgerung weitergeben. ✓

15

Ich kann einen Film über Sehenswürdigkeiten in New York verstehen. ✓

(Task) A city profile

Work in groups of three students. Each group chooses an American city and finds out some basic facts about it and its population. Each group makes a poster and compares the city with another one.

Step 1

Get into groups. Choose an American city.

Choose one of America's big cities like Los Angeles. Look at the map at the back of the book to find an interesting place.

Step 2

Find the basic facts and photos.

City: Los Angeles
Location: in the state of California
History: first belonged to Spain; became part of Mexico in 1821; the USA bought California in 1847

Step 3

Find statistical data.

Find data on the internet to answer these questions:

1. What's the total population of the city that you chose?
2. What are the sizes of the different age groups?
3. Which ethnic groups are part of the city's population? How many people are in each one?

STUDY SKILLS

Suche offizielle Webseiten der Regierung, um die korrekten Zahlen herauszufinden. Daten zu Städten in den USA findest du auf der Webseite des US Census Bureau.
Du kannst die Angaben dort runden.

Step 4

Make one or two charts.

You can make a pie chart (A) and/ or a bar chart (B).
Remember that your chart must have a title, labels and a key. Your charts should take up about 50% of your poster.

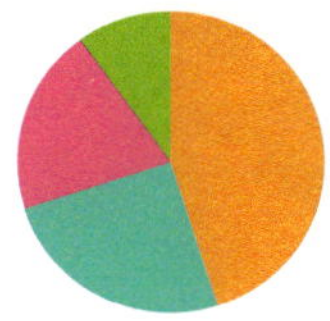

A

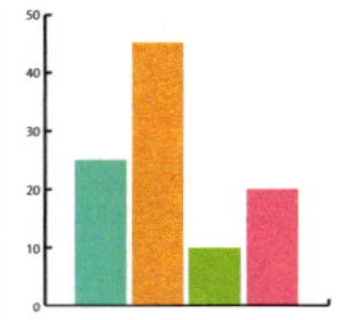

B

STUDY SKILLS

Du kannst Säulen- oder Kreisdiagramme auch mit einem Computerprogramm erstellen. Das ist recht einfach und sieht sauber und ordentlich aus.

Step 5

Write a short text for your chart(s).

This text should explain the most important information.

most | the majority | the minority
half of | two-thirds | the total number

Step 6

Finish your poster.

Arrange your photo(s), chart(s) and texts.
Can you read everything from two metres away?
Did you cite your sources?

STUDY SKILLS

Überprüfe, ob dein Poster Aufmerksamkeit erregt. Ist es gut strukturiert und sieht gut aus?

Step 7

Put up your poster. → M Gallery walk, p. 173

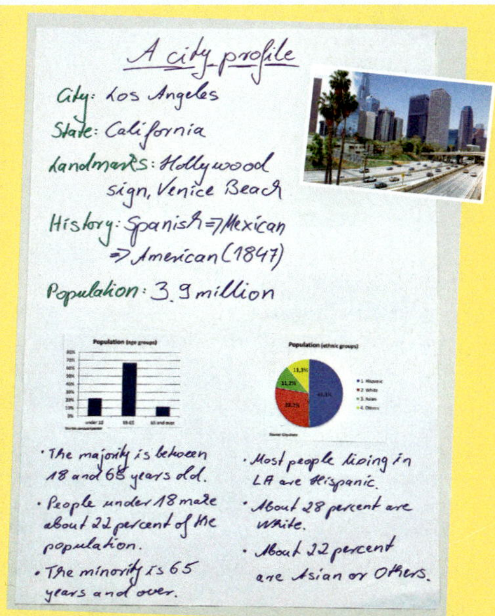

Step 8

Choose one of the other groups' cities and compare it with your city.

Is it bigger? Smaller? Are there any other differences? …

0.7 = zero point seven

Extra practice

1 Find the words. (nach 15/4)

roadwork

rush hour

skyline

lights

subway

traffic jam

1. The fastest way to travel in Manhatten is by —— .
2. At six in the evening it's —— . After work there are lots of people on the road.
3. At night the —— of New York is very beautiful.
4. The cars are going slowly because there is —— here.
5. The —— are green. You can go.
6. The cars aren't moving. This is a really big —— .

2 Match the phrases with the pictures and present the places. (nach 15/5)

Enjoy the view ... | Go for a walk... | Try the best... | Take the subway... | Finish the day ... | Buy a ...

1

2

3

4

5

6
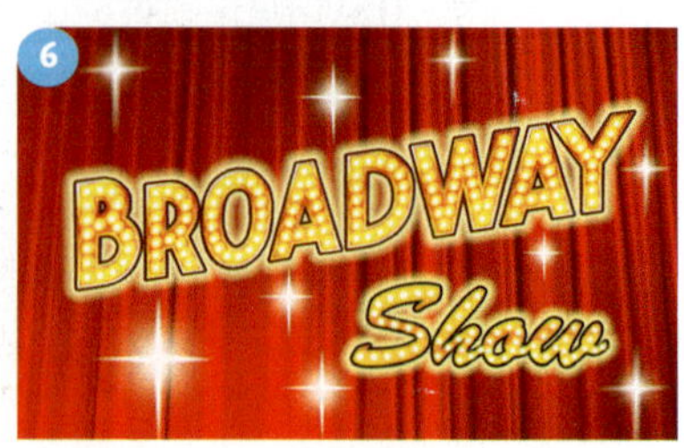

1. Buy a sandwich and a drink and walk in the park.

3 Answer the questions. (nach 18/2)

1. Did José answer questions for a magazine? (✓ lots of questions)
   Yes, he did. He answered lots of questions.
2. Did he come to the USA when he was a baby? (✗ ten years old)
   No, he didn't. He came when he was ten years old.
3. Did he arrive with his father? (✗ mother and sisters)
4. Did his parents have problems? (✓ speak English)
5. Did they have a supermarket? (✗ small shop)
6. Did he start his career when he was ten? (✗ when he was 15)
7. Did José become a football star in high school? (✓ in high school)

4 Put the verbs in the past perfect. (nach 20/7)

1. I became a taxi driver in New York after I hadn't found (not find) a job in my town.
2. Before that I — (be) a bus driver.
3. After a passenger — (leave) my taxi, I found her bag with $10,00.
4. Once it smelled funny. A passenger — (not finish) his fish burger.
5. A passenger was late for his plane because he — (forget) his passport.
6. A movie star got out in a traffic jam because I — (not know) who he was.
7. We arrived after the show — (start).

5 Complete the questions with the verbs in the past perfect. (nach 21/8)

1. Had you been (you • be) to New York before we went together?
2. — (she • want) to see a Broadway show before I invited her?
3. What sights — (you • visit) before we met?
4. — (they • take) the subway before you met them?
5. — (he • go) to a baseball game before he went to the USA?
6. How much coffee — (you • drink) before I saw you?
7. Where — (they • decide) to go before Beth got sick?

6 What are the questions? (nach 22/3)

1. The immigrants arrived on Ellis Island.
   Where did the immigrants arrive?
2. Most immigrants came between 1892 and 1954.
3. When they arrived, people first saw the Statue of Liberty.
4. Poor immigrants traveled in crowded spaces on the ship.
5. They were sick because the food was bad and there was very little fresh air.
6. The doctors sent back people who were too weak to work.

INTERNET

Alaska: Denali National Park

wild and wonderful

SEARCH MENU

Wild and wonderful Alaska is a state full of extremes – freezing winters and warm summers. You can have fantastic adventures and enjoy the amazing wildlife in the USA's most northern state. The park is also the home of Denali, the highest mountain in the United States.

▶ Park history

A The life of a Denali husky

Denali National Park is also home to a group of Alaskan huskies. They make travel and transport easier in the park. Denali rangers teach the huskies how to run and pull sleds. In winter the dogs help the rangers patrol the park and transport supplies. These trips can take from one day to six weeks. They travel on paths with the sled where cars and trucks cannot go because of the snow.

▶ Visiting the kennels

B Do not feed the bears!

One reason tourists come to Alaska is to see the grizzly bears. If you are lucky to see them, you will never forget these large, beautiful animals. Grizzly bears are intelligent and have a great sense of smell. Campers in Denali National Park must keep food and waste away from bears. One good way to do this is to build a 'food cache'. You can also buy special containers to store your food and garbage in.

▶ What bears eat in the wild

▶ Bus tours ▶ Park alerts ▶ Contact us ▶ FAQ

Last updated: 02/20/2016
(security information)

1 Find out information.

First look at the website on the left. What could the keywords be to find a website like this? Make a list. Compare it with a partner.

Je genauer du deine Schlüsselwörter eingibst, desto eindeutiger werden deine Suchergebnisse.
Wenn du nach Tieren im Denali Nationalpark suchst, beginne mit „animals" und „Denali National Park".
Benötigst du spezielle Informationen, kannst du in deiner Suchmaschine auch Folgendes eingeben:

Animal Denali National Park
Large animals Denali National Park
What animals are in Denali National Park?

2 Check the information.

Look at the website on the left again. Do you think it is an official website, an ad or a blog? Give reasons.

Es ist wichtig zu wissen, woher die Informationen kommen, die du gefunden hast. Offizielle Webseiten sind verlässlicher als Werbeseiten oder Seiten von Einzelpersonen. Sieh dir immer mehrere Webseiten an.

official website	ad	blog
– Datum, Update, – Geschäfts-/Sicherheits-informationen …	– Slogan – kurz, einfach – große Fotos …	– eigene Meinung – wie ein Journal oder Tagebuch …

3 Collect information.

Choose text A or B on the left. Write down the most important keywords.

19/1-3 ## 4 Do a search.

Search for more facts about your topic. Present at least three different things you find most interesting.

1. List keywords.
2. Search the internet.
3. List two to three different websites.
4. Prepare a short presentation.

Here are some ideas:
- Huskies: Training? Typical day?
- Bears: Food? Size? Weight?

Benutze deine eigenen Worte, wenn du die Informationen der Webseiten weitergibst. Kopiere nicht einfach den Text. Aber ändere keine Fakten.

Find more online: fe76m3

Am Ende dieser Unit kann ich …
- Informationen über den Mittleren Westen verstehen.
- das Schulleben in den USA und in Deutschland vergleichen.
- über Schülerjobs sprechen.
- einen Comic über das Highschool-Leben verstehen.
- Informationen über den Führerschein weitergeben.
- einen Film über den ersten Tag an einer neuen Schule verstehen.

3 1,8

Unit 2

Teens in the Midwest

1

The American Midwest is famous for its big areas of flat farmland and small towns. The summers are very hot and the winters are very cold. In the Tornado Alley there can be terrible storms.

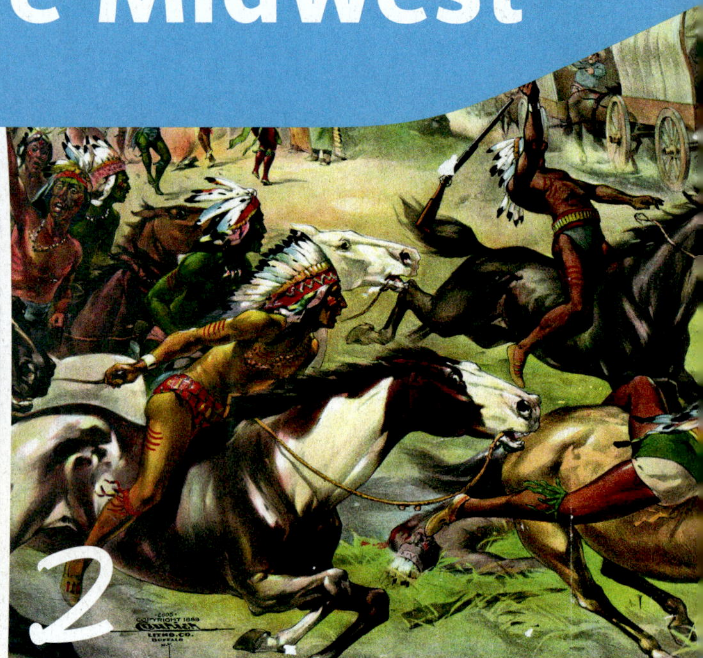

2

In the 1840s many European settlers moved west. They were looking for land and gold. The Native Americans lost their land and had to move to reservations.

1 (SPEAKING) Talk about the photos.

20/1

a) Match the headings with the photos.

History | Country life | School life | A special event | Working life

b) Which photos would you like to know more about? Say why.

→ M Round robin, p. 176

I'm interested in … . / I really like … . / Photo x looks great. / …

2 Read the texts and answer the questions.

1. What's the Midwest famous for?
2. What happened to the Native Americans?
3. What do students often do after school?
4. What's special about the grades?
5. When is Homecoming?

High school students over 14 often have a job. They're allowed to work in stores, help in restaurants or serve ice cream in cafés.

American high schools are usually big. There can be over 2,000 students in a school. Students are 15 to 18 years old. They get grades from A to F. The schedule is almost the same every day.

At the start of the new school year students celebrate Homecoming. There's a football game and a dance. Students vote for a Homecoming King and Queen.

3 (LISTENING) Listen to a radio report about a tornado.

1,9 20/2

a) Before you listen. What do you think a storm chaser does?

b) Listen. Take notes. How much information do you find? Compare with a partner. Add the information to your mind map.

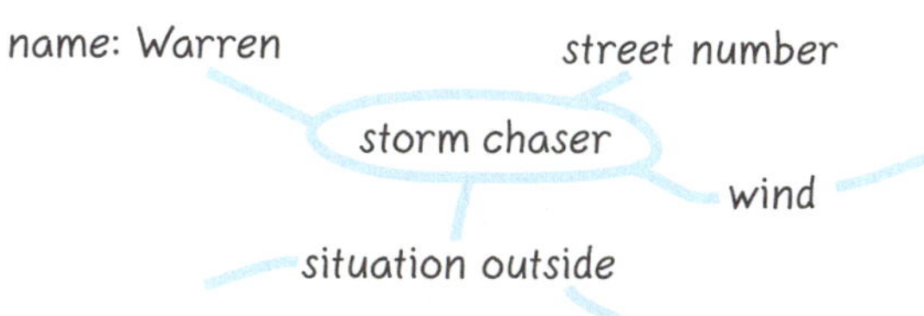

storm chaser [ˈstɔːm ˌtʃeɪsə] – Sturmjäger/in
to report (on) [rɪˈpɔːt] – berichten (über)
to drive [draɪv] – fahren
direction [dɪˈrekʃn] – Richtung
cloud [klaʊd] – Wolke

Ich kann Informationen über den Mittleren Westen verstehen. ✓

Hier lerne ich, das Schulleben in den USA und in Deutschland zu vergleichen.

A student exchange

1 What can you see in the photos? What's new to you? → M Think-pair-share, p. 177

A

B

C

D

E

2 (READING) Read Luise's report.

1,10

"No! I'll be stuck in the middle of nowhere," I thought. "An exchange year in South Dakota? Really?" But after that year I can say that it was the best time of my life.

In the beginning it felt like living in a movie. It all looked so familiar.

My American school was huge. Teachers usually stay in their classrooms, and students go to them for each lesson. So we weren't allowed to keep things in the classrooms. We had to put everything into our lockers. After two weeks I got used to it, and I was able to find the way to the classrooms by myself.

Every day school started at 8:00 with a morning message from the principal and the Pledge of Allegiance. Everyone stood and promised to be true to the United States. That was strange.

The first class started at 8:30. I had to take Math, English, Science and History. But I was able to choose 'electives' like Journalism too. There were lots of interesting subjects to choose from. We also had six study hall periods a week, where you do your homework or study. You weren't allowed to talk there.

School rules were strict. Much stricter than at home. You had to get a hall pass from the teacher to go to the bathroom, for example.

Classes ended at 3:30 p.m. Then there were many extracurricular activities. I wanted to join the cheerleaders. There was a lot of competition for places, and exchange students were allowed to try too, so I did. And I got a place! Awesome!

My host family was great too. They even took me on a trip to the east coast, so I was able to see the Atlantic. Anyway, my year in the USA was a blast.

CULTURE

Eltern müssen ihre Kinder nicht in die Schule schicken. Sie dürfen sie auch zu Hause unterrichten. Das tun aber nur sehr wenige (ca. 3%). Gibt es Homeschooling auch in Deutschland?

3 Find the information in the text.

a) Answer the questions. → ○ p. 118

1. How long was Luise in the USA?
2. Who had to change classrooms?
3. When did classes start and end?
4. What do students do during study hall?
5. What do students need a hall pass for?
6. What did Luise do after school?

b) What does 'elective' mean? What do 'extracurricular activities' mean? Give examples.

4 Find the words. → M Peer correction, p. 175 → V At American schools, p. 190

a) Match the photos with the right word. → ○ p. 119

21/1-2a)

1

2

3

4
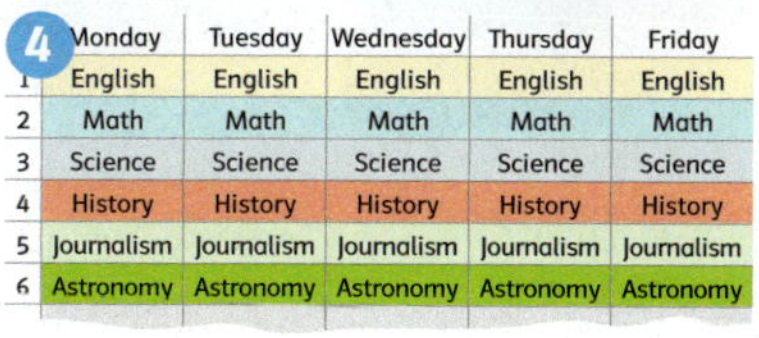

	Monday	Tuesday	Wednesday	Thursday	Friday
1	English	English	English	English	English
2	Math	Math	Math	Math	Math
3	Science	Science	Science	Science	Science
4	History	History	History	History	History
5	Journalism	Journalism	Journalism	Journalism	Journalism
6	Astronomy	Astronomy	Astronomy	Astronomy	Astronomy

5
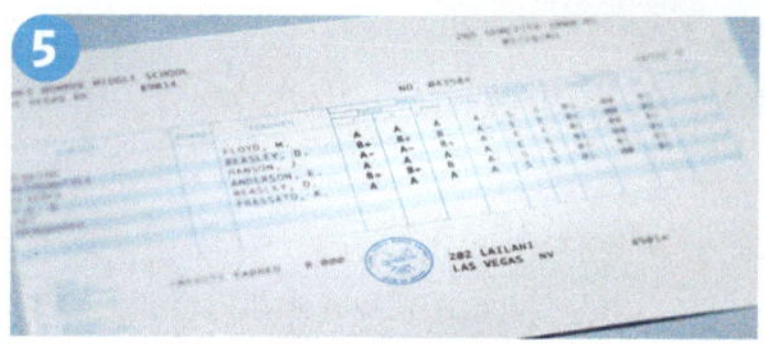

grade | principal | detention | schedule | locker

b) Explain these words: class | campus | vacation A class is a place where …

21/2b)

5 (SPEAKING) Describe a school day. → M Bus stop, p. 172

21/3
22/4

a) Describe a day at an American high school.

Most students go to school by … . School starts at … . Then there is … . After that … . Students have/don't have … . They can … .

b) Describe a day at your school.

SPEAKING SKILLS

Benutze Wörter wie *then, after that, next, finally*, um Ereignisse zu verbinden.

6 (SONG) Cool kids

1,11

Listen to the song. How does the singer describe the 'cool kids'?

She sees them walking in a straight line,
that's not really her style.
And they all got the same heartbeat,
but hers is falling behind.
Nothing in this world could
ever bring them down.
Yeah, they're invincible, and she's just in the
background.
And she says,

I wish that I could be like the cool kids,
'cause all the cool kids, they seem to fit in.
I wish that I could be like the cool kids,
like the cool kids.

Language detectives → G3, p. 160

I had to take Math, English, Science and History.
We weren't allowed to keep things in the classrooms.
I was able to choose 'electives'.

Welches Wort benutzen wir für must im simple past?
Was ist der Unterschied zwischen be allowed to und be able to?

7 (SPEAKING) Talk about school rules.

22/5 a) What was or wasn't Luise allowed to wear at high school? Use these verbs.

1. She was allowed to wear jeans. She wasn't allowed to …

b) What are you allowed to do at school? What aren't you allowed to do?
We're (not) allowed to keep/chose/take … .

8 (WRITING) Find out about two other exchange students.

a) Make sentences. → ○ p. 119

22/6 23/7

During the exchange (not) allowed to	Aileen	Jannik
1. bring any boys/girls to the bedroom	–	+
2. go out until 10 p.m. during the week	+	+
After the exchange (not) be able to		
3. get used to the old life easily	+	–
4. speak English a lot better	+	+

1. During the exchange Aileen wasn't allowed to … but Jannik …
2. They were able to …

23/8 b) What do you think? What were or weren't Aileen and Jannik allowed to do during the exchange? What were or weren't they able to do after the exchange? Make more sentences.

9 Complete the sentences about Luise's practice. Use had to or didn't have to.

23/9

1. When Luise joined the cheerleaders, she **had to** • **didn't have to** learn new dance moves.
2. Before it started she **had to** • **didn't have to** get the right clothes.
3. She was fit, so she **had to** • **didn't have to** be afraid.
4. She **had to** • **didn't have to** be on time.
5. During her first practice she **had to** • **didn't have to** shout loudly.
6. She was very good at it, so she **had to** • **didn't have to** worry.

10 Make a dialogue. → M Read and look up, p. 176

a) Complete the dialogue. Act it with a partner. → ○ p. 120

Sarah: Did you have to (have to) do jobs around the house in the USA?
Luise: No, I didn't. —— (be able to) decide when I wanted to help.
Sarah: —— (be allowed to) stay up late? When —— (have to) be in bed?
Luise: During the week —— (have to) be in bed at 9.
Sarah: —— (be able to) travel around with the family?
Luise: Yes, I was. But I —— (not be allowed to) travel without another person.

Was she allowed to go?
Were you able to choose?
Did you have to go?
When did you have to go?

b) Think about the last time you were a guest. What were(n't) you allowed to do? What were(n't) you able to to? What did(n't) you have to do?

11 (YOUR TURN) A comparison → V Comparing schools, p. 194 → M Writers' conference, p. 177

a) Look at this station again. Collect information about American and German schools. Compare them.

b) Would you like to go to an American school? Say why (not).

WRITING SKILLS

So vergleichst du zwei Dinge:
1. Stelle dein Thema vor.
2. Gib Fakten für beide Seiten im Hauptteil an. Konzentriere dich auf fünf Aspekte, die du vergleichen möchtest.
3. Gib deine Meinung am Ende wieder.

You can start like this:
I would like to compare … to … .
In American high schools … but in …
You are allowed to … in Germany.
You aren't allowed to …
For … this is the same.
But … is different.
Finally …

Ich kann das Schulleben in den USA und in Deutschland vergleichen. ✓

Hier lerne ich über Schülerjobs zu sprechen.

A lesson outside school

1 Have you ever tried to earn some extra money? What did you do?

2 (READING) Read the story.

1,12

Like many American teenagers 16-year-old Michael Adams needed money. His allowance wasn't enough. He wanted to get a car, he needed new clothes, and he had a new girlfriend. So when he read the ad for a job, he thought, "That's the perfect one for me." He applied for the job.

The job interview was tough. The manager asked many questions. "What will you do if you see someone steal something?" or "What will you do if you are late?" Michael answered all the questions and got the job. Ten hours a week and the minimum wage was OK.

His co-workers were helpful and cooperative. One of them said, "If you have any questions, I'll help you." First, everything was exciting. After two weeks, however, Michael learned that jobs have their good and bad sides. There were days when there wasn't much to do. He just sorted the shirts. The blue ones on the right, the green ones on the left. On other days, he was very busy.

One Saturday two students from school came into the store. When they saw him, they started teasing him. "Your job is boring! You'll miss all the fun if you work here every weekend. Just look at you. If you wear a uniform like that, you won't be one of the cool kids."

Michael became angry. He got into a fight with them and in the end, he threw them out. Later, his manager called him into his office. "I understand," he said. "But such behavior is very bad. What will our customers think? Be more responsible. If this happens again, you'll lose your job. Now please go back to work."

INTERNET

Student Jobs

JIMMY'S SPORTING GOODS Lincoln, NE

Job title: Sales associate

Job type: Part-time (weekends)

Education: High school

Bring your love of sports to Jimmy's.

3 Work with the text.

24/1

a) Find the right order.

A The boys have a fight.
B Two students start teasing Michael.
C He gets the job.
D Michael needs money for many things.
E There's a job interview.
F He applies for a job.
G Michael's job has good and bad sides.
H The manager talks about Michael's behavior.

b) What do you think about the manager's reaction at the end?

I think he's right because Michael must be friendly. / He's wrong because …

4 (SPEAKING) What do you think? → M Think-pair-share, p. 177

a) What should or shouldn't Michael say to the manager? → ○ p. 120

1. "I'm sorry."
2. "It won't happen again."
3. "But they started it."
4. "It wasn't me."
5. "I don't think you're right."
6. "Next time I'll try to be cooler."

b) Your friend is trying on a pair of jeans. You think that they don't suit him or her. What do you do? Act a short role play.

A: Tell your friend that they look great.

B: You aren't sure.

C: Tell your friend that they don't suit him or her.

5 (LISTENING) Listen to Marie on her first day at work at Fruit4U. Answer the questions.

1,13

1. Who is Stacey?
   manager • co-worker
2. What day is it?
   Marie's first day • Marie's last day
3. What does Marie have to learn about?
   different salads • different fruit
4. What are Marie's working hours?
   9 a.m. to 2 p.m. • 9:30 a.m. to 2 p.m.
5. How long is Marie's lunch break?
   30 min • 40 min
6. How can she get a bonus?
   has many customers • gets good feedback

6 Practise words to describe people at work.

24/2 a) Copy and complete the table. → ○ p. 120

bossy · unmotivated · cooperative ✓ · responsible · lazy · hard-working

good behavior (+)	bad behavior (–)
cooperative	...

24/3 b) Find the opposites. → V Describing people, p. 191

1. confident · 2. generous · 3. polite · a. rude · b. selfish · c. shy

7 (SPEAKING) Describe the most ... job. → V Jobs, p. 195

25/4

What jobs do you know? Make a list in two minutes. Then decide which job is the ...

most dangerous · most exciting · most boring · the easiest

Present your results to the class.
Give reasons.
I think being a/an ... is the ... job because ...

CULTURE

Viele Amerikaner benutzen Kreditkarten, kein Bargeld. Man kann sogar einen einzigen Bagel mit der Kreditkarte bezahlen.

Language → G4, p. 161

If you have any questions, I'll help you.
If you wear a uniform like that, you won't be one of the cool kids.

Die Sätze bestehen aus zwei Teilen. In welchem Teil steht die Bedingung? In welchem die Konsequenz? Was sind die Zeiten in den beiden Satzteilen?

25/5

8 What does Marie think after her first day? Complete the sentences. → M Bus stop, p. 172

1. If I watch everything, I'll learn (learn) quickly.
2. If I have to cut fruit all day, it ___ (not be) easy.
3. What ___ (happen) if I get sick?
4. The manager will give me a bonus if I ___ (do) well.
5. Will I get fed up if a customer ___ (get) unfriendly?
6. When will we meet if my friends ___ (work) every weekend too?

9 (WRITING) What will happen if …?

25/6
26/7

a) Look at the pictures. Make sentences. → ○ p. 121

1. find student job • earn money

2. need help • ask co-worker

3. be late • lose job

4. steal T-shirt • talk to her

5. bring back • get new one

6. buy two • get one free

1. If Michael finds a student job, he'll earn some money.

b) What will happen if …?

- Michael • get sick
- he • buy something from the store
- he • leave soon
- computer • not work

1. If Michael gets sick, he'll stay at home.

Language detectives → G5, p.162

He read the ad for the student job. "That's the perfect one for me."
He sorted the shirts. The blue ones on the right, the green ones on the left.

Warum benutzt man hier one und ones?

10 Complete the sentences.

a) Use one or ones. → ○ p. 121

26/8

1. I really like this jacket. This one suits me perfectly.
2. We have lots of helmets. The best — are over there.
3. Is there a bathroom? – Yes, there's — over there.
4. This towel is a bit dirty. Do you have a clean — ?
5. How about these trousers? – No, I prefer those — .
6. I need some new sport sunglasses. I don't like my old — .

b) Make questions with Which one/ones …?

26/9

1. These are all the trainers that we have in our store. (you/like/?)
2. We have that pair in different sizes. (you/need/?)

Benutze „ones", um Pluralwörter wie „sunglasses" und „trousers" zu ersetzen.

11 (YOUR TURN) A job for me → V Jobs, p. 195

27/1

Which student job would you like to do? Choose one and talk about it.

- Why did you choose the job?
- Why will you be good at it (and not so good at the others)?
- How will your life change if you take the job?

I chose/didn't choose … because … .
Another reason why … .
I like to work … .
I'm a … person, so a job like this … .
I'm very/quite/not good at … .
If I earn money, I'll be able to … .
If I work in my free time, I won't be able to … .

JOBS FOR TEENS

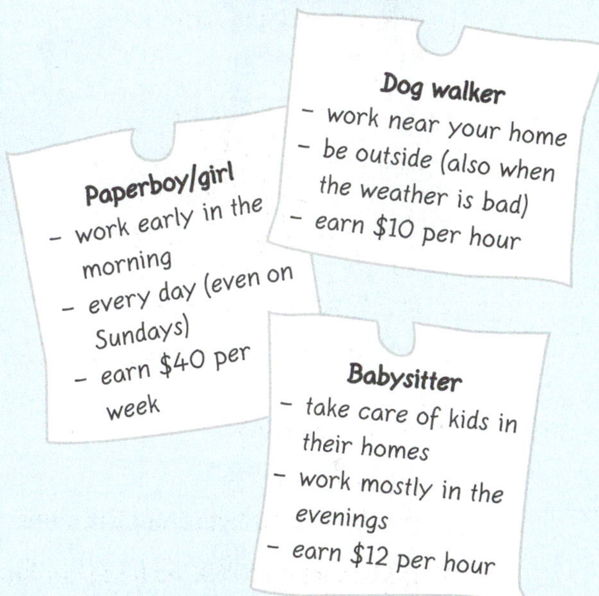

Ich kann über Schülerjobs sprechen. ✓

A first date

1 Which stereotypes of American high schools characters do you know from movies and TV shows?

2 (READING) Read the comic strip.

1,14

1. Dylan often thought about Abby. He really liked her. But he was too shy to ask her out on a date.

2. One day his books fell out of his locker right when Abby showed up. With Scott in tow, of course. How embarrassing.

3. A few days later they had lunch together. Dylan helped Abby with her Science project. They didn't notice Scott and his football friends.

4. When Dylan went to the gym, the boys attacked him. Scott pushed him really hard and Dylan couldn't do anything about it.

3 Talk about the story.

a) Did you like the story? Talk about it with a partner and say why or why not.

b) Answer the questions.

1. Why didn't Dylan ask Abby out on a date?
2. What did Scott think of Dylan?
3. What did Dylan do at lunch?
4. Why did Scott and his friends attack Dylan?
5. How did Dylan feel before and during the Homecoming party?
6. What did Abby's dad do at the end?

5. A few days later Dylan asked Abby "So, are you coming to the dance with me?" And she said yes. He was very nervous when he picked her up.

6. The party was great. Everybody enjoyed the music and dancing. There was a big surprise that evening. Dylan and Abby were so proud.

7. At the end of the evening Dylan took Abby home. There it was, the perfect moment. But …

4 (SPEAKING) Retell the story.

→ M Read and look up, p. 176

a) Take notes. Don't write more than two or three notes for each picture.

b) Tell the story in your own words.

Dylan and his friends …

First … | Then … | After that … | In the end …

STUDY SKILLS

Wenn du einen Comic nacherzählst, benutze auch die Informationen aus den Bildern. Sie bieten manchmal weitere interessante Details zum Nacherzählen.

5 Choose one of these tasks. → M Tip top, p. 177

P

28/1
29/2-3

a) Do Dylan and Abby stay together? What happens next? Write the last paragraph.

OR

b) Work in groups. Make freeze frames for each part of the story. Let other groups guess.

Ich kann einen Comic über das Highschool-Leben verstehen. ✓

How to get your driver's license

Classroom Driver Ed

Length: 9 weeks

Classroom driver education is a course for all students who will be 15 years before the last day of instruction and who have successfully completed eight out of ten courses in eighth grade. The course introduces students to basic skills of driving.
To take the written and practical driving test, please contact your local driving school.

DRIVER EDUCATION APPROVAL FORM

Name and Address of Driver Training School:

Sally's Driving School Inc., 524 Bird Highway, Park Ridge 60068 IL

Student's Full Name: (last) Jenkins (first) Caitlin (middle) Amy

Street Address: 1815, Baxendale Road

City or Town: Chicago ZIP Code: 60004 IL

Caitlin A. Jenkins 12/16/2016
Signature of Student Date

Steve. M. Jenkins
Signature of Parent

CULTURE

Amerikaner haben keinen Personalausweis. Sie benutzen stattdessen ihren Führerschein. Nach fünf Jahren muss man einen neuen beantragen (aber man muss die Prüfung nicht wiederholen).

1 Berichte darüber, wie man in den USA den Führerschein macht.

2 Pass on the information in a conversation about how to get a driver's license.

30/1-2

A *(from Germany)*: In welchem Alter kann man bei euch in Illinois den Führerschein machen?
You: At what age … ?
B *(from Illinois)*: At the age of 15. And in Germany?
You: …
A: Mit 18. Aber man kann ihn auch schon mit 17 machen, wenn eine weitere Person mit Führerschein im Auto dabei ist.
You: …
B: So, do you need a parent's signature for that too?
You: …
A: Ja, das stimmt. Muss man in den USA auch eine theoretische und eine praktische Prüfung ablegen?
You: …
B: …

Wenn du ein bestimmtes Wort auf Englisch nicht weißt, sage es mit anderen Worten.

Ich kann Informationen über den Führerschein weitergeben.

The new kid at school

1 Talk about a new school.

a) What would you show a new kid at your school?

b) How would you feel if you were the 'new kid' at school? What could be good or or bad about it?

2 (VIEWING) Watch the film.

4

a) Watch the film until 02:48. Right or wrong? Correct the wrong sentences.

1. A buddy is a teacher's favourite student.
2. CJ and Ronan are in the same homeroom.
3. Ruby has had seven detentions this year.
4. They have Math first period.
5. All students say the Pledge of Allegiance.

b) Watch the film from 02:48 to the end. Name the places that Ronan and CJ go to. Say one sentence about what they do there.

3 (WRITING) Write about the film.

Write Ronan's e-mail to Roy, his best friend at his old school, to tell him about his first day at the new school.

E-MAIL

Hi Roy,
I must tell you about my first day at school.
I met CJ who's my buddy. He's really … . We went … .
Then I met … . Can you believe that … ?
Bye,
Ronan

CULTURE

In den USA beginnen viele Schulen jeden Tag mit dem Treueschwur. Die Schüler stehen auf, legen ihre rechte Hand aufs Herz, sehen zur amerikanischen Flagge und geloben der Nation und Gott ihre Treue.
Hältst du einen Treueschwur für eine gute Idee? Warum? Warum nicht?

VIEWING SKILLS

Die meisten Filme beginnen mit einer Eröffnungsszene. Sie zeigt die Tageszeit, den Ort des Geschehens und die beteiligten Personen etc. an.
Sieh dir die Eröffnungsszene im Film an. Was erfährst du dort?

Ich kann einen Film über den ersten Tag an einer neuen Schule verstehen.

Checklist

Ich kann Informationen über den Mittleren Westen verstehen. ✓

31

Ich kann das Schulleben in den USA und Deutschland vergleichen. ✓

In American high schools … • However, in German schools … . • School rules … stricter. • … is the same. • But … is different.

31

Ich kann über Schülerjobs sprechen. ✓

I'm very/quite/(not) good at … . • If I earn money, I'll be able to … . • If I work in my free time, I won't be able to … .

32

Ich kann einem Comic über das Highschool-Leben verstehen. ✓

32

Ich kann Informationen über den Führerschein weitergeben. ✓

33

Ich kann einen Film über den ersten Tag an einer neuen Schule verstehen. ✓

❀ (TASK) A speech

Every year your class votes for a class president. You would like to be the next one. Give a 1-minute speech. Then answer your classmates' questions.

Step 1

Collect ideas.

What's important for you and your class?
(atmosphere, relationships, …)

What topics interest you?
(field trips, projects, …)

What are you good at?
(listening to …, talking to …, …)

What will you do if your class elects you?
(try to paint the classroom in a new colour, have a party every month, …)

Step 2

Structure and write your speech.

→ M 1-minute-presentation, p. 172

1. Think about how to address your listeners.
2. Say that you would like to be the next class president. Use one paragraph for each topic to tell your listeners why you are the right person for the job.
3. Think of an ending.

WRITING SKILLS

Eine Rede hat ähnliche Merkmale wie die meisten geschriebenen Texte: Einleitung, Hauptteil, Schluss.

Step 3

Practise your speech.

→ M Read and look up, p. 176

Find different partners.
Practise your speech in front of them.
Read your speech a couple of times.
Then make notes and repeat your speech again and again.

SPEAKING SKILLS

Um gewählt zu werden, musst du deine Klasse überzeugen. Es ist wichtig, dass sie dir zuhört. Du kannst z. B. Dinge mehrmals wiederholen, die dir wichtig sind. Sprich nicht zu schnell oder zu langsam.

Step 4

Give your speech.

- Stand straight and get organized.
- Look at your listeners from time to time. Eye contact is important.
- Don't make hectic movements. They distract your listeners.
- Speak loudly and clearly.

Dear class,
Next Friday will be a big day for all of us because we're going to elect our class president. …
I think our class is already a really good team already. If you vote for me, I'll … . I'll listen and … . If you have any problems, I am sure … . I promise … because I'm hard-working and motivated.
You think classes could be more fun? You think we should have …?
Come and talk to me. I'll try to talk to the staff and the principal.
Thanks for listening. I'll be happy to answer your questions now.

Step 5

Answer your listeners' questions.

Answer the questions politely.
If you didn't understand the question, ask the person to repeat it.

Extra practice

1 Find the right word. (nach 35/4)

1. Where do students keep their books and other things?
2. What's another word for the manager of a high school?
3. How do students know how good their work is? What do they get?
4. Where can students see when the next lesson is?
5. What do they call a period when students can do their homework?
6. In British English it's a 'History lesson'. What is it in American English?

2 Complete last year's school rules. Use (not) be allowed to and (not) be able to. (nach 36/8)

1. Steve was allowed to leave early when he finished his homework. (✓ allowed to)
2. Teachers — give detentions. (✓ allowed to)
3. Jackie, you — bring your skateboard to school. (✗ allowed to)
4. Students — eat during classes. (✗ allowed to)
5. Mr. Grant — speak German. Talk to him if you need help. (✓ able to)
6. Students — use computers in class when the teacher says it's OK. (✓ able to)
7. Matt and Ramon — work together. They always fight. Don't put them together. (✗ able to)
8. Kayla — listen very well. She needs the teachers' help. (✗ able to)

3 Ask and answer Sue's questions. Use have or had to. (nach 37/10)

1. Sue: (wear a uniform)
   Did you have to wear a uniform? – Kate: No, I didn't. I just had to wear nice clothes.
2. Sue: (arrive early) — ? – Kate: Yes, — . I — be there at 7:30.
3. Sue: (take extra classes) — ? – Kate: Yes, — . I — take American history.
4. Sue: (get a hall pass) — ? – Kate: No, — . I just — ask the teacher.
5. Sue: (where • go after lunch) — ? – Kate: I always — to the library.
6. Sue: (what • parents • do) — ? – Kate: My parents — agree.

4 Put in the right words. (nach 39/5)

co-workers | **customers** | **lose her job** | **job** | **serve** | **help**

This summer Susan has found a — (1). It's in a restaurant which needs summer — (2). It's her job to — (3) ice cream. She has five — (4), and they are all very friendly. The — (5) are usually happy too when the sun is shining. Susan works hard and is friendly to everyone. She doesn't want to — (6)!

5 Match the photos with the adjectives. (nach 39/6)

busy | hard-working | helpful | lazy | unmotivated | responsible

1

2

3

4

5

6

6 Complete what a manager tells his workers. (nach 40/9)

1. John, if you always leave (leave) early, you will get (get) a bad report card.
2. Louise, if you don't talk (not talk) to the customers, they ___ (think) that you aren't polite.
3. Carol, if you ___ (wear) that short skirt again, I ___ (send) you home.
4. George, if you ___ (work) with a partner, it ___ (be) easier to carry the heavy boxes.
5. José, if you ___ (not have) your card with you, you ___ (get) into trouble.
6. Laura, if you ___ (want) to get a bonus, you ___ (have) to work harder.
7. Janet, if you ___ (need) extra holidays, we ___ (talk) about it later.
8. Michael, if you ___ (not follow) the rules, you ___ (not be) here for a long time.

7 Complete the dialogues with one or ones. (nach 41/10)

1. A: Those flowers are beautiful.
   B: Which ___ ?
   A: The yellow ___ .
2. A: I know a better store.
   B: Which ___ ?
   A: The ___ just opposite.
3. A: Are those CDs cheaper?
   B: Which ___ ?
   A: The ___ on the small table.
4. A: Have you got a credit card?
   B: I don't need ___ . I've got $50.
5. A: Do you know that girl?
   B: Which ___ ?
   A: The ___ with the red top.

Ersetze Wörter in der Einzahl durch „one", Wörter in der Mehrzahl durch „ones".

Hier kannst du lernen, wie du eine Präsentation vorbereitest und hältst.

American football

A

- Super Bowl: most famous sporting event
- first Sunday in February
- famous sports event on TV
- like a national holiday
- final match of the season
- game first played in USA in 1869

B

C

- team of supporters
- motivate players and fans
- today: 95% girls
- dance, jump, yell, do stunts
- 1–3 minutes per performance (= routine)

D

- pass the ball by throwing and kicking
- allowed: running with the ball, hands
- aim: take the ball as far as possible into the other team's half
- score: touchdown, field goal

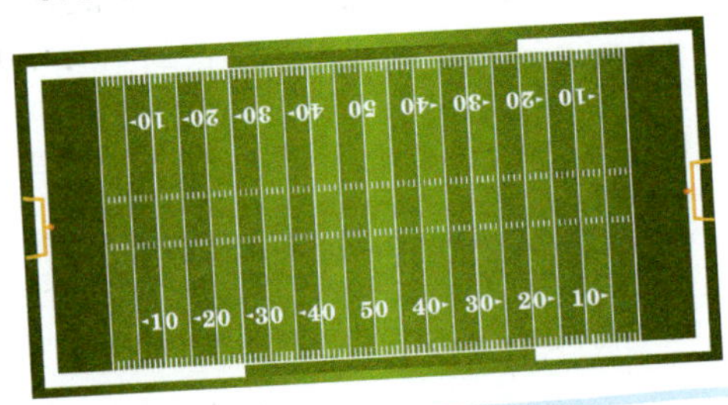

E

F

- team sport
- each team: 11 players on the field
- one game: 60 minutes (+ breaks)
- 4 quarters (one quarter = 15 minutes)

1 Organize the cards on the left.

a) Give each card and each photo a heading.
You can start like this:
- General facts
- ...

b) Put the information cards and the photos in a suitable order.

Schlage neue Wörter nach. Achte darauf, dass du die richtige Bedeutung auswählst und die Wörter richtig aussprechen kannst. Überlege dir, wie du deiner Klasse unbekannte Wörter erklärst. Nutze dazu Fotos oder Skizzen.

2 Prepare your presentation about American football.

a) Prepare your poster, transparency or computer presentation.

Prüfe, ob deine Präsentation gut ist:
- große Überschrift
- keine Rechtschreibfehler
- Fotos

b) Use the prompt cards from page 50 or prepare your own prompt cards.

Das sollte auf deinen Karteikarten stehen:
- kurze Stichpunkte
- die Erklärung neuer Wörter

3 Practise your presentation.

You can practise your presentation in front of the mirror or with family and friends.

1. Give a general introduction.
2. Present the different aspects of your information.
3. End your presentation. Emphasize the most important facts and come to a conclusion.

Hilfreiche Redewendungen für den Einstieg:
My presentation is about ... .
First, I'd like to talk about ... .

So kannst du zum nächsten Punkt deiner Präsentation überleiten:
Now I'm going to talk about ... .
My next topic is ... .
Second, ... Finally, ...

Bedanke dich bei deinen Zuhörern für ihre Aufmerksamkeit und biete an, Fragen zu beantworten:
That's the end of my presentation. Thank you for listening. Do you have any questions?

37/1-3 ## 4 Give your presentation.

Sieh dein Publikum an, während du sprichst. Sprich langsam, klar und deutlich. Beziehe dein Poster oder deine Folie in deine Präsentation mit ein. Achte auf die Zeit.

Find more online: fe76m3

Am Ende dieser Unit kann ich ...
- Informationen über den Nordosten der USA verstehen.
- einen Text ausdrucksstark vorlesen.
- meine Meinung sagen und begründen.
- eine Geschichte über Freunde verstehen.
- Informationen über Reisemöglichkeiten weitergeben.
- einen Film über Thanksgiving verstehen.

5 1,15 Unit 3

In the Northeast

The Northeast of the United States is from the border with Canada to Washington, D.C. You can visit the amazing Niagara Falls, enjoy the beaches or the sea. In the fall you can go through beautiful forests.

The USA is a very big country. From Boston to L.A., for example, it's a six and a half hour flight. Families often live and work thousands of miles away from each other. So they like to meet for important celebrations.

1 (SPEAKING) Talk about the photos.

a) Choose your favourite photo.
What can you see? Why do you like it best?
Tell a partner.

I like photo X best because ... .
In the photo I can see .../there's ... .

b) Add information from the texts.

Photo 1 is in the Northeast of ... .

2 Match the people's statements with the texts.

40/1-2

1. "I couldn't live without modern inventions. I need my phone."
2. "We always eat too much turkey on that day."
3. "I really love the beautiful colors of the trees in the fall."
4. "I like to read creepy stories."
5. "Let's all meet in Pittsburgh for Christmas."

On Thanksgiving almost everybody eats turkey. However, a new tradition started. The president 'pardons' a turkey and the bird goes back to a farm in Virginia.

Maine is a favorite location for creepy movies and books. It's 90 percent forest, has few people and long, dark winters. So it's popular with writers of mystery stories.

The USA is called the 'land of the free'. People can choose how they want to live. The Amish are an old Christian community who have chosen to live without most modern inventions.

3 (LISTENING) Listen to a story about a Niagara daredevil.

1,16

Right or wrong?

1. A boat went down Niagara Falls.
   That's **wrong**. It was a barrel.
2. A woman climbed out of it.
3. The man signed autographs.
4. He hadn't planned anything.
5. Steve survived a second time too.
6. Steve had to pay money.

daredevil ['deəˌdevl] – Draufgänger/in
barrel ['bærl] – Faß; Tonne
to sign autographs [ˌsaɪn 'ɔːtəgrɑːfs] – Autogramme geben

Ich kann Informationen über den Nordosten der USA verstehen. ✓

A family Thanksgiving

1 What is the biggest celebration in your family? → M Round robin, p. 176

2 (READING) Read the dialogue.

1,17

The Millers from Boston are getting ready for dinner. Julia is in the kitchen. Her husband Mark, their teenage son Jacob and Grandma Brenda are in the living room.

Grandma: Last year we had such a terrible storm. I got stuck in my car. Do you remember?

Mark: Yes, that's right. Did you have a hard time again yesterday?

(The doorbell rings. Mark opens the door. It's their neighbor.)

Robert: Happy Thanksgiving, Mark!

Mark: You too, Robert. How are you?

Robert: Great, thanks. Brr. It's freezing, isn't it?

Mark: Come on in. I'm so glad you could make it. *(They enter the living room.)* Grandma, this is Robert. He's our new neighbor. He doesn't have family here, so we've invited him. Robert, this is Brenda.

Robert: Nice to meet you, Brenda. You came all the way from Miami, didn't you?

Grandma: Yes, I did. Please have a seat. When did you move here?

Mark: *(shouting across the room)* Jacob, why don't you say hello? You can't spend all your time on your phone.

Jacob: What's up Robert?

Robert: How's it going? Are you enjoying the holiday? Do you like turkey?

Jacob: Not really. I'm a vegetarian, so I won't eat any.

Julia: *(coming out of the kitchen)* You always used to eat everything. *(noticing the guest)* Oh, hi Robert.

Robert: Hey Julia. Thanks so much for inviting me. Here's a little present. You eat chocolates, don't you? *(giving her a box as a present)*

Mark: OK everybody. I'm making a video. Please, answer this question. 'What do you feel thankful for?' Julia, you go first, please. *(he starts filming)*

Julia: Me? Well, err, I am most thankful for my husband and my two children who …

(Mark's phone rings.)

Mark: That's probably Lily and her new boyfriend. Hello Lily. … Oh, no! *(to the others)* Their plane from Washington, D.C. had engine trouble. They had to land in New York. *(to Lily)* So when does your plane arrive? … OK. … Will you call us when you know more? I promise we'll keep you some turkey!

CULTURE

Small Talk ist in den USA sehr wichtig.
Man unterhält sich über sehr einfache Dinge.
Was sind für euch alltägliche Dinge?

Language tip → G6, p. 163

You eat chocolates, **don't you**?
You came all the way from Miami, **didn't you**?

3 Work with the text about the Miller family. → M Peer correction, p. 175

a) Put the pictures in the right order. → ○ p. 122

A Mark and Julia

B Mark on the phone

C Robert and Julia

D Mark and Robert

E Mark and Brenda

F Robert and Jacob

b) Write one or two sentences for each picture.

1,18
4 (LISTENING) Listen to Lily introduce her boyfriend Evan.

a) Listen to the conversation. Match the questions and answers. → ○ p. 123

41/1

1. How are you doing?
2. What's new?
3. So what have you been up to?
4. How is she?

A She's good, thanks.
B Good, thanks.
C I'd like you to meet Evan.
D Not much.

LISTENING SKILLS

Keine Sorge, wenn du beim ersten Hören nicht alles verstehst. Beim zweiten Hören wirst du schon mehr verstehen.

b) Listen again. Which other phrases can you understand?

1. What's …? 2. Nice to … . 3. We've heard … . 4. What about …?

5 (SPEAKING) Make small talk.

41/2

a) Make a table. Fill in the phrases from the text on page 54 and Ex. 4. → V Small talk, p. 196

Saying 'How are you?'	*Saying 'I'm fine.'*
What's new?	

b) Use the phrases from a) to have small talk conversations. → M Milling around, p. 174

6 (SOUNDS) Listen, read and say.

1,19

1. Do you like turkey? ↗
2. Yes, I love turkey. ↘
3. Did you come by car? ↗
4. No, I flew from Miami. ↘

Language → G7, p. 164

Do you like turkey?
Why don't you say hello?
Did you have a hard time yesterday?
Will you call us?

Wie bildest du Fragen in der Gegenwart, der Vergangenheit und der Zukunft? Welche Signalwörter außer „yesterday" kennst du noch?

7 Make questions in the right tense.

42/3-4

1. Do you usually prefer turkey or ham? (prefer)
2. ___ your mum ___ at 6:30 a.m. to have breakfast every day? (get up)
3. ___ you ___ the snowstorm on the news yesterday? (see)
4. ___ you ___ by plane last year? (travel)
5. ___ you ___ me how to make a great cake like this tomorrow? (teach)
6. ___ Grandma ___ with you next Thanksgiving? (stay)

8 (SPEAKING) Ask questions about holidays.

a) Interview your partner. → p. 123

43/5

1. Which • holidays • your family • celebrate?
2. What • you • usually • eat?
3. What • you • like • about • last *(name of holiday)?*
4. How many • guests • your family • invite • last time?
5. Where • it • take place • next year?
6. Who • you • call • next *(name of holiday)?*

b) Think of more questions like these that Grandma asks at a family party.

GRAMMAR → G7, p. 164

Who did you invite?
Who will you call?

How old ...?
Do you already have ...?
When will you ...?

9 (WRITING) Write Jacob's questions to his grandma.

a) What did Jacob ask his grandma? Write his questions for the underlined answers. → ○ p. 124

43/6

What? | Where? | When? | Who? | Why?

E-MAIL

Dear Jacob,
Yes, it's true, it'll be my 65th birthday soon! I'm planning (1) a big family party. I'll have it (2) at my house in Miami. It'll be (3) on May 1. I'll invite (4) everybody who can come to Miami. And of course you can ask your new girlfriend to come too. Yes, I already know about her. That's (5) because your dad told me about her.
Love,
Grandma

1. What are you planning for your birthday?

b) Jacob has some more questions about her birthday. Write an answer with three more questions.

❀10 (YOUR TURN) A holiday dialogue → M Dramatic reading, p. 173

a) Work in groups of five. Each of you chooses a role from the dialogue on page 54.

b) Practise and read the dialogue.

c) Give feedback to the other groups.

READING SKILLS

Wenn ihr einen Dialog vorlest, benutzt eure Stimme, um die Gefühle der Personen gut auszudrücken. Lest z. B. schneller, wenn es aufgeregt klingen soll.

Ich kann einen Text ausdrucksstark vorlesen. ✓

One country, different worlds

1 How much electricity have you used so far today?

2 (READING) Read the texts about two American teenage girls.

1,20

I live in a small Amish community in Pennsylvania. We lead a simple life. We don't have any modern devices like a TV, a fridge or a computer. If we had these things, we couldn't concentrate on our community life enough. I also cover my hair, wear long dresses, and never use make-up. We grow our own food too.
The people in our community look after each other. To us it's more important who you are and what you do than what you wear or how you look.
We usually don't have much contact with the outside world. But at 16 we're allowed to do 'forbidden things'. I went to parties and drank alcohol.
Now I have to make the most important decision of my life: Do I join the Amish community or not?
Living in the outside world was not what I had expected. I felt lost. Just think: if I didn't return, I would really miss my family. This is where I belong. I'm sure I won't regret it.

I'm a pretty average American girl. I'm interested in fashion and yes … gossip too. I love being on the phone at all times. What would I do if I had to live without it? My friends and I chat a lot about everyone and everything.
My first big decision of the day is: What am I going to wear?
When I'm on the school bus, I think about what's going on at school. Mostly it's about who is wearing what or who's going out with whom.
I often hang out with my friends. If I had a car, I would drive around town with them. But I don't have one yet. So we often meet in town to have something to eat, go bowling or watch movies.
Some of my friends go to church, but I don't. That isn't part of my life.
I wouldn't like to change anything about my life.

CULTURE

Die Amischen sind eine religiöse Gruppe, die im 18. Jahrhundert aus Europa ausgewandert ist. Sie führen in ihren Gemeinschaften ein einfaches Leben. Die Amischen sprechen einen deutschen Dialekt. Welche anderen Lebensstile kennst du?

3 Match the headings with the texts. There are two headings for each text.

1. Modern times
2. Life as an Amish girl
3. Different from others
4. It's all about fashion and people

4 Compare the girls' lives.

	Clothes?	Modern devices?	Free time?
Ruth	…	…	…
Jennifer	…	…	…

5 Sort the phrases. → M Peer correction, p. 175

a) Sort the phrases into the table. → ○ p. 124

44/1a)

I agree	I disagree
…	…

That's true. | I don't think so. | Exactly. | That's for sure. | Absolutely not. | No way!

b) Put the phrases into the right list. → V Agreeing and disagreeing, p. 197

44/1b)

- I'm sure: …
- I'm not sure: …

I guess … | I'm convinced that … | It's clear to me that … | I doubt that …

6 (SPEAKING) Talk about devices.

a) Make a list. → ○ p. 125

44/2
45/3

Talk to your partner and agree on a ranking list. Rank the devices from the most (++) to the least (--) important.

microwave

TV

phone

computer

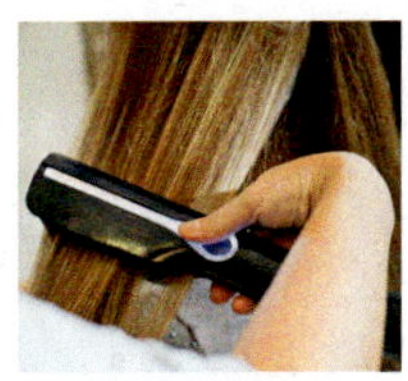
hair straightener

The most important thing for me is … . / I don't think … is more important than … . / … comes first/second/third/ … is next.

b) Which device could you live without? Discuss it with other students. → V Devices, p. 198

fan | electric toothbrush | dishwasher | vacuum cleaner | electric razor

Language → G8, p. 165

Jennifer: If I had a car, I would drive around town with my friends.
Ruth: If I didn't return, I would miss my family.
Jennifer: What would I do if I had to live without it?

Wie heißt die Zeit der Verben im if-Satz? Was passiert mit den Verben im Hauptsatz? Mit welcher Wahrscheinlichkeit werden Ruth oder Jennifer die Dinge tun oder nicht tun? 100%? 50% oder gar nicht?

7 Complete the sentences. → M Bus stop, p. 172

45/4-5

1. If Jennifer met Ruth, they would compare their different lives. (compare)
2. If Ruth stayed with Jennifer, Jennifer —— bowling with her. (go)
3. If Ruth didn't know how to use a computer, Jennifer —— her. (help)
4. Ruth would show Jennifer how to grow her own food if she —— Ruth's family. (visit)
5. Jennifer wouldn't worry about her clothes if she —— with the Amish. (live)
6. Jennifer wouldn't be able to phone her friends if she —— to talk to them. (want)

8 What would make Jennifer's life easier?

a) Look at the pictures. Complete the sentences. → ○ p. 125

46/6

1. Jennifer would be less worried in the morning if she chose her clothes … .

2. She would be at school much earlier if … .

3. She wouldn't feel so tired in the morning if … .

4. She would hear what her dad said if … .

5. She wouldn't get cold if … .

6. It would be better if … .

b) What would make your life easier? Make sentences.

have breakfast • not hungry   call parents when you're late • no trouble   …

If I had breakfast, …

9 (SPEAKING) What would you do if …? → M Round robin, p. 176

a) Answer the questions. Then ask your partner. What would you do if you … → ○ p. 126

46/7

1. were president of the USA for a day?
2. were a superhero?
3. traveled through time?
4. had a million dollars?
5. knew the answers to your next English test before the test?
6. got a place in a talent show?

b) Make more questions for your partner.

46/8

meet an alien · have no brothers/sisters · be a teacher · …

10 (YOUR TURN) Giving your opinion → V Giving opinions, p. 201

a) Could you live without electricity? Why (not)?
Write a short text. Give three reasons.

47/1

(1) The question is "Could I live …?"
(2) I could (not) live without electricity
(3) because … • I also think that … • Another reason is …
(4) For example, … • If I only had / If I had no …
(5) So all in all …

WRITING SKILLS

Nenne dein Thema (1). Sage deine Meinung (2). Begründe nun deine Aussage (3) und gib Beispiele (4). Fasse deine Argumente am Schluss kurz zusammen (5).

b) Work in groups of three. One of you reads his or her text to the others. The other two give feedback. Then take turns.

I (don't) agree with you. / I think you're right/wrong there. / That's true. / I don't think so because … .

Ich kann meine Meinung sagen und begründen. ✓

The Body by Stephen King, 1982

1 What do you do when you spend time with your friends?

2 (READING) Read the story.

1,21

In The Body *Gordie Lachance and his three friends learn that a boy from their area, in the state of Maine, has disappeared and is probably dead. They decide to go on a trip to find the boy's body. In this scene they prepare for the trip.*

The Gun

My room was on the second floor, and it was really hot. I was happy. I wasn't sleeping there that night, and the thought of where we were going made me excited again. I rolled up two blankets and tied an old belt around them. I grabbed all my money, which was less than a dollar. Then I was ready to go.

I went down the back stairs to avoid meeting my dad. I was walking up Carbine Street towards the clubhouse when Chris caught up with me.

"Gordie! You want to see something?"

"Sure. What?"

"Come down here first." He pointed down a small street between two shops.

"What is it, Chris?"

"Come on, I said!"

He ran down the alley and I ran after him. The smell from the rubbish was horrible. "Chris, I'm going to puke, I'm – "

But I forgot about the smell when Chris put his hand into his backpack and pulled out a big gun.

"Where did you get that?"
"From my dad's desk."
"Man, your dad's going to beat you when he finds out."
Chris's eyes just went on dancing. "He isn't going to find out. I'll put it back before then." Chris hated alcohol – he'd already seen too much of what it can do to people.
"Have you got bullets for it?"
"Nine of them."
"Any in it at the moment?"
"No, of course not. What do you think?"
I finally took the gun. I liked the heavy way it sat in my hand.
I pointed the gun at a large tin.
KA – BLAM!
The gun jumped in my hand. Fire shot from the end. It felt as if my wrist was broken. My heart was in my mouth. A big hole appeared in the tin.
"Wow!" I screamed.
Chris was laughing wildly; I couldn't tell if he was amused or scared.
"You did it, you did it! Gordie Lachance is shooting Castle Rock to pieces. Be careful, everyone! Here comes Gordie!"
"Shut up! Let's go!" I screamed.
I gave the gun to Chris and he pushed it into his backpack as we ran up the alley. When we reached Carbine Street we started to walk slowly, so that no one would notice us. Chris was still laughing.
"Man, it's a pity you couldn't see your face. Oh, man, that was really great."
"You knew there was a bullet in it, didn't you? That was a trick, Chris."
"I didn't know, Gordie, honestly. I just took it out of my dad's desk. He always takes the bullets out of it. I guess he was too drunk to remember last time."
Chris looked as innocent as a baby, but when we got to the clubhouse we found Vern and Teddy waiting, and he started to laugh again. He told them the whole story, and after everyone had had a good laugh Teddy asked Chris, "What do you think we need a gun for?"
"Nothing, really," Chris said. "Except we might see a wild animal. And anyway, it's scary out in the forest at night." Everyone agreed with that.
Chris was the strongest and bravest guy of us, and he could say things like that.

"Did you put your tent up in the field?" Teddy asked Vern.

"Yeah, and I put two lamps in it and turned them on, so it'll look as if we're there."

"Hey, man, great!" I said. For him that was real thinking.

He grinned.

"So let's go," Teddy said. "It's nearly twelve already."

Chris stood up and we gathered round him.

"We'll walk across Beeman's field," he said, "and then we'll meet the railway tracks and just walk across the bridge into Harlow."

"How far is it?" Teddy asked.

"I don't know," said Chris. "Harlow's big. We're going to have to walk at least twenty miles. Does that sound right to you, Gordie?"

"Yeah. Maybe more — thirty miles."

"Come on, you guys," Chris said, and picked up his backpack, blankets and water bottle.

CULTURE

In den USA sterben jährlich ungefähr 30.000 Menschen durch Schusswaffen. Das Gesetz besagt, dass jeder Amerikaner das Recht hat eine Waffe zu besitzen. Viele Amerikaner glauben, dass sie eine Waffe brauchen, um sich selbst zu schützen.

Wer darf in Deutschland eine Waffe tragen? Wie findest du das?

3 Did you like the story? Say why or why not.

I think the story was .... | I didn't like/I liked the story because ... | I liked ... best.

4 Work with the story.

a) Put the sentences in the right order.

A The boys tell their friends what happened.
B Gordie takes a gun and shoots.
C They leave before twelve.
D Gordie and Chris meet in Carbine Street.
E Chris shows Gordie his father's gun.
F Gordie gets ready to leave home.

b) Who tells the story? How do you know? Find sentences in the text that tell you.

5 Find out about Chris and Gordie.

a) Who says it? Chris or Gordie?

1. ll. 3–4: … the thought of where we were going made me excited again.
2. ll. 21–24: "… when he finds out." […] "He isnt going to find out. I'll put it back before then."
3. ll. 37–38: My heart was in my mouth. […] "Wow!" I screamed.
4. ll. 41–42: "Be careful, everyone! […]" "Shut up! Let's go!" I screamed.
5. l. 46: "Man, it's a pity you couldn't see your face. Oh man, that was really great."
6. l. 54: "Nothing, really, […]. Except we might see a wild animal."

b) What do the sentences from a) tell about Chris and Gordie?

crazy | excited | strong | worried | scared | amused

1. Gordie seems … .
2. Chris seems … .

STUDY SKILLS

Der Erzähler nutzt Adjektive, um einen Charakter zu beschreiben ("The boy was quiet.") oder er beschreibt dessen Verhalten ("The boy listened to his friends but he never talked much.").

c) Exchange your answers with your partner.

d) "Chris was laughing wildly; I couldn't tell if he was amused or scared." (l. 39)

Read lines 18–42. What do you think? Was Chris really amused or really scared of the situation? Discuss with your partner.

6 Choose one of these tasks.

48/1
49/2-4

a) Play a game: Who am I?
1. Make groups of four.
2. Write the name of a famous person on a sticky note.
3. Put your sticky note on the student next to you.
4. The first player starts asking Yes/No-questions.
5. If an answer to a question is No, it's the next player's turn.

OR

b) Work in groups of four.
1. Take notes about something really exciting that you did together with your friends.
2. Talk about the stories in your group.
3. Choose the best story and tell it to the class.

When I was … | I always wanted to … | One day I … | I was afraid to tell … | I didn't expect …

Ich kann eine Geschichte über Freunde verstehen.

From Chicago to Boston

INTERNET

A

OUTGOING TRIP		**September 16 (Fri)**		**Price (USD)**
Chicago, IL 08:05 a.m.	>	24h 25m	> Boston, MA 09:30 a.m. (+ 1 days)	Fare total for 1 Adult $89
RETURN TRIP		**September 18 (Sun)**		
Boston, MA 05:00 p.m.	>	22h 30m	> Chicago, IL 02:30 p.m. (+ 1 days)	Fare total for 1 Adult $89
			Subtotal	$178
			Taxes and fees	$ 5
			YOUR TOTAL	**$183**

INTERNET

B

Sep 16 (Fri)				
1:39 p.m. Chicago, IL	>	5:05 p.m. Boston, MA	2h 26m	
Sep 18 (Sun)				
5:30 p.m. Boston, MA	>	9:17 p.m. Chicago, IL	4h 47m Philadelphia 1 stop	
			Flight	$141.85
			Tax & Fee	$ 47.35
			Trip total (round trip)	**$189.20**

C

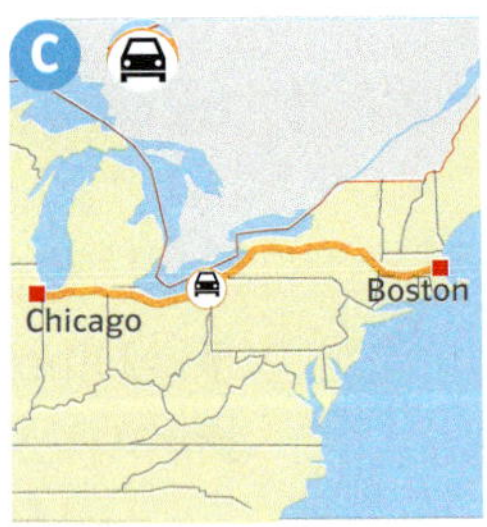

One-way
Time: 14h 46m
Distance: 982 miles
Price of gas: about $160

1 Beantworte die Fragen.

Finde die Vor- und Nachteile jedes Verkehrsmittels heraus. Welche Reise ist am kürzesten? Welche die billigste?

CULTURE

In den USA gibt es neun Zeitzonen. In Boston ist es immer eine Stunde später als in Chicago. Wie viele Zeitzonen hat Europa?

2 What do you think?

50/1-2

If you had to go from Berlin to Frankfurt/Main, how would you get there? By train, plane or bus? Say why. Find information on the internet.

Ich kann Informationen über Reisemöglichkeiten weitergeben.

Trouble at Thanksgiving

1 Look at the photo and guess.

a) What is Jessica making? What is her Dad making?

b) What could the trouble be? Collect ideas in class and vote on the best idea.

Now watch the beginning of the film. Were you right?

2 (VIEWING) Watch the film.

6

a) What else goes wrong that day? Complete the table.

People	Food	Places
...	...	...

b) Thanksgiving Day: Which five things are not in the film?

big parade · balloons · turkey dinner · barbecue party · nice presents · football game · special songs · pecan pie · president's pardon · volunteer work · terrible traffic

3 (SPEAKING) Talk about the film.

a) Watch the film from 03:19 again. What activities do people do at Thanksgiving?

b) Which of these activities are most interesting to you? Say why.

CULTURE

Thanksgiving bedeutet „give thanks“ (sich bedanken). In den USA kommt an diesem Tag die Familie zusammen. Mit einem Festessen wird die gute Ernte gefeiert und meistens wird dabei ein Dankgebet gesprochen.
Gibt es bei euch so eine ähnliche Tradition?

VIEWING SKILLS

Filme beinhalten oft Fotos oder Videos mit zusätzlichen Informationen oder Nebenhandlungen.

Ich kann einen Film über Thanksgiving verstehen. ✓

Checklist

Ich kann Informationen über den Nordosten der USA verstehen. ✔

51

Ich kann einen Text ausdrucksstark vorlesen. ✔

What's up? • How's it going? • I'm glad you could make it. • What have you been up to? • Are you enjoying …?

51

Ich kann meine Meinung sagen und begründen. ✔

I really like that. • I wouldn't change … • I don't think so. • That's for sure. • Absolutely not. • That's true. • I couldn't live without …

52

Ich kann eine Geschichte über Freunde verstehen. ✔

52

Ich kann Informationen über Reisemöglichkeiten weitergeben. ✔

53

Ich kann einen Film über Thanksgiving verstehen. ✔

❀ (TASK) A talk show

"Living without your phone for one day – piece of cake or total nightmare?" Organize a 5 to 10-minute talk show. At the end decide if you want to live without your phone for one day. Do more than one show for practice and for fun.

Step 1

Brainstorm ideas. → M Think-pair-share, p. 177

Collect arguments for both sides:
What's good about a day without a phone? What isn't?

Step 2

Get into groups: 'piece of cake', 'total nightmare' or 'hosts'.

It's always easier to present your own opinion. However, you sometimes have to take a different perspective. Think of that when you make groups.

A host loves talking, keeps the show running, is well-informed and has to be very flexible.

Step 3

Prepare for the show.

Guests

1. Decide on three to four arguments.
2. Explain your arguments, give reasons and examples.
3. Decide who is going to present which argument in the show.
4. Write your arguments on cards (keywords only).
5. Practise your talk.

1. parents control us
2. out with friends
3. phone rings > Mum
4. annoying situation

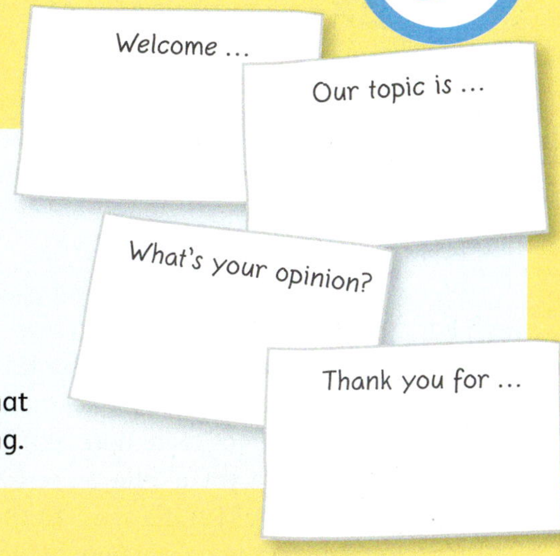

Hosts

1. Think of introductions for the show and the guests.
2. Think of questions that you can ask your guests. Write them on cards.
3. Think of ways to react: What will you say if your guests stop talking or nobody has any questions?
4. Practise.

Welcome to today's talk show. / Our topic today is … / David, what do you think about …? / That's all for today. Thank you for coming.

Step 4

Set the scene and act the show.

1. Prepare the classroom for the show: Arrange the tables and chairs.
2. Decide which groups are going to be in the first show.
3. Decide who is going to be the host.
4. Act the show.

SPEAKING SKILLS

Vergiss nicht, zuerst deine Meinung zu sagen. Sprich das Publikum direkt an, um dessen Aufmerksamkeit zu erregen. Sprich flüssig, aber nicht zu schnell.

Step 5

Make a decision.

What does your class think? Should you live without phones for one day?

Step 6

Do more shows for practice and for fun.

Extra practice

1 Choose the most polite answer. (nach 55/5)

1. Can I help you with anything?
   a) No, thanks, everything's organized. • b) No, I like to do it myself.
2. You came by car, didn't you?
   a) Yes, I did. • b) Yes, and you?
3. How are you doing?
   a) Everything is fine, thanks. • b) I'm doing my homework.
4. I'm so glad you could come.
   a) It's great to be here. • b) I'm glad too.
5. I bought you a little present.
   a) Really? Let me see. • b) That's so nice.
6. So what have you been up to?
   a) Oh, I got up early every day. • b) Oh, it's been a busy time.

2 Ask questions. (nach 56/7)

a) Put the signal words in the right sentences.

always · next year · two months ago · tomorrow · yesterday · this morning

1. Did you arrive — ?
2. Do you — drive there?
3. Will you go home — ?
4. Did you make the pumpkin pie — ?
5. Did you move here — ?
6. Will you come for Thanksgiving again — ?

b) Make questions in the right tense.

1. — your children often — you in the kitchen? (help)
2. — you — everything yesterday evening? (cook)
3. — you always — cooking? (enjoy)
4. — you usually — the same people? (invite)
5. — you — to tea with us next weekend? (come)

3 Complete the questions with where, what, when, who, why and choose the right answer. (nach 56/8)

1. — are you flying to? a) I flew to Portland. • b) I fly to Portland. • c) To Portland, Maine.
2. — will you stay with there? a) I stay with grandpa. • b) I'll stay with grandpa. • c) I will want to stay with grandpa.
3. — does he live? a) He lives on a farm. • b) He lives many years. • c) He lives with his daughter.
4. — time will you get there? a) I'll arrive late. • b) I arrive late. • c) I arrived late.
5. — did you visit him the last time? a) I did last Thanksgiving. • b) I do last Thanksgiving. • c) Last Thanksgiving, I think.
6. — do you like it there? a) So I often like the beach. • b) Because I can often go to the beach. • c) Because I do often the beach.

4 Which of the devices (1–6) do the people need? (nach 59/6)

1. "These clothes are still wet."
2. "She likes to listen to music, but the room is so noisy."
3. "I'll make a quick meal."
4. "Let's send him a message. Have you got your —— ?"
5. "It's raining outside and my hair got very wet."
6. "Could I have a cold drink?"

5 What did the two girls say? Make sentences with If I . . . . (nach 60/8)

Rachel (Amish):

1. have • electricity • at home • iron • all my clothes
2. own • TV • evenings • not be so boring
3. not live • the Amish community • still go • church • Sundays

Maisie (high school student):

4. If I didn't have a cell phone, talk • more • my friends.
5. If I didn't go to school by car, walk • and be fitter.
6. If I didn't always make meals in the microwave, cook • better food.
7. If I didn't hang out with my friends so much on the weekends, help • Mum • at home.

1. If I had electricity at home, I would iron all my clothes.

6 Make the questions and answer them. (nach 61/9)

What would you do if …

1. live • Amish community • for a day?
2. go • Northeast of America?
3. live thousands of kilometres away • from family?
4. have • only one day • America?
5. find • gun?
6. your friend • be unhappy?

1. A: What would you do if you lived in an Amish community for one day?
   B: If I lived in an Amish community, I would miss my phone.

Hier kannst du lernen, wie du eine Zusammenfassung schreibst.

1,22

Healthy and active at Thanksgiving?

written by Pam Warner
(published 07/12/16 in Health & Style)

What is your Thanksgiving like? Turkey and pumpkin pie? American football on the sofa? In the last couple of years a new trend has become popular in the USA: More people like to eat better quality food and live a more active life.

It is slowly going out of fashion to live off convenience and frozen food. A number of people shop for organic food at special supermarkets instead. In some states farmers' markets offer a great variety of fresh vegetables and fruit from the region. "There are also dairy products, bread and meat without chemical additives at these markets. Organic food is not only much healthier but it tastes a lot better as well," explains Emma from Boston. So how about some healthy recipes for Thanksgiving? Maybe pumpkin soup or mashed sweet potatoes? A roast turkey breast or a turkey roulade filled with apples and cranberries is delicious too.

But there's more to a healthy lifestyle than just food. A lot of trend sports show that you can have fun, spend time with friends and stay fit at the same time.
Have you found the right sport for you yet? If not, here is a suggestion: How about standup paddleboarding? If you like water, that's the ideal kind of sport for you. You stand on the board and you use a paddle to move through the water. Don't worry, you don't have to travel to the sea. A lot of clubs offer standup paddleboarding on lakes and rivers.

Of course living healthy also means avoiding alcohol and drugs. Finn, a fitness instructor from Cleveland, says: "Drinking too much alcohol isn't good for your health. Most alcoholic drinks have a lot of calories and negative effects on your fitness too. So why not try a smoothie instead?" Drugs are even worse. You can easily get addicted, and they often cause problems with your family or at school.

To sum up, you can say that organic food together with doing sports is a great way to stay fit. You don't have to do without your favorite meals. Just changing your lifestyle a bit will make you a much happier person.

headline
author, date, source
introduction
main part
conclusion

1 Read the text and take notes.

Find the most important keywords in each paragraph and make a list. Look at the examples in the introduction and the first paragraph on the left.

Notiere keine Beispiele, keine Zahlen, keine Vergleiche, keine Zitate oder direkte Rede. Sie sind für eine Zusammenfassung nicht nötig.

2 Write a summary of the text.

Use your notes to write your summary.

Normalerweise ist eine Zusammenfassung nicht länger als ein Drittel vom Originaltext. Sie kann natürlich auch kürzer sein. Benutze immer deine eigenen Worte.

1. Start with the introduction. Name the title, the author and where the text comes from. Don't forget to say what the text is about.

The article "…" was written by … on … .
The text/article/story is about … It explains …/describes …/deals with …

2. Now summarise each paragraph of the main part in a few sentences. Use your notes to help you.

Benutze immer das simple present für die Zusammenfassung.
Pam Warner talks about organic food and farmers' markets. She explains what these markets offer. …
First/Second/Third …/Then/After that …

3. Write a conclusion. Say what you think about the article.

To sum up, I can say …
In general the article explains …
I think …
In my opinion …

57/3-5
3 Check your summary.

Read your text again and check:

- Spelling (all words correct?)
- Grammar (correct tense?)
- Style (linking words?)
- Content (the most important information?)

Kontrolliere deinen Text mit Hilfe der Checkliste auf Seite 179.

Find more online:
fe76m3

Am Ende dieser Unit kann ich ...
- Informationen über Kalifornien und den Westen der USA verstehen.
- eine Werbeanzeige gestalten.
- über Trends sprechen.
- einen Text über den Goldrausch verstehen.
- Informationen über Kinderarbeit weitergeben.
- einen Film über Beruf und Karriere verstehen.

7 2,1

Unit 4
California dreams

With its 840 miles of coast, California has something for everyone – giant redwood trees in the north, sunny beaches in the south. People live a relaxed lifestyle here. They enjoy surfing and beach volleyball.

You can take cable cars which go up and down the hills in San Francisco or visit the largest Chinatown outside of Asia. The Golden Gate Bridge is San Francisco's famous landmark.

1 What do you know about California?

a) Work in groups of five. Each of you reads a text and its photo. Then tell the others about it.

b) Find headings for all the texts and photos.

2 Find another word for ....

58/1-2

Text 1: 'very big'
Text 2: 'sight'
Text 3: 'not a real name'
Text 4: 'modern'
Text 5: 'to go and see something'

In 1849 the California Gold Rush started. Thousands moved to the west, hoping to find gold and get rich. California's nickname 'The Golden State' comes from that time.

Many high-tech companies have settled in Silicon Valley near San Francisco. Some have developed into the world's largest companies.

Hollywood is the capital of the world's movie industry. You can visit the movie studios there and see the Walk of Fame.

3 (LISTENING) **Listen to the information and take notes.**

2,2

The Golden Gate Bridge

1. bridge: almost —— miles long
2. Joseph Strauss: —— of the bridge
3. bridge: opened in ——
4. safety net: saved —— workers
5. help in foggy weather: —— colour of the bridge
6. symbol of: —— and ——

huge [hjuːdʒ] – riesig
architect [ˈɑːkɪtekt] – Architekt/in
safety net [ˈseɪfti ˌnet] – Sicherheitsnetz
foggy [fɒgi] – neblig
to paint [peɪnt] – (an)streichen

Ich kann Informationen über Kalifornien und den Westen der USA verstehen. ✓

Enjoy the sunny west!

1 Describe the photos in the ads.

In photo 1 I can see … .
In the upper right corner there is … .
In the middle I can see … .
A man is standing next to … .

STUDY SKILLS

Wenn du ein Bild beschreibst, fange mit deinem ersten Eindruck an. Dann beschreibe Details und sage, was die Personen auf dem Bild tun.

1

2

3

You'll love Yosemite Family Adventures

4

2,3 59/1

2 (LISTENING) Listen to a conversation about an ad from exercise 1.

a) Add the missing information. → ○ p. 127

1. Daniel is talking to — and — .
2. They are talking about ad number — in exercise 1.
3. Daniel and — like the ad, but — doesn't.

b) What do Daniel and one girl like about the ad? Why doesn't the other girl like it? Take notes.

3 (SPEAKING) What do you think of the ads? → M Think-pair-share, p. 177

59/2 a) Use these words to talk about the ads. → ○ p. 128

catchy · (not) informative · clear · funny · (un)appealing · fascinating

I think ad number 2 looks … .

59/3 b) Match each word with one of the ads. Does your partner agree? → V Adjectives for ads, p. 202

spectacular · pointless · unusual · dull

4 (SPEAKING) What makes a good ad?

60/4 a) Rank ads 1–4 from best to worst.

b) Give reasons for your choice.
Say something about …

The layout and design:
appealing / simple / boring / …

The headline or slogan:
funny / catchy / too long / …

Text with a message:
informative / too long / clear / …

A: The layout of number … is simple and appealing.
B: Yes, I agree. And the headline is quite …

5 (SONG) Surfin' U.S.A.

2,4 Listen to the song. What does the song sound like? How does it make you feel?

If everybody had an ocean
Across the U.S.A.
Then everybody'd be surfing
Like Californ-i-a

You'd see 'em wearin' their baggies
Huarache sandals, too
A bushy, bushy blond hairdo
Surfin' U.S.A.

You'd catch 'em surfin' at Del Mar
Ventura County Line
Santa Cruz and Trestles
Australia's Narrabeen

All over Manhattan
And down Doheny way
Everybody's gone surfin'
Surfin' U.S.A.

Language → G9, p. 166

A surfer is standing next to a small bus.
At the moment Daniel is looking at his phone.
I never go in the water.
Summers here are always terrible.

Wann benutzt du das present progressive? Wann das simple present?
Was ist an der Schreibweise von 'running' und 'coming' besonders?

60/5 **6 What are the people in the ads doing? Make sentences.**

INTERNET

1. A boy is riding a mountain bike.

carry | sit | walk | ride ✓ | run | hold

61/7 **7 (WRITING) Simple present or present progressive?**

a) Complete the e-mail. → ○ p. 128
61/6

E-MAIL

Hi Becky,
Right now I 'm sitting (sit) next to the swimming pool, and I ___ (have) some ice cream. Well, my life here in California is the same as the one in the Midwest. Every day I ___ (get up), ___ (go) to school and ___ (go) to bed. ☺
But some things are different. It's always warm. We usually ___ (spend) the weekends at the beach. At the moment I ___ (learn) how to surf.
What ___ you ___ (do) right now? I miss you.
Sandy

b) Write a short answer to Sandy's e-mail. Tell her what you usually do and what you're doing now.

Hi Sandy,
Great to hear from you. I often think about you too. Right now I'm waiting for a call from …

Language → G10, p. 167

I'm a terrible swimmer.
It would be nice to sit quietly on the beach.

In welchem der Sätze steht das Adjektiv? In welchem das Adverb?
Woran kannst du beide Formen in der Regel erkennen?

8 Read the advertising text about a helicopter tour. Choose: Adjective or adverb?

61/8

Our Grand Canyon Helicopter Tour is a (1) fantastic • fantastically thing to do. The flight leaves at 9:30 every day. We will fly you there (2) **quick** • **quickly**, and you will arrive at 10 o'clock. After a (3) **delicious** • **deliciously** picnic, our pilots will (4) **happy** • **happily** answer your questions. This (5) **fascinating** • **fascinatingly** tour takes about three hours. The Grand Canyon looks (6) **good** • **well** in photos, but it looks even better in real life.

GRAMMAR → G10, p. 167

to feel sad
to look happy
to seem easy

9 (YOUR TURN) Making an ad → V Talking about a region, p. 207

a) In groups of four make an ad about region in Germany.

1. Decide on a region.
2. Collect ideas. → M Placemat, p. 175
3. Make a quick draft.
4. Divide the tasks:
   - find pictures or make drawings (two students)
   - write the text (two students)

Use the ads on page 76 as examples.
Write a slogan plus two or three sentences.

b) Present your ad. Describe the actions in the photos. Look at the ads. Which one is the most appealing or the most informative? Say why.

STUDY SKILLS

Überlege zuerst, für welche Zielgruppe deine Werbung gedacht ist. Ist sie für Kinder oder für Erwachsene? Wähle dann ein Bild aus, das für sich spricht.

Der Text sollte kurz und einfach sein, und die Botschaft klar. Sprich die Leser direkt an, benutze Fragen und Aufforderungen. Du kannst im Internet auch *Slogan Maker* nutzen.

Ich kann eine Werbeanzeige gestalten. ✓

Hier lerne ich über Trends zu sprechen.

Made in California

1 How often do you go online? How often do you text in a day? → M Round robin, p. 176

2 (READING) Read the blog of a Californian teenager.

2,5

BLOG

A quick look back

Thursday, March 16, 2017

California has always welcomed new ideas – just think of the high-tech companies or the movie industry.

The World Wide Web is one of these ideas. It started in the early 1990s, so it's been around for almost 30 years. And it has really changed the world.

The social media sites that we use came with it. I've had an account since I was 13. Why have they been so successful? Well, that's easy: you can post your photos, share what you think and keep in touch with friends. Most of the time you don't even have to look for information. It'll find you. We should give that a big 'like'.

Online videos have become extremely popular too. They have a huge impact on our lives. Of course, there are the lots of funny videos, but I like the tutorials best. You can find videos on how to do almost anything. People often watch video clips or their favorite shows online.

Nobody watches much TV anymore.

Smartphones and tablets became the next big thing. They have strongly influenced how we communicate. I don't have a radio, write letters or use a map. I use my smartphone instead.

I've been thinking about all this and did a small survey with my friends. What I've found is that more than 90 percent of them go online every day, and half of them are online almost all the time. Most use more than one social media site. Some say it's difficult to stop using them. They get messages every minute and feel that they have to answer right away. Others are worried about cyberbullying because if a person writes bad things about you online, a lot of people can read it.

It looks like we haven't really found any good answers yet.

Posted by Derek Lee   at 8:51 a.m.   2 comments: Links to this post

CULTURE

In den USA können sich Kinder ab 13 Jahren in sozialen Netzwerken anmelden, wenn deren Eltern das erlauben. Wie ist das in eurem Land?

3 Find it in the text.

a) Where in the text is it? → ○ p. 129

1. Derek talks about an invention which started at the end of the 20th century.
2. Derek gives reasons why some social media sites are successful.
3. Derek loves shows which tell people how to do things.
4. Derek asked his friends some questions.
5. Derek talks about some problems of social media.

b) Why have social media become popular? What problems do people have with them?

4 (LISTENING) Listen to the survey. Choose the right answer.

2,6
62/1

1. It's **the latest thing** • **out of fashion**.
2. Didn't it become **outdated** • **popular** in Europe first?
3. Jumping fitness is **in fashion** • **trendy** at the moment.
4. I think it will soon go **out of fashion** • **outdated** again.
5. The instructor was **trendy** • **great**.
6. I don't think it will be **in fashion** • **outdated** so soon.

62/3

5 (SPEAKING) Explain the words.

62/2a)

a) Explain these social media words to your partner. → p. 130

(dis)like · friend request · post · share · unfriend

When you 'like' a video, you show people that you've liked it.

62/2b)

b) Explain three more words to a partner. → V Social media, p. 203

follower · subscribe · trending

6 (SPEAKING) What is the cartoon about?

STUDY SKILLS

Beschreibe zuerst nur das, was du siehst. Fange erst dann mit der Interpretation an. Was will der Zeichner dem Leser sagen? Was will er kritisieren? Gib zum Schluss deine eigene Meinung wieder. Stimmst du dem Zeichner zu? Wird seine Botschaft deutlich?

Language → G11, p. 168

The internet has changed the world.
Smartphones have influenced how we communicate.
We haven't found answers for these problems yet.

Welche Zeitform steht in den Sätzen? Wie wird sie gebildet?
Wann benutzen wir sie?

63/4

7 What have or haven't they done? → M Bus stop, p. 172

1. Derek • just • make • fresh orange juice

2. Linda • already • start • computer

3. already • read • his e-mail

4. not finish • her blog • yet

5. not see • each other • in real life • yet

6. just • meet • first time

1. Derek has just made fresh orange juice.

8 Say for how long or since when.

63/5

a) Choose since or for. Make sentences. → ○ p. 130

1. I've had my smartphone	since	more than three years.
2. Millions have seen the cat photos	for	Tuesday.
3. 5,000 people have watched that tutorial		May.
4. He hasn't answered his e-mails		five days.
5. Have you posted a new comment		last week?
6. The book has been successful		years.

63/6

b) Make sentences with for or since.

1. I sent Linda a message 20 minutes ago. She didn't answer.
2. She couldn't live without the internet. She started using it when she was five.

GRAMMAR → G11, p. 168

since 10 o'clock
for an hour

9 Complete the survey questions and answers.

a) Use the simple past or the present perfect to complete the sentences. → ○ p. 131

64/7

1. Interviewer: How much did you spend (spend) on food and clothes last month?
   Person A: I'm not sure but it —— (be) a lot of money.
2. Interviewer: —— you —— (buy) a book or a magazine this week?
   Person B: No, I haven't. But I —— (get) a magazine two days ago for my Mum.
3. Interviewer: —— you ever —— (use) tutorials to learn how to do something?
   Person C: Yes, sure. I —— (learn) to play the guitar that way.
4. Interviewer: —— you —— (find) any new music videos that you liked in the last two weeks?
   Person D: Oh, yes. Yesterday I —— (see) one that I really enjoyed.

b) Make more sentences from the survey.

1. I • not see • that movie • yet
2. who • invent • the internet • 30 years ago?
3. I • not think about • that question • yet

Achte auf die Signalwörter wie „yesterday" oder „ever".

10 (YOUR TURN) Talking about trends → V Giving opinions, p. 201

a) Hot or not? What do you think? Sort these trends into the table.

64/8
65/1-2

selfies | torn jeans | veganism

hot	not

b) Think of more trends and put them in the table.

c) Work with a partner. Exchange your tables. Give your opinion: Do you agree with your partner's table?

Do you know …?
Is the trend hot or not?
What do you think of …?
Have you tried it?
Has it had an impact on your life?

Ich kann über Trends sprechen. ✓

Gold rush! → M Jigsaw, p. 174

1 (READING) **Home group: Find two partners. Each of you chooses one of the texts (A, B or C). Read your text and answer the questions.**

2 **Expert group: Find students who read the same text. Compare your answers with them.**

STUDY SKILLS

Wenn ihr in Gruppen verschiedene Aufgaben bearbeitet, seid ihr dafür verantwortlich, eure Ergebnisse an die anderen weiterzugeben. Denkt daran, wenn ihr eure Aufgabe löst. Welche Informationen und welche Vokabeln brauchen die anderen, die den Text nicht gelesen haben, damit sie das Thema verstehen?

2,7 **Text A: A newspaper report**

California Star

December 6, 1848

GOLD! GOLD! GOLD! Found in California

Washington. Yesterday the President of the United States confirmed the discovery of gold in California. The race for gold has just begun. Who will win?

It began in Coloma, 40 miles away from Sacramento, when one of Mr. Sutter's workers found gold in January this year. Mr. Sutter, a German-Swiss immigrant and businessman, wanted to keep the gold a secret because he didn't want to give up his farming plans. At the same time he tried to buy more land and become the official landowner. His workers weren't allowed to talk about the gold, but the news got out. Sutter now has a big problem. He has to prove that he officially owns the land.

First, many local people didn't believe it. Then in May the news got to San Francisco and half of the city's population left to look for gold in the American River. Men stopped working and moved to the West where they hoped to become rich easily. You have probably heard stories about some of these men.

Landowners in the West now worry that the gold fever will increase even more, and the problems will get worse. We will tell you more in our next edition.

1. When did the President confirm the discovery of gold?
2. Who is Mr Sutter?
3. How did Sutter react when he learned about the gold?
4. What didn't Sutter allow his workers to do?
5. What happened when the news came to San Francisco?
6. What are landowners in the West worried about?

2,8

Text B: A letter from a gold hunter

February 15, 1850
San Francisco

Dear Maddy,

It's been weeks since I left you. Finally, I've found the time to rest and send you some news.

I arrived safely. There were heavy storms when we crossed the sea to Panama. A lot of men got sick, and some died. Sometimes I wanted to give up, but then I thought of you and our children. Ninety days after I had left you in New York, we arrived at San Francisco Bay. We were happy, and the weather was great.

However, it took another week to get to the place where we got horses and wagons. At night we slept under the stars. A few days later we arrived at our camp.

I've now made friends with some of the men who have come from all over the country. We often sit around the fire at night, tell stories and sing. All of us still dream of making money and then returning home to our families. Sometimes there are fights in the camps. But don't worry, Maddy, I'm OK.

Finding gold isn't easy, but I get better every day. Do you know how happy I was when I found my first little piece of gold? Some days are better than others, but you keep me going. One day I got terribly sick. I hadn't eaten or slept much, and I had worked in very cold water for hours. The fever was gone after a week.

My thoughts are with you, Maddy. Write soon.

Always yours,
Edward

1. Who is writing to whom?
2. What happened on the way to Panama?
3. How did the men feel when they reached San Francisco Bay?
4. How long did the journey take from the start to the end?
5. How is life in the camp?
6. What does Edward say about his job?

2,9

Text C: An encyclopedia entry

A history of California and the Gold Rush

News of the discovery of gold in California in 1848 caused huge excitement not only in America. Thousands of people went there from all over the world and in 1849 the Gold Rush started.
By 1852 it became more and more difficult and expensive to find gold. But many more immigrants arrived. Before the Gold Rush, not even 1,000 non-native people lived in California. Ten years later the population was almost 400,000. San Francisco went from a small village of 500 people to a town of 150,000 in a few years. Many other new towns were built.
Because of all this, California quickly became the 31st state of the United States in 1850. The money from the gold helped to connect California with the rest of the country: in 1869 the First Transcontinental Railway to San Francisco opened.
However, the impact on the Native American population was terrible. The immigrants killed them or made them their slaves. Thousands died. In 1870 the Native American population was only 20 % of what it had been before the Gold Rush.
The gold fever did not last long. When there was no more gold, there was no more work. So people moved away and left the towns behind. Some of them are still there today. The town of Bodie, for example, once had 8,000 inhabitants. Now visitors can walk through it.

1. Where did people come from to find gold?
2. What happened until 1852?
3. How much did the population grow in California after 1848?
4. Where did the money from the gold go?
5. What was the impact of the Gold Rush on the Native Americans?
6. What happened to Bodie?

CULTURE

Der Goldrausch wurde zum Symbol des „Kalifornischen Traums“ und Kalifornien ein Ort des Neuanfangs, wo man mit Glück sehr schnell sehr reich werden konnte. Würdest du so viele Stunden unter schwierigsten Bedingungen arbeiten wollen, um reich zu werden?

3 Home group: present what you have found out about your text to the group. Take notes about the other texts.

Text A / B / C is a …
The most important information from the text is …
It's about …
First …
The writer is …
Then …

4 Do a quiz in class.

Each expert writes one right or wrong sentence about his or her text.
Read the sentence to the class.
Is it right or wrong?

5 Choose one of these tasks.

66/1
67/2-5

a) Do an interview: It's 1848. One of you is a reporter for the *California Star*. Your partner is a gold hunter who has just found a lot of gold.

Reporter: Prepare questions.
Where did you …?
When did you …?
What did you …?
Who …?
How long …?
How much …?

Gold hunter: Prepare your story and your plans for the future.
Make notes to answer the reporter's questions.
I came to … in … . / I looked for … in … . /
I found … . / … went with me. /
I stayed for … . / I made … .

OR

b) Make a timeline about the history of the Gold Rush. Collect information from the texts.

1848	events in January, May, December
1849	
1850	California
1852	…
1858	population
1869	…
1870	Native Americans

Ich kann einen Text über den Goldrausch verstehen.

Too young to work?

CULTURE

Fast die Hälfte des US-amerikanischen Obsts, Gemüses und der Nüsse kommt aus dem Central Valley, Kalifornien. Hohe Temperaturen von 40°C (100°F) und wenig Regen bieten ideale Bedingungen. Aber die Arbeitsbedingungen sind hart.

Many big farms in California employ children, mostly from Latin America, to pick fruit or vegetables. They sometimes work more than ten hours a day and only earn the minimum wage or even less. "We have to get up at 4:30 in the morning. Buses drive us to the fields, where we work all day in the heat," explains Matteo (12) from Sacramento.

Children like Matteo have to help their parents because migrant parents often don't have enough income. It is difficult for them to get a better job because many of them don't have the qualifications or hardly speak English. Some are in the USA illegally.

All laborers have the legal right to take breaks and drink water. But the reality is different: the long hours in the fields make them tired and some get hurt or sick. "I always have difficulties breathing, and I have a constant headache out there," says Matteo's brother Ramon (14), who has been working on different farms since he was ten. "But I'm glad Matteo and I have the jobs. If we hadn't found work, it would have been a bad year for our family."

A federal law from 1938 allows farm owners to employ children from the age of twelve on big farms and even younger children on small farms. From the age of 14 teenagers can do farm work without their parents' consent. Officially, they are only allowed to work outside school hours. There are no statistics about how many children spend their days as farm helpers, but the estimate is about half a million. All recent attempts to change the law have failed.

1 Beantworte die Fragen.

1. In welchem Bereich arbeiten Kinder in Kalifornien? Warum?
2. Unter welchen Bedingungen arbeiten sie?
3. Wie sind die gesetzlichen Bestimmungen?

2 Talk to your class.

68/1

What jobs are you allowed to do?

Ich kann Informationen über Kinderarbeit weitergeben.

Talking about jobs

1 Talk about the ad on the right.

a) Which question in the ad is the most important to you? Why?

b) Would the job interest you? Give reasons.

2 (VIEWING) Watch the film.

8

a) Watch the film until 02:08. Jessica, Wesley or Ronan: Who …

1. helps neighbours in their gardens?
2. walks the neighbours' dogs?
3. works as a waitress?
4. helps students with their homework?
5. puts groceries in bags for customers?

b) Watch the film from 02:08 to the end.

1. What does Wesley want to be?
2. What animals would Jessica like to work with?
3. Where would Ronan like to work?

CULTURE

Die Rocky Mountains (the Rockies) liegen im Westen Kanadas und der USA. Sie sind beliebt bei Kletterern, Campern, Wanderern und Skifahrern. Teile der Rockies sind in National-parks. Finde die Rockies auf der Karte hinten im Buch.
Welche Gebirge kennst du?

3 (SPEAKING) Talk about the film.

a) Choose one of the jobs from the film. Find two or three reasons why you'd like this job.

I'd love/My big dream is to become a …
I'd like to work with …

b) You partner argues against it.

I don't think so.
No, that's …!
Really? But you must …

at the weekends/after school/on Saturdays
out in the country/in the city
at a computer/outside/alone/… all day
famous/interesting/rich/boring/hard work/…

VIEWING SKILLS

In einem Film bewegen sich die Menschen oder Dinge – oder die Kamera bewegt sich stattdessen (z. B. durch Schwenken oder Näherkommen). Das kann den Film interessanter machen.

Sieh dir die zweite Hälfte des Films erneut an. Wer oder was bewegt sich – die Schauspieler, die Kamera oder beide?

Ich kann einen Film über Beruf und Karriere verstehen. ✓

Checklist

Ich kann Informationen über Kalifornien und den Westen der USA verstehen. ✓

69

Ich kann eine Werbeanzeige gestalten. ✓

The ad looks spectacular. • Its layout is simple and .... • The headline is funny. • In the picture there is ...

69

Ich kann über Trends sprechen. ✓

Almost everyone uses it. • It has had a huge impact. • ... isn't trendy/popular • It's out of fashion. • Have you tried it?

70

Ich kann einen Text über den Goldrausch verstehen. ✓

70

Ich kann Informationen über Kinderarbeit weitergeben. ✓

71

Ich kann einen Film über Beruf und Karriere verstehen. ✓

(TASK) A blog

Write a blog about a trend that you like. Add pictures. Share your blog with others. Which trends do you find interesting? Which ones not? Why?

Step 1

Collect ideas.

Work with a partner.
Make a mind map of trends.

trends: fashion, food, technology, entertainment

Step 2

Choose your topic.

Decide which trend you would like to write about.
Collect words and phrases.

- It's a kind of ...
- You can use it for / when ...
- It comes from ...

Step 3

Collect information.

- Say where you learned about the trend.
- Say what you like about it.
- Say where the trend comes from.
- Talk about the trend. What is it? What's special about it?
- Say which people like this trend.

WRITING SKILLS

In einem Blog schreibst du deine eigene Meinung. Vergiss also nicht zu sagen, was du denkst.

Step 4

Write your draft and check it.

Check the content and spelling.

BLOG

Have you ever heard of bento boxes? No? Well, I hadn't either until a friend of mine introduced them to me. If you like being creative, try out this fun way of organizing food. It's awesome. My brothers and sisters love it. And it's great for parties too. I once made a box as a present. It was a blast.

Bento originally comes from Japan and usually means a "home-packed meal". Bentos have been around since the fifth century. Modern bento boxes are made of plastic or metal. Traditional boxes are made of bamboo. They can have rice, fish or meat and vegetables.

Here's mine ...

You can make your own bento easily.
Just follow these simple steps:
- The food must be easy to eat.
- You must be able to eat it with your fingers.
- Your food must be cut into small pieces.
- Your food must be nice to look at.

Comment:
September 7, 2016
cookie: AWESOME. What a great idea! ...

Step 5

Share your blog with other groups. → M Gallery walk, p. 173

Read at least three blogs from other groups.
Which one do you find the most interesting? Why?

Step 6

Comment on a blog.

Choose one blog. Discuss it and write a short comment.

Extra practice

1 Read these sentences from ads. Fill in the missing adjectives. (nach 77/3)

special | boring | informative ✓ | fascinating | funny | interesting | great

1. We have an informative brochure with lots of tips for you.
2. You will find the Grand Canyon f — .
3. What makes California so s — ? Come and find out!
4. Our trips are never b — .
5. We promise you'll have a g — time.
6. There are lots of i — activities for families.
7. Come to the show. It's so f — , so you will laugh a lot.

2 Describe the ad. (nach 77/4)

a) Name the parts of the ad 1–4.

layout | headline | slogan | message

b) Describe the parts. Use these adjectives.

catchy | clear | informative | simple

The layout is … .

3 Simple present or present progressive? (nach 78/7)

The Brown family lives (1 live) in Chicago. They always — (2 go) to California in the summer. At the moment they — (3 rent) a house in San Francisco. Their daughter is there, but their son Bruce — (4 not travel) with them this time because he — (5 ski) in Canada. Mr Brown usually — (6 go) shopping for the family, and he — (7 do) that now. But sometimes he — (8 not understand) what people say because many people — (9 speak) Spanish in California. So he — (10 learn) Spanish during this trip!

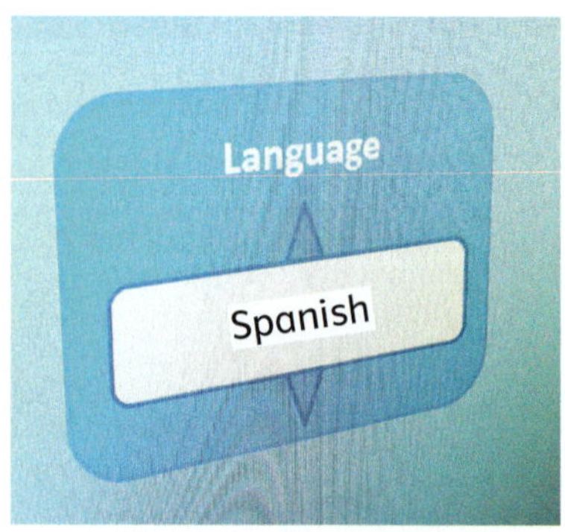

4 Complete the sentences with an adjective or an adverb. (nach 79/8)

1. My American friend Olivia gets excited easily. (easy)
2. And she often talks — about her home. (excited)
3. She enjoys telling lots of — jokes. (funny)
4. But sometimes Olivia has a — day. Then she misses California and feels — . (bad; sad)
5. She had a — life there. She liked the — beaches. (good; beautiful)
6. She is a — surfer, and she can swim very — . (good; fast)
7. She lived there — , but her friend didn't feel — in Berlin. (happy; good)

5 Find the opposites. (nach 81/5)

1. in fashion
2. trendy
3. make a friend request
4. share
5. funny

serious | outdated | unfriend | keep | out of fashion

6 Make sentences with the present perfect and use for or since. (nach 82/8)

1. California has become (become) more and more important since the Gold Rush.
2. Silicon Valley — (be) the home of high-tech industry — the 1990s.
3. We — (live) here — 2014.
4. I — (follow) the best trends here — years.
5. I — (not watch TV) — two weeks because I prefer online videos.
6. Today's teenagers — (know) the internet — they were little.
7. — a number of years people — (buy) more phones than computers.

7 Complete the dialogue with the present perfect or the simple past. (nach 83/9)

1. A: Have you seen (you • see) my new smartphone yet? I bought (buy) it last week.
2. B: Yes, you — (show) it to me yesterday afternoon.
3. A: But what — (you • think) of it? You — (not • tell) me.
4. B: Well, I — (take) some cool photos with it yesterday. But I — (always • prefer) having a bigger one.
5. A: Really? I — (not • choose) a big one because my bag — (be) too small. I — (have) the phone for about a week, but I — (not • learn) half the things I can do with it yet.
6. B: — (you • try) e-books yet? I — (not • buy) a paper book since last year. I — (already • read) lots of e-books on my phone.

Hier kannst du lernen,
wie du ein Gespräch führst.

2,10

A podcast interview

Wow, that sounds cool!

Isn't that the same every year?

No way!? That's amazing!

That doesn't sound like much fun.

Tell me more.

Is that really interesting?

Thanks so much.

I can imagine that.

I have to interrupt here.

1 Look at the photos on the left.

a) Talk about the photos with a partner. How do the people feel in each photo? Why?

> Wenn ihr herausfinden wollt, wie Menschen sich fühlen, achtet auf den Gesichtsausdruck und Körperhaltung.

b) Listen to the interviews.
1. Which interview matches which photo?
2. Which interview is the better one?

2 Listen to the interviews again.

Match the sentences from page 94 with the interviews.

> Der Tonfall und die Art, wie Menschen reden, können euch viel über die Situation verraten.

Interview A
- showing interest
- sounding surprised
- saying thank you

Interview B
- sounding bored
- interrupting

74/1
75/2-4

3 Interview your partner about the last movie that he or she saw.

a) Work in pairs. Decide who will ask the questions and who will answer.

> Macht euch zuerst Stichpunkte. Schreibt alles auf, was euch zu dem Film einfällt, über den ihr reden wollt. Beantwortet die W-Fragen (Who? What? When? Where? Why? How did you like it?).

b) Think of some questions and answers together.

> Wenn ihr das Interview vorbereitet, vergesst nicht, die Sätze aus Interview A zu verwenden.

c) Act the interview.

> Denkt bei eurem Interview an euren Gesichtsausdruck, eure Körperhaltung und euren Tonfall.

Find more online: fe76m3

Am Ende dieser Unit kann ich ...
- Informationen über die Südstaaten der USA verstehen.
- über Einflüsse verschiedener Kulturen im täglichen Leben sprechen.
- andere über Freizeitaktivitäten informieren.
- einen Bericht über Rassismus verstehen.
- Informationen über Rituale weitergeben.
- einen Film über die Sommerferien verstehen.

9 2,11 Unit 5

Southern life

The Southern Appalachian Mountains, the Gulf Coast beaches, the Florida swamps and the Mississippi River – the South has many exciting places for fans of the outdoors.

Until the 1950s African Americans in the South had few rights. There was a lot of discrimination. The Civil Rights Movement was a peaceful protest movement. It forced the government to change the laws.

1 (SPEAKING) Talk about the photos.

a) Choose a photo. How do you feel when you look at it? What does it make you think of?

b) Talk about it with a partner.

2 Which text is it?

A In the middle of the last century African Americans got more rights.
B The southern way of life is different.
C Music is important in the South.
D In the past black people were forced to work for white people on very big farms.
E The countryside in the South is great.

3

In the 18th century, people from France, England, Scotland and Ireland went to the South. Soon they brought in African slaves to work on their plantations.

4

More than any other region of the United States, the South has its own lifestyle, culture and customs. People here are proud to be both Americans and Southerners.

5

Some styles of music come from the South like gospel, blues or rock 'n' roll. New Orleans is the home of jazz, and Nashville is the home of country music.

3 (LISTENING) Listen to the online radio broadcast about Taylor Swift.

2,12
78/1-2

What do these numbers mean?
Match them with the right words.

A 10
B 14
C 2006
D 2.5 million
E under 30

1. moved to Nashville
2. number of copies of first album
3. best-paid celebrity
4. started playing the guitar
5. released her first single

career [kəˈrɪə] – Karriere
to release [rɪˈliːs] – veröffentlichen
copy [ˈkɒpi] – Exemplar
best-paid [ˈbest peɪd] – höchstbezahlt
celebrity [səˈlebrəti] – Prominente/r

Ich kann Informationen über die Südstaaten der USA verstehen. ✓

Hier lerne ich, über Einflüsse verschiedener Kulturen im täglichen Leben zu sprechen.

Living together

1 (READING) Read the text.

2,13
79/1

Rich food, rich culture
by Anna Williams

A Southern food

The South is famous for its great food. This food shows the history of the Southerners. So I went on a trip down there. Here's what I found.
First, there was the food of the Native Americans. Then new dishes were brought in by European settlers. Slaves from West Africa had a big influence too.
The delicious southern fried chicken is a good example. It was introduced by Scottish people. The dish is made with chicken, flour and different spices. The spices are mixed with the flour. The chicken pieces are washed and then covered in the flour. Finally, they are fried in oil.

B The city of New Orleans

In New Orleans different cultures and traditions come together. The city was founded by the French in 1718 then it became Spanish. New Orleans was the most important cotton and slave market in the South until the middle of the 19th century. Later it became the country's biggest harbor after New York where immigrants arrived. Thousands who came from Europe entered the country there.
When you walk through New Orleans today, you can see that it's a multicultural city.

New Orleans

The best example is the famous Mardi Gras carnival.

C The Confederate flag

But living together doesn't come without problems. The Confederate flag is one example. I talked to some people about it. For many white people in the South this historic flag is a symbol that they are proud of. Others just tolerate it. But most African Americans think that it is a symbol of racism.
The flag flew over the South Carolina State House for years until 2015. But after the people had learned about a number of killings of black teenagers, protests started. The people and the state government had to find a solution. Many big shops have now stopped selling the flag.
Anyway, many visitors come to see the rich multicultural life of the South like I did.

CULTURE

Die Südstaaten benutzten eine eigene Fahne im amerikanischen Bürgerkrieg. Der Norden wollte die Sklaverei abschaffen, der Süden nicht. Heute ist die Fahne bei vielen umstritten.

The Confederate flag

2 Take notes about multicultural influences.

a) Work in groups of three. Take notes.

Student 1: Read text A.
- Where from and who?
- Recipe?

Student 2: Read text B.
- Historic facts?
- Harbour?

Student 3: Read text C.
- The Confederate flag?
- Things that changed?

b) Talk to your partners and exchange your results. Which fact did you find most interesting?

3 What's the nationality?

79/2

a) Match the nationalities with the flags. → ◯ p. 131

Chinese · Greek · Italian · Russian · Polish · Turkish

1. 中国

2. Россия

3. Polska

4. Ελλάδα

5. Türkiye

6. Italia

b) Which is typical? Match the food with the nationality. → V Nationalities, p. 209

paella

cheese

sushi

Japanese · Spanish · Swiss

80/4

4 Work with words to talk about conflicts and solutions.

79/3a)

a) Find the word with the same meaning. → ◯ p. 131

1. accept: say no • say yes to something
2. tolerate: disagree • do nothing
3. ban: say no to something • find a solution
4. disagree: have a different opinion • think the same
5. protest: be against something • agree
6. agree: refuse • have the same opinion

STUDY SKILLS

Beim Vokabellernen kann es dir helfen, wenn du Synonyme (Wörter mit gleicher Bedeutung) und Antonyme (Wörter mit gegensätzlicher Bedeutung) gleichzeitig lernst.

79/3b)

b) Sort the words into the table. Add the words from a) too. → V Conflicts and solutions, p. 209

appreciate · reject · resent · respect

👍	👎
…	…

Language detectives → G12, p. 169

The dish is made with chicken.
Chicken pieces are washed.

Wann benutzt du das Passiv?
Wie bildest du es?

80/5

5 Choose is or are.

1. Pork — used in many southern dishes.
2. Southern food — eaten across the USA.
3. Vegetables and meat — kept in the fridge.
4. All these dishes — made with rice.
5. The chicken and rice — not cooked for a long time.
6. Black rice — not sold in all shops.

80/6

6 (SPEAKING) Describe how southern fried chicken is made.

1. The spices and flour are — (mix).

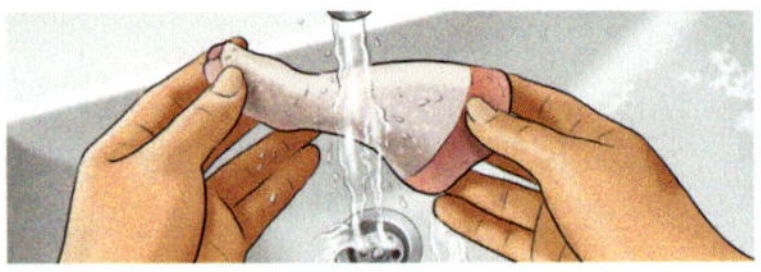

2. Then the chicken pieces are — (wash).

3. The chicken is — in flour (cover).

4. Next the chicken pieces are — (put) in hot oil.

5. Finally, the chicken is — (fry) until it's golden.

Sieh im Anhang nach, wenn du die dritte Form des Verbs nicht mehr weißt.

7 (WRITING) Make sentences about living together.

81/7

a) Make sentences. → ○ p. 132

1. People from other countries are welcomed (welcome) in multicultural societies.
2. More than one language — (speak) there.
3. In some schools classes — (teach) in different languages.
4. Special classes — (organize) for new people.
5. Dishes from all around the world — (serve) in restaurants.
6. Racism — (not accept) in multicultural societies.

b) Change these sentences to passive sentences.

1. Multicultural societies accept new ideas.
2. Visitors enjoy New Orleans' cultural life.
3. Some people don't respect immigrants.

Wenn du in einem Passivsatz sagen willst, wer etwas getan hat, ergänze 'by+ …'

8 Make passive sentences in the simple past. → M Bus stop, p. 172

81/8

a) Complete the information about the city of Raleigh. → ○ p. 132

The city of Raleigh (1) was founded in the 18th century as the capital of North Carolina. It's an example of a city that (2) — (plan) from the beginning. The city (3) — (give) the name of Sir Walter Raleigh, an English adventurer and writer. The streets (4) — (build) in a special way; like on a grid.
The tallest skyscraper in the city, the PNC Plaza, (5) — (not complete) until 2008. In 2014 the city (6) — (choose) as one of the Top 10 of the cities that have grown the fastest.

GRAMMAR → G12, p. 169

choose	– was / were chosen
found	– was / were founded
build	– was / were built
give	– was / were given
plan	– was / were planned
complete	– was / were completed

b) Complete the sentences to find out more about Raleigh.

1. The land for the city — (sell) by a man who owned a plantation in the 1780s.
2. The first African-American college of the South — (open) in Raleigh in 1865.
3. The work on the first airport — (not finish) until 1929.
4. During the 1960s the laws about black people — (change).

9 (YOUR TURN) Different cultures where I live → V Talking about culture, p. 213

81/9

What is the influence of other cultures where you live? Prepare a short presentation.
→ M Tip top, p. 177

- Describe where you live.
  I live in … / There are many Turkish / Chinese / … there.
- Say what multicultural influences you find in:
  - shops
  - restaurants
  - signs
  - music

  Most of the …
  When you look around, you see …
  The … is written in …
  People like to buy/go to … because …
- Choose a dish or a piece of music from another culture and describe it.
  'Paella' is a famous … dish. It's usually made … . But often other things are added, like … .

STUDY SKILLS

1. Sammle Informationen und mache dir Notizen.
2. Teile deine Präsentation in klare Abschnitte ein.
3. Stelle dein Thema vor.
4. Beantworte mögliche Fragen nach der Präsentation.

Ich kann über Einflüsse verschiedener Kulturen im täglichen Leben sprechen. ✓

Hier lerne ich, andere über Freizeitaktivitäten zu informieren.

A trip to Florida

1 Look at the websites. Which trip would you choose? Why?

INTERNET

Be there for the most important NASCAR race!

Our Daytona 500 race packages:

- excellent Daytona 500 race tickets,
- large choice of hotels
- transfer to the race track
- booklet with all details

INTERNET

Go into the Florida Everglades!

Airboat rides, alligators, wildlife show

- hotel pick-up,
- exciting 30-minute boat tour (with lots of 360-degree turns!)
- alligator, snake and wildlife show
- jungle trail through the swamps

2 (READING) Read the friends' dialogue. → M Dramatic reading, p. 173

2,14
82/1

Anna: Dad can take us to Daytona or to the Everglades. He says that he needs an answer today. These are the websites that he's found.
Matt: Well, I know. I'd like to go to the race. It's the biggest NASCAR event of the year. And I'm sure we'll get great seats.
Anna: That's not my idea of fun. All those noisy people! I prefer the Everglades. I've never seen an alligator in the wild.
Matt: Why do you want to spend the day in the heat?
Anna: What does Ethan think?
Ethan *is speech impaired. He can hear, but he uses sign language. Matt understands sign language and translates for Anna.*
Matt: Ethan says that he doesn't like crowds much either.
Anna: There you are. He wants to see the alligators too.
Ethan *makes more signs.*
Matt: I'm sorry, I didn't get that, Ethan. Can you repeat it, please? (Ethan *repeats it.*) I see. But he also says that he has always wanted to watch a NASCAR race.
Anna: Oh, no! I'm outnumbered!
Ethan *makes signs.*
Matt: I'm sorry, I didn't catch that, Ethan.
Ethan *repeats it.* Oh, right. He says the jungle trail sounds really interesting too. He'd like to see big snakes. He wants to know if your dad can take us to the Everglades another time. Maybe next month?
Anna: Hmm. I can ask him again tonight.

3 Answer the questions.

1. Where does Anna want to go? Why?
2. Where do Ethan and Matt want to go? Why?

2,15 · 82/2

4 (LISTENING) Listen to the text about a visit to an alligator farm.

a) Read notes A–C. Which one is correct? → ○ p. 132

A
- trainer fed alligators
- trainer put hand in alligator's mouth
- photo of Ethan with snake

B
- trainer fed snakes
- trainer put hand in alligator's mouth
- photo of Anna with alligator

C
- trainer fed alligators and snakes
- trainer had fight with snake
- photo of Matt with snake

b) Which answer is right?

1. Where did they go back to after the day in Daytona? — Florida • Georgia
2. How did Matt feel after the 360-degree turns? — sick • strong
3. What did Ethan think of the last part of the day? — best part • most boring part

5 Say that you understand or don't understand.

a) Put the sentences into two groups: "I understand ☺" or "I don't understand ☹": → ○ p. 133

82/3a)

Could you please explain? · I get it. · I know what you mean. · I see. · I'm sorry, but I didn't catch that. · Excuse me?

Saying "I understand": …   Saying "I don't understand": …

b) Match the phrases with the definitions. → V Understanding things, p. 210

82/3b)

Please repeat that. · Absolutely! · What do you mean by '…'?

1. Ask somebody to explain a word.
2. Ask somebody to say something again.
3. Tell somebody that you agree with them.

SPEAKING SKILLS

Wenn du etwas nicht verstehst, sag nicht einfach nur „Hä?" oder „Was?". Das ist unhöflich.

6 Use sign language.

Look at the signs. Then close your books and practise them with a partner.

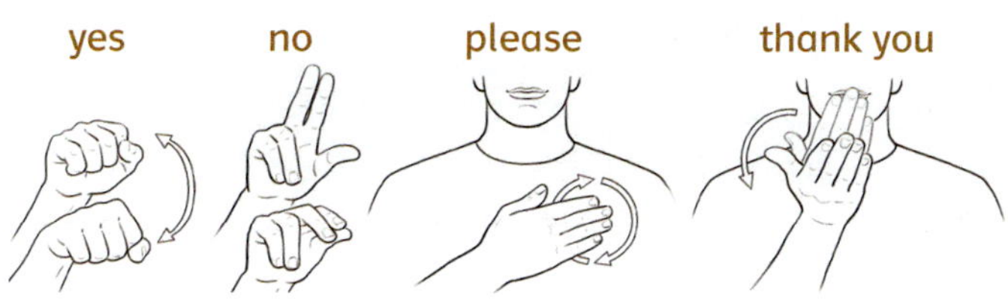

STUDY SKILLS

Verbindest du beim Vokabellernen bestimmte Gesten mit bestimmten Wörtern, wirst du dir diese leichter merken können.

Language detectives → G13, p. 170

Dad: "I need an answer today." → Dad says he needs an answer today.
Ethan: "I don't like crowds much either." → Ethan says that he doesn't like crowds much either.
Ethan: "Can your dad drive us? → He wants to know if your dad can drive us.

Diese Sätze geben wieder, was der Vater und Ethan sagen. Sieh dir die Sätze an.
Welche Wörter verändern sich?

83/4

7 Report what other people say. → M Peer correction, p. 175

a) Report what Anna says. → ○ p. 133

1. "I love the warm weather in Florida."
2. "It's awesome."
3. "We just wear T-shirts."
4. "We often go to the beach."
5. "I don't have time to take lots of photos."
6. "I don't like the thousands of insects."

1. Anna says that she loves the warm weather in Florida.

Pronomen und Verben ändern sich in der indirekten Rede:
I → he/she
I love → he/she loves
we → they

b) Play the game: Your teacher gives a sentence to the first student in your group. He or she whispers the sentence to the next person .... Are the sentences still the same at the end?

Teacher: "I don't want to be alone with an alligator."
Student 1: He/She says ...

Fragen in der indirekten Rede kannst du mit „He/She asks how/where/what ..." oder „He/She wants to know if ..." beginnen.

83/5

8 Report the questions in the speech bubbles.

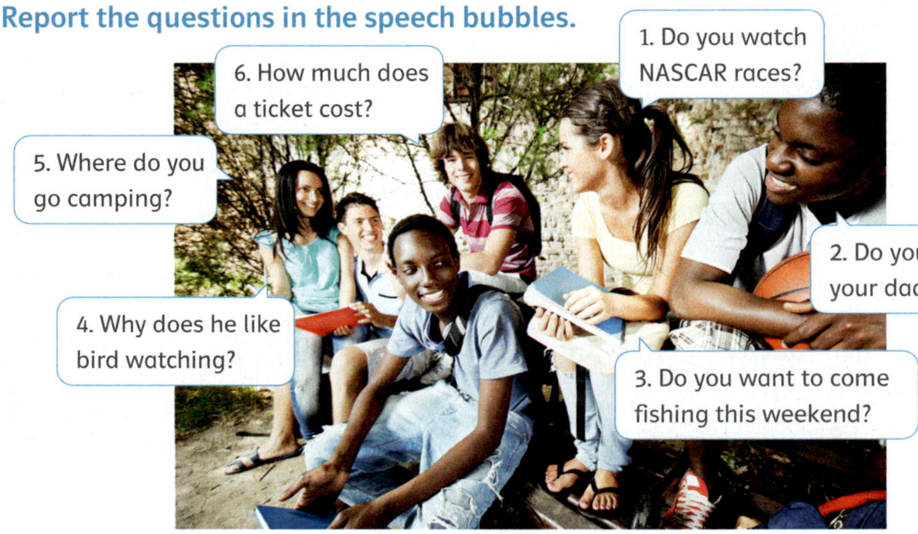

1. She asks if he watches the NASCAR races.
2. He wants to know if ... .

9 (WRITING) Report the statements with the simple past.

a) Report what the animal trainer said. → ○ p. 133

84/6

Al Lane, the animal trainer, talked about an exciting day at Florida Alligator Farm:

1. "I get up at 6 a.m.
2. I have breakfast.
3. Then I clean the alligator cage.
4. I don't feed my alligators until 10 o'clock.
5. I also count them.
6. There are only 19 in the cage, not 20!"

1. Al Lane said that he got up at 6 a.m. He said …

GRAMMAR → G14, p. 171

"I live in Florida."	–	He said that he lived in Florida.
"We love NASCAR races."	–	They told me that they loved NASCAR races.

b) Say other things that Al said to the reporter.

84/7

1. "We don't get a lot of visitors."
2. "Most tourists go to my brother's bigger farm."
3. "My daughter doesn't like alligators."
4. "But she still often visits me."

1. Al said that …

10 (YOUR TURN) Information for a day trip → V A day trip, p. 214

85/1

Tell an English friend about Berlin Zoo.

Can you tell me where it is?
– The website says it's in the centre of Berlin.

Which animals can you see there?
– It says here that …

What activities can you do there?
What are the opening times?
Where can we buy tickets?
… ?

STUDY SKILLS

Es ist nicht nötig, immer alles Wort für Wort zu übersetzen. Du musst nur die wichtigsten Informationen weitergeben. Benutze deine eigenen Worte.

INTERNET

Herzlich willkommen im Zoo Berlin!
Besuchen Sie uns im Zentrum Berlins. Unter unseren über 17.000 Zoo-Tieren finden Sie Affen, Elefanten, Schlangen, Tiger, Giraffen und viele mehr.

» Erleben Sie die Fütterungen und Tiershows.
» Feiern Sie Kindergeburtstage bei uns.
» Nehmen Sie am Fotospaziergang teil.

Öffnungszeiten
Heute, 2.6.2018, 9:00 – 18:30 Uhr
Jetzt Online Ticket kaufen!

Ich kann andere über Freizeitaktivitäten informieren. ✓

The girl who fought segregation

1 If you know something is wrong or unfair, what do you do about it? → M Think-pair-share, p. 177

2 (READING) Read the report.

2,16

Claudette Colvin, 2016

Montgomery is a nice, small town in Alabama. But in the 1950s the people there were segregated. Black people had to go to separate movie theaters. They weren't allowed to try on clothes in stores. The seats in the front of the buses were for whites, people of color had to sit at the back.

Claudette Colvin was an African-American teenager in Montgomery at the time. She believed that segregation was unfair. On March 2, 1955, Claudette was on a bus with three other girls. They were sitting in the middle of the bus. More and more white people got on and it was soon full. When this happened, the rule was that people of color had to give up their seats to whites and move to the back. The bus driver told them to do so. Three of them got up and went to the back. But Claudette didn't move.

CULTURE

Der Ku Klux Klan ist eine geheime Organisation weißer Amerikaner, die sich gegen Menschen anderer Kulturen und Religionen richtet. In den 1950er und -60er Jahren griffen sie Afro-Amerikaner und Mitglieder der Bürgerrechtsbewegung an oder brachten sie um.
Gibt es solche Gruppierungen auch in deinem Land?

3 Which statements about the story are right?

1. There were different laws for different people in the 1950s.
2. When a bus was full, white people had to sit at the back of the bus.
3. A police officer talked to Claudette and brought her home.
4. Many of Claudette's friends stayed away from her after that.
5. Claudette moved because she couldn't find a job in Montgomery.
6. Claudette wasn't the first who refused to give up her seat. It was Rosa Parks.

4 Make notes about these things and explain them. → M 1-minute-presentation, p. 172

Segregation | What Claudette did | The result of her protest

READING SKILLS

Die meisten Texte haben ein Hauptthema oder eine Hauptaussage. Es ist wichtig, diese zu finden und zu verstehen. Du findest es oft in der Überschrift, im ersten Absatz oder am Ende. Lies deshalb genau. Das Hauptthema wird oft durch Beispiele unterstützt. Findest du diese im Text?

The bus driver called the police. A police officer got on the bus, but Claudette still refused to move. She said that she paid her fare like other people. It was her right to sit there. In the end, they had to drag her off the bus and arrest her. Her parents brought her home later that day, but her father was awake all night because he was afraid of the Ku Klux Klan.

The next week she had problems in school too. Some students were impressed by her courage. Many others felt that her action made things more difficult for African Americans. Claudette lost a lot of friends: their parents told her friends that Claudette was crazy.

Claudette's life became very difficult, but her protest was a success. A year later she took part in the court case which ended segregation on all public transport in the state of Alabama. In that same year she left Montgomery and moved to New York because it was very difficult for her to find work.

Claudette's story has been forgotten by most people. Instead, the fight against segregation on buses is linked with Rosa Parks, a woman who did the same thing nine months later. When Claudette was asked about this, she said that it was OK.

There were hundreds of brave people like Claudette who fought to end segregation. You never see their names or their faces but they played an important role in the long fight to abolish an unfair system. Their courage will always be remembered.

5 Choose one of these tasks.

86/1
87/2-4

a) Search the internet for information about these people who fought for their rights:

- Martin Luther King
- Mahatma Gandhi
- Malala Yousafzai

Choose one and write a short biography of him or her. Add pictures.

→ M Gallery walk, p. 173

OR

b) A quote:

"It is the greatest mistake to do nothing because you can only do a little. Do what you can."
– Sydney Smith

Explain the meaning. Discuss: Do you agree? Say why or why not. Write your opinion. Your notes from Ex. 1 can help you.

Ich kann einen Bericht über Rassismus verstehen. ✓

Going out in style

INTERNET

The 'jazz funeral' came with African slaves about 400 years ago. It was first called 'funeral with music'. People celebrated the end of slavery for the dead person. They wanted to help them find their way to heaven. It was used mainly for poorer African Americans and later also for musicians. In the mid-20th century it became an accepted form of funeral.

When the parade is on its way to the church, the brass band usually plays some call-and-response-style music. It's like a dialogue. Some musicians play a part and other musicians answer. On the way to the cemetery the band plays slow and sad songs. But on the way back there's happy music. One of the most famous songs is "When the Saints Go Marching In".

One of the biggest jazz funerals in New Orleans took place on August 29, 2006 for the 1,700 people who died during Hurricane Katrina. The communities remembered the people who lost their lives in 2005. That shows how much the jazz funeral has become a symbol of life and death, of being sad and happy at the same time.

1 Beantworte die Fragen.

1. Was feierten die Menschen bei einer Jazz Beerdigung?
2. Was macht einen 'call-and-response-style' aus?
3. Welche Art Musik wird vor und nach der Beerdigung gespielt?
4. An welches Ereignis und an wen erinnerte die Jazz Beerdigung am 29. August 2006?

2 Which funeral traditions do you know in your country or in other countries?

88/1-2

Ich kann Informationen über Rituale weitergeben. ✓

The great outdoors?

1 Talk about the summer holidays.

a) Do you prefer outdoor or indoor activities in your free time?

b) What's your favourite activity? Why?

CULTURE

In den USA dauern die Sommerferien 8–12 Wochen. Während dieser Zeit besuchen viele Kinder ein Ferienlager. Manche haben Schwerpunkte wie Reiten oder andere Sportarten oder Computerspiele. Gibt es in deiner Nähe ein Ferienlager? Würdest du gerne eins besuchen?

2 (VIEWING) Watch the film.

10

a) Match the statements with the right scene.

1. "I got the job interview at Silverley."
2. "That was last year. I'm 16 now."
3. "That's for really young kids ..."
4. "Very reliable. You can trust her."

b) Watch from 01:31 to 01:55. Make notes about five of the activities there.

Which one of them would you like to try? Give your reasons.

3 (SPEAKING) Talk about the film.

Watch the sequence at Silverley again from 03:17. Practise an interview for a job.

A: So do you have experience in ...
B: Well, I've worked/helped/done ...
A: As a ... you will ... / To be honest, you won't ...
B: Oh! OK, I ...
A: Excellent! You've got the job!
B: Oh, ...

VIEWING SKILLS

Achte darauf, wie die Person, die das Interview durchführt, auf ihren Gesprächspartner eingeht (indem sie ihn z. B. anlächelt).
Wie kann eine Person in einem Gespräch sonst noch auf ihren Partner eingehen?

Ich kann einen Film über die Sommerferien verstehen. ✓

Checklist

Ich kann Informationen über die Südstaaten der USA verstehen. ✓

89

Ich kann über Einflüsse verschiedener Kulturen im täglichen Leben sprechen. ✓

... had a big influence on .... • ... living together is ... • When you look around, you see ... • ... is a famous dish from ...

89

Ich kann andere über Freizeitaktivitäten informieren. ✓

He says that he needs ... • What does ... think? • I'm afraid I didn't get that. • He wants to know if ...

90

Ich kann einen Bericht über Rassismus verstehen. ✓

90

Ich kann Informationen über Rituale weitergeben. ✓

91

Ich kann einen Film über die Sommerferien verstehen. ✓

❀ (TASK) A feature story

Imagine you are a reporter. Choose a topic. Then choose a place, watch the people there and take notes. Write a feature story. Make a wall newspaper in class.

Early birds
(by Mika Hensing)
May 13, 2016 — *headline, writer, date*

It's still dark. I can see hardly any people on the street. However, the smell of fresh bread is in the air. And at the bright baker's stall there's a crowd of people in a long line. They are all waiting their turn. — *describing the scene*

Some are looking at their phones. Some are counting their money; others are talking to each other. — *describing details*

Almost everyone looks tired except the saleswoman who ... . I feel ... . — *describing emotions*

Bakers usually get up at ... . — *background information*

"I come here every day," a woman says ... . — *direct speech*

Step 1

Look for an interesting place to go.

You can go to the campus, a bus stop, the park or any other place where you can watch other people. Make sure that your place is relevant to your topic. Find other students who chose the same place.

Step 2

Take notes about the scene at your place.

What do you see, hear, smell, feel?
What other details are important to describe the atmosphere?
Take photos too. If you take photos of single people or small groups, you have to ask them if that's OK.

Step 3

Find facts about your place.

You can find facts on location or on the internet. If you choose a bus stop, for example, you can find out how many buses there are every day and where they go.

Step 4

Use your notes to write a draft.

- Find a catchy headline, an interesting opening and an appealing photo.
- Describe the scene, the people and the atmosphere.
- Name the place and give interesting facts and details.
- Say what is special about the place or the people.
- Use a computer programme to format your text.

WRITING SKILLS

Benutze Adjektive und die direkte Rede, um deinen Text lebendiger zu machen.

Step 5

Check your draft. → M Writers' conference, p. 177

WRITING SKILLS

Nutze diese Liste, um deinen Entwurf zu prüfen:
- Hast du eine Überschrift, einen Einleitungssatz und ein Foto? ✓
- Hast du deinen Namen und das Datum angegeben? ✓
- Hast du den Ort und die Menschen allgemein und im Detail beschrieben? ✓
- Hast du alle Wörter richtig geschrieben? ✓
- Ist die Grammatik richtig? ✓

Frage jemanden aus deiner Klasse, wenn du Hilfe benötigst.

Step 6

Make a wall newspaper in class. Find the most interesting feature story. → M Gallery walk, p. 173

Read the headlines, the first lines and look at the photos. Vote for the best headline, the most interesting first line and the most interesting photo. Read these three feature stories in class.

Extra practice

1 Find the country. (nach 99/3)

1. Chicken curry comes from this country.
2. New Orleans was founded by this country.
3. Many slaves in the South came from this part of the world.
4. The north of this country is part of the United Kingdom.
5. Pizza comes from this country.
6. This country is south of France.

2 How does New Orleans get ready for Mardi Gras? Make sentences in the simple present passive. (nach 100/6)

1. fantastic costumes • make

2. special food • cook

3. small plastic baby • put • in some cakes

4. lots of parties • celebrate • before Mardi Gras

5. faces • guests • not see

6. small presents • buy • to throw at • crowds

1. Fantastic costumes are made.

3 Choose was or were. (nach 100/7)

After a terrible storm in 2005 many workers from Mexico came to New Orleans.

1. New homes **was** • **were built** with their help.
2. The workers **wasn't** • **weren't tolerated** by some people.
3. The smell of their food **wasn't** • **weren't liked** by others.
4. But many other people disliked that their jobs **was** • **were taken** away.
5. The new immigrants **was** • **were accepted** as part of the multicultural society.
6. These different opinions **was** • **were accepted** by the city government.
7. It **was** • **were decided** to find solutions quickly.

4 Make passive sentences in the simple past about New Orleans. (nach 101/8)

1. New Orleans was founded in 1718 by the French. (found)
2. French houses — in the city centre. (build)
3. In 1763 the city — to Spain. (give)
4. At the end of the 18th century the French houses — in two terrible fires. (lose)
5. New houses — by Spanish people. (build)
6. The state — to the United States in 1803. (sell)
7. In the 20th century cheap houses — (rent) by many artists.

5 Put the sentences in each of the dialogues in the correct order. (nach 103/5)

1. – I know what you mean. (A)
   – I get it. Let's find a quieter place. (B)
   – I can't stand noisy crowds. (C)
   – I really want to leave. (D)

2. – Sleep. I'm always tired. (A)
   – I don't have enough. (B)
   – I see. (C)
   – Could you explain, please? (D)

6 Report what the people say at an alligator farm. (nach 104/8)

1. "I plan to see and do everything on the farm." (Sarah, New York)
   Sarah says (that) she plans to see and do everything on the farm.
2. "I love the boat trips." – Luke (Boston)
3. "Do I get wet on the boat trip?" – Carol (San Francisco)
4. "Does a boat trip cost extra?" – Alice (Houston)
5. "We find the guides very friendly and helpful." Sophie and Ken (San Diego)
6. "I don't think the cages are very clean." – Jeff (Atlanta)
7. "Can I hold a baby alligator?" – Angela (New Orleans)

7 Report what a girl told you yesterday about life in Florida. (nach 105/9)

1. "We play outside from January to December."
   She said (that) they played outside from January to December.
2. "I don't need a winter coat."
3. "I often go to an outdoor movie."
4. "My parents take me to Disney World every year."
5. "We learn to swim before we can walk."
6. "We never have to drive in the snow."
7. "I wear flip flops every day."

Pronomen und Verben ändern sich in der indirekten Rede:
I → he/she
I love → he/she loves
we → they

Diff corner

Unit 1, p.15

○ **4** Work with the city words.

Find one or more words from the text.

1. street • road • —— (l.24)
2. skyscraper • building • —— (l.9 or l.16)
3. taxi • traffic jam • —— (l.2)
4. take the subway • get into the city • —— (l.20)

Unit 1, p.15

○ **5** (SPEAKING) Act as a guide.

Present what is in the picture. Look at the numbers for help.

1. Over there you can see …
2. Don't miss …
3. Right ahead …
4. Just around this corner we'll come to …
5. You must visit …

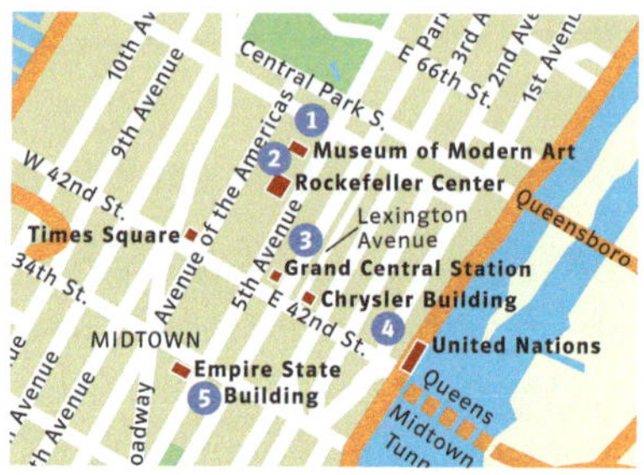

Unit 1, p.16

○ **7** (WRITING) Tell the taxi driver's story.

Make two sentences for each picture.

gave | got | found | was (4x) | didn't see | talked | didn't take | looked

be at the airport • get in

be cold • heavy snow

talk to • be in a traffic jam

not take with her • find it

not see her • look for her

give back • be happy

1. Last winter I was at the airport. A woman …

Unit 1, p.17

8 (SPEAKING) What did they do at One World Trade Center yesterday?

Ask and answer questions about the people in the picture.

A: What did Henry eat?
B: He ate a sandwich.

B: Did Susan take a photo?
A: No, she didn't. She phoned her mother.

What did Where did Who did Did	+	Lisa Nancy Frank Susan Linda Henry	+	drink eat look at sit take a photo phone	+	…?

Unit 1, p. 18

2 Collect facts about José and his family.

1,4

Interviewer: Hello José. Can I ask you some questions for our magazine?

José: Hi. Sure.

Interviewer: You're new on the baseball team. Are you happy?

José: Yes, I am.

Interviewer: When did you immigrate from Cuba to the USA?

José: I arrived with my mom and sisters when I was ten. My dad had arrived in New York two years before I came.

Interviewer: That was a big decision for your parents. They left their home and moved to a foreign place.

José: Yes, and they were very poor. My father hadn't had a job for a long time. My parents wanted to give my sisters and me the best chances.

Interviewer: What were the first years like?

José: My parents had problems because they hadn't learned English. But there's a strong community. So my parents opened a small shop.

Interviewer: How did you feel? Had you seen skyscrapers before?

José: No, I hadn't. It was exciting. Later I was homesick. But I knew I had a better future here.

Interviewer: When did you start your career?

José: I hadn't taken baseball seriously before I was 15. Then I wanted to be successful. I think people who leave their countries are more motivated. After I had become the star of the my team in high school, I had lots of opportunities.

Interviewer: You've been successful!

José: Yes, I have. For most people it's much harder. My story is a perfect example of the American Dream.

Interviewer: So, what about your plans?

José: I have become a US citizen. But I talk to people in Cuba, and I plan to help them.

Interviewer: Thank you. All my best wishes.

Complete the fact card. Take notes.

Name: —
From: —
Lives in: —
Family: —
Reasons why they emigrated: —
Career: —

Unit 1, p.19

○ 4 Imagine you want to leave your country.

Complete the sentences with these words.

immigrate | get used | cross | emigrate | opportunities | foreign

1. I will have many —— .
2. I want to —— to the USA.
3. I want to —— the border by car.
4. I will —— to my new life soon.
5. I want to —— from Mexico.
6. I will feel —— .

Unit 1, p. 20

○ 7 (WRITING) Write about one of Angela's days.

Make sentences with the simple past and the past perfect.

After ...

invite to his party • buy a present

walk through the park • take the subway home

buy tickets • visit Ellis Island

1. After Pablo had invited Angela to his party, she bought a present.
2. After they had ...

Before ...

eat pizza • order a milkshake

go to the stadium • put on their fan T-shirts

Die Liste mit den unregelmäßigen Verben findest du auf S. 216.

4. Before Angela ate a pizza, she ...
5. Before they ...

Unit 1, p. 21

8 (SPEAKING) Ask and answer questions.

What had José done before his first important baseball game? What hadn't he done? Ask questions and answer them.

1. Interviewer: Had you played every day before your first big game?
   José: Yes, I had.
2. Interviewer: Had you …
   José: …

1. played every day ✓
2. bought new sports shoes
3. ordered tickets for his friends ✓
4. watched the other team ✓
5. phoned his dad ✓
6. gone to bed early

Unit 2, p. 35

3 Find the information in the text.

1,10

"No! I'll be stuck in the middle of nowhere," I thought. "An exchange year in South Dakota? Really?" But after that year I can say that it was the best time of my life.

In the beginning it felt like living in a movie. It all looked so familiar.

My American school was huge. Teachers usually stay in their classrooms, and students go to them for each lesson. So we weren't allowed to keep things in the classrooms. We had to put everything into our lockers. After two weeks I got used to it, and I was able to find the way to the classrooms by myself.

Every day school started at eight o'clock with a morning message from the principal and the Pledge of Allegiance. Everyone stood and promised to be true to the United States. That was strange.

The first class started at 8:30. I had to take Math, English, Science and History. But I was able to choose 'electives' like Journalism too. There were lots of interesting subjects to choose from. We also had six study hall periods a week, where you can do your homework or study. You weren't allowed to talk there.

School rules were strict. Much stricter than at home. You had to get a hall pass from the teacher to go to the bathroom, for example. Classes ended at 3:30 p.m. Then there were many extracurricular activities. I wanted to join the cheerleaders. There was a lot of competition for places, and exchange students were allowed to try too, so I did. And I got a place! Awesome!

My host family was great too. They even took me on a trip to the east coast, so I was able to see the Atlantic. Anyway, my year in the USA was a blast.

Answer the questions.

1. How long was Luise in the USA?
2. Who had to change classrooms?
3. When did classes start and end?
4. What do students do during study hall?
5. What do students need a hall pass for?
6. What did Luise do after school?

Unit 2, p. 35

4 Find the words. → M Peer correction, p. 175 → V At American schools, p. 190

Choose the right words.

1 

grade • detention

2 

principal • locker

3 

schedule • locker

4

	Monday	Tuesday	Wednesday	Thursday	Friday
1	English	English	English	English	English
2	Math	Math	Math	Math	Math
3	Science	Science	Science	Science	Science
4	History	History	History	History	History
5	Journalism	Journalism	Journalism	Journalism	Journalism
6	Astronomy	Astronomy	Astronomy	Astronomy	Astronomy

schedule • grade

5 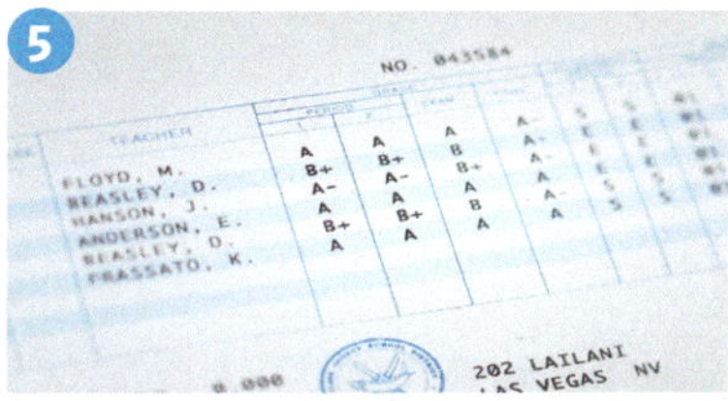

principal • grade

Unit 2, p. 36

8 (WRITING) Find out about two other exchange students.

Make sentences. Use (not) be allowed to and (not) be able to.

During the exchange (not) allowed to	Aileen	Jannik
1. bring any boys/girls to the bedroom	–	+
2. go out until 10 p.m. during the week	+	+

Aileen/Jannik was allowed to … or wasn't allowed to … .
They were allowed to … or weren't allowed to … .

After the exchange (not) allowed to	Aileen	Jannik
1. get used to the old life easily	+	–
2. speak English a lot better	+	+

Aileen/Jannik was able to … or wasn't able to … .
They were able to … or weren't able to … .

Unit 2, p. 37

○ 10 Make a dialogue. → M Read and look up, p. 176

Put the verbs into the simple past. Complete the dialogue. Then act it with a partner.

Sarah: Did you have (have) to do jobs around the house in the USA?
Luise: No, I didn't. I — (be) able to decide when I wanted to help.
Sarah: — (be) you allowed to stay up late?
When — you — (have) to be in bed?
Luise: During the week I — (have) to be in bed at 9.
Sarah: — (be) you able to travel around with the family?
Luise: Yes, I was. But I — (not be) allowed to travel without another person.

Was she allowed to go?
Were you able to choose?
Did you have to go?
When did you have to go?

Unit 2, p. 39

○ 4 (SPEAKING) What do you think? → M Think-pair-share, p. 177

What should or shouldn't Michael say to the manager?

1. "I'm sorry."
2. "It won't happen again."
3. "But they started it."
4. "It wasn't me."
5. "I don't think you're right."
6. "Next time I'll try to be cooler."

Achte auf Verneinungen. Sie drücken meist etwas Negatives aus.

Unit 2, p. 39

○ 6 Practise words to describe people at work.

Copy and complete the table.

good behavior (+)	bad behavior (–)
cooperative	u...
r...	l...
h...	b...

bossy · unmotivated · cooperative ✓ · responsible · lazy · hard-working

Unit 2, p. 40

○ 9 (WRITING) What will happen if …?

Look at the pictures. Make sentences.

1. If Michael —— (find) a student job, he —— earn money.

2. If he needs help, he —— ask his co-workers.

3. If he is late, he —— lose his job.

4. If the girl —— (steal) a T-shirt, Michael will talk her.

5. If the man —— (bring back) the pullover, he'll get a new one.

6. If the woman —— (buy) two pairs, she'll get another one for free.

1. If Michael finds a student job, he'll earn some money.

Unit 2, p. 41

○ 10 Complete the sentences.

Benutze „ones", um Pluralwörter wie „sunglasses" und „trousers" zu ersetzen.

Use one or ones.

1. I really like this jacket. This one suits me perfectly.
2. We have lots of helmets. The best —— are over there.
3. Is there a bathroom? – Yes, there's —— over there.
4. This towel is a bit dirty. Do you have a clean —— ?
5. How about these trousers? – No, I prefer those —— .
6. I need some new sport sunglasses. I don't like my old —— .

Unit 3, p. 55

3 Work with the text about the Miller family. → M Peer correction, p. 175

1,17

Put the pictures in the right order.

Mark

Julia

Jacob

Brenda

Robert

The Millers from Boston are getting ready for dinner. Julia is in the kitchen. Her husband Mark, their teenage son Jacob and Grandma Brenda are in the living room.

Brenda: Last year we had such a terrible storm. I got stuck in my car. Do you remember?

Mark: Yes, that's right. Did you have a hard time again yesterday?

(The doorbell rings. Mark opens the door. It's their neighbor.)

Robert: Happy Thanksgiving, Mark!

Mark: You too, Robert. How are you?

Robert: Great, thanks. Brr. It's freezing, isn't it?

Mark: Come on in. I'm so glad you could make it. *(They enter the living room.)* Grandma, this is Robert. He's our new neighbor. He doesn't have family here, so we've invited him. Robert, this is Brenda.

Robert: Nice to meet you, Brenda. You came all the way from Miami, didn't you?

Brenda: Yes, I did. Please have a seat. When did you move here?

Mark: *(shouting across the room)* Jacob, why don't you say hello? You can't spend all your time on your phone.

Jacob: What's up, Robert?

Robert: How's it going? Are you enjoying the holiday? Do you like turkey?

Jacob: Not really. I'm a vegetarian, so I won't eat any.

Julia: *(coming out of the kitchen)* You always used to eat everything. *(noticing the guest)* Oh, hi Robert.

Robert: Hey Julia. Thanks so much for inviting me. Here's a little present. You eat chocolates, don't you? *(gives her a box as a present.)*

Mark: OK everybody. I'm making a video. Please, answer this question. 'What do you feel thankful for?' Julia, you go first, please. *(starts filming)*

Julia: Me? Well, err, I am most thankful for my husband and my two children who …

(Mark's phone rings.)

Mark: That's probably Lily and her new boyfriend. Hello Lily. … Oh, no! *(to the others)* Their plane from Washington, D.C. had engine trouble. They had to land in New York. *(to Lily)* So when will you arrive? … OK. … Will you call us when you know more? I promise we'll keep you some turkey!

Mark and Julia

Mark on the phone

Robert and Julia

Mark and Robert

Mark and Brenda

Robert and Jacob

Unit 3, p. 55

○ 4 (LISTENING) Listen to Lily introduce her boyfriend Evan.

1,18

Listen to the conversation. Match the questions and answers.

1. How are you doing?
2. What's new?
3. So what have you been up to?
4. How is she?

A She's good, thanks.
B Good, thanks.
C I'd like you to meet Evan.
D Not much.

Unit 3, p. 56

○ 8 (SPEAKING) Ask questions about holidays.

Interview your partner. Choose do, does, did or will.

1. What holidays **do** • **does** your family celebrate?
2. What **do** • **will** you usually eat?
3. What **did** • **do** you like about last *(name of holiday)*?
4. How many guests **do** • **did** your family invite last time?
5. Where **did** • **will** it take place next year?
6. Who **did** • **will** you call next *(name of holiday)*?

GRAMMAR → G7, p. 164

Who did you invite?
Who did you talk to?

Unit 3, p. 57

9 (WRITING) Write Jacob's questions to his grandma.

What did Jacob ask his grandma? Match his questions with the underlined answers.

E-MAIL

Dear Jacob,
Yes, it's true, it will be my 65th birthday soon! I'm planning (1) a big family party. I'll have it (2) in my home in Miami. It will be (3) on May 1. I'll invite (4) everybody who can come to Miami. And of course you can ask your new girlfriend to come too. Yes, I already know about her. That's (5) because your dad told me about her.
Much love,
Grandma

A What are you planning for your birthday? (1)
B Who will you invite?
C When will it take place?
D Why do you know about her?
E Where will you have your birthday party?

Unit 3, p. 59

5 Sort the phrases. → M Peer correction, p. 175

Sort the phrases into the table.

I agree	I disagree
Exactly.	Absolutely — .
That's — .	No — !
That's for — .	I don't think — .

not | Exactly. ✓ | so | sure | true | way

Unit 3, p. 59

6 (SPEAKING) Talk about devices.

Make a list.

microwave

TV

phone

computer

hair straightener

The most important thing for me **is my phone.** • I don't think **phones** are more important than **computers.** • **TVs** come first/second/third. • **A microwave** is next.

Unit 3, p. 60

8 What would make Jennifer's life easier?

Look at the pictures. Complete the sentences.

prepare | have | walk | chose ✓ | go | not listen

1. Jennifer would be less worried in the morning if she chose her clothes … .

2. She would be at school much earlier if she — her clothes before.

3. She wouldn't feel so tired in the morning if she — to bed early.

4. She would hear what her dad said if she — to music.

5. She wouldn't get cold if she — a warm coat.

6. It would be better if she — to school.

Unit 3, p. 61

9 (SPEAKING) What would you do if …?

Answer the questions. Then ask your partner.

What would you do if you …

1. were president of the United States for a day?
2. were a superhero?
3. traveled through time?
4. had a million dollars?
5. knew the answers to your next English test before the test?
6. didn't have the money to buy a ticket for the bus home?

Here are some ideas:

- travel around the world
- do funny things
- get an A
- save the world
- call my parents
- play tricks on people
- walk home
- take my bike to
- buy my family a big house
- fight against the bad guys

Unit 4, p. 76

2 (LISTENING) Listen to a conversation about an ad from exercise 1.

2,3

Emily: ... the store is this way. Look, there's Daniel. Where's he going?
Carol: I don't know. He's looking at his phone. He's nearly running into people. Let's call him.
Daniel: Hi Carol.
Carol: Hi Daniel. Look behind you.
Daniel: Err ... What? ... Oh ... Hi Carol. Hey Emily.
Emily: Where are you going, Daniel?
Daniel: I'm walking to the mall. It's too windy and cold outside. Summers here are always terrible, aren't they? Hey, see the ad on that building over there? California! That's where I'd love to be. You look at that photo, and you can almost smell the sea. And it's always a lot sunnier and warmer there. That's what I call a great ad!
Emily: Really? It doesn't look special to me. It's boring. Just a guy who is carrying a surf-board. And that bus looks really old.
Carol: I think it's interesting, Emily. It looks like a great place. Anyway, the guy is cute, don't you think?
Daniel: Girls, the ad says a lot more! Wouldn't that be a great – surfing, music, cold drinks? I've always dreamed of something like that. And that bus is really cool.
Emily: Sorry, but I don't see any of that in the photo. Probably because I don't dream about that kind of lifestyle. I'm a terrible swimmer, you know. I never go in the water.
Carol: Oh, come on, Emily. You could do a lot more there. If you ask me, it would be nice to just sit quietly on the beach and watch the sea.
Daniel: I agree, Carol. I still think the ad is good. And one day I'm off to California.
Carol: OK, Daniel. Then we'll come with you, and you can teach us how to surf!
Daniel: Sounds good. Anyway, where are you two going now?
Carol: We're going to the computer store. It's on the way to the mall. Wanna join us?
Daniel: Yeah, sure. Let's go.

Listen and read. Add the missing information.

1. Daniel is talking to —— and —— .
2. They are talking about ad number —— in exercise 1.
3. Daniel and —— like the ad, but —— doesn't.

Unit 4, p. 77

3 (SPEAKING) What do you think of the ads? → M Think-pair-share, p. 177

Talk about the ads.

catchy | (not) informative | clear | funny | (un)appealing | fascinating

Ad number 1 is/isn't .... / I think ad number 2 looks/doesn't look .... / But number 3 looks .... / And 4 is ....

Unit 4, p. 78

7 (WRITING) Simple present or present progressive?

Choose the correct verb form to complete the e-mail.

E-MAIL

Hi Becky,
Right now I'm sitting • sit next to the swimming pool, and **I'm having** • **have** some ice cream.
Well, my life here in California is the same as the one in the Midwest. Every day **I'm getting up** • **get up**, **am going** • **go** to school, and **am going** • **go** to bed.
But some things are different. It's always warm. We usually **are spending** • **spend** the weekends at the beach. At the moment I'**m learning** • **learn** how to surf.
What **are you doing** • **do you do** right now? I miss you.
Sandy

Unit 4, p. 80

3 Find it in the text.

2,5

BLOG

A quick look back

Thursday, March 16, 2017

California has always welcomed new ideas – just think of the high-tech companies or the movies industry. The World Wide Web is one of these ideas. It started in the early 1990s, so it's been around for almost 30 years. And it has really changed the world. The social media sites that we use came with it. I've had an account since I was 13. Why have they been so successful? Well, that's easy: you can post your photos, share what you think and keep in touch with friends. Most of the time you don't even have to look for information. It'll find you. We should give that a big 'like'. Online videos have become extremely popular too. They have a huge impact on our lives. Of course, there are the lots of funny videos, but I like the tutorials best. You can find videos on how to do almost anything. People often watch video clips or their favorite shows online. Nobody watches much TV anymore. Smartphones and tablets became the next big thing. They have strongly influenced how we communicate. I don't have a radio, write letters, or use a map. I use my smartphone instead. I've been thinking about all this and did a small survey with my friends. What I've found is that more than 90 percent of them go online every day, and half of them are online almost all the time. Most use more than one social media site. Some say it's difficult to stop using them. They get messages every minute and feel that they have to answer right away. Others are worried about cyberbullying because if a person writes bad things about you online, a lot of people can read it. It looks like we haven't really found good answers yet.

Posted by Derek Lee at 8:51 a.m. 2 comments: Links to this post

Where in the text is it?

1. Derek talks about an invention which started at the end of the 20th century.
   ll. 3–4: The World Wide Web is one of these ideas. It started in the early 1990s.
2. Derek gives reasons why some social media sites are successful.
3. Derek loves shows which tell people how to do things.
4. Derek asked his friends some questions.
5. Derek talks about some problems of social media.

Unit 4, p. 81

○ 5 (SPEAKING) Explain the words.

Match the sentence parts.

1. When you 'like' something, →
2. When you 'dislike' something,
3. When you make a 'friend request',
4. When you 'post' something,
5. When you 'share' something,
6. When you 'unfriend' somebody

a) you tell people something they will probably find interesting.
b) you tell people that you've enjoyed what they posted.
c) you put it on social media so that other people can see or read it.
d) you don't want to be friends with him or her.
e) you tell people that you haven't enjoyed what they posted.
f) you ask somebody to be your friend.

Unit 4, p. 82

○ 8 Say for how long or since when.

Complete the sentences with for or since.

1. I've had my smartphone **since** • for more than three years.
2. Millions have seen the cat photos **since** • **for** Tuesday.
3. 5,000 people have watched that tutorial **since** • **for** May.
4. He hasn't answered his e-mails **since** • **for** five days.
5. Have you posted a new comment **since** • **for** last week?
6. The book has been successful **since** • **for** years.

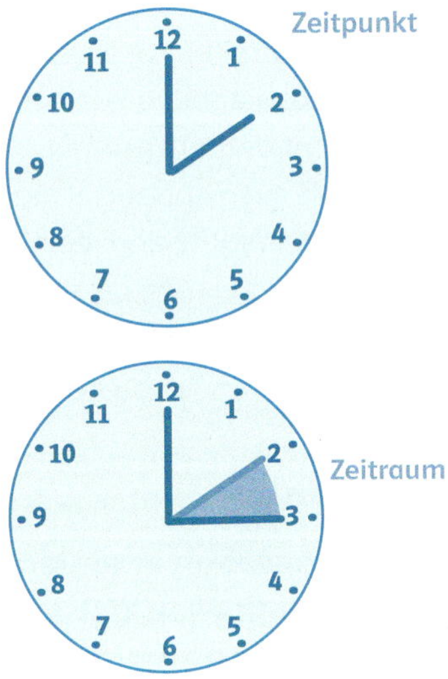

D

Unit 4, p. 83

9 Complete the survey questions and answers.

Use the simple past or the present perfect to complete the sentences.

1. Interviewer: How much **did you spend** • **have you spent** on food and clothes last month?
   Person A: I'm not sure but it **was** • **has been** a lot of money.
2. Interviewer: **Did you buy** • **Have you bought** a book or magazine this week?
   Person B: No, I haven't. But I **got** • **have got** a magazine two days ago for my Mum.
3. Interviewer: **Did you** ever **use** • **Have you** ever **used** tutorials to learn how to do something?
   Person C: Yes, sure. I **learnt** • **have learnt** to play the guitar that way.
4. Interviewer: **Did you find** • **Have you found** any new music videos that you liked in the last few weeks?
   Person D: Oh, yes. Yesterday I **saw** • **have seen** one that I really enjoyed.

Unit 5, p. 99

3 What's the nationality?

Match the nationalities with the flags.

Chinese | Greek | Italian | Russian | Polish | Turkish

1 2 3 4 5 6

1. 中国 (China)
2. Россия (Russia)
3. Polska (Poland)
4. Ελλάδα (Greece)
5. Türkiye (Turkey)
6. Italia (Italy)

Unit 5, p. 99

4 Work with words to talk about conflicts and solutions.

Find the word with the same meaning.

1. accept: say no • say yes to something → Some people liked having the flag.
2. tolerate: disagree • do nothing → They could live with it. It was OK.
3. ban: say no to something • find a solution → Most people didn't want to have the flag.
4. disagree: have a different opinion • think the same → Other people didn't accept it.
5. protest: be against something • agree → Other groups said no too.
6. agree: refuse • have the same opinion → Some people thought the same thing.

Unit 5, p. 100

○ 7 (WRITING) Make sentences about living together.

Choose the right verbs.

1. People from other countries **is welcomed** • **are welcomed** in multicultural societies.
2. More than one language **is spoken** • **are spoken** there.
3. In some schools classes **is taught** • **are taught** in different languages.
4. Special classes **is organized** • **are organized** for new people.
5. Dishes from all around the world **is served** • **are served** in restaurants.
6. Racism **isn't accepted** • **aren't accepted** in multicultural societies.

Unit 5, p. 101

○ 8 Make passive sentences in the simple past. → M Bus stop, p. 172

Complete the information about the city of Raleigh.

were built | was chosen | wasn't completed
was founded ✓ | was given | was planned

The city of Raleigh (1) was founded in the 18th century as the capital of North Carolina. It's an example of a city that (2) — (plan) from the beginning. The city (3) — (give) the name of Sir Walter Raleigh, an English adventurer and writer. The streets (4) — (build) in a special way; like on a grid.
The tallest skyscraper in the city, the PNC Plaza, (5) — (not complete) until 2008. In 2014 the city (6) — (choose) into the Top 10 of the cities that have grown the fastest.

Unit 5, p. 103

○ 4 (LISTENING) Listen to the text about a visit to an alligator farm.

2,15

Read the notes A–C. Which one is correct?

A
- trainer fed alligators
- trainer put hand in mouth of alligator
- photo of Ethan with snake

B
- trainer fed snakes
- trainer put hand in mouth of alligator
- photo of Anna with alligator

C
- trainer fed alligators and snakes
- trainer had fight with snake
- photo of Matt with snake

Unit 5, p. 103

5 (SPEAKING) Say that you understand or don't understand.

Copy the chart and complete the sentences.

catch that · explain · get · Pardon? · see · you mean

Saying "I understand":	Saying "I don't understand":
I — it. I know what — . I — .	Could you — , please? I'm sorry, but I didn't — . —

Unit 5, p. 104

7 Report what other people say. → M Peer correction, p. 175

Report what Anna says.

she doesn't have · it's · they go · she loves ✓ · they wear · she doesn't like

1. "I love the warm weather in Florida."
2. "It's awesome."
3. "We just wear T-shirts."
4. "We often go to the beach."
5. "I don't have time to take lots of photos."
6. "I don't like the thousands of insects."

Pronomen und Verben ändern sich in der indirekten Rede:
I → he/she
I love → he/she loves
we → they

1. Anna says (that) she loves the warm weather in Florida.

Unit 5, p. 105

9 (WRITING) Report the statements with the simple past.

Report what the animal trainer said. Choose the right verb form.

1. He said that he **got up** • **has got** up at 6 a.m.
2. He said that he **will have** • **had** breakfast.
3. He said that he **cleaned** • **had cleaned** the alligator cage.
4. He said he **won't feed** • **didn't feed** his alligators until 10 o'clock.
5. He said he also **counted** • **will count** them.
6. He said **there were** • **there had been** only 19 in the cage, not 20.

2,17 Art and culture in NYC

Big city lights

1

New York City has great museums, lots of movie theaters, the finest restaurants, street markets, …
Walk down Broadway at night, and you'll see the lights of 40 theaters. Watch popular actors in world-class shows, plays and musicals.
Or experience the different communities of New York. The Puerto Ricans celebrate their national day with a parade along Fifth Avenue every June, for example.
In the summer the parks in New York's five boroughs have hundreds of free events.
There's a great number of things to see and do here …

Hip hop culture

2

It's the end of the 1960s in the Bronx. Here African-American teenagers start a new cultural movement, hip hop.
Rap, DJing, breakdancing and graffiti were the main parts of hip hop culture. DJs took parts of older songs to create a new style of music.
Rappers often talked about life in street gangs and about social questions. Breakdancers became famous for their robotic moves. Graffiti artists used subway trains and buildings as their canvas.
Hip hop has gone global.

D

Street art

3

In the past street art meant large murals, often in poorer parts of the city. Today you can go on guided tours and see the best of these murals. But people always find new ways to change the face of their city, and you can find many examples in New York City.
Some think it's art, some don't.

The city in comics

4

Spiderman lives in Queens, Iron Man's company is in Long Island, and Batman's Gotham City is a fictional version of New York. And there are lots of other examples – the city is the home of superheroes.
Comics are an art form that comes from the United States. The biggest comic book companies are located in New York City, and famous writers like Stan Lee and artists like Jack Kirby and Steve Ditko have worked here.

1 **What did you find interesting about the texts? Talk about them with a partner.**

movie theater *(AE)* – *Kino*; to experience – *erleben*; social – *gesellschaftlich*; artist – *Künstler/in*; canvas – *Leinwand*; global – *weltweit*; fictional – *erfunden*; to be located in – *sich befinden*

2,18 Native Americans then and now

Christopher Columbus didn't discover America!

The history of Native Americans in our country is fascinating and tragic. When Europeans made first contact around 1500, about ten million people lived in North America. They had come from Siberia to Alaska about 10,000 BC.
They spoke different languages and had many different lifestyles. The ones in the north were hunters and fishermen. They built houses of wood and made canoes. Others lived in villages by rivers and were farmers and traders. On the Great Plains tribes lived in tepees and hunted buffalo with bows and spears.

"I was born on the prairie where the wind blew free [...]. I want to die there and not within walls. I know every stream and every wood between the Rio Grande and the Arkansas. [...] So, why do you ask us to leave the rivers and the sun and the wind and live in houses?"

Chief Ten Bears in 1867

The Europeans arrive

From the 17th century, the large numbers of Europeans had a terrible impact on the Native Americans. They brought illnesses which killed thousands. When more Europeans arrived, they wanted land, so the tribes had to leave theirs. The settlers pushed them further away, until in the 1830s many tribes had to move west of the Mississippi River. On this terrible journey hundreds died of cold, hunger, and illness.
On the Great Plains, however, it was different. The tribes had got horses from the Europeans, so they were able to hunt buffalo more easily. They didn't want to give up their freedom, and they attacked settlers who crossed the plains. Many bloody battles followed. By 1900 most tribes had to go and live on reservations.
In 1924, after they had fought in the First World War, Native Americans became full American citizens.

D

Native Americans today

Today five million Native Americans live on reservations. Some reservations make money from the casino business, but people there are poor, and there's a lot of unemployment.

Among younger people there's a new interest in their Native American culture. Alaqua (16), for example, lives in Oklahoma, and he is typical of this new generation: "The government took my grandad away and sent him to boarding school, together with thousands of others. They didn't let him learn about his language or culture. So my dad never learned anything either. We lost a lot of things.

"Even in school today nobody teaches us about our history before Europeans arrived. But many of us want to change this situation. My history is part of me. I feel like we Native Americans are picking up the pieces of our culture and moving forward. I want to help rebuild things."

By Pat Smith
September 15, 2016
Junior History Magazine

1 Talk about the text.

What did you already know about Native Americans?
What didn't you know?
Talk with a partner.

tragic – *tragisch*; BC (= before Christ) – *vor Christus*; hunter – *Jäger/in*; trader – *Händler/in*; Great Plains – *Flachland in den USA*; tepee – *Tipi, Indianerzelt*; impact – *Einfluss*; tribe – *(Volks-)Stamm*; *Auswirkung*; further – *weiter*; to attack – *angreifen*; unemployment – *Arbeitslosigkeit*; government – *Regierung*; boarding school – *Internat*

2,19 Holidays in the USA

JANUARY Martin Luther King Day

1

This day is the birthday of the civil rights activist. Martin Luther King lived at a time when African Americans didn't have the same rights as white Americans. He used peaceful ways to protest against this situation. He also was a great public speaker. His speech 'I have a dream' is famous. Martin Luther King was assassinated in 1968.

FEBRUARY Presidents' Day

2

This holiday celebrates the birthdays of two great presidents – George Washington and Abraham Lincoln. Washington led the American army which defeated Great Britain. He became the first American president in 1789.
In 1865, after a terrible civil war, Lincoln ended slavery in the United States. He was assassinated in the same year.

MAY Memorial Day

3

On this day people remember all the soldiers who have died for their country since the Civil War. Flags fly at half-mast and many people visit cemeteries. Others see it as a day to relax with family and friends. People often see Memorial Day as the start of the summer.

D

JULY Independence Day

4

The Fourth of July celebrates the USA's independence from Great Britain. That's the day in 1776 when the 13 American states signed the Declaration of Independence, now a famous document. People dress in red, white and blue – the color of the flag. They have picnics or barbecues and there are fantastic fireworks across the country.

OCTOBER Columbus Day

5

Columbus first saw America in 1492. Today there are parades and dinners in memory of the event. Some people don't like this holiday because Columbus didn't actually discover America. But the day remembers a man of ideas, dreams and great ambition. That's something most Americans understand very well.

NOVEMBER Thanksgiving

6

The history of Thanksgiving began in 1621 when the Pilgrim settlers celebrated their first year in their new country. They invited some local Native Americans to share their meal. Thanksgiving is a family day. A traditional Thanksgiving dinner has turkey, cranberry sauce, and pumpkin pie for dessert. Football games are usually a big part of the day too.

1 **What celebration would you like to take part in? Why? Talk with a partner.**

civil rights – *Bürgerrechte*; was assassinated – *wurde ermordert*; to defeat – *schlagen*; civil war – *Bürgerkrieg*; slavery – *Sklaverei*; cemetery– *Friedhof*; in memory of – *in Erinnerung an*

2,20 Hollywood

The movie industry

1

Since the silent movies of the early 20th century, Hollywood has been the centre of the movie industry. The sign was originally an ad from 1923 which read HOLLYWOODLAND. They changed it to HOLLYWOOD in 1949. Today the sign is famous all over the world.

Movie classics

2

The 1930s was the Golden Age of Hollywood, starting with the introduction of sound into movies. New types of movies appeared – musicals, documentaries, westerns, action and horror movies. *Snow White and the Seven Dwarfs* (1937), *Gone with the Wind* (1939) and *The Wizard of Oz* (1939) are just three examples of the hundreds of movies that came out every year.
In the 1970s, Hollywood found new markets for younger people with high-action movies and lots of special effects like *Jaws* and *Star Wars*. In the 21st century, more successful blockbusters came out like *Avatar*, *The Hobbit* and *Jurassic World*.

"And the Oscar goes to ... "

3

The highest honor in the movie business is an Oscar or Academy Award. The ceremony has taken place every year since 1929. Millions of people around the world watch the stars arrive and walk the Red Carpet. There are many different categories of awards, but the most famous are Best Picture, Best Actor, and Best Director.

D

Walk of Fame

4

The Walk of Fame – a boulevard about two kilometers long – remembers famous or important people in the entertainment industry. There are the names of more than 2,500 actors, musicians, directors, authors and many others from the past and present written on pink stars.

Hollywood or Bollywood

5

Hollywood is famous, but the biggest film industry in the world is in India. 'Bollywood' is its nickname. Here's the difference:
- Bollywood makes way more films. But Hollywood spends more and earns more.
- One Bollywood movie has action, drama, romance, and comedy. In Hollywood you need to see four movies for that.
- Hollywood movies with music are called musicals. All Bollywood films have music and dance.
- Hollywood movies are shorter (two hours) than Bollywood movies (three hours), which have a short break.

1 What did you find interesting? What did you already know? Talk with a partner.

honor (AE) – *Ehre*; audience – *Publikum*; entertainment – *Unterhaltung*; to attract – *anziehen*

2,21 Life in the South

Plantation houses Southern hospitality

1

When Louisiana and other territories were bought by the United States from the French in 1803, rich Anglo-American landowners moved there. They built large houses on their plantations to show off their wealth. Many of these were destroyed after the American Civil War (1861-65), but some have remained.
Oak Alley Plantation was built by slaves on a sugar plantation and was completed in 1839. Today the house is open to the public.

Paddle steamers

2

The Mississippi, one of the longest rivers in the USA, is nearly 4,000 miles long.
In the 19th century paddle steamers were the most popular way to transport people and goods up and down the river. Because of their paddlewheels, they could go far up the river, even when the water level was low.
Later there were also "showboats", on which passengers could enjoy music and theater on the journey. Today there are many modern riverboats for tourists to explore the Mississippi.

D

Fishing in the Florida Keys

3

In the Florida Keys you can find all kinds of fishing, for beginners and experts. If you love the sea and fishing, there's no better place. Here you can find some of the best fishing guides and captains in the world. And when you return to the harbor, take your fish back to one of the local restaurants and a great meal will be prepared for you.

Line dance

4

Line dancing as we know it today goes back to the 1970s. Its origins, however, lie in the different folk dances of the 18th and 19th century Europe.
What is line dance? A group of people dances in one or more lines. They all face the same direction and they all do the same steps at the same time. Each dance has its own choreography. People can dance to country and western music but also to rock and pop. Even the internet sensation video "Gangnam Style" had elements of line dancing in it.

1 Read the texts and ask your partner four questions about them.

hospitality – *Gastfreundschaft*; manner – *Manieren*, Benehmen; territory – *Gebiet*; to show off – *angeben*; to destroy – *zerstören*; public – *Öffentlichkeit*; paddle steamer – *Raddampfer*; origin – *Ursprung*

Extra

When the earth shakes

1 What's an earthquake?

Every day there are minor or major earthquakes[1] around the world. The ground shakes for seconds or sometimes even minutes. Earthquakes can occur at any time, and we don't notice most of them. You can't tell when or where they will happen. In the USA the West Coast is most at risk[2] because of its special geological structure. However, there can be earthquakes in the Midwest or on the East Coast too.

2 What causes an earthquake?

The earth's crust consists[3] of about 20 different (tectonic) plates which slowly move. The place where two plates meet is called a fault line[4]. Each plate rubs[5] against another one. This puts both plates under stress. When the force[6] gets too strong, it comes apart with a jerk[7]. The released energy makes the earth move in waves.

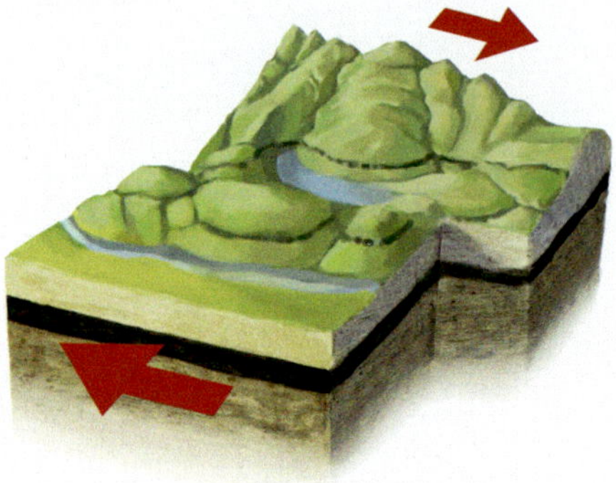

3 What can earthquakes do?

Major earthquakes can cause many problems. Buildings or bridges can collapse[8] or pipelines burst[9]. There can be mudslides[10], fires or tsunamis too. A large number of people can be hurt or even die after the earthquake.

1 earthquake ['ɜ:θkweɪk] – *Erdbeben*; 2 be at risk [rɪsk] – *einem Risiko ausgesetzt sein*; 3 consist of [kən'sɪst‿əv] – *bestehen aus*; 4 fault line ['fɔ:lt,laɪn] – *Verwerfungs-, Bruchlinie*; 5 rub [rʌb] – *reiben*; 6 force [fɔ:s] – *Kraft, Stärke*; 7 jerk [dʒɜ:k] – *Ruck*; 8 collapse [kə'læps] – *zusammenbrechen*; 9 burst [bɜ:st] – *platzen*; 10 mudslide ['mʌdslaɪd] – *Schlammlawine*

4 How are earthquakes measured?

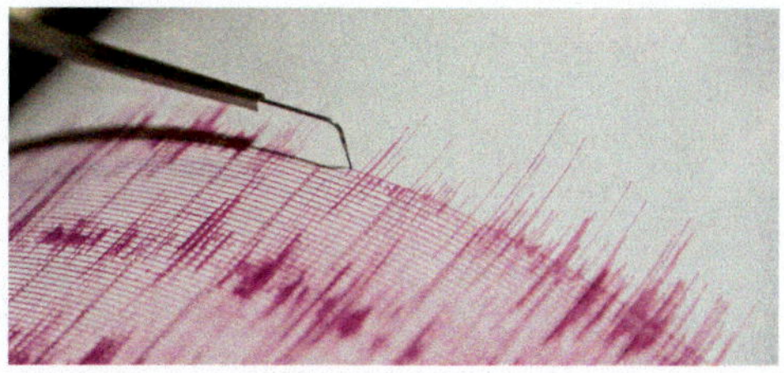

Scientists[1] record earthquakes with the help of a special instrument – the seismograph. It measures[2] the magnitude of an earthquake.
The Richter scale shows how destructive[3] earthquakes can be:

The Richter scale

0 – 1.9	only recorded by seismograph; not felt
2.0 – 2.9	objects may swing; hardly any damage
3.0 – 3.9	comparable to a passing truck
4.0 – 4.9	may break windows; smaller objects may fall
5.0 – 5.9	loose objects may fall from walls; furniture moves
6.0 – 6.9	damage to buildings
7.0 – 7.9	major ground breaks; buildings destroyed in large numbers
8.0 – 8.9	bridges and most houses destroyed
9.0 and over	total devastation

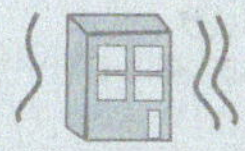

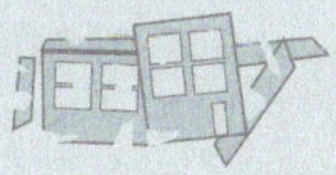

5 Find out about recent earthquakes worldwide.

Search the internet for a 'map of latest earthquakes'. Where did the last earthquakes happen?

6 Earthquake facts – What do you find most interesting?

Animals seem to sense[4] an earthquake is going to happen. No one knows how they do it.

An earthquake on the moon is called a moonquake. But they happen less and are smaller than earthquakes on earth.

There are about 500,000 earthquakes in the world each year. 100 of them cause heavy damage[5].

Because of the earth's movements, San Francisco and Los Angeles will meet in a few million years.

In Japanese mytholgy, a giant fish makes the earth move.

1 scientist ['saɪəntɪst] – *Wissenschaftler/-in;* 2 measure ['meʒə] – *messen;* 3 destructive [dɪ'strʌktɪv] – *zerstörerisch;* 4 sense [sens] – *spüren, fühlen;* 5 damage ['dæmɪdʒ] – *Schaden*

Static electricity

1 Are you 'electrified'?

Have you ever …

- ☐ … rubbed[1] a balloon on your hair and made it stand on end[2]?
- ☐ … touched a person or a metal object and felt an electric shock[3]?
- ☐ … taken off a pullover which made your hair crackle[4]?
- ☐ … felt like your clothes were clinging[5] to you?

All of these situations happen because of static[6] electricity. Sometimes your hair does funny things. Sometimes you may feel a small electric shock. It doesn't hurt badly, but it's a strange feeling. The most spectacular example of static electricity is lightning[7].

2 Why does static electricity happen?

Static electricity happens because everything is made of atoms. Atoms are tiny particles that are so small we can't see them. Inside of atoms are protons, neutrons and electrons. Protons, neutrons and electrons are very different from each other. Protons have a positive charge[8] (+). Neutrons have no charge. Electrons have a negative charge (–). Protons and neutrons make the center of the atom, the nucleus. The electrons move around this center.

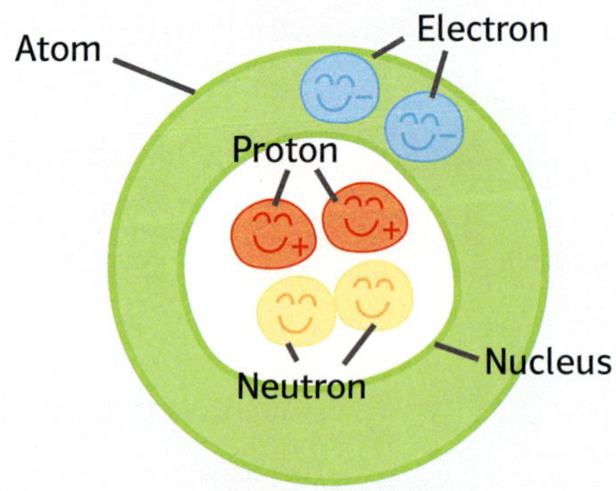

Usually atoms have no charge, because there are as many electrons as protons. But some electrons can move between atoms. This happens when two atoms come in contact or rub against each other. If electrons move from one atom to another, the charge of the atom changes. If there are more protons than electrons in an atom, the atom has a positive charge. If there are more electrons than protons, it has a negative charge.

If two atoms meet and they have the same charge, they move away from each other. If two atoms have different charges, they move towards each other.

1 rub [rʌb] – *reiben;* 2 stand on end [stænd‿ɒn‿end] – *die Haare zu Berge stehen lassen;* 3 electric shock [ɪ'lektrɪk ʃɒk] – *elektrischer Schock;* 4 crackle ['krækl] – *knistern;* 5 cling [klɪŋ] – *sich festhalten, klammern, hängenbleiben;* 6 static ['stætɪk] – *statisch;* 7 lightning ['laɪtnɪŋ] – *Blitz;* 8 charge [tʃɑːdʒ] – *Ladung*

3 Why does your hair stand on end?

When two objects with different charges touch[1] or rub against each other, the charges react and we sometimes see sparks[2] or feel an electric shock. When you rub a balloon on your hair, for example, electrons move from your hair to the balloon. The balloon then has more negative charge and the tips[3] of your hair have more positive charge. That's why your hair moves towards the negative charge of the balloon and away from all the other positively charged hair – suddenly your hair stands on end!

4 Some experiments

a) You need these materials:

balloons

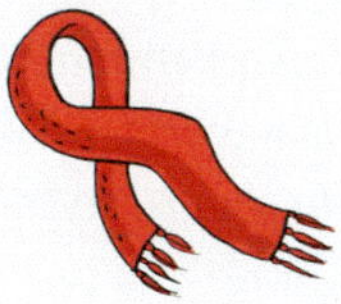

a wool scarf

pieces of paper

an empty can[4]

a string[5]

b) Try these experiments and write what happens.

1. Rub a balloon on a wool scarf. Hold it against a wall and let go[6].
2. Rub a balloon on a wool scarf. Hold the balloon over some small pieces of paper (e.g. confetti).
3. Put an empty can on the floor or a table. Rub a balloon with a wool scarf. Hold the balloon in front of the can without touching it.
4. Cut a piece of string (~70cm). Tie a balloon to each end of the string. Rub both balloons with a wool scarf and then hold up the middle of the string so that the balloons hang down.

1 touch [tʌtʃ] – *berühren, antippen;* 2 spark [spɑːk] – *Funke;* 3 tip [tɪp] – *Spitze;* 4 can [kæn] – *Dose, Getränkedose;* 5 string [strɪŋ] – *Schnur, Bindfaden;* 6 let go [ˌlet ˈɡəʊ] – *loslassen*

2,22

The Absolutely True Diary of a Part-Time Indian by S. Alexie (2007)

This is the diary of Arnold 'Junior' Spirit. He is small, very skinny[1], wears big glasses and has a stutter[2] and a lisp[3]. He is also really intelligent, and he loves to draw cartoons. This is a cartoon Arnold 'Junior' drew of himself:

Arnold 'Junior' Spirit is a Spokane[4] Indian. He lives in Wellpinit, a small town on an Indian reservation. He calls it the 'rez'. A lot of people there are very poor and never leave the rez.

One day Arnold 'Junior' decides that he has to change his life. He doesn't want to be poor all his life, and he wants to see the world. So Arnold 'Junior' decides to go to school in Reardan, a little town outside the reservation. At Reardan High School, all the kids are white, rich and amazing. Arnold is scared because he will be the only Indian at the school. But he also knows that it is his only chance to make his life better.

That's how Arnold 'Junior' becomes a part-time[5] Indian: He goes to school in Reardan where everyone calls him Arnold, but he lives on the reservation with his family where everyone calls him Junior.

This is his diary entry from his first day at the new school:

The next morning, Dad drove me the twenty-two miles to Reardan.

"I'm scared," I said.

"I'm scared, too," Dad said.

He hugged[6] me. "You don't have to do this," he said. "You can always go back to the rez school."

"No," I said. "I have to do this."

1 skinny [ˈskɪni] – *dünn, mager*; 2 stutter [ˈstʌtə] – *Stottern*; 3 lisp [lɪsp] – *Lispeln*; 4 Spokane [spəʊˌkæn] – *„Kinder der Sonne" oder „Sonnenvolk", ein Indianerstamm im Nordwesten der USA (Bundesstaat Washington)*; 5 part-time [ˌpɑːtˈtaɪm] – *Teilzeit-*; 6 hug sb [hʌg] – *jmd. umarmen*

"Just remember this," my father said. "Those white people aren't better than you."

But he was so wrong. And he knew he was wrong. He was the loser Indian father of a loser Indian son living in a world built for winners.

But he loved me so much. He hugged me again.

"This is a great thing," he said. "You're so brave. You're a warrior[1]."

It was the best thing he could have said.

"Hey, here's some lunch money," he said and gave me a dollar.

We were poor enough to get free lunch, but I didn't want to be the only Indian and the only one who needed charity[2].

"Thanks, Dad," I said.

"I love you," he said.

"I love you, too."

I felt stronger so I stepped out of the car and walked to the door. It was closed.

I watched my father drive away.

2,23 I stood at the door for a few very long minutes. It was still early.

Then the white kids arrived for school. They surrounded[3] me.

Most of the kids were my size or smaller, but there were ten or twelve monster dudes[4]. Giant white guys. They looked like men, not boys. Some of them looked like they had to shave[5] two or three times a day.

They stared[6] at me, the Indian boy. Those white kids couldn't believe their eyes. They stared at me like I was a UFO. What was I doing at Reardan, whose mascot[7] was an Indian, thereby making me the only other Indian in town?

So what was I doing in racist[8] Reardan, where more than half of every graduating[9] class went to college? Nobody in my family had ever gone near a college.

Reardan was the opposite of the rez. It was the opposite of my family. It was the opposite of me. I didn't deserve to be there. I knew it; all of those kids knew it. Indians don't deserve anything.

So, feeling worthless[10] and stupid[11], I just waited. And pretty soon, a janitor[12] opened the door and all of the other kids strolled inside.

1 warrior ['wɒriə] – *Krieger/-in*; 2 charity ['tʃærɪti] – *Almosen, Wohltätigkeit*; 3 surround [sə'raʊnd] – *umgeben, umringen*; 4 dude [du:d] – *Mann (ugs.)*; 5 shave [ʃeɪv] – *sich rasieren*; 6 stare [steə] – *starren*; 7 mascot ['mæskɒt] – *Maskottchen*; 8 racist ['reɪsɪst] – *rassistisch*; 9 graduating ['grædʒueɪtɪŋ] – *Abschluss-*; 10 worthless ['wɜ:θləs] – *wertlos*; 11 stupid ['stju:pɪd] – *blöd, dumm*; 12 janitor ['dʒænɪtə] – *Hausmeister/-in*

I walked into the school, made my way to the office, and told them who I was.

"Oh, you're the one from the reservation," the secretary said.

"Yeah," I said.

I couldn't tell if she thought the reservation was a good or bad thing.

"My name is Melinda," she said. "Welcome to Reardan High School. Here's your schedule and a Student ID. We've got you in Mr. Grant's homeroom[1]. You better walk there quickly. You're late."

"Ah, where is that?" I asked.

"We've only got one hallway[2] here," she said. She had red hair and green eyes. "It's all the way down on the left."

I put the paperwork into my backpack and walked to my homeroom. I waited a second at the door and then walked inside.

2,24 Everybody, all of the students and the teacher, stopped to stare at me. They stared hard.

Like I was bad weather.

"Take your seat," the teacher said. He was a muscular[3] guy. He had to be a football coach.

I sat down in the back and tried to ignore[4] all the stares and whispers[5], until a blond girl leaned[6] over toward me.

Penelope!

Yes, there are places left in the world where people are named Penelope!

"What's your name?" Penelope asked.

"Junior," I said.

She laughed and told her girlfriend at the next desk that my name was Junior. They both[7] laughed. Word spread[8] around the

1 homeroom [ˈhəʊmruːm] – *Zimmer des/der Klassenlehrers/-in*; 2 hallway [ˈhɔːlweɪ] – *Flur*; 3 muscular [ˈmʌskjələ] – *muskulär*; 4 ignore [ɪgˈnɔː] – *ignorieren*; 5 whisper [ˈwɪspə] – *Geflüster*; 6 lean over to sb [liːnˈəʊvə] – *sich zu jmd. rüberbeugen*; 7 both [bəʊθ] – *beide, beides*; 8 word spread [wɜːd‿spredðə] – es *sprach sich herum*

room and pretty soon everybody was laughing. They were laughing at my name.

I had no idea that Junior was a weird[1] name. It's a normal name on my rez, on any rez. You walk into any trading post[2] on any rez in the United States and shout, "Hey, Junior!" and seventeen guys will turn around. And three women.

But there were no other people named Junior in Reardan, so I was being laughed at because I was the only one who had that silly name.

And then I felt smaller because the teacher was taking roll[3] and he called out my name name.

"Arnold Spirit," the teacher said. No, he yelled[4] it.

"Here," I said as quietly as possible.

"Speak up," the teacher said.

"Here," I said.

"My name is Mr. Grant," he said.

"I'm here, Mr. Grant."

He moved on to other students, but Penelope leaned over toward me again, but she wasn't laughing at all. She was very angry now.

"I thought you said your name was Junior," Penelope said.

She accused[5] me of telling her my real name. Well, okay, it wasn't completely my real name. My full name is Arnold Spirit Jr. But nobody calls me that. Everybody calls me Junior. Well, every other Indian calls me Junior.

"My name is Junior," I said. "And my name is Arnold. It's Junior and Arnold. I'm both."

I felt like two people inside of one body. No, I felt like a magician[6] cutting myself in half, with Junior living on the north side of the Spokane River[7] and Arnold living on the south.

"Where are you from?" she asked.

She was so pretty and her eyes were so blue. She was the prettiest girl I had ever seen. She was movie star pretty.

"Hey," she said. "I asked you where you're from."

Wow, she was tough.

"Wellpinit," I said. "Up on the rez, I mean, the reservation."

"Oh," she said. "That's why you talk so funny."

And yes, I had that stutter and lisp, but I also had that singsong reservation accent that made everything I said sound like a bad poem.

Man, I was scared. I didn't say another word for six days.

1 weird [wɪəd] – *komisch*; 2 trading post ['treɪdɪŋ‿peʊst] – *Laden, Handelsposten*; 3 take roll [teɪk‿rəʊl] – die *Anwesenheitsliste durchgehen*; 4 yell [jel] – *brüllen, schreien*; 5 accuse sb of sth [ə'kju:z] – *jmd. beschuldigen*; 6 magician [mə'dʒɪʃn] – *Magier, Zauberer*; 7 Spokane River [spaʊˌkæn' rɪva] – *Flussname*

2,25

Deep water by C. Gardiner (2009)

Henry Jackson is sixteen years old, and he lives with his grandmother in a small town in Nebraska. Their house is outside of town; near a dam[1] and a lake that were built some years ago. Every day when Henry comes home, his grandmother tells him to not go to The Lake. It is dangerous and people die there. That's why Henry is afraid of deep[2] water, and he still cannot swim. Henry's best friend is Alice. She is a great swimmer, and Henry likes her a lot.

One day Alice tells him that she is going to have a picnic and go swimming with some friends. Henry doesn't go because he hates swimming. But later in the evening he realizes[3] that Alice and the other kids from his class probably went to The Lake. Some strange things have been happening at The Lake and Henry is afraid that something bad will happen, so he quickly leaves the house to go find Alice …

Henry ran into the woods at the back of the house. It was nearly night and the moon was just rising. Now Henry was glad that he was a good runner. No other kid in the school could have got through the woods so fast.

He wished he had Alice's cell phone number. Then he could call her and warn her. But then what could he say – 'don't swim in The Lake! There's something evil[4] there'? She wouldn't believe him and he would just look stupid[5].

He had to go to The Lake. Grandma's worries[6] weren't important. His friend Alice, the girl he liked more than anyone else in the whole school, was in danger[7]. He had to help her.

The moon was up as Henry burst[8] out of the woods. He heard kids laughing. He could see the dam wall not far away. The surface[9] of The Lake was shining in the moonlight. Everything looked calm[10].

The whole class was there with their picnic baskets. But they were over on the other side of The Lake. Henry shouted, "Alice!" She looked up and saw him. She waved to him and shouted something. But she was too far away so he couldn't hear her. He shouted again, "Don't go swimming, it's dangerous!" Alice shook[11] her head to show that she didn't understand what he was saying.

Henry looked around quickly. There was a path all along The Lake. But it was a long way to the other side. Even at his fastest, it'd take time to get to Alice. He was tired from his run through the woods but he had to try.

"Oh, Alice – please, please don't go swimming before I get there," Henry said softly to himself.

1 dam [dæm] – *Damm, Staumauer*; 2 deep [di:p] – *tief*; 3 realize ['rɪəlaɪz] – *erkennen, realisieren*; 4 evil ['i:vl] – *böse, schlecht*; 5 stupid ['stju:pɪd] – *dumm, blöd*; 6 worry ['wʌri] – *Sorge*; 7 danger ['deɪndʒə] – *Gefahr*; 8 burst out of [bɜ:st] – *herausstürzen*; 9 surface ['sɜ:fɪs] – *Oberfläche*; 10 calm [kɑ:m] – *ruhig, friedlich*; 11 shake [ʃeɪk] – *schütteln*

Then Matt jumped. Henry heard the splash as Matt went under the water. Henry ran faster. He was afraid that Matt would just disappear, that something would grab his foot and pull him down.

But then Matt's head came up again. He was laughing as he shook the water out of his hair. Henry shouted but the kids paid no attention[1]. He was still a long way away. Most of the other kids followed Matt into the water. Henry could see their heads as they splashed each other. Alice stood at the waterside. She didn't go in right away. She was watching Henry racing[2] round the path.

Henry ran on although it was getting hard to breathe. He waved and waved, trying to get the kids' attention. Then Alice went into the water. Henry almost fell to the

1 pay attention to sth [ˌpeɪ‿əˈtenʃn] – *seine Aufmerksamkeit auf etw. richten*; 2 race [reɪs] – *(sehr schnell) rennen*;

ground. “Alice! No!” Henry was shouting as loudly as he could. Suddenly something started moving towards the swimmers. It was big and black, like a shadow[1], moving smoothly[2] just under the surface of the water. The kids couldn’t see it.

They were busy with their game. They were playing with a ball, throwing it and trying to catch[3] it before it hit the water.

Alice started to swim towards Henry and away from the other kids. Henry could not run another step. He could hardly get his breath.

He fell down onto his knees.

2,26 Then Chet threw the ball up high into the air instead of throwing it to the next kid. He laughed loudly and he looked over at Henry. So Henry could see how surprised Chet was as something pulled him under the water. His head went down so fast that he didn’t even have time to shout.

His mouth was wide open as he went under.

The ball that Chet had thrown was still up in the air. At that same moment every other kid disappeared under the water. Every head just went down

1 shadow [ˈʃædəʊ] – *Schatten*; 2 smooth [smuːð] – *geschmeidig, gleichmäßig*; 3 atch [kætʃ] – *fangen*

without making any waves in the water. Except Alice. She was quite a bit away. She was moving fast towards Henry and didn't notice anything behind her.

The surface of the water was smooth again. The Lake was quiet. The black shadow was gone and the kids were gone. It all happened in just a few seconds. The ball landed back on the surface of the water with a splash.

Alice heard the splash. She looked back. The ball floated[1] on the water. There was nothing else, no kids anywhere. She turned round and started to swim faster and faster towards Henry.

Henry stood up again. The dark water of The Lake came right up to the path. He wanted to save Alice. But he was afraid of the black shadow in the water. She was still swimming fast towards him.

Something moved on the other side of The Lake, where the picnic baskets were. Henry didn't want to look but he could not control his eyes. He saw a tall, thin[2] man standing there.

"Henry!" Alice screamed, and he tore[3] his eyes away from the man. She was much nearer Henry now but still too far for him to reach[4] her. He put one foot into the water. It was very cold. It was like putting his foot into ice. He stepped in a bit deeper. Alice swam closer[5]. Behind her Henry saw the black shadow in the water again. It was coming very close to her. Henry went into the water as fast as he could. The water was up to his knees. The black shadow was right at Alice's feet. Her hand came towards him, her fingers just touched[6] his fingers – then a shout came from the other side of The Lake.

"Henry! Henry!" That was Grandma's voice! Henry automatically looked up towards her.

And then suddenly he couldn't feel Alice's hand any more. He looked back at The Lake.

Alice was gone.

What happened? Will Henry be able to save Alice?

1 float [fləʊt] – *gleiten, treiben*; 2 thin [θɪn] – dünn; 3 tear one's eyes away [teə] – *die Augen losreißen*; 4 reach [ri:tʃ] – *erreichen, greifen*; 5 close [kləʊs] – *nah*; 6 touch [tʌtʃ] – *berühren, antippen*

Grammar

G2

Mit G sind die Grammatikkapitel gekennzeichnet und der Reihe nach durchnummeriert. Eine Übersicht über alle Themen in diesem Band findest du auf der nächsten Seite.

Language tip G6

Die Seiten kennzeichnen zusätzliche Grammatikkapitel. Du kannst dir die neuen Formen dort wie neue Vokabeln merken oder – wenn du es genau wissen willst – ein paar Regeln dazu lernen.

Hier stehen Besonderheiten und Tipps.

(TEST YOURSELF)

Hier kannst du üben.
Die Lösungen findest du auf S. 293.

(FÜR PROFIS)

Hier findest du knifflige Extras zum Thema.

R = Revision (Wiederholung)

G

	Englisch	Deutsch	Beispiel	Seite
G1	R: simple past	einfache Vergangenheit	He opened a shop. • We didn't see the zoo. • It wasn't a safe place.	158
G2	past perfect	Vorvergangenheit	After I had come home, I took a shower. • Before I went to work, I had had breakfast.	159
G3	modal auxiliaries and their substitutes	Modale Hilfsverben und ihre Ersatzformen	I was allowed to go to bed late, but I had to get up early.	160
G4	R: If-clauses I	Bedingungssätze Typ I	If you ask me, I'll help you.	161
G5	one / ones	Stützwort one / ones	I need new jeans. The old ones are too short.	162
G6	question tags	Bestätigungsfragen	It is hot today, isn't it? • You like hip hop, don't you?	163
G7	R: questions – with who	Fragen – mit who	Do you like turkey? • Who likes you? • Who do you like?	164
G8	R: If-clauses II	Bedingungssätze Typ II	If I had a car, I would drive around town.	165
G9	R: simple present and present progressive	Gegenwartszeiten	She never forgets her smartphone. • She's talking on the phone right now.	166
G10	R: adjectives and adverbs	Adjektive und Adverbien	The flight is quick. • They fly us there quickly. • The place looks good.	167
G11	R: present perfect – since and for	Perfekt – since und for	The internet has changed the world. • I haven't seen Tom for a long time.	168
G12	passive voice – simple present – simple past	Passiv	A lot of T-shirts are made of cotton. • The city was founded by the French.	169
G13	reported speech – without backshift	Indirekte Rede – ohne Zeitverschiebung	She says (that) she likes New York.	170
G14	reported speech – with backshift	Indirekte Rede – mit Zeitverschiebung	He said (that) he had a problem.	171

Unit 1

G1 R: Die einfache Vergangenheit

Revision: The simple past

Um über Dinge zu sprechen, die in der Vergangenheit passiert und vorbei sind, verwendest du die einfache Vergangenheit (**simple past**).

Signalwörter	
yesterday	gestern
last year	letztes Jahr
a week ago	vor einer Woche
in 2015	(im Jahr) 2015

Das **simple past** bildest du so:
Hänge die Endung **-ed** an das Verb.
Achte auf unregelmäßige Verben, z. B. have → **had**; do → **did**; get → **got**; build → **built**; go → **went** etc.

Eine Liste der unregelmäßigen Verben findest du ab Seite 216.

They **started** roadwork last Monday.	Sie begannen am letzten Montag mit Straßenarbeiten.
Two years ago they **had** a lot of snow in New York.	Vor zwei Jahren hatten sie in New York viel Schnee.

Um zu sagen, was in der Vergangenheit nicht passiert ist, setzt du **didn't** (= did not) vor das Verb.

David **didn't get** into the city.	David kam nicht in die Stadt.

Und so kannst du im **simple past** Fragen stellen:

Did you **have** a good time in New York?	Yes, I **did**.	No, I **didn't**.
When **did** your friend **visit** Manhattan?	Last weekend.	

Aussagen und Verneinungen mit **be** bildest du so:

I **was** in New York.	Ich war in New York.
I **wasn't** in Washington.	Ich war nicht in Washington.
The Statue of Liberty **was** a present from France. It **wasn't** a present from Germany.	Die Freiheitsstatue war ein Geschenk von Frankreich. Sie war kein Geschenk von Deutschland.
We **were** in New York, but we **weren't** in Brooklyn.	Wir waren in New York, aber wir waren nicht in Brooklyn.

Fragen mit **be** bildest du so:

Were you at the zoo in Central Park?	Yes, I **was**.	No, I **wasn't**.
What **was** special in New York?	The Brooklyn Bridge.	

(TEST YOURSELF) Put the verbs in the simple past.

1. Tom — (have) a great time in NYC last summer.
2. He — (like) the New York skyline.
3. We — (not take) a taxi.
4. What — you — (do) in Manhattan?
5. — (be) you in the USA last year?
6. I — (not be) in Chicago.

G2 Die Vorvergangenheit

The past perfect

After I had built my new house, I felt much better.

Um über Ereignisse zu sprechen, die noch **vor** einem vergangenen Ereignis stattfanden, verwendest du die Vorvergangenheit, das **past perfect: had / hadn't + 3. Form** des Verbs (past participle).

Signalwörter

after	nachdem
before	bevor

Bei den meisten Verben hängst du für die 3. Form ein **-ed** an das Verb: visit → visit**ed**
Achte auf unregelmäßige Verben, z. B. go → **gone**; see → **seen**; be → **been** etc.

Eine Liste der unregelmäßigen Verben findest du ab Seite 216.

Was in der Vergangenheit weiter zurückliegt, wird mit dem **past perfect** ausgedrückt!

She wasn't at home. She **had gone** to Tim's (house).	Sie war nicht zu Hause. Sie war zu Tim gegangen.
After I **had been** in NYC for two months, I moved to Chicago.	Nachdem ich zwei Monate in NYC gewesen war, zog ich nach Chicago um.
I **hadn't seen** skyscrapers before I went to New York.	Ich hatte noch keine Wolkenkratzer gesehen, bevor ich nach New York ging.

Und so kannst du im **past perfect** Fragen stellen:

Had you ever **been** to the USA before you left Cuba?	Yes, I **had**.	No, I **hadn't**.
Which countries **had** you **visited** before you went to the USA?	I **hadn't visited** any other countries at all.	

(TEST YOURSELF) **Put the verbs in the past perfect.**

1. After I — (leave) the shop, I lost my shopping bag.
2. I couldn't go to the swimming pool because I — (not do) my homework.
3. When I arrived, the concert — already — (start).
4. What — you — (do) before you phoned me?
5. My grandad didn't want to move because he — (live) in Cuba all his life.
6. Yesterday I saw an animal which I — (not see) before.

Unit 2

G3 Modale Hilfsverben und ihre Ersatzformen

Modal auxiliaries and their substitutes

I didn't have to book a holiday,
I only had to swim to this lovely rock.

Modale Hilfsverben kannst du nur im **simple present** verwenden. Für alle anderen Zeiten benötigst du **Ersatzformen.** Ausnahme **can**: Für **can** kannst du im **simple past** auch **could** verwenden.

Mit **can/could** und der Ersatzform **be able to** sagst du, was du tun **kannst** (Fähigkeit).

Simple present	Simple past
Kim **can/is able to** speak English. Kim **kann** Englisch sprechen. **Can** he/**Is** he **able to** speak English? **Kann** er Englisch sprechen?	Kim **could/was able to** understand it. Kim **konnte** es verstehen. **Could** he/**Was** he **able to** speak English? **Konnte** er Englisch sprechen?

Mit **can** und der Ersatzform **be allowed to** sagst du, was du tun **darfst** (Erlaubnis).

She **can't/isn't allowed to** use her phone. Sie **darf** ihr Handy **nicht** benutzen. **Can** you/**Are** you **allowed to** wear jeans? **Darfst** du Jeans tragen?	She **couldn't/wasn't allowed to** use it. Sie **durfte** es **nicht** benutzen. **Could** you/**Were** you **allowed to** wear jeans? **Durftest** du Jeans tragen?

Mit **must** und der Ersatzform **have to** sagst du, was du tun **musst** (Verpflichtung).

Sarah **must** take English and History. Sarah **muss** Englisch und Geschichte nehmen. We **don't have to** worry. Wir **müssen** uns keine Sorgen machen. **Must** you help your parents? **Musst** du deinen Eltern helfen?	Sarah **had to** take Biology too. Sarah **musste** auch Biologie nehmen. We **didn't have to** worry. Wir **mussten** uns **keine Sorgen** machen. **Did** you **have to** help in the house? **Musstest** du im Haus helfen?

Bei **must** musst du die Ersatzform schon in **verneinten Sätzen** im **simple present** benutzen!

(TEST YOURSELF) Use the correct forms in the simple past.

1. When Luise was in the USA, she —— (not can) keep her things in the classrooms.
2. She —— (must) put her books into lockers.
3. She —— (can) travel around in the USA.
4. She —— (not must) take lessons in basketball.
5. The students —— (can) wear jeans.
6. When she was ten, she —— (not can) dance like she dances today.

G4 R: Bedingungssätze Typ I

Revision: If-clauses type I

Um Bedingungen und Folgen auszudrücken, benutzt man **if**-Sätze.
Dabei steht im **if-Satz** das **simple present**, im Hauptsatz das **will-future**.
Geht der **if**-Satz voran, steht am Ende des **if**-Satzes ein Komma.

Bedingung (condition)	Folge (consequence)	
If Michael **finds** a job,	he **will earn** some money.	Wenn Michael einen Job findet, wird er etwas Geld verdienen.
If you **don't work** well,	you **won't get** a bonus.	Wenn du nicht gut arbeitest, bekommst du keine Prämie.

Bedingungssätze können auch mit dem Hauptsatz beginnen. Dann entfällt das Komma.

Folge (consequence)	Bedingung (condition)	
You **will be** late	if you **walk.**	Du wirst zu spät kommen, wenn du zu Fuß gehst.
You **won't be** successful	if you **don't work** more carefully.	Du wirst nicht erfolgreich sein, wenn du nicht sorgfältiger arbeitest.

Das **will-future** drückt allgemein Zukünftiges aus. Im **if**-Satz steht nie **will** oder **won't**!

Für das **will-future** kannst du im Deutschen die Zukunft oder die Gegenwart benutzen. Beides ist richtig. Vergleiche:

He will earn some money.	Er wird etwas Geld verdienen. Er verdient etwas Geld.

(TEST YOURSELF) Complete the sentences.

1. If you — (need) me, I — (help) you.
2. If you — (not phone) me, I — (be) sad.
3. If she — (not come) on time, she — (lose) her job.
4. Matt — (not find) a job if he — (not look) on the internet.
5. I — (talk) to Sue if I — (meet) her.
6. You — (not sleep) well if you always — (read) scary stories.

(FÜR PROFIS)

Im Deutschen können **if** (falls, wenn) und **when** (dann, wenn) mit wenn übersetzt werden.
Im Englischen kommt es darauf an, welche **Absicht** du ausdrücken möchtest.

If I go shopping, I'll get you a T-shirt.
(Ich weiß noch nicht, **ob** ich einkaufen gehe. Aber **falls** ich gehe, dann kaufe ich dir ein T-Shirt. Es ist nicht sicher und nur eine Möglichkeit.)

When I go shopping, I'll get you a T-shirt.
(Ich gehe auf jeden Fall einkaufen. Das weiß ich schon sicher. Ich weiß nur noch nicht, **wann**. Aber dann kaufe ich dir ein T-Shirt. Es ist sicher und nur eine Frage des Zeitpunkts.)

G5 Stützwort one / ones

One / ones

Which cave is better?
The right one or the left one?

Um eine unnötige Wiederholung von Nomen zu vermeiden, kannst du sie durch **one** (Einzahl) und **ones** (Mehrzahl) ersetzen. **One / ones** werden nicht übersetzt. Sie stehen oft nach einem Adjektiv. Auch nach der Steigerungsform eines Adjektivs kommt **one** oder **ones** häufig vor.

Who are those boys over there?	Wer sind diese Jungs dort drüben?
The tall ~~boy~~ **one** is Jim and the short ~~boy~~ **one** is Tim.	Der große ~~Junge~~ ist Jim und der kleine ~~Junge~~ ist Tim.
Which towels did you buy?	Welche Handtücher hast du gekauft?
– The cheaper **ones.**	– Die billigeren.
Which books do you prefer?	Welche Bücher bevorzugst du?
– Exciting **ones.**	– Spannende.

One oder **ones** stehen auch oft nach Fragen mit **which.**

You can borrow my CDs.	Du kannst dir meine CDs ausleihen.
Which ones would you like?	**Welche** möchtest du?
There are lots of nice T-shirts here.	Es gibt hier viele schöne T-Shirts.
Which one do you like best?	**Welches** gefällt dir am besten?

(TEST YOURSELF) **Use one or ones.**

1. You should try on some shoes. What about these black ___?
2. The short skirt is much nicer than the long ___.
3. The new computers are much better than the old ___.
4. I like these sunglasses. – Yes, they are nice. Which ___ would you like to buy?
5. I've missed my bus. Now I have to wait for the next ___.
6. That shop doesn't look very good. – You're right. Let's look for another ___.

(FÜR PROFIS)

Auch nach **the**, **this**, **that** und **these**, **those** kann one oder ones stehen.

Look at these beautiful dresses.	Schau dir diese schönen Kleider an.
These ones here are really cheap.	**Diese** hier sind wirklich günstig.
I like **this one**, **the one** with the flowers.	Ich mag **dieses**, **das** mit den Blumen.

G

Language tip

G6 Bestätigungsfragen

Question tags

You didn't eat the turkey, did you?

Um ein Gespräch nicht abreißen zu lassen, kannst du eine Bestätigungsfrage (question tag) benutzen. Im Deutschen sagt man dafür Ausdrücke wie **nicht wahr?**, **nicht?**, **oder?**
Für negative **question tags** benutzt du immer Kurzformen.
Alle **question tags** werden mit einem Komma vom Aussagesatz abgetrennt.

Ist der Aussagesatz positiv +, so wird die Bestätigungsfrage negativ –.

Aussagesatz +	Question tag –
It's cold,	**isn't** it?
You **are** fifteen,	**aren't** you?
She **can** play the guitar,	**can't** she?
Robert **was** in Boston,	**wasn't** he?
You **were** in New York,	**weren't** you?

Ist der Aussagesatz negativ –, so wird die Bestätigungsfrage positiv +.

Aussagesatz –	Question tag +
Your shirt **isn't** new,	**is** it?
You **weren't** in the USA last year,	**were** you?

Bei Vollverben musst du **do**, **does**, **did** oder **don't**, **doesn't**, **didn't** benutzen:

You **like** chocolates,	**don't** you?
Julia **wants** to go to Miami,	**doesn't** she?
You **met Brenda**,	**didn't** you?
You **don't like** turkey,	**do** you?
Nick **doesn't drink** coke,	**does** he?
Robert **didn't see** the Niagara Falls,	**did** he?

(TEST YOURSELF) **Use the correct question tags.**

1. You are from Boston, —?
2. The USA is a huge country, —?
3. You were in Chicago last year, —?
4. You like Thanksgiving, —?
5. You enjoyed your holiday, —?
6. Jacob doesn't eat meat, —?

G7 R: Fragen

Revision: Questions / questions with who

So bildest du unterschiedliche Fragen mit Vollverben, z. B. like, go etc.:

Fragen, auf die man mit yes oder no antwortet (Ja/Nein-Fragen)
– Fragen im **simple present** beginnst du mit **do** oder **does** (he, she, it).

Do you **like** turkey?	Magst du Truthahn?
Does Jacob **like** chocolate?	Mag Jacob Schokolade?

– Fragen im **simple past** beginnst du mit **did** für alle Personen.

Did you **travel** by car last year?	Bist du letztes Jahr mit dem Auto verreist?
Did it **rain** last December?	Hat es im letzten Dezember geregnet?

– Fragen im **will-future** beginnst du mit **will** für alle Personen.

Will you **call** us again tomorrow?	Wirst du uns morgen nochmal anrufen?

Fragen mit Fragewörtern

What do you **like**?	Was magst du gerne?
Where did you **spend** your summer?	Wo hast du deinen Sommer verbracht?
When will you **go** to Boston?	Wann wirst du nach Boston fahren?

Fragen mit who
– Das Fragewort **who?** kann **verschiedene Bedeutungen** haben:
– Heißt es **Wer?** wird **keine Form von do** verwendet.
– Heißt es **Wen?** oder **Wem?** muss **eine Form von do** verwendet werden.

Who lives in Boston?	**Wer** lebt in Boston?
Who do you **like**?	**Wen** magst du?
Who did you **help** last week?	**Wem** hast du letzte Woche geholfen?

Präpositonen bleiben in Fragen meistens beim Verb stehen. Im Deutschen dagegen steht die Präposition meistens beim Fragewort. Vergleiche:

Who did you **talk to?**	**Mit wem** hast du dich unterhalten?
Where do you **come from?**	**Woher** kommst du?

(TEST YOURSELF) Put in do, does, did, will – if necessary.

1. — you often have a turkey dinner?
2. Where — your uncle live?
3. Who — you invite next Friday?
4. — you see the snow storm on TV last Sunday?
5. Who — got stuck in his car last night?
6. Who — Mark talk to yesterday?

G8 R: Bedingungssätze Typ II

Revision: If-clauses type II

Bei den Bedingungssätzen Typ II ist eine Bedingung unwahrscheinlich oder nicht erfüllbar. Du verwendest im **if**-Satz **simple past**. Im Hauptsatz steht **would / wouldn't + Grundform des Verbs.**

Bedingung (condition)	Folge (consequence)	
If it **rained**,	I **would stay** at home.	Wenn es regnen würde, würde ich zu Hause bleiben.
If you **didn't call**,	I **would be** very sad.	Wenn du nicht anrufen würdest, wäre ich sehr traurig.

Bedingungssätze können auch mit dem Hauptsatz beginnen. Dann entfällt das Komma.

Folge (consequence)	Bedingung (condition)	
I **would buy** new clothes	if I **had** more money.	Ich würde mir neue Kleidung kaufen, wenn ich genug Geld hätte.
I **wouldn't have** problems with my clothes	if I **lived** in the Amish community.	Ich hätte keine Kleidungsprobleme, wenn ich in der Gemeinschaft der Amish leben würde.

Statt **If I was** … wird oft **If I were** … gebraucht.

If I **were** a film star,	I **would live** in Beverly Hills.	Wenn ich ein Filmstar wäre, würde ich in Beverly Hills wohnen.

Im **if**-Satz steht nie **would / wouldn't**!

Im Deutschen verwendet man in beiden Satzteilen **würde**, **wäre** oder **hätte (Konjunktiv)**.

(TEST YOURSELF) Complete the sentences.

1. If you — (visit) your grandma on Sundays, she — (be) very glad.
2. If she — (have) less time, she — (not meet) her friends every week.
3. If I — (be) in Pennsylvania, I — (like) to see the Amish community.
4. I — really — (miss) you if you — (not come) back.
5. Jennifer — (not worry) about clothes if she — (live) with the Amish community.
6. Maybe it — (be) better if you — (not phone) me every day.

Unit 4

G9 R: Gegenüberstellung: Simple present – present progressive

Revision: Simple present – present progressive

Du kennst schon die Zeiten **simple present** und **present progressive**. Hier findest du noch einmal die Situationen, in denen du sie benutzen kannst und siehst, wie sie gebildet werden.

Simple present

Das **simple present** verwendest du, wenn du sagen willst, dass jemand etwas häufig oder regelmäßig tut.

Signalwörter: always, never, sometimes, often, usually, every …

Aussagen bildest du mit der Grundform des Verbs.

I **work** every day. You never **listen**.

Achtung: **He**, **she**, **it** – das **s** muss mit:
He works. She talks. It rains. Aber: He goes.

Sätze mit Vollverben verneinst du mit **don't** und **doesn't**:

I **don't play** football.

Bei Fragen mit Vollverben musst du mit **do** oder **does** beginnen:

Do you **eat** fish? **Does** he **like** games?

Present progressive

Mit dem **present progressive** kannst du sagen, was jemand gerade tut oder was im Augenblick passiert.

Signalwörter: now, at the moment

Aussagen bildest du so:
am / are / is + Verb + -ing

I**'m working** at the moment. It **is raining** now.

Achtung Schreibweise: make → mak**ing**; write → writ**ing**; run → run**ning**; sit → sit**ting**

So verneinst du Sätze:
am / are / is not **+ Verb + -ing**:

He **isn't eating** at the moment.

Bei Fragen stellst du **am / are / is** an den Satzanfang:

Are you **listening**? **Is** she **dancing**?

Simple present und present progressive kannst du auch einsetzen, um ein **Bild** zu beschreiben. Zunächst sagst du, wen oder was du siehst. Dann beschreibst du, was jemand tut.

Simple present

Du benutzt es, um zu sagen, wer oder was auf dem Bild zu sehen ist, oder in welchem Zustand etwas ist.

There is a boy in the picture.
There are a man and a woman.
She **looks** happy.
She **has** two dogs.
The weather **is** nice. It **is** warm.

Present progressive

Du benutzt es für alle Handlungen, die im Bild zu sehen sind und für alles, was jemand tut.

The boy **is riding** a mountain bike.
They**'re sitting** in camping chairs.
She**'s wearing** boots.
They **are playing** with a ball.
The sun **is shining**. It **isn't raining**.

(TEST YOURSELF) Use present progressive or simple present.

1. Sandy often —— (go) surfing.
2. But at the moment she —— (not surf).
3. "—— you really —— (listen), Sandy?"
4. Students —— (not like) tests.
5. What —— you usually —— (do) after school?
6. We sometimes —— (meet) some friends.

G10 R: Adjektive und Adverbien

Revision: Adjectives and adverbs

Ein **Adjektiv** (Eigenschaftswort) beschreibt eine Person oder eine Sache.

Sandra is a **good** surfer.	Sandra ist eine gute Surferin.
A helicopter tour is **fantastic**.	Ein Hubschrauberflug ist fantastisch.

Ein **Adverb** beschreibt, wie jemand etwas tut oder wie etwas geschieht.
Man erkennt Adverbien durch ein angehängtes **-ly**.

Look, she is running **slowly**.	Schau, sie läuft langsam.
It happened **quickly**.	Es geschah schnell.

Achtung Schreibweise: happy – happ**ily**; careful – careful**ly**; comfortable – comfortab**ly**; fantastic – fantasti**cally**

Es gibt Adverbien, die sich nicht verändern:

Basketball is a **fast** game.	(Adjektiv)	Basketball ist ein schnelles Spiel.
Look, the players are running **fast**.	(Adverb)	Schau, die Spieler rennen schnell.
That was a **hard** exercise.	(Adjektiv)	Das war eine schwierige Übung.
Tom has to work **hard** every day.	(Adverb)	Tom muss jeden Tag schwer arbeiten.

Es gibt auch unregelmäßige Adverbien:

This is a **good** surfboard.	(Adjektiv)	Das ist ein gutes Surfbrett.
I can surf very **well** with it.	(Adverb)	Ich kann sehr gut damit surfen.

Achtung Ausnahme! Manche Verben drücken **keine** Tätigkeit aus, z. B. **look**, **feel**, **seem**, **sound**.
Nach diesen Verben verwendest du ein **Adjektiv**:

I **feel** so **sad**.	Ich fühle mich so traurig.
You **look** **happy** today.	Du siehst heute glücklich aus.
This exercise **seems** **easy**.	Diese Aufgabe scheint leicht zu sein.
That **sounds** **good**.	Das klingt gut.

(TEST YOURSELF) **Use adjectives or adverbs.**

1. Don't speak so — (fast). Speak more — (slow), please.
2. She surfed so — (good) that she — (easy) won the race.
3. Sandy looks — (pretty) in her new dress.
4. I don't feel — (good) today. I think I've worked too — (hard).
5. Yesterday it rained — (heavy).
6. You seem — (unhappy) with the results of the last test.

G11 R: Das Perfekt

Revision: The present perfect

Wenn eine Handlung in der Vergangenheit beginnt und in der Gegenwart zu einem Ergebnis führt, verwendest du das **present perfect**:
have/has + 3. Form des Verbs (past participle).
Bei den meisten Verben hängst du ein **-ed** an das Verb: help → help**ed**

Signalwörter	
already	schon
just	gerade
not ... yet	noch ... nicht
never	noch nie
ever (in Fragen)	jemals (in Fragen)
since	seit (Zeitpunkt)
for	seit (Zeitspanne)

Eine Liste der unregelmäßigen Verben findest du ab Seite 216.

Einige Verben haben unregelmäßige 3. Formen: z. B. be → **been**; write → **written**

I **have** just **posted** a photo.	Ich habe gerade ein Foto verschickt.
She **has** already **written** ten text messages.	Sie hat schon zehn SMS geschrieben.

Um Sätze zu verneinen, benutzt du **haven't** oder **hasn't** (bei he, she, it):

I **haven't been** to California yet.	Ich bin noch nicht in Kalifornien gewesen.
She **hasn't seen** Los Angeles yet.	Sie hat Los Angeles noch nicht gesehen.

Fragen und Kurzantworten bildest du so:

Have you ever **been** to San Francisco?	Yes, I **have**.	No, I **haven't**.
Has your sister ever **met** a famous star?	Yes, she **has**.	No, she **hasn't**.

Present perfect mit **for** und **since**
since (seit) verwendest du vor einem **Zeitpunkt**, z. B. **since** 5 o'clock, **since** July, **since** 2013.
for (seit) verwendest du vor einer **Zeitspanne**, z. B. **for** five hours, **for** three years, **for** a long time.

I haven't seen Lara **since** Monday.	Ich habe Lara **seit** Montag nicht gesehen.
I haven't seen Lara **for** a week.	Ich habe Lara **seit** einer Woche nicht gesehen.

Wie im Präsens gibt es im Perfekt eine Verlaufsform (present perfect progressive).
Damit betonst du die Dauer der Handlung. Vergleiche.

I **have been living** in Los Angeles **for** two years.	Ich **lebe seit** zwei Jahren in Los Angeles.

(TEST YOURSELF) Put the verbs in the present perfect.

1. Linda — never — (meet) a Hollywood star.
2. I — (not see) you for two months.
3. Why — your sister — (not call) yet?
4. — you — (forget) your homework again?
5. We — (not be) on holiday since 2010.
6. — you ever — (watch) video clips?

G12 Das Passiv

Passive voice (simple present
and simple past)

English is important.
It is spoken all over the world.

Mit dem Passiv kannst du über eine Handlung Auskunft geben, ohne zu sagen, wer die Handlung ausführt. Im Vordergrund steht die Handlung.

So bildest du das **Passiv** im **simple present: am / are / is + 3. Form des Verbs** (past participle)

English **is spoken** in a lot of countries.	Englisch **wird** in vielen Ländern **gesprochen**.
Racism **isn't accepted**.	Rassismus **wird nicht akzeptiert**.
Spices and flour **are mixed**.	Gewürze und Mehl **werden gemischt**.

So bildest du das Passiv im **simple past: was / were + 3. Form des Verbs** (past participle)

Raleigh **was founded** in the 18th century.	Raleigh **wurde** im 18. Jahrhundert **gegründet**.
The airport **wasn't finished** until 1929.	Der Flughafen **wurde nicht** vor 1929 **fertiggestellt**.
The streets **were built** in a special way.	Die Straßen **wurden** auf besondere Weise **gebaut**.

Willst du in einem Passivsatz sagen, **wer** die Handlung ausführt, ergänzt du ihn oder sie mit **by**.

The city of Raleigh **was founded** by the French.	Die Stadt Raleigh **wurde** von den Franzosen **gegründet**.
New dishes **were brought** here by the slaves.	Neue Gerichte **wurden** von den Sklaven hierher **gebracht**.

(TEST YOURSELF) Use the passive voice, simple present or simple past.

1. The fried chicken — (introduce) by people from Scotland hundreds of years ago.
2. Today this dish — (make) with flour and spices.
3. The chicken and the rice — (not cook) for a long time.
4. Many cities in the South — (found) by the French in the 18th century.
5. Every year the famous Mardi Gras carnival — (celebrate) in New Orleans.
6. The city — (not build) by Sir Walter Raleigh.

G13 Indirekte Rede (ohne Zeitverschiebung)

Reported speech (without backshift)

Mit der indirekten Rede kannst du über das berichten, was jemand anderes **gerade gesagt hat**. Du beginnst mit **He says that … / She says that …** usw. Das Wort **that** kann man auch weglassen.

Positive Aussagen und verneinte Sätze in der indirekten Rede bildest du so:

Direkte Rede	Indirekte Rede
Anna says, "**I like** Florida." Anna says, "**We want** to see the alligators." Anna says, "**I don't need** a hotel."	Anna says (that) **she likes** Florida. Anna says (that) **they want** to see the alligators. Anna says (that) **she doesn't need** a hotel.

Beachte die Änderungen:

I	→ **he/she**	**my**	→ **his/her**
we	→ **they**	**our**	→ **their**
(I) **like**	→ (he/she) **likes**		
(I) **don't …**	→ (he/she) **doesn't …**		

Fragen in der indirekten Rede werden so wiedergegeben:

Du beginnst z. B. mit	**She asks if …**	Sie fragt, **ob …**
Bei Fragen mit Fragewörtern beginnst du z. B. mit	**He asks where …**	Er fragt, **wo/wohin …**

Direkte Rede	Indirekte Rede
Anna asks Ethan, "**Do you like** alligators?" Nick asks, "**Where do you go** camping?"	She asks Ethan **if he likes** alligators. He asks **where they go** camping.

Erkenne die Zeitform in der **Frage** der direkten Rede (hier: **simple present**) und bilde in der indirekten Rede einen **Satz** im **simple present** nach der Regel **S**ubjekt – **V**erb – **O**bjekt!

(TEST YOURSELF) Report what Anna says.

1. "We prefer the Everglades."
2. "I want to go on a boat tour."
3. "I don't like all those crowds."
4. "I don't want to feed the alligators."
5. "Ethan, do you know Florida?"
6. "Ethan, what do you think?"

G14 Indirekte Rede (mit Zeitverschiebung)

Reported speech (with backshift)

Look, I've got a new boyfriend.
But he's a bat!
And he told me he was a pilot.

Mit der indirekten Rede kannst du über etwas berichten, was jemand **vor einiger Zeit gesagt hat.** Du beginnst mit **He said that ... / She told me that ...** usw. Das Wort **that** kann man auch weglassen. Das Verb des Satzes wird vom **simple present** in das **simple past** zurückgesetzt. Das nennt man **backshift.**
Backshift gilt auch für die Verneinung: aus **don't / doesn't** wird **didn't**.

Positive Aussagen und verneinte Sätze in der indirekten Rede bildest du so:

Direkte Rede	Indirekte Rede
Al Lane said, "I **get up** at 6 a.m." He said, "There **are** 20 alligators." He said, "We **don't get** a lot of visitors."	Al Lane told me (that) he **got up** at 6 a.m. He said (that) there **were** 20 alligators. He said (that) they **didn't get** a lot of visitors.

(TEST YOURSELF) Report what Al Lane said.

1. "I often work with the alligators."
2. "Some tourists don't like alligators."
3. "We feed the animals at 10 o'clock."
4. "It's too late to feed the alligators."
5. "I don't speak German."
6. "The visitors love the warm weather."

(FÜR PROFIS)

Fragen werden in der indirekten Rede so wiedergegeben:

Du beginnst z.B. mit	**She asked if ...**	Sie fragte, **ob** ...
Bei Fragewörtern beginnst du z.B. mit	**He asked when ...**	Er fragte, **wann** ...

Direkte Rede	Indirekte Rede
Al Lane asked, "Anna, **do** you **want** to feed the alligators?" Anna asked, "**When does** the alligator show **start**?"	Al Lane asked Anna **if** she **wanted** to feed the alligators. Anna wanted to know **when** the alligator show **started**.

Erkenne die Zeitform in der **Frage** der direkten Rede (hier: **simple present**) und bilde in der indirekten Rede einen **Satz** im **simple past** nach der Regel **S**ubjekt – **V**erb – **O**bjekt!

Methods

1-minute-presentation

Step 1
Nimm ein Blatt DIN A4-Papier quer und falte es so, dass das untere Drittel nach hinten wegknickt.

Step 2
Schreibe den Vortragstext auf die oberen zwei Drittel.

Step 3
Streiche nun die wichtigsten Stichpunkte im Text an. Notiere sie noch einmal auf dem unteren Drittel. Das ist dein Spickzettel.

Step 4
In deiner Präsentation verwendest du nur den Spickzettel. Wenn du steckenbleibst, darfst du ihn umknicken und kurz auf den Text oben schauen.

Bus stop
(Lerntempoduett)

Step 1
Bearbeite die Aufgabe zunächst allein. Schreibe deine Lösungen auf.

Step 2
Wenn du fertig bist, gehe zum „bus stop“. Warte dort auf die nächste Person bzw. triff die Person, die dort schon wartet. Vergleicht und korrigiert eure Ergebnisse.

Step 3
Gehe danach wieder zu deinem Platz zurück. Bearbeite die nächste Aufgabe.

Dramatic reading
(Szenisches Lesen)

Step 1
Verteilt die Rollen innerhalb eurer Gruppe.

Step 2
Lies dir deinen Text lautlos oder ganz leise immer wieder vor, bis du ihn gut kennst.

Step 3
Übt euren Text in der Gruppe mit der Methode „Read and look up" (Seite 176).

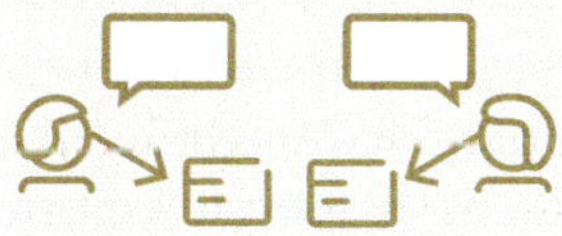

Step 4
Überlegt euch, wie ihr euch in der Rolle fühlt und wie ihr euch bewegen würdet. Tragt euren Text so frei wie möglich vor.

Gallery walk

Step 1
Hängt nach eurer Gruppenarbeit euer Produkt gut sichtbar im Klassenzimmer auf.

Step 2
Einer von euch, der „Experte", bleibt bei eurem Produkt stehen und erklärt es den anderen. Die anderen gehen herum. Nach jedem Durchgang wechselt der Experte.

Step 3
Seht euch die Produkte der anderen an und bewertet sie.

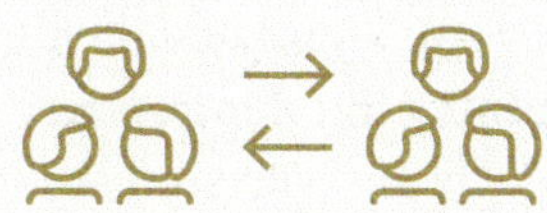

Step 4
Wertet im Anschluss eure Ergebnisse in der Klasse aus.

Jigsaw
(Gruppenpuzzle)

Step 1
Bildet Stammgruppen („home groups“).
Jedes Gruppenmitglied wählt einen Text aus, liest ihn und bearbeitet ihn. Macht euch Notizen dazu.

Step 2
Trefft euch in Expertengruppen („expert groups“) mit den Mitgliedern der anderen Stammgruppen, die denselben Text wie ihr bearbeitet haben. Vergleicht eure Notizen, besprecht sie gemeinsam und ergänzt sie.

Step 3
Geht zurück in eure Stammgruppe. Präsentiert dort die Informationen aus eurem Text. Macht euch Notizen zu den Texten der anderen, so dass am Ende jeder die Informationen aus allen Texten hat.

Milling around
(Marktplatz)

Step 1
Bearbeite die Aufgabe zunächst allein.
Auf ein Zeichen vom Lehrer oder der Lehrerin steht ihr auf und geht durch den Raum.
Nimm die Aufgabe und einen Stift mit.

Step 2
Wenn ein Signal ertönt, bleibt ihr stehen.
Besprecht mit der Person die Aufgabe, die euch am nächsten steht.

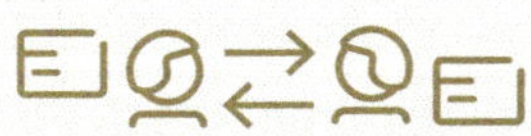

Step 3
Beim nächsten Signal trennt ihr euch und geht weiter durch den Raum. Wiederholt den Vorgang.

Peer correction
(Partnerkontrolle)

Step 1
Bearbeite die Aufgabe zunächst selbstständig.

Step 2
Tausche deine Lösungen mit einem Partner/einer Partnerin. Kontrolliere seine oder ihre Lösungen.

Step 3
Tauscht euch danach zu der Aufgabe aus und korrigiert den Text.

Placemat
(Platzdeckchen)

Step 1
Bildet Vierergruppen.

Step 2
Teilt ein großes Blatt Papier in fünf Bereiche ein.

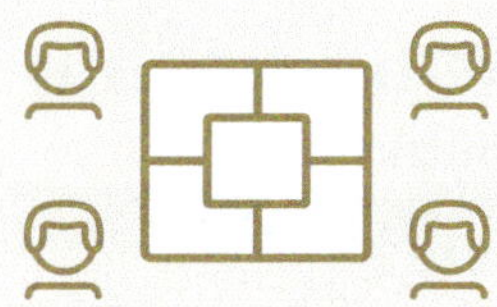

Step 3
Setzt euch so hin, dass alle in eine Ecke des Blattes schreiben können.

Step 4
Jedes Gruppenmitglied denkt allein über das Thema nach und schreibt Ideen auf seinen Teil des Blattes.

Step 5
Tauscht euch über die Ideen aus. Einigt euch auf die besten Ideen und schreibt diese in die Mitte des Blattes.

Read and look up

(Lesen und Aufschauen)

Step 1

Schaue auf deinen Text und präge dir die erste Zeile oder den ersten Satz ein. Schaue hoch und sprich deine Zeile/deinen Satz lautlos oder leise vor dich hin. Nimm dir die nächste Zeile/den nächsten Satz vor.

Step 2

Übe nun mit einer Partnerin/einem Partner. Erzähle deinen Text, Zeile für Zeile oder Satz für Satz. Dazwischen schaust du immer wieder nach unten auf deinen Text.

Step 3

Wiederhole alles, bis es gut klappt. Überlege dir, wo du stehen und wie du dich bewegen willst.

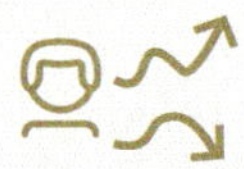

Round robin

(Blitzlicht)

Step 1

Bildet Gruppen und setzt euch in einen Kreis.

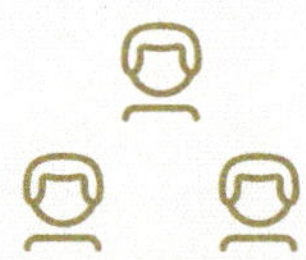

Step 2

Jedes Gruppenmitglied überlegt sich kurz einen Satz, der seine persönliche Meinung zum Thema ausdrückt.

Step 3

Wenn alle bereit sind, sagen die Gruppenmitglieder der Reihe nach ihre Meinung.

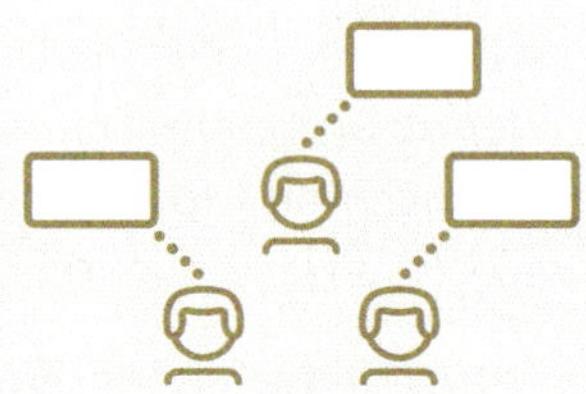

Step 4

Die anderen Gruppenmitglieder dürfen die Sätze nicht kommentieren.

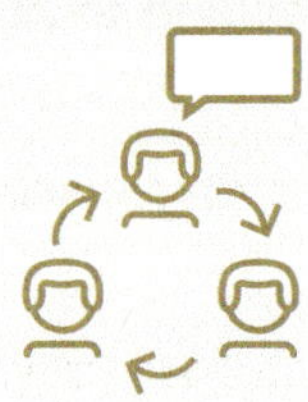

Think – pair – share

Step 1
Schreibe deine Ideen, Gedanken oder Lösungen zur Aufgabe auf.

Step 2
Tauscht eure Notizen zu zweit aus und besprecht sie.

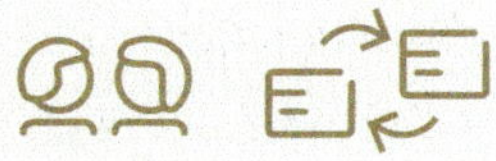

Step 3
Präsentiert euer Ergebnis anderen Paaren oder der gesamten Klasse.

Tip top

Step 1
Sage zunächst, was dir gut gefallen hat – was „top" war.

Step 2
Sage nun, was noch nicht so gut war, und gib einen Tipp, was man noch verbessern könnte.

Writers' conference

(Schreibwerkstatt)

Step 1
Bildet Vierergruppen.

Step 2
Lest euch eure Sätze/Texte gegenseitig vor.

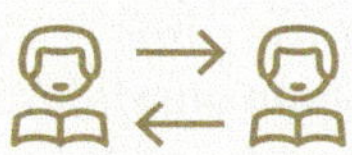

Step 3
Die anderen sagen, was ihnen gefallen hat.

Step 4
Die Zuhörer machen Verbesserungsvorschläge.

Step 5
Jede Gruppe wählt den besten Text aus und liest ihn der Klasse vor.

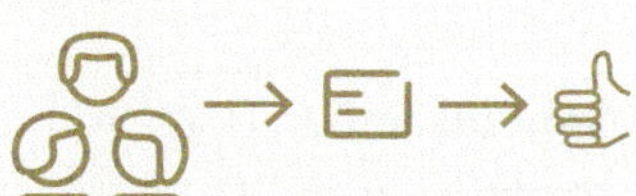

Du kennst schon einige Tipps und Tricks zum Vokabellernen. Erinnerst du dich? Hier gibt es weitere Tipps.

Vocabulary

Vocabulary tips

Lerntipp: Englisch im Alltag

Achte während des Tages auf alle englischen Wörter, die dir begegnen. Ob im Supermarkt, im Fernsehen, in Büchern, auf Werbeplakaten oder Schildern am Bahnhof, Flughafen etc.: Du wirst erstaunt sein, wie oft man im Alltag auf die englische Sprache stößt. Das ist ein gutes Training, um auf noch unbekannte Vokabeln aufmerksam zu werden. Deinen Sprachschatz erweiterst du ganz leicht, indem du dir ein schönes Heft oder Notizbuch kaufst, das speziell für solche Vokabeln da ist. Nimm es so oft wie möglich mit, vor allem, wenn du verreist! Die noch unbekannten Wörter kannst du dann zu Hause in einem Wörterbuch nachschlagen. Da du mit jedem Wort eine kleine Geschichte oder bestimmte besondere Umstände verbindest (zum Beispiel: „Ach ja! Dieses Wort habe ich am Bahnhof gesehen, im Kino gehört" etc.), wirst du es dir sehr leicht merken können!

Wortbildung

Es gibt verschiedene Möglichkeiten, um aus einem Verb ein Nomen abzuleiten.

1. Du kannst die Endung *-ing* anhängen:
   to build → a building
   to meet → a meeting
2. Manche Nomen werden mit der Endung *-er* oder *-or* gebildet.
   Solche Nomen bezeichnen meistens eine Person:
   to ride → a rider
   to visit → a visitor
3. Es gibt auch die Endung *-ion*:
   to define → a definition
   to invent → an invention
4. Sehr oft haben auch Verb und Nomen dieselbe Form:
   to call → a call
   to dream → a dream

Diese Checkliste kann dir helfen, Fehler zu vermeiden und deine Rechtschreibung zu verbessern. Prüfe alle deine Texte damit.

- **Schreibung:**
  - ☐ *gh* wird meist nicht gesprochen. Vergiss es beim Schreiben nicht.
  - ☐ *k* kommt vor *t* so gut wie nie vor, z. B. action – Aktion, October – Oktober
- **Gleiche Aussprache, unterschiedliche Schreibung:**
  - ☐ [iː] z. B. teacher, meeting, media, magazine, people, field
  - ☐ [uː] z. B. food, route, to do, swimsuit, supermarket, true, crew
- **Gleiche Aussprache, unterschiedliche Schreibung und Bedeutung:**
  - ☐ [iː] z. B. see – sehen, sea – Meer; meet – treffen, meat – Fleisch
  - ☐ [uː] z. B. two – zwei, too – auch
- **Verdoppelung der Endkonsonanten:**
  - ☐ to stop – stopping, stopped
  - ☐ to plan – planning, planned
- ***y* wird zu *ie*:**
  - ☐ in der 3. Person Singular: z. B. to carry – he carries; aber: to buy – she buys
  - ☐ im Plural: z. B. city – cities, party – parties; aber: boy – boys
  - ☐ bei der Steigerung von Adjektiven: z. B. happy – happier – (the) happiest; easy – easier – (the) easiest
- **Ähnlich und doch anders:**
  - ☐ Wortendung *le*: z. B. engl. title – dt. Titel; engl. middle – dt. Mittel
  - ☐ *ph* statt *f*: z. B. engl. phone – dt. Telefon; engl. photo – dt. Foto
- **Großschreibung:**
  - ☐ Monatsnamen: z. B. January, July, December
  - ☐ Wochentage: z. B. Monday, Wednesday, Saturday
  - ☐ Eigennamen: z. B. Tom, Lisa, the Brooks, the London Eye, the Thames
  - ☐ geografische Namen: Bristol, Greenwich, Germany, Italy
- **Plural:**
  - ☐ Der Plural bekommt normalerweise ein *-s*: z. B. friend – friends, chair – chairs, film – films
  - ☐ Endet ein Wort auf *s* oder *x*, wird *-es* angehängt: z. B. bus – buses, box – boxes
  - ☐ Manche Wörter haben einen unregelmäßigen Plural: z. B. man – men, child – children, shelf – shelves, mouse – mice
- **Apostroph:**
  - ☐ bei Kurzformen: z. B. she is → she's; they are → they're
  - ☐ beim Genitiv-s: z. B. Sam's bike, Emma's family, the Jacksons' house, the children's games
- **Wörterbuch:**
  - ☐ Prüfe die Schreibung aller Wörter, bei denen du dir nicht ganz sicher bist, indem du sie im Wörterbuch nachschlägst.

Vocabulary

Das Vocabulary enthält alle neuen Wörter und Wendungen. Sie stehen in der Reihenfolge, wie sie im Buch vorkommen.

Die Wortliste ist in drei Spalten aufgeteilt:

Links findest du das englische Wort mit der Lautschrift in Klammern. (Die Lautschrift wird ganz unten auf jeder Seite im *Dictionary* erklärt.)

In der mittleren Spalte steht die deutsche Übersetzung.

Rechts findest du Beispielsätze, Hinweise und Tipps, die dir beim Lernen helfen.

Die **fett** gedruckten Wörter musst du lernen.
Die blau gedruckten Wörter kannst du lernen, musst du aber nicht.
Die Wörter aus den Checkpoints musst du nicht lernen.

Symbole und Abkürzungen:

👄	Achte auf die Aussprache!	=	entspricht
✎	Achte auf die Schreibung!	*(sg)*	Einzahl (Singular)
↔	ist das Gegenteil von	*(pl)*	Mehrzahl (Plural)
→	ist verwandt mit	R	ähnlich wie im Russischen
sth	something	T	ähnlich wie im Türkischen
sb	somebody		

Die *Word bank*-Seiten helfen dir, die *Your turn*-Aufgaben in den *Units* zu bearbeiten.
Du findest dort nützlichen individuellen Wortschatz zum Thema der *Unit*, der dir hilft, über deine eigene Situation zu sprechen oder zu schreiben. Diese Wörter findest du auch im *Dictionary*.

Wenn du ein Wort nicht weißt und im Wörterbuch nachschlagen willst, schau auf den *Dictionary*-Seiten ab S. 220 nach. Oder bei den *Instructions* auf S. 215.

Zoom in – The USA

p. 8	**fall** *(AE)* [fɔ:l]	Herbst	AE: **fall** BE: autumn
	state [steɪt]	Staat; Bundesstaat; Land	There are 50 **states** in the USA.
	to shine [ʃaɪn], **shone** [ʃɒn], **shone** [ʃɒn]	scheinen; glänzen	The sun is **shining** today.
	bright [braɪt]	hell; leuchtend; strahlend	**bright** ↔ dark
	color *(AE)* ['kʌlə]	Farbe	AE: **color** BE: colour
p. 9	**area** ['eəriə]	Fläche; Gegend; Gebiet; Areal	The USA has an **area** of over 9,000,000 km².
	corn [kɔ:n]	Korn; Mais; Getreide	
	soy bean ['sɔɪ ˌbi:n]	Sojabohne	You can see **soy beans** in the Midwest.

	field [fiːld]	Feld; Wiese; Weide	There are corn **fields** in the Midwest.
	surfer ['sɜːfə]	Wellenreiter; Wellenreiterin; Surfer; Surferin	[T] sörfçü 
	paradise ['pærədaɪs]	Paradies	Hawaii is a surfer's **paradise**.
	perfect ['pɜːfɪkt]	perfekt; vollkommen	Today is the **perfect** weather for a picnic.
	wave [weɪv]	Welle	
p. 8	**North America** [ˌnɔːθ‿ə'merɪkə]	Nordamerika	Denali is the highest mountain in **North America**.
p. 9	**landscape** ['lændskeɪp]	Landschaft	Tourists enjoy the beautiful **landscape**.
	American [ə'merɪkən]	amerikanisch; Amerikanisch; aus Amerika; Amerikaner; Amerikanerin	**American** → America
	swamp [swɒmp]	Sumpf	There are **swamps** in the American south.
	alligator ['ælɪgeɪtə]	Alligator	[R] аллигатор [T] alligator 
p. 8	**rose** [rəʊz]	Rose	[R] роза 
	bald eagle [ˌbɔːld 'iːgl]	Weißkopfseeadler	The **bald eagle** is an American symbol.
	population [ˌpɒpjə'leɪʃn]	Einwohner; Einwohnerzahl; Bevölkerung	The **population** of New York is over eight million.
	total ['təʊtl]	Gesamt-; gesamt	The **total** area is all of the area.
	square mile (= sq. mi.) [ˌskweə 'maɪl]	Quadratmeile	The United States' total area is about 3,600,000 **square miles**.
	currency ['kʌrnsi]	Währung	The **currency** in Germany is the euro.
	dollar ['dɒlə]	Dollar *(amer. Währungseinheit)*	[R] доллар [T] dolar
	time zone ['taɪm ˌzəʊn]	Zeitzone	There are nine **time zones** in the USA.
	major ['meɪdʒə]	Haupt-; wichtig; bedeutend	There are three **major** rivers in the USA.
p. 9	**to name** [neɪm]	benennen	to **name** → name
	north of ['nɔːθ‿əv]	nördlich von	Denmark is **north of** Germany.
	south of ['saʊθ‿əv]	südlich von	Italy is **south of** Germany.
	ocean ['əʊʃn]	Ozean; Meer	[R] океан [T] okyanus
	east of ['iːst‿əv]	östlich von	Poland is **east of** Germany.
	west of ['west‿əv]	westlich von	France is **west of** Germany.
	distance ['dɪstns]	Entfernung; Distanz	Find out the **distance** from A to B.

Unit 1 Gateway NYC

p. 12	**gateway** ['geɪtweɪ]	Tor; Eingangstor	NYC is the **gateway** to America.

Way in

	over ['əʊvə]	über	**Over** eight million people live in NYC.
	borough ['bʌrə]	Stadtteil; Bezirk	NYC has five **boroughs**.
	skyline ['skaɪlaɪn]	Skyline	
	to **replace** [rɪ'pleɪs]	ersetzen	I **replaced** my old car.
	attack [ə'tæk]	Angriff; Attacke	There were **attacks** on September 11, 2001.
p. 13	**baseball** ['beɪsbɔ:l]	Baseball	R бейсбол T beyzbol 
	New Yorker [ˌnju: 'jɔ:kə]	New Yorker; New Yorkerin	**New Yorkers** live in New York City.
	center *(AE)* ['sentə]	Zentrum; Mitte; Center	AE: **center** BE: centre
	theater *(AE)* ['θɪətə]	Theater	AE: **theater** BE: theatre
	cultural movement [ˌkʌltʃrl 'mu:vmənt]	Kulturbewegung	There are many **cultural movements**.
	independence [ˌɪndɪ'pendəns]	Unabhängigkeit	They celebrated 100 years of **independence**.
	immigrant ['ɪmɪgrənt]	Immigrant; Immigrantin; Einwanderer; Einwanderin	A lot of **immigrants** went to America.
	symbol ['sɪmbl]	Symbol	R символ T sembol
	hope [həʊp]	Hoffnung	**hope** → to hope
	billion ['bɪliən]	Milliarde	R биллион
	event [ɪ'vent]	Ereignis; Veranstaltung	My birthday was a big **event**.
	on TV [ɒn ˌti:'vi:]	im Fernsehen	You could see everything **on TV**.
	elevator *(AE)* ['elɪveɪtə]	Aufzug; Lift	AE: **elevator** BE: lift
	to **produce** [prə'dju:s]	herstellen; produzieren; anbauen; erzeugen; verursachen	The elevators **produce** electricity.
	light [laɪt]	Licht	There was **light** at the end of the tunnel.
	top [tɒp]	Spitze; oberer Teil; oberes Ende	It took 30 seconds to travel to the **top**.
	grounds *(pl)* [graʊndz]	Gebiet; Gelände	The house is in the **grounds** of the school.

Station 1

City words

traffic jam ['træfɪk ˌdʒæm]	Stau	**avenue** ['ævənju:]	Allee; Boulevard
rush hour ['rʌʃ ˌaʊə]	Hauptverkehrszeit	**lights** [laɪts]	Ampel
roadwork *(AE)* ['rəʊdwɜ:k]	Straßenbauarbeiten	**parking lot** *(AE)* ['pɑ:kɪŋ ˌlɒt]	Parkplatz
landmark ['lænmɑ:k]	Wahrzeichen	**commuter** [kə'mju:tə]	Pendler; Pendlerin
skyscraper ['skaɪskreɪpə]	Wolkenkratzer	**construction site** [kən'strʌkʃn ˌsaɪt]	Baustelle
story *(AE)* ['stɔ:ri]	Stock; Stockwerk; Etage	**suburb** ['sʌbɜ:b]	Vorort
subway *(AE)* ['sʌbweɪ]	U-Bahn		

p. 14	**ride** [raɪd]	Fahrt; Ritt	A taxi **ride** in NYC is very interesting.
	traffic ['træfɪk]	Verkehr	There's lots of **traffic** on the road today.
	snow [snəʊ]	Schnee	
	to **get into** [ˌget‿'ɪntə]	hineinkommen; hineingelangen	I usually **get into** town by bus.
	anyway ['eniweɪ]	jedenfalls; trotzdem; sowieso	**Anyway**, it's a long way to walk.
	look [lʊk]	Blick; Anblick; Sicht	**look** → to look
	financial [faɪ'nænʃl]	finanziell; Finanz-	Where is the **financial** centre of the world?
	view [vju:]	Aussicht; Sicht; Ausblick; Blick	The **view** from the top is amazing.
	star sign ['stɑ: ˌsaɪn]	Sternzeichen	Look at the **star signs** at the station.
	ceiling ['si:lɪŋ]	Zimmerdecke	There are pictures on the **ceiling**.
	around [ə'raʊnd]	um … herum	The café is **around** the corner.
	hot dog ['hɒt ˌdɒg]	Hot Dog *(Würstchen im Brötchen)*	[R] хот-дог [T] hot dog 
	cart [kɑ:t]	*hier:* Stand	We can get a hot dog from that **cart**.
	to **belong (to)** [bɪ'lɒŋ (tə)]	gehören (zu)	**it belongs to me** = it's mine
	to **make sure** [ˌmeɪk 'ʃɔ:]	sich versichern	Please **make sure** he gets the letter.
p. 15	**right ahead** [ˌraɪt‿ə'hed]	geradeaus	Look, the museum is **right ahead**.

Station 2

Going to a new country

decision [dɪ'sɪʒn]	Entscheidung
foreign ['fɒrɪn]	fremd; ausländisch
community [kə'mju:nəti]	Gemeinde; Gemeinschaft
career [kə'rɪə]	Beruf; Laufbahn; Karriere
motivated ['məʊtɪveɪtɪd]	motiviert
opportunity [ˌɒpə'tju:nəti]	Gelegenheit; Chance
citizen ['sɪtɪzn]	Staatsbürger; Staatsbürgerin; Staatsangehöriger; Staatsangehörige
to **emigrate** ['emɪgreɪt]	auswandern; emigrieren
visa ['vi:zə]	Visum; Einreisebewilligung
to **get used to (sth)** [ˌget 'ju:zd tə]	sich an (etw.) gewöhnen
to **succeed (in)** [sək'si:d (ɪn)]	Erfolg haben (mit / bei); nachfolgen
to **fail (at)** [feɪl (ət)]	versagen (in/bei); ausfallen; fehlschlagen
support [sə'pɔ:t]	Unterstützung; Hilfe
papers *(pl)* ['peɪpəz]	Unterlagen; Papiere

p. 18	**interviewer** ['ɪntəvju:ə]	Interviewer; Interviewerin; Befrager; Befragerin	**interviewer** → interview → to interview
	Cuba ['kju:bə]	Kuba	R Куба T Küba
	poor [pɔ:]	arm	**poor** ↔ rich
	future ['fju:tʃə]	Zukunft	I had a better **future** in the USA.
	to **take sth seriously** [ˌteɪk 'sɪəriəsli]	etw. ernst nehmen	I don't **take sport seriously**, I do it for fun.
	high school ['haɪ ˌsku:l]	Highschool *(weiterführende Schule, Oberstufe)*	I worked hard at **high school**.
	example [ɪg'zɑ:mpl]	Beispiel	Give me an **example** of a good book.
	US [ˌju:'es]	US-amerikanisch	It is a **US** school, not a British one.
p. 19	**college** ['kɒlɪdʒ]	College; Institut	Angela goes to **college** too.
	Mexico ['meksɪkəʊ]	Mexiko	R Мексика T Meksika
p. 21	**Cuban** ['kju:bən]	kubanisch; aus Kuba; Kubaner; Kubanerin	**Cuban** → Cuba
	reader ['ri:də]	Leser; Leserin	**reader** → to read

Reading corner

p. 22	**immigration** [ˌɪmɪ'greɪʃn]	Immigration; Zuwanderung	**immigration** → to immigrate → immigrant
	to **save** [seɪv]	sparen	I'm **saving** my money to buy a bike.

	statistics *(no pl)* [stə'tɪstɪks]	Statistik	R статистика T istatistik
	the rest [ðə 'rest]	der Rest	They sent for **the rest** of the family.
	condition [kən'dɪʃn]	Bedingung; Zustand	The **conditions** were very hard.
	crowded ['kraʊdɪd]	überfüllt	**crowded** → crowd
	little ['lɪtl]	wenig; kaum	We had very **little** space on the ship.
	air [eə]	Luft	You have to put **air** in the tyres.
	majority [mə'dʒɒrəti]	Mehrheit; Mehrzahl	The **majority** of people were sick.
	harbor *(AE)* ['hɑ:bə]	Hafen	AE: **harbor** BE: harbour
	powerful ['paʊəfl]	stark; mächtig; bedeutend; beeindruckend	America is a **powerful** country.
	future ['fju:tʃə]	zukünftig	past – today – **future**
	check [tʃek]	Kontrolle	**check** → to check
	disease [dɪ'zi:z]	Krankheit	Doctors checked for **diseases**.
p. 23	**percent (%)** [pə'sent]	Prozent	50 **percent** of ten is five.
	to return [rɪ'tɜ:n]	zurückkehren; zurückgeben	My friends had to **return** home.
	minority [maɪ'nɒrəti]	Minderheit	**minority** ↔ majority
	Scandinavia [ˌskændɪ'neɪviə]	Skandinavien	Denmark is in **Scandinavia**.
	Greece [gri:s]	Griechenland	**Greece** is in the south of Europe.
	Eastern Europe ['i:stn jʊərəp]	Osteuropa	Poland is in **Eastern Europe**.
	Russia ['rʌʃə]	Russland	**Russia** is to the east of Germany.
	religious [rɪ'lɪdʒəs]	religiös; gläubig	Are you **religious**?
	political [pə'lɪtɪkl]	politisch	People have different **political** opinions.
	freedom *(no pl)* ['fri:dəm]	Freiheit; Unabhängigkeit	**Freedom** hat keine Mehrzahl.
	to escape [ɪ'skeɪp]	entkommen; fliehen; entfliehen; flüchten	They wanted to **escape** their problems.
	poverty ['pɒvəti]	Armut	**Poverty** is when you have no money.
	China ['tʃaɪnə]	China	Achtung Aussprache!
	The Dominican Republic [ðə dəˌmɪnɪkn rɪ'pʌblɪk]	Dominikanische Republik	**The Dominican Republic** is to the east of Cuba.
	Vietnam [ˌvjet'næm]	Vietnam	**Vietnam** is south of China.
	few [fju:]	wenige	**Few** people come from Cuba.

Film corner

p. 25	**once** [wʌns]	einst; einmal	at a time in the past
	honor *(AE)* ['ɒnə]	Ehre	There's a Wall of **Honor** on Ellis Island.
	great-grandparents [ˌgreɪt'græn͵peərənts]	Urgroßeltern	My **great-grandparents** are my grandparents' parents.
	inside [ˌɪn'saɪd]	innen; drinnen	In summer it can get hot **inside**.

Checkpoint

ethnic ['eθnɪk]	ethnisch; Volks-

Word bank: City guide

skyscraper

cathedral

tower

museum

gallery

station

bridge

building

monument

Over there you can see …
Don't miss …
Around this corner we'll come to …
Right/Straight ahead are …
You must visit …
In the distance you can see …
Have a look at/Look at …
Make sure you visit …
I'd like to point out …
Down there/Over there is …
From here …
… built it in …
It opened in …
It is special because …

Word bank: Presenting personal information

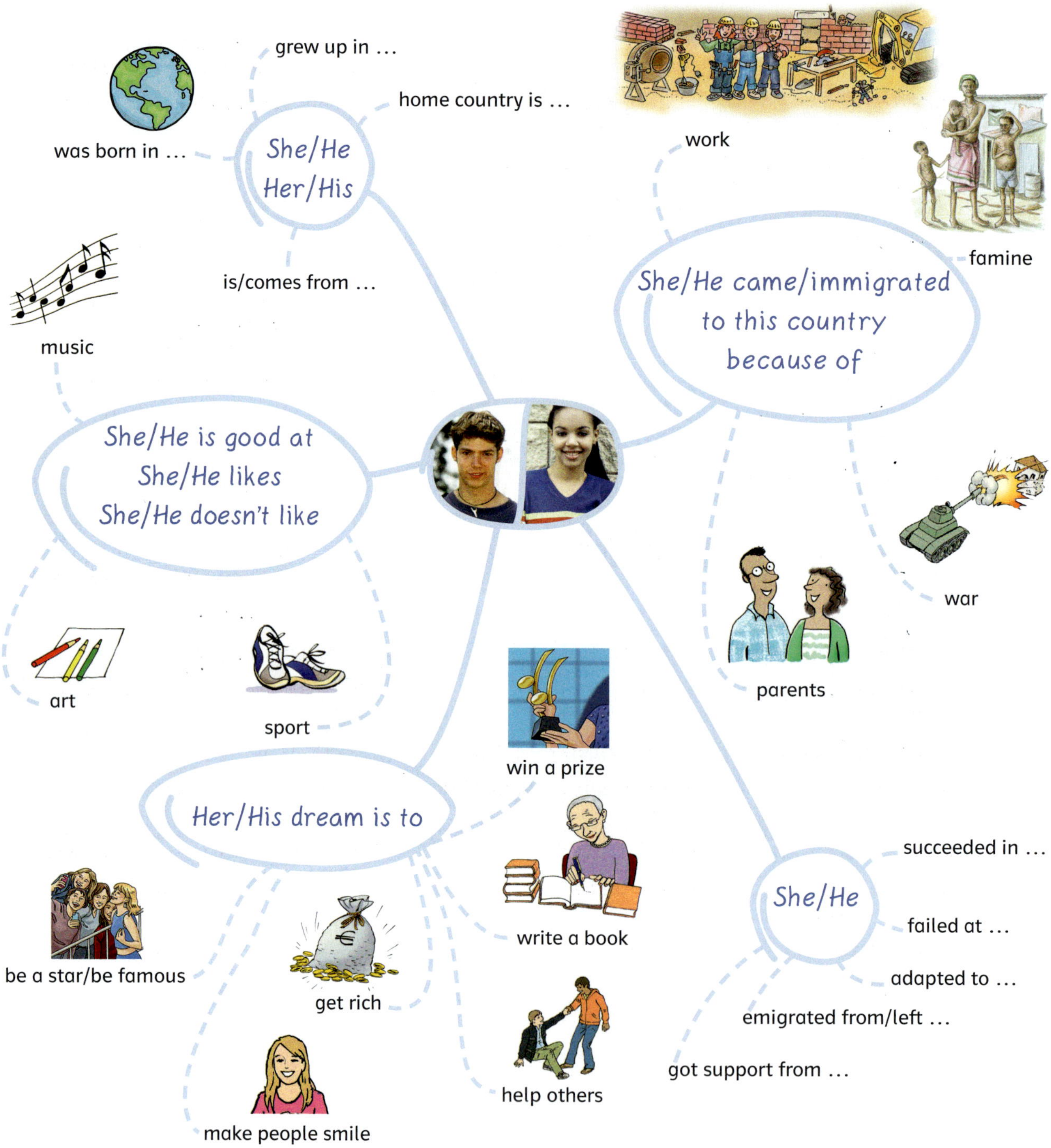

Unit 2 Teens in the Midwest

Way in

p. 32	**flat** [flæt]	flach; platt	When the land is **flat** you can see lots.
	farmland ['fɑːmlænd]	Ackerland; Ackerboden; Landwirtschaftsflächen	You can see corn on **farmland** in the Midwest.
	tornado [tɔː'neɪdəʊ]	Tornado; Wirbelsturm	R торнадо
	alley ['æli]	Gasse; Weg	An **alley** is a small street.
	terrible ['terəbl]	schrecklich; furchtbar	There can be **terrible** storms.
	European [ˌjʊərə'piːən]	europäisch; Europäisch; aus Europa; Europäer; Europäerin	T Avrupalı
	settler ['setlə]	Siedler; Siedlerin	Thousands of **settlers** came to the West.
	Native American [ˌneɪtɪv‿ə'merɪkən]	Ureinwohner Amerikas; Ureinwohnerin Amerikas	**Native Americans** live in the USA.
	reservation [ˌrezə'veɪʃn]	Reservat	We had to live on **reservations**.
p. 33	**to be allowed to (do sth)** [biː ə'laʊd tə]	(etw.) dürfen	We **were allowed to** talk in class.
	store *(AE)* [stɔː]	Laden; Geschäft	AE: **store** BE: shop
	to serve [sɜːv]	servieren	Sarah **serves** ice cream in the new café.
p. 32	**grade** *(AE)* [greɪd]	Note; Klasse	AE: **grade** BE: mark; class
	schedule *(AE)* ['skedʒuːl]	Stundenplan; Fahrplan	AE: **schedule** BE: timetable
p. 33	**Homecoming** *(AE)* ['həʊmˌkʌmɪŋ]	Ehemaligentreffen	The **Homecoming** Dance is always fun. 
	to vote for ['vəʊt fə]	abstimmen über; wählen	
	chaser ['tʃeɪsə]	Jäger; Jägerin; Verfolger; Verfolgerin	Warren is a storm **chaser**.
	to report (on) [rɪ'pɔːt (ɒn)]	berichten (über)	They **reported** the storms on the radio.
	to drive [draɪv], **drove** [drəʊv], **driven** ['drɪvn]	fahren; treiben	
	direction [dɪ'rekʃn]	Richtung	The wind comes from all **directions**.
	cloud [klaʊd]	Wolke	

Station 1

At American schools

locker ['lɒkə]	Schließfach; Spind
morning message ['mɔ:nɪŋ ˌmesɪdʒ]	morgendliche Ansprache
principal *(AE)* ['prɪnsɪpl]	Schulleiter; Schulleiterin
pledge of allegiance [ˌpledʒ‿əv‿ə'li:dʒns]	Treueeid
pledge [pledʒ]	Versprechen
class [klɑ:s]	Unterrichtsstunde; Kurs
Math *(AE)* [mæθ]	Mathematik; Mathe
elective [ɪ'lektɪv]	Wahlfach
study hall period ['stʌdi hɔ:l ˌpɪəriəd]	Freistunde
pass [pɑ:s]	Ausweis; Pass
extracurricular [ˌekstrəkə'rɪkjələ]	außerhalb des Lehrplans; außerunterrichtlich *(Zusatzunterricht)*
cheerleader ['tʃɪəˌli:də]	Cheerleader *(Mädchen, das in einer Gruppe eine Sportmannschaft anfeuert)*
detention [dɪ'tenʃn]	Nachsitzen
campus ['kæmpəs]	Campus; Schulgelände
vacation *(AE)* [və'keɪʃn]	Ferien; Urlaub
dress code ['dres ˌkəʊd]	Kleiderordnung; Bekleidungsvorschriften

p. 34	**exchange** [ɪks'tʃeɪndʒ]	Austausch	Luise did a student **exchange** in the USA.
	nowhere ['nəʊweə]	nirgendwo; nirgendwohin	We live in the middle of **nowhere**.
	familiar [fə'mɪliə]	vertraut; bekannt	Everything was so **familiar**.
	to keep [ki:p], **kept** [kept], **kept** [kept]	aufbewahren; behalten	You can't **keep** things in the classroom.
	to be able to (do sth) [bi: 'eɪbl tə]	(zu etw.) fähig sein; (etw.) können; (etw.) dürfen	I **was able to** find my own way.
	to promise ['prɒmɪs]	versprechen	I **promise** to work hard at school.
	true [tru:]	*hier:* treu	The students are **true** to the US.
	journalism ['dʒɜ:nlɪzm]	Journalistik; Journalismus	R журналистика
	to study ['stʌdi]	studieren; lernen	You can **study** or do your homework here.
	strict [strɪkt]	streng; strikt	The school rules are very **strict**.
	hall [hɔ:l]	Flur; Korridor; Diele	
	bathroom *(AE)* ['bɑ:θrʊm]	Toilette; Bad(ezimmer)	AE: **bathroom** BE: toilet
	for example [fər‿ɪg'zɑ:mpl]	zum Beispiel	I like fruit, **for example** apples.
	to end [end]	enden; beenden; aufhören	Classes **ended** at 3:30 p.m.
	competition [ˌkɒmpə'tɪʃn]	Konkurrenz	There was lots of **competition** for places.

awesome ['ɔ:səm]	super; spitze	**awesome** = amazing, great
host family ['həʊst ˌfæmli]	Gastfamilie	I really liked my **host family.**
blast [blɑ:st]	*hier:* Wahnsinnsspaß	My exchange year was a **blast.**

Station 2

Describing people

helpful ['helpfl]	hilfsbereit	**hard-working** [ˌhɑ:d'wɜ:kɪŋ]	fleißig
cooperative [kəʊ'ɒprətɪv]	kooperativ; hilfsbereit	**generous** ['dʒenrəs]	großzügig
responsible [rɪs'pɒnsəbl]	verantwortlich; verantwortungsvoll	**rude** [ru:d]	unhöflich; unverschämt
bossy ['bɒsi]	rechthaberisch	**selfish** ['selfɪʃ]	selbstsüchtig
unmotivated [ˌʌn'məʊtɪveɪtɪd]	unmotiviert	**shy** [ʃaɪ]	schüchtern
lazy ['leɪzi]	faul		

p. 38	**outside** [ˌaʊt'saɪd]	außerhalb	Extracurricular activites are **outside** school.
	to **earn** [ɜ:n]	verdienen	I have a job and **earn** money.
	year-old [ˌjɪər‿'əʊld]	jährig; Jahre alt	My sister is 16. I've got a 16-**year-old** sister.
	allowance *(AE)* [ə'laʊəns]	Taschengeld; Unterhaltsgeld	AE: **allowance** BE: pocket money
	girlfriend ['gɜ:lfrend]	Freundin *(in einer Paarbeziehung)*	Sarah is Michael's **girlfriend.**
	ad(vert) (= advertisement) ['æd(vɜ:t) (əd'vɜ:tɪsmənt)]	Anzeige; Annonce; Werbespot	I saw an **advert** for a student job.
	job title ['dʒɒb ˌtaɪtl]	Stellenbezeichnung; Berufsbezeichnung	What is the **job title** of your new job?
	sales associate *(AE)* [ˌseɪlz ə'səʊʃiət]	Verkäufer; Verkäuferin	AE: **sales associate** BE: sales assistant
	part-time [ˌpɑ:t'taɪm]	Teilzeit-; Halbtags-	Students often have **part-time** jobs.
	education [ˌedʒʊ'keɪʃn]	Ausbildung; Erziehung; Bildung	My **education** was at the local school.
	to apply (for) [ə'plaɪ (fə)]	sich bewerben (für/um)	He **applied for** the student job.
	interview ['ɪntəvju:]	Vorstellungsgespräch	He had an **interview** on Thursday.
	manager ['mænɪdʒə]	Manager; Managerin; Geschäftsführer; Geschäftsführerin	R менеджер
	someone ['sʌmwʌn]	jemand	There was **someone** in the house.
	to steal [sti:l], **stole** [stəʊl], **stolen** ['stəʊlən]	stehlen	I saw the boy **steal** a T-shirt.

	minimum ['mɪnɪməm]	Minimum; minimal; Mindest-	[T] minimum
	wage [weɪdʒ]	Lohn	He earned the minimum **wage**.
	co-worker ['kəʊˌwɜːkə]	Arbeitskollege; Arbeitskollegin	My **co-workers** are friendly.
	to **sort** [sɔːt]	sortieren	He **sorted** the colourful T-shirts.
	to **tease** [tiːz]	hänseln; sticheln; reizen	People came in and **teased** Michael.
	to **throw** [θrəʊ], **threw** [θruː], **thrown** [θrəʊn]	werfen	He **threw** them out of the store.
	such [sʌtʃ]	solch	It was **such** a nice day.
	behavior *(AE)* [bɪ'heɪvjə]	Verhalten	AE: **behavior** BE: behaviour
p. 39	**working hours** *(pl)* ['wɜːkɪŋ ˌaʊəz]	Arbeitszeit	9:00 to 5:00 are my **working hours**.
	break [breɪk]	Pause	My **break** was at one o'clock.
	bonus ['bəʊnəs]	Bonus; Prämie	I worked hard and got a **bonus**.
	feedback ['fiːdbæk]	Feedback; Rückmeldung	She got good **feedback**.
p. 41	**pair** [peə]	Paar	Do you like my new **pair** of trainers?
	dog walker ['dɒg ˌwɔːkə]	Hundeausführer; Hundeausführerin	a person who takes dogs for a walk
	per [pɜː]	pro	I earn $40 **per** week.
	paperboy ['peɪpəˌbɔɪ]	Zeitungsausträger	I'm Dave, I'm a **paperboy**.
	papergirl ['peɪpəˌgɜːl]	Zeitungsausträgerin	A paperboy or **papergirl** works every day.
	babysitter ['beɪbɪˌsɪtə]	Babysitter; Babysitterin	a person who looks after children
	to **take care of sb** [ˌteɪk 'keər‿əv]	sich um jmdn. kümmern; für jmdn. sorgen	I **take care** of my neighbour's kids.

Reading corner

p. 42	**date** [deɪt]	Verabredung; Date	They went on their first **date**.
	to **ask sb out** [ˌɑːsk … 'aʊt]	sich mit jmdm. verabreden	Dylan **asked** Abby **out** on a date.
	to fall out of [ˌfɔːl‿'aʊt‿əv]	herausfallen aus	All my books **fell out of** my locker.
	right [raɪt]	gerade; genau; in dem Moment als	It happened **right** when he walked past.
	to show up [ˌʃəʊ‿'ʌp]	auftauchen; erscheinen	He **showed up** late for school.
	in tow [ɪn 'təʊ]	im Schlepptau	Abby had Scott **in tow**, of course.
	embarrassing [ɪm'bærəsɪŋ]	peinlich	It was so **embarrassing**, I went red.
	to **notice** ['nəʊtɪs]	bemerken; wahrnehmen	The didn't **notice** Scott and his friends.

	gym(nasium) [dʒɪm (dʒɪm'neɪziəm)]	Turnhalle	the room in a school where PE lessons are
	to attack [ə'tæk]	angreifen	The boys **attacked** him in the gym.
p. 43	**to pick up** [ˌpɪk‿'ʌp]	abholen	Dylan **picked** Abby **up** at seven o'clock.
	dancing ['dɑ:nsɪŋ]	Tanzen; Tanz-	T dans

Film corner

p. 45	**buddy** *(infml)* ['bʌdi]	Kumpel	David is my best **buddy**.
	homeroom ['həʊmru:m]	erste Stunde *(in der Schule)*	We are in the same **homeroom**.

Checkpoint

atmosphere ['ætməsfɪə]	Atmosphäre; Stimmung	to interest ['ɪntrəst]	interessieren
relationship [rɪ'leɪʃnʃɪp]	Beziehung	field trip ['fi:ld ˌtrɪp]	Schulausflug

Presentation skills

p. 51	**presentation** [ˌprezn'teɪʃn]	Präsentation; Vortrag	My **presentation** is about cats.
	topic ['tɒpɪk]	Thema	My next **topic** is the rules of the game.
	second ['seknd]	zweitens	**Second**, the cats are loud.

Word bank: Comparing schools

dress code

pledge of allegiance

cheerleading

marching band

school bus

locker

Homecoming Dance

schedule

grade

hall pass

class

I would like to compare …
In/At American high schools …
In/At German schools …
Both countries have detention/principals/…

In America there is … but not in Germany.
… is the same.
… is different.

V

Word bank: Jobs

waitress

waiter

serve ice cream

work on a market stall

shop assistant

wash up in a café/ restaurant

babysitter

dog walker

paperboy/girl

help in the garden/ mow the lawn

do the shopping for people

I earn …
I work inside/outside.
I work every day/at the weekends/in the holidays/on …
I work in the mornings/afternoons/evenings.
I start work at …
I like it/don't like it because …
I'm a … person.
It's hard/easy work.
It's fun/boring.
I work with nice/interesting/fun/strange/quiet/… people.

Unit 3 In the Northeast

Way in

p. 52	**forest** ['fɒrɪst]	Wald	
	flight [flaɪt]	Flug	It's a six and a half hour **flight**.
	celebration [ˌseləˈbreɪʃn]	Feier	**celebration** → to celebrate
p. 53	**Thanksgiving** [ˌθæŋksˈgɪvɪŋ]	Erntedankfest	**Thanksgiving** is the 4th Thursday in November.
	everybody ['evribɒdi]	jeder; alle	**Everybody** meets at our house. 
	turkey ['tɜ:ki]	Truthahn; Pute	
	to pardon ['pɑ:dn]	begnadigen; entschuldigen; verzeihen	The President **pardons** a turkey.
	creepy ['kri:pi]	gruselig	**Creepy** films are often made in Maine.
	mystery story ['mɪstri ˌstɔ:ri]	Krimi (= Kriminalgeschichte); Detektivgeschichte	Maine is very popular for **mystery stories**.
	land of the free [ˌlænd‿əv ðə 'fri:]	Land der Freien	The USA is called the **land of the free**.
	the Amish [ði 'ɑ:mɪʃ]	die Amischen	**The Amish** don't have mobile phones.
	Christian ['krɪstʃn]	christlich	T Hıristiyan
	daredevil ['deəˌdevl]	Draufgänger; Draufgängerin	The **daredevil** did dangerous tricks. 
	barrel ['bærl]	Fass; Tonne	
	to sign autographs [ˌsaɪn 'ɔ:təgrɑ:fs]	Autogramme geben	The actor **signed autographs** for us.

Station 1

Small talk

What's up? [ˌwɒts‿'ʌp]	Wie geht's?	**How are you doing?** [ˌhaʊ‿ə jə 'du:ɪŋ]	Wie geht's dir?
How's it going? [ˌhaʊz‿ɪt 'gəʊɪŋ]	Wie geht's?; Wie läuft's?	**What have you been up to?** [ˌwɒt‿əv ju: bi:n 'ʌp tə]	Was hast du (in letzter Zeit) gemacht?; Wie läuft's bei dir?

p. 54	**to get ready** [get 'redi]	sich vorbereiten; sich fertig machen	We have to **get ready** for the party.
	husband ['hʌzbənd]	Ehemann	**husband** ↔ wife

teenage ['ti:neɪdʒ]	jugendlich	**teenage** → teenager
to **get stuck** [ˌget 'stʌk]	stecken bleiben	I **got stuck** in my car for two hours.
doorbell ['dɔ:bel]	Türklingel	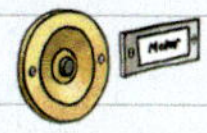
neighbor *(AE)* ['neɪbə]	Nachbar; Nachbarin	AE: **neighbor** BE: neighbour
freezing ['fri:zɪŋ]	eiskalt; gefrierend	Come in, it's **freezing** outside.
glad [glæd]	froh	We were **glad** you liked the flowers.
to **make it** ['meɪk‿ɪt]	es schaffen	I'm glad you could **make it**.
to **enter** ['entə]	hineingehen; hereinkommen; betreten; eintreten	**to enter** ↔ to leave
Have a seat. [ˌhæv‿ə 'si:t]	Setzen Sie sich.; Setz dich.	Come in. **Have a seat.**
across [ə'krɒs]	über; hinüber; herüber; quer durch	He shouted **across** the room.
to **used to** *(+ infinitive)* ['ju:st tə]	pflegte(n) zu; tat(en) früher	You **used to** eat everything I made.
chocolate ['tʃɒklət]	Praline	T çikolata 
video ['vɪdiəʊ]	Video	I'm making a **video** of Thanksgiving.
thankful ['θæŋkfl]	dankbar	**thankful** → Thank you.
boyfriend ['bɔɪfrend]	Freund *(in einer Paarbeziehung)*	**boyfriend** ↔ girlfriend
engine ['endʒɪn]	Motor	Cars don't work without an **engine**.
to **land** [lænd]	landen	Our plane **lands** at seven o'clock.
p. 56 **Easter** ['i:stə]	Ostern	**Easter** is in March or April.
p. 57 **bored** [bɔ:d]	gelangweilt	I was so **bored** in Math today.
stress [stres]	Stress	Phew, I had so much **stress** today.

Station 2

Agreeing and disagreeing

Exactly. [ɪg'zæktli]	Genau.	I'm convinced that … [ˌaɪm kən'vɪnst ðət]	Ich bin überzeugt, dass …
Absolutely not. [ˌæbsə'lu:tli nɒt]	Ganz und gar nicht.; Auf keinen Fall!	It's clear to me that … [ɪts 'klɪə tə ˌmi: ðæt]	Mir ist klar, dass …
I guess … [aɪ 'ges]	Ich nehme an, dass …	I doubt that … [aɪ 'daʊt ˌðæt]	Ich bezweifle, dass …

Devices

device [dɪ'vaɪs]	Gerät; Vorrichtung	dishwasher ['dɪʃˌwɒʃə]	Spülmaschine
hair straightener ['heə ˌstreɪtnə]	Haarglätter	vacuum cleaner ['vækju:m ˌkli:nə]	Staubsauger
fan [fæn]	Ventilator	razor ['reɪzə]	Rasierer; Rasierapparat

p. 58	**Amish** ['ɑ:mɪʃ]	amisch	We live in an **Amish** community.
	to lead [li:d], **led** [led], **led** [led]	führen; anführen	We **lead** a simple life.
	to concentrate ['kɒnsntreɪt]	(sich) konzentrieren	This is hard. I have to **concentrate**.
	to cover ['kʌvə]	bedecken; abdecken	Amish girls often **cover** their hair.
	make-up ['meɪkʌp]	Make-up; Schminke	T makyaj
	to grow [grəʊ], **grew** [gru:], **grown** [grəʊn]	anbauen; züchten; ziehen; wachsen	We **grow** our own vegetables.
	contact ['kɒntækt]	Kontakt	I don't have much **contact** with my aunt.
	forbidden [fə'bɪdn]	verboten	I never do **forbidden** things.
	alcohol *(no pl)* ['ælkəhɒl]	Alkohol	R алкоголь T alkol
	really ['rɪəli]	wirklich	I will **really** miss you.
	to regret [rɪ'gret]	bedauern	I'm sure I won't **regret** my decision.
	pretty ['prɪti]	ziemlich	AE: **pretty** BE: really
	average ['ævrɪdʒ]	durchschnittlich	I'm an **average** American teenager.
	fashion *(no pl)* ['fæʃn]	Mode	I love clothes and the newest **fashion**.
	gossip ['gɒsɪp]	Klatsch; Tratsch; Gerede	I read the **gossip** about the stars too.
	mostly ['məʊstli]	meistens; hauptsächlich	We talk **mostly** about boys and music.
	to go out with [ˌgəʊ‿'aʊt wɪð]	(aus)gehen mit	She's **going out** with him.
	whom [hu:m]	wem; wen	They ask who has a date with **whom**.
	to hang out (with) [ˌhæŋ‿'aʊt (wɪð)]	rumhängen (mit); sich treffen (mit); sich herumtreiben (mit)	I **hang out** with my friends after school.
	bowling ['bəʊlɪŋ]	Bowlen	R боулинг T bowling
p. 59	electric [ɪ'lektrɪk]	elektrisch	T elektrik
p. 61	**superhero** ['su:pəˌhɪərəʊ] *(sg)*, **superheroes** ['su:pəˌhɪərəʊz] *(pl)*	Superheld	Spiderman is a **superhero**.

	before [bɪ'fɔː]	vor	**before** ↔ after
	test [test]	Test; Klassenarbeit; Prüfung	Who likes class **tests**?

Reading corner

p. 62	**body** ['bɒdi]	Leiche	There was a man's **body** on the beach.
	to **disappear** [ˌdɪsə'pɪə]	verschwinden	The man **disappeared** two weeks ago.
	gun [gʌn]	Schusswaffe	He had a **gun** in his hand.
	floor [flɔː]	Stockwerk; Etage	Our flat is on the second **floor**.
	thought [θɔːt]	Gedanke	The **thought** of dinner made me happy.
	to **roll up** [ˌrəʊl‿'ʌp]	zusammenrollen; aufrollen; aufkrempeln	We **rolled up** our clothes.
	blanket ['blæŋkɪt]	Decke; Bettdecke; Wolldecke	
	to **tie** [taɪ]	binden; zubinden; fesseln	Be careful! **Tie** your shoes right.
	belt [belt]	Gürtel	
	back [bæk]	Hinter-	We went in the **back** door.
	to **avoid** [ə'vɔɪd]	vermeiden; meiden; aus dem Weg gehen; ausweichen	We have to **avoid** the teachers.
	towards [tə'wɔːdz]	in Richtung; auf … zu	We were walking **towards** the station.
	clubhouse ['klʌbhaʊs]	Klubhaus; Vereinsheim	We meet at the **clubhouse** on Tuesdays.
	to **catch up with** [ˌkætʃ‿'ʌp wɪð]	einholen	I was slow so they **caught up with** me.
	to **point** [pɔɪnt]	zeigen	I **pointed** to the book I wanted.
	smell [smel]	Geruch; Gestank; Duft	**smell** → to smell
	to **puke** [pjuːk]	erbrechen; sich übergeben	**to puke** = to be sick
	backpack ['bækpæk]	Rucksack	
	desk [desk]	Schreibtisch	
	to **beat** [biːt], **beat** [biːt], **beaten** [biːtn]	schlagen; verprügeln; prügeln	He will **beat** me when he knows.
p. 63	**bullet** ['bʊlɪt]	Kugel; Geschoss	There are no **bullets** in the gun.
	sat [sæt]	simple past, past participle von *to sit* (sitzen)	I **sat** = ich saß/ich habe gesessen
	tin [tɪn]	Dose; Büchse; *hier:* Mülleimer	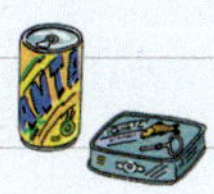
	to **jump** [dʒʌmp]	springen	
	to **shoot (at)** [ʃuːt (ət)], **shot (at)** [ʃɒt (ət)], **shot (at)** [ʃɒt (ət)]	schießen (auf)	He **shot** at the bottles on the wall.

	wrist [rɪst]	Handgelenk	It is between your hand and your arm.
	heart [hɑ:t]	Herz	
	to scream [skri:m]	schreien; kreischen	I was scared and I **screamed** loudly.
	to shut up [ʃʌt‿'ʌp]	die Klappe halten	**Shut up** and listen to me!
	to reach [ri:tʃ]	erreichen	We **reached** the station at two o'clock.
	it's a pity [ˌɪts‿ə 'pɪti]	(es ist) schade	**It's a pity** it rained.
	honestly ['ɒnɪstli]	ehrlich	**Honestly**, I didn't know it was broken.
	drunk [drʌŋk]	betrunken	He was too **drunk** to remember.
	innocent ['ɪnəsnt]	unschuldig	He didn't do it, he is **innocent**.
	laugh [lɑ:f]	Lachen	**laugh** → to laugh
p. 64	**to put up** [ˌpʊt‿'ʌp]	aufstellen; errichten	We **put** the pictures **up** next to each other.
	to turn on [ˌtɜ:n‿'ɒn]	einschalten	It was dark and I **turned on** the lamp.
	to grin [grɪn]	grinsen	He **grinned** from ear to ear.
	to gather ['gæðə]	(sich) sammeln	We **gathered** round him and listened.
	railway track ['reɪlweɪ ˌtræk]	Gleis	We went across the bridge on the **railway tracks**.
	at least [ət 'li:st]	mindestens; wenigstens	It is **at least** twenty miles away.
	to seem [si:m]	scheinen	He **seems** to be happy.

Film corner

p. 67	**pecan** ['pi:kæn]	Pekannuss	**Pecan** pie is my favourite pie.
	pardon ['pɑ:dn]	Begnadigung; Entschuldigung; Verzeihung	The President's **pardon** is for a turkey.

Checkpoint

to control [kən'trəʊl]	kontrollieren	annoying [ə'nɔɪɪŋ]	ärgerlich; lästig
out [aʊt]	aus; draußen; außerhalb		

Writing skills

p. 73	**to describe** [dɪ'skraɪb]	beschreiben	The text **describes** the country.
	to deal (with) [di:l (wɪð)], **dealt (with)** [delt (wɪð)], **dealt (with)** [delt (wɪð)]	sich befassen (mit); umgehen (mit)	The text **deals with** the culture.
	to sum up [ˌsʌm‿'ʌp]	zusammenfassen	To **sum up** you can say this food is better.
	in general [ɪn 'dʒenrl]	allgemein; generell	**In general** the news is good.

Word bank: **Giving opinions**

- I agree with the statement …
- I agree with you.
- I think you're right (there).
- That's true.
- I think so because …
- In my opinion …
- I think …
- I also think that … because …

- So my answer is …
- I tried it when I was …
- One reason is …
- Another reason is …
- To conclude I would like to say …
- It had an impact on my life because …

- I don't agree/disagree with the statement …
- I don't agree/disagree with you.
- That's false.
- I don't think so because …
- In my opinion …
- I think …
- You can't be serious!

- I think you're wrong (there).
- I tried it when I was …
- Another reason is …
- One reason is …
- To conclude I would like to say …
- It had an impact/influence on my life because …

Unit 4 California dreams

Way in

p. 74	**giant** [dʒaɪənt]	Riesen-; riesig	Look at the **giant** sandwiches. 
	redwood (tree) ['redwʊd (tri:)]	Mammutbaum	
	relaxed [rɪ'lækst]	entspannt; locker; gelassen	People are very **relaxed** in California.
	lifestyle ['laɪfstaɪl]	Lebensart; Lifestyle	the way you live your life
	surfing ['sɜ:fɪŋ]	Wellenreiten; Surfen	I love **surfing** in the summer. 
	cable car ['keɪbl ˌkɑ:]	Seilbahn	
	hill [hɪl]	Berg; Hügel	
	Asia ['eɪʒə]	Asien	R азия T Asya
p. 75	**nickname** ['nɪkneɪm]	Spitzname	Most US cities have a **nickname**.
	golden ['gəʊldn]	golden; Gold-	California is called 'The **Golden** State'.
	high-tech [ˌhaɪ'tek]	Hightech-	I work for a **high-tech** company.
	to **settle** ['setl]	besiedeln; sich niederlassen	We moved from NYC and **settled** here.
	to **develop** [dɪ'veləp]	entwickeln	We have **developed** two new games.
	studio ['stju:diəʊ]	Studio	They make movies in **studios**.
	safety net ['seɪfti ˌnet]	Sicherheitsnetz	There's a **safety net** to catch you.
	foggy ['fɒgi]	neblig	You can see the bridge in **foggy** weather.
	huge [hju:dʒ]	riesig; riesengroß; gewaltig	**huge** = very big
	architect ['ɑ:kɪtekt]	Architekt; Architektin	R архитектор 
	to **paint** [peɪnt]	streichen; anmalen; malen	

Station 1

Adjectives for ads

catchy ['kætʃi]	eingängig; einprägsam	**fascinating** ['fæsɪneɪtɪŋ]	faszinierend
informative [ɪn'fɔ:mətɪv]	informativ	**spectacular** [ˌspek'tækjələ]	spektakulär
clear [klɪə]	klar; eindeutig; deutlich	**pointless** ['pɔɪntləs]	sinnlos
appealing [ə'pi:lɪŋ]	ansprechend	**unusual** [ʌn'ju:ʒl]	ungewöhnlich; außergewöhnlich
unappealing [ˌʌnə'pi:lɪŋ]	uninteressant	**dull** [dʌl]	langweilig

p. 76	**to chill out** [ˌtʃɪlˈaʊt]	chillen; sich entspannen	**Chill out** in sunny California.
	reservation [ˌrezəˈveɪʃn]	Reservierung	T rezervasyon
	to book [bʊk]	buchen; reservieren	We booked our **flights** yesterday.
	lifetime [ˈlaɪftaɪm]	Leben; Lebenszeit	It will be the holiday of a **lifetime**.
	tour [tʊə]	Tour; Fahrt; Reise	We went on the Grand Canyon **tour**.
p. 77	**layout** [ˈleɪaʊt]	Layout; Anordnung	Look at the **layout** of this ad.
	design [dɪˈzaɪn]	Design; Gestaltung	I like the **design** of this one.
	headline [ˈhedlaɪn]	Überschrift; Schlagzeile	We need a good **headline** for our ad.
	slogan [ˈsləʊgən]	Slogan; Werbespruch	We thought of a catchy **slogan** too.
	message [ˈmesɪdʒ]	Botschaft	What is the **message** in this text?
	expert [ˈekspɜːt]	Experte; Expertin	R эксперт
p. 78	**climbing** [ˈklaɪmɪŋ]	Kletter-	Always wear a good **climbing** helmet.
p. 79	**swimmer** [ˈswɪmə]	Schwimmer; Schwimmerin	
	helicopter [ˈhelɪkɒptə]	Helikopter; Hubschrauber	T helikopter 
	pilot [ˈpaɪlət]	Pilot; Pilotin	

Station 2

Social media

social media [ˌsəʊʃl ˈmiːdiə]	soziale Medien	to **friend** [frend]	befreunden *(jmdn. zu seiner Freundesliste hinzufügen)*
account [əˈkaʊnt]	Konto	to **unfriend** [ʌnˈfrend]	entfreunden *(jmdn. von seiner Freundes-liste streichen)*
to **post** [pəʊst]	online stellen; posten	**follower** [ˈfɒləʊə]	Follower; Followerin; Anhänger; Anhängerin
tutorial [tjuːˈtɔːriəl]	Anleitung; Tutorial	to **subscribe** [səbˈskraɪb]	abonnieren
clip [klɪp]	Clip; Ausschnitt; Kurzfilm	**trending** [ˈtrendɪŋ]	trendsetzend
smartphone [ˈsmɑːtˌfəʊn]	Smartphone	to **update** [ˈʌpdeɪt]	updaten; auf den neu-esten Stand bringen
tablet [ˈtæblət]	Tablet	**status** [ˈsteɪtəs]	Status
cyberbullying [ˈsaɪbəˌbʊliɪŋ]	Cyber-Mobbing	**selfie** [ˈselfi]	Selfie *(Schnappschuss von sich selbst)*
to **dislike** [dɪˈslaɪk]	nicht mögen		
request [rɪˈkwest]	Anfrage		

p. 80	**to welcome** [ˈwelkəm]	willkommen heißen	California **welcomes** new ideas.

	to **be around** [bi: ə'raʊnd]	geben; existieren	The WWW has **been around** for 30 years.
	for [fɔ:]	seit	I have lived here **for** two months.
	site [saɪt]	*hier:* Seite *(im Internet)*	I visit many **sites** when I'm on the internet.
	since [sɪns]	seit; seitdem	I have lived here **since** March.
	extremely [ɪk'stri:mli]	äußerst; sehr	Climbing is **extremely** popular.
	impact ['ɪmpækt]	Einfluss; Auswirkung	Social media had a big **impact** on us.
	favorite *(AE)* ['feɪvrɪt]	Lieblings-	AE: **favorite** BE: favourite
	to **influence** ['ɪnfluəns]	beeinflussen	Social media **influences** our lives.
	to **communicate** [kə'mju:nɪkeɪt]	kommunizieren; sich verständigen	Today we **communicate** differently.
	instead [ɪn'sted]	stattdessen; anstelle von	I don't like ham, let's have cheese **instead**.
	half *(sg)* [hɑ:f], **halves** *(pl)* [hɑ:vz]	(die) Hälfte	**half** a lemon 
	right away [ˌraɪt‿ə'weɪ]	sofort; gleich	I answer my messages **right away**.
p. 81	**jumping fitness** ['dʒʌmpɪŋ ˌfɪtnəs]	Jumping Fitness *(Trendsportart)*	**Jumping fitness** is a new sport.
	out of fashion [ˌaʊt‿əv 'fæʃn]	altmodisch; nicht mehr aktuell	**out of fashion** ↔ in fashion
	outdated [ˌaʊt'deɪtɪd]	veraltet	Listening to CDs is very **outdated**.
	trendy ['trendi]	trendy; modisch	**trendy** ↔ outdated
p. 82	**orange juice** ['ɒrɪndʒ ˌdʒu:s]	Orangensaft	
	comment ['kɒment]	Kommentar	I wrote a **comment** under the picture.
p. 83	**trend** [trend]	Trend; Entwicklung; Richtung	There are always new **trends** to follow.
	torn [tɔ:n]	zerrissen; aufgerissen	The jeans are **torn**. 
	veganism *(no pl)* ['vi:gənɪzm]	Veganismus	T veganizm

Reading corner

p. 84	**gold rush** ['gəʊld ˌrʌʃ]	Goldrausch	Everyone wanted gold in the **gold rush**.
	report [rɪ'pɔ:t]	Bericht	T rapor
	to **confirm** [kən'fɜ:m]	bestätigen; bekräftigen	Can you **confirm** when you arrive?
	discovery [dɪ'skʌvri]	Entdeckung	I made an awesome **discovery** – gold!
	Swiss [swɪs]	schweizerisch; aus der Schweiz; Schweizer; Schweizerin	He was a **Swiss** immigrant.
	businessman ['bɪznɪsmæn]	Geschäftsmann	R бизнесмен

	to give up [ˌgɪv‿'ʌp]	aufgeben	The spider never **gives up**.
	farming ['fa:mɪŋ]	Landwirtschaft; Ackerbau	He gave up his **farming** plans.
	landowner ['lændˌəʊnə]	Grundbesitzer; Grundbesitzerin	He owns the land, he's the **landowner**.
	to allow [ə'laʊ]	erlauben; gestatten	He didn't **allow** us to say anything.
	to prove [pru:v]	beweisen	He has to **prove** he owns the land.
	fever ['fi:və]	Fieber	The gold rush is also called gold **fever**.
	to increase [ɪn'kri:s]	zunehmen; vergrößern	The population has **increased**.
	edition [ɪ'dɪʃn]	Ausgabe; Auflage; Edition	Find out more in our next **edition**.
p. 85	**hunter** ['hʌntə]	Jäger; Jägerin	Lots of gold **hunters** went to California.
	bay [beɪ]	Bucht	
	wagon ['wægən]	Waggon; Planwagen	The horses pulled the **wagons** for us.
	to keep going [ki:p 'gəʊɪŋ]	weitergehen; weitermachen	I will **keep going** until I find more gold.
p. 86	**encyclopedia** [ɪnˌsaɪklə'pi:diə]	Enzyklopädie; Lexikon	Achtung Schreibweise! encyclopedia
	entry ['entri]	Eintrag	What does the **entry** for Gold Rush say?
	to cause [kɔ:z]	verursachen	The driver **caused** the accident.
	excitement [ɪk'saɪtmənt]	Aufregung	**excitement** → exciting
	transcontinental [ˌtrænsˌkɒntɪ'nentl]	transkontinental *(über den Kontinent hinweg)*	**Transcontinental** trains make long journeys. 
	railway ['reɪlweɪ]	Eisenbahn	
	slave [sleɪv]	Sklave; Sklavin	There were **slaves** before the Civil War.

Film corner

p. 89	**helper** ['helpə]	Helfer; Helferin	**helper** → to help → help
	as soon as [əz 'su:n‿əz]	sobald	**as soon as** → soon
	regular ['regjələ]	regelmäßig; normal; üblich; gleichmäßig	I work **regular** hours in my job.
	to respect [rɪ'spekt]	respektieren	I love and **respect** animals.
	to care (for) ['keə (fɔ:)]	sich kümmern (um)	He **cares for** old people.
	energetic [ˌenə'dʒetɪk]	tatkräftig	I am **energetic** and fit for the job.
	practical ['præktɪkl]	praktisch	I like making things, I'm **practical**.
	attitude ['ætɪtju:d]	Einstellung; Haltung	I have a practical **attitude** to work.
	waitress ['weɪtrəs]	Kellnerin; Bedienung	She is a **waitress** in the new café.
	groceries *(pl)* ['grəʊsriz]	Lebensmittel	We buy our **groceries** at the supermarket.

Checkpoint

entertainment *(no pl)* [ˌentəˈteɪnmənt]	Unterhaltung	Japan [dʒəˈpæn]	Japan
to introduce [ˌɪntrəˈdjuːs]	*hier:* zeigen	home-packed [ˌhəʊmˈpækt]	zu Hause gemacht
creative [kriˈeɪtɪv]	kreativ	bamboo [ˌbæmˈbuː]	Bambus

Communication skills

p. 94	**podcast** [ˈpɒdkɑːst]	Podcast	I got the new **podcast** last night.
	Thanks so much. [ˌθæŋk‿səʊ ˈmʌtʃ]	Vielen Dank.; Herzlichen Dank.	**Thanks so much** for your help!
	to **interrupt** [ˌɪntəˈrʌpt]	unterbrechen	I have to **interrupt** here.

Word bank: Talking about a region

Which region?

north

west  east

south

How many people live in the region/visit the region?

thousands millions billions

What does it look like?

mountains

beach

countryside

town

city

coastline

What can you do there?

museum

amusement park

zoo

church

skiing

shopping

hiking

sightseeing

It's in the … of …
It's near the …
There are …
There is …

… people live in the region/visit the region.
I like it because …
It's nice/quiet/busy/beautiful/…

Unit 5 Southern Life

p. 96	**southern** ['sʌðən]	südlich	**northern** ↔ southern

Way in

the outdoors [ˌði 'aʊtdɔ:z]	die freie Natur	They are fans of **the outdoors**.
African American [ˌæfrɪkən ə'merɪkən]	Afroamerikaner; Afroamerikanerin	There were lots of **African Americans** in the South.
right [raɪt]	Recht	African Americans wanted the same **rights**.
discrimination [dɪˌskrɪmɪ'neɪʃn]	Diskriminierung	There was a lot of **discrimination**.
civil rights *(pl)* [ˌsɪvl 'raɪts]	Bürgerrechte	King fought for **civil rights** in the 1950s.
peaceful ['pi:sfl]	friedlich	Protests aren't always **peaceful**.
protest ['prəʊtest]	Protest; Demonstration	R протест
to **force** [fɔ:s]	zwingen	We were **forced** to sell our land.
government ['gʌvnmənt]	Regierung	Achtung Schreibweise! gover<u>n</u>ment
law [lɔ:]	Gesetz; Recht	The government changed the **laws**.

p. 97	**African** ['æfrɪkən]	afrikanisch; aus Afrika; Afrikaner; Afrikanerin	T Afrikalı
	plantation [plæn'teɪʃn]	Plantage	People had to work on the **plantations**.
	region ['ri:dʒn]	Region; Gegend	The USA has many different **regions**.
	culture ['kʌltʃə]	Kultur	Each country has its own **culture**.
	custom ['kʌstəm]	Brauch; Sitte	The South has its own culture and **customs**.
	Southerner ['sʌðənə]	Südstaatler; Südstaatlerin	**Southern** → south → southern
	copy ['kɒpi]	Exemplar	The CD sold two million **copies**.
	best-paid ['bestˌpeɪd]	bestbezahlt	He is the **best-paid** actor.
	celebrity [sə'lebrəti]	Prominenter; Prominente; berühmte Person	**celebrity** = famous person
	to **release** [rɪ'li:s]	veröffentlichen; herausgeben; freigeben; freisetzen; loslassen	In 2006 Taylor Swift **released** her first CD.
	single ['sɪŋgl]	Single	A **single** is one song.

Station 1

Nationalities

Spanish ['spænɪʃ]	spanisch; Spanisch; aus Spanien	**Russian** ['rʌʃn]	russisch; Russisch; aus Russland; Russe; Russin
Chinese [tʃaɪ'ni:z]	chinesisch; Chinesisch; aus China; Chinese; Chinesin	**Polish** ['pəʊlɪʃ]	polnisch; Polnisch; aus Polen
Greek [gri:k]	griechisch; Griechisch; aus Griechenland	**Turkish** ['tɜ:kɪʃ]	türkisch; Türkisch; aus der Türkei
Italian [ɪ'tæliən]	italienisch; Italienisch; aus Italien; Italiener; Italienerin	**Japanese** [ˌdʒæpən'i:z]	japanisch; Japanisch; aus Japan; Japaner; Japanerin

Conflicts and solutions

to **tolerate** ['tɒlreɪt]	tolerieren; dulden	to **appreciate** [ə'pri:ʃieɪt]	schätzen; anerkennen; würdigen
solution [sə'lu:ʃn]	Lösung	to **reject** [rɪ'dʒekt]	zurückweisen; ablehnen
to **accept** [ək'sept]	akzeptieren; annehmen; hinnehmen	to **resent** [rɪ'zent]	übelnehmen; verübeln
to **ban** [bæn]	verbannen; verbieten; sperren		

p. 98	**down there** [ˌdaʊn 'ðeə]	dahin; da unten	I went on a trip **down there**.
	West Africa [ˌwest 'æfrɪkə]	Westafrika	The slaves were from **West Africa**.
	influence ['ɪnfluəns]	Einfluss	He has a bad **influence** on her.
	to **introduce** [ˌɪntrə'dju:s]	einführen; vorstellen; einleiten	They **introduced** new food ideas.
	flour [flaʊə]	Mehl	We need **flour** and spices.
	to **mix** [mɪks]	mischen; vermischen; mixen	If you **mix** blue and yellow, you get green.
	to **cover in flour** [ˌkʌvər‿ɪn 'flaʊə]	in Mehl wenden	First **cover** the chicken **in flour**.
	to **fry** [fraɪ]	braten; frittieren	
	oil [ɔɪl]	Öl	
	to **found** [faʊnd]	gründen	The city was **founded** in 1718.
	the French [ðə 'frenʃ]	die Franzosen	It was founded by **the French**.
	multicultural [ˌmʌlti'kʌltʃrl]	multikulturell	The south is a **multicultural** area.

	carnival ['kɑːnɪvl]	Karneval; Fasching	[R] карнавал [T] karnaval
	historic [hɪ'stɒrɪk]	historisch	**historic** → history
	racism ['reɪsɪzm]	Rassismus	Some say the flag is a symbol of **racism**.
	State House *(AE)* ['steɪt ˌhaʊs]	Regierungsgebäude	The US flag flies over the **State House**.
	a number of [ə 'nʌmbər‿əv]	einige; mehrere	I spoke to **a number of** people.
	killing ['kɪlɪŋ]	Tötung; Ermordung	There have been a number of **killings**.
	state government ['steɪt ˌɡʌvnmənt]	Landesregierung	Protesters confronted the **state government**.
p. 99	**paella** [paɪ'elə]	Paella	[T] paella
	sushi ['suːʃi]	Sushi	[R] суши [T] sushi
	nothing ['nʌθɪŋ]	nichts	**nothing** ↔ something
p. 100	**society** [sə'saɪəti]	Gesellschaft	We live in a multicultural **society**.
p. 101	**grid** [ɡrɪd]	Gitter; Raster	
	to complete [kəm'pliːt]	fertigstellen; vervollständigen	The building was **completed** in 2015.
	African-American [ˌæfrɪkənə'merɪkən]	afroamerikanisch	Obama was the first **African-American** president of the USA.

Station 2

Understanding things

I didn't get that. [aɪ ˌdɪdnt 'ɡet ðæt]	Ich habe es nicht verstanden.	**to explain** [ɪk'spleɪn]	erklären
I didn't catch that. [aɪ ˌdɪdnt 'kætʃ ðæt]	Das habe ich nicht verstanden.; Das habe ich nicht gehört.	**I know what you mean.** [aɪ ˌnəʊ wɒt jə 'miːn]	Ich verstehe, was du meinst.
		I see. [aɪ 'siː]	Ich verstehe.
		Absolutely! [ˌæbsə'luːtli]	Auf jeden Fall!

p. 102	**package** ['pækɪdʒ]	Paket	[T] paket
	excellent ['ekslnt]	exzellent; hervorragend	The ticket prices are **excellent**.
	choice [tʃɔɪs]	Auswahl; Wahl	**choice** → to choose
	transfer [træns'fɜː]	Transport; Transfer	There is a free **transfer** by bus.
	track [træk]	Strecke	The race **track** isn't far away.
	booklet ['bʊklət]	Broschüre; Heft	
	detail ['diːteɪl]	Detail; Einzelheit	[T] detay

	airboat ['eəbəʊt]	Propellerboot	We can go on an **airboat** there.
	wildlife ['waɪldlaɪf]	Tierwelt *(in freier Wildbahn)*	There is lots of **wildlife** in Florida.
	show [ʃəʊ]	Show; Schau; Aufführung	There is a **show** every 30 minutes.
	pick-up ['pɪkʌp]	Abholung; Pick-up	Look, there is a free hotel **pick-up** too.
	degree [dɪ'gri:]	Grad	It was really hot, 35 **degrees**.
	turn [tɜ:n]	Drehung	**turn** → to turn
	jungle ['dʒʌŋgl]	Dschungel	
	trail [treɪl]	Wanderweg; Spur	There is a **trail** through the swamps.
	seat [si:t]	Sitzplatz; Platz	If we book early, we'll get good **seats**.
	the wild [ðə 'waɪld]	Wildnis; freie Wildbahn	I've never seen a cat in **the wild**.
	heat [hi:t]	Hitze	This **heat** is too much for me.
	speech impaired ['spi:tʃ ɪm,peərd]	sprachbehindert	He can't speak, he's **speech impaired**.
	to translate [trænz'leɪt]	übersetzen	I can **translate** the text for you.
	outnumbered [,aʊt'nʌmbəd]	in der Unterzahl	I think I'm **outnumbered**, aren't I?
p. 103	**trainer** ['treɪnə]	Trainer; Trainerin	The **trainer** fed the alligators.
	to feel sick [,fi:l 'sɪk]	Übelkeit verspüren; sich schlecht fühlen	I **felt sick** after the airboat ride.
p. 104	**vacation** *(AE)* [və'keɪʃn]	Ferien; Urlaub	AE: **vacation** BE: holiday
	fishing ['fɪʃɪŋ]	Angeln; Fischen	
p. 105	**to count** [kaʊnt]	zählen	I can **count** in English, German and French.
	opening times ['əʊpənɪŋ ,taɪmz]	Öffnungszeiten	We have to look at the **opening times**.

Reading corner

p. 106	**segregation** [,segrɪ'geɪʃn]	Rassentrennung; Trennung	Not everyone believed in **segregation**.
	segregated ['segrɪgeɪtɪd]	getrennt	**segregated** → segregation
	separate ['seprət]	getrennt; separat; verschieden	**separated** = segregated
	movie theater *(AE)* ['mu:vi ,θi:ətə]	Kino	AE: **movie theater** BE: cinema
	at the back [ət ðə 'bæk]	hinten; am Ende; im hinteren Teil	**at the back** ↔ at the front
	full [fʊl]	voll	The bus was **full** of people.
p. 107	**to refuse** [rɪ'fju:z]	sich weigern; ablehnen	Claudette **refused** to move.
	to drag [dræg]	schleppen; schleifen; ziehen	They **dragged** him away from the dog.

off [ɒf]	von … weg	They pulled the dog **off** the man.
to **arrest** [ə'rest]	festnehmen; verhaften	She was **arrested** by the police.
courage ['kʌrɪdʒ]	Mut; Tapferkeit; Courage	She showed a lot of **courage** on the bus.
action ['ækʃn]	Handlung; Action	Did her **actions** make things worse?
court case ['kɔ:t ˌkeɪs]	Gerichtsverhandlung; Rechtsfall	The **court case** ended segregation.
to **link** [lɪŋk]	verbinden	The man was **linked** with the shop.
role [rəʊl]	Rolle	I played an important **role** in the fight.
to **abolish** [ə'bɒlɪʃ]	abschaffen	It took a long time to **abolish** segregation.
system ['sɪstəm]	System	They abolished an unfair **system**.

Film corner

p. 109	**reliable** [rɪ'laɪəbl]	verlässlich; zuverlässig; vertrauenswürdig	She's very **reliable**. She's always on time.
	to **trust** [trʌst]	vertrauen	She's reliable and you can **trust** her.
	experience [ɪk'spɪəriəns]	Erfahrung	I have **experience** of working with animals.

Checkpoint

feature story ['fi:tʃə ˌstɔ:ri]	Leitartikel; Sonderbericht	saleswoman ['seɪlzˌwʊmən]	Verkäuferin
stall [stɔ:l]	Stand; Bude	emotion [ɪ'məʊʃn]	Gefühl; Emotion
line [laɪn]	Schlange		

V

Word bank: Talking about culture

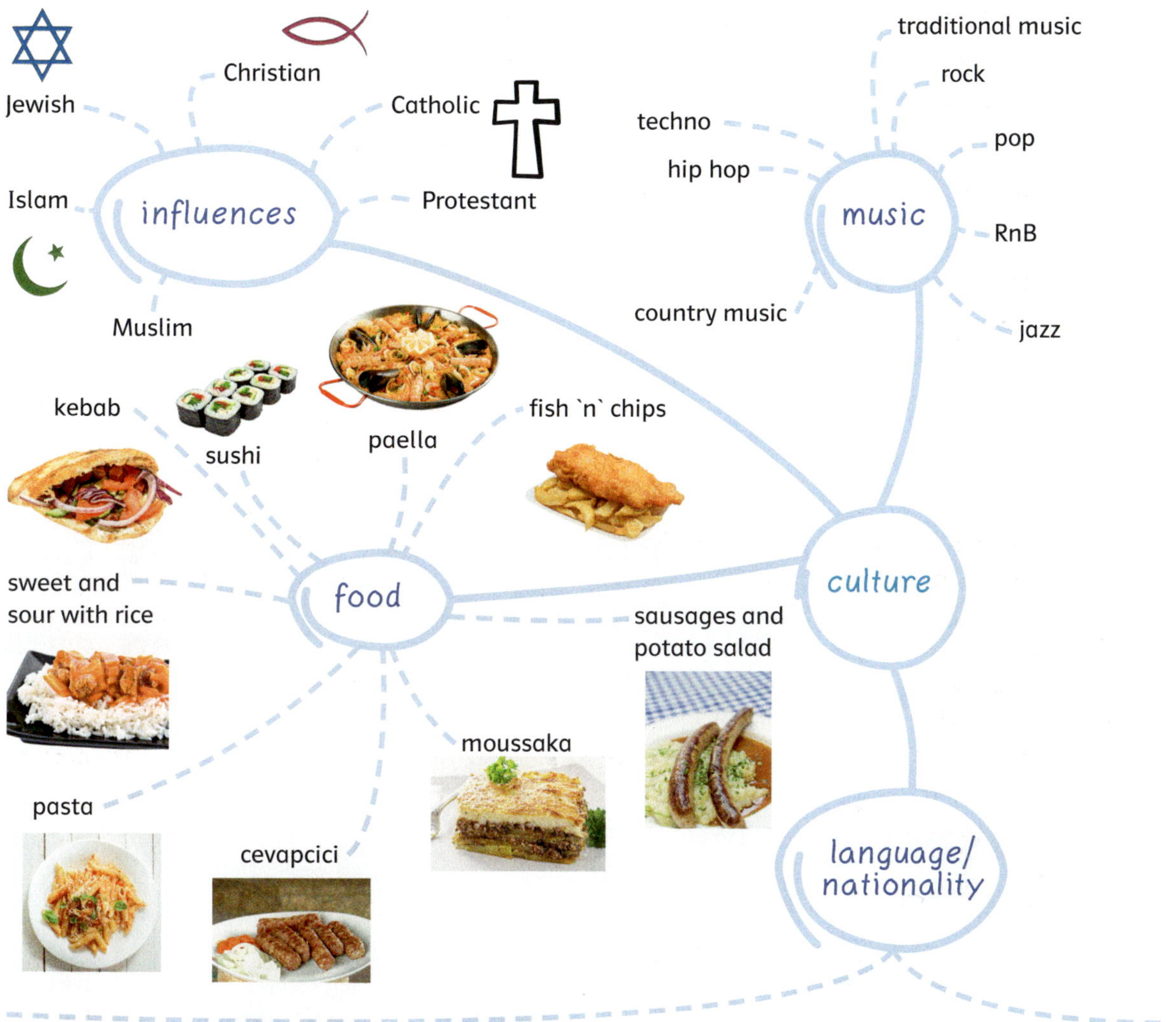

Word bank: A day trip

opening times

all day half day
from 9:00 a.m. until 5:00 p.m.
weekends only
last entry one hour before closing time
afternoons/morning only
closed on Mondays

tickets

adults	£ 10.00
children (under 14)	£ 5.00
senior citizens/OAPs	£ 5.00
students	£ 5.00
family (2 adults + 2 children)	£ 17.50

places

museum

zoo

amusement/
theme park

city

beach

transport

coach

train

tram

car

bike

boat

activities

hiking

sightseeing

fishing

a guided tour

cycling

Instructions

Arbeitsanweisungen mit Operatoren

Act the dialogue • the role play.	**Spielt** den Dialog • das Rollenspiel.
Add more words.	**Ergänze** mehr Wörter.
Answer the questions.	**Beantworte** die Fragen.
Ask a partner.	**Frage** eine Partnerin/einen Partner.
Check the sentences.	**Überprüfe** die Sätze.
Choose one of the tasks • the right answer.	**Wähle** eine der Aufgaben • die richtige Antwort **aus.**
Collect ideas.	**Sammle** Ideen.
Compare with your partner.	**Vergleicht** zu zweit.
Complete the sentences • the dialogue.	**Vervollständige** die Sätze • den Dialog.
Copy the list.	**Schreibe** die Liste **ab.**
Correct the wrong sentences.	**Verbessere** die falschen Sätze.
Decide on the best order.	**Entscheide dich für** die beste Reihenfolge.
Describe the picture.	**Beschreibe** das Bild.
Discuss in groups.	**Besprecht euch** in Gruppen.
Draw a picture.	**Zeichne** ein Bild.
Exchange your lists.	**Tauscht** eure Listen aus.
Explain the rules.	**Erkläre** die Regeln.
Finish the sentences.	**Vervollständige** die Sätze.
Give feedback.	**Gib** Rückmeldung.
Give reasons.	**Gib Gründe an.**
Guess.	**Überlege.**
Interview your partner.	**Interviewe** deine Partnerin/deinen Partner.
Label the picture.	**Beschrifte** das Bild.
Listen to the dialogue.	**Höre** dir den Dialog **an.**
Look at the photos • pictures (again).	**Schau** dir die Fotos • Bilder (noch einmal) **an.**
Make a list • a chart • a mind map.	**Erstelle** eine Liste • eine Tabelle • ein Wörternetz.
Make notes.	**Mache** dir **Stichpunkte.**
Make up more verses.	**Denke dir** weitere Strophen **aus.**
Match the sentences with the pictures.	**Ordne** den Bildern die richtigen Sätze **zu.**
Name the place.	**Nenne** den Ort.
Plan your role play.	**Plant** euer Rollenspiel.
Practise with a partner.	**Übe** mit einer Partnerin/einem Partner.
Present your profile to the class.	**Stelle** dein Profil deiner Klasse **vor.**
Put in the right verbs.	**Setze** die richtigen Verben **ein.**
Put the words **in the right order.**	**Bringe** die Wörter **in die richtige Reihenfolge.**
Read the story **again.**	**Lies** die Geschichte **noch einmal.**
Record your dialogue.	**Nehmt** euren Dialog **auf.**
Rewrite the sentences.	**Schreibe** die Sätze **um.**

Say how you feel.	**Sage**, wie du dich fühlst.
Show your text to a partner.	**Zeige** deinen Text einer Partnerin/einem Partner.
Sort the words **into groups**.	**Sortiere** die Wörter **in Gruppen**.
Take notes.	**Mache** dir **Notizen**.
Talk about the photos.	**Rede** über die Fotos.
Tell the class.	**Erzähle** es der Klasse.
Think about the story.	**Denke über** die Geschichte **nach**.
Think of a number.	**Denke** dir eine Nummer **aus.**
Use your own ideas.	**Benutze** deine eigenen Ideen.
Watch the film.	**Schau** den Film **an**.
Write a poem • a heading • a draft.	**Schreibe** ein Gedicht • einen Titel • einen Entwurf.

Classroom phrases

You and your teacher

I'm sorry I'm late.	Tut mir leid, dass ich mich verspätet habe.
I'm sorry I don't have my exercise book.	Tut mir leid, ich habe mein Heft nicht dabei.
What's the homework?	Was haben wir als Hausaufgabe auf?
Can you help me, please?	Können Sie / Kannst du mir bitte helfen?
Can you say that again, please?	Können Sie / Kannst du das bitte wiederholen?
Can I go to the toilet, please?	Kann ich bitte auf Toilette gehen?
Mr / Mrs / Miss ..., I don't feel well.	Herr / Frau ..., mir geht es nicht gut.
What page is it, please?	Auf welcher Seite ist das?
What's the German / English word for ...?	Was ist das deutsche / englische Wort für ...?
How do you spell ...?	Wie schreibt man ...?
What does that mean?	Was heißt / bedeutet das?
Sorry, I don't understand/ I don't know.	Tut mir leid, ich verstehe das nicht/ ich weiß es nicht.

Working together

Can we work in pairs / groups?	Können wir zu zweit / in Gruppen arbeiten?
Do you want to work with me / us?	Willst du / Wollt ihr mit mir / uns arbeiten?
Let's make a / draw a ...	Lass(t) uns ein ... machen / zeichnen.
Whose turn is it? – It's my / your turn.	Wer ist dran? – Ich bin dran. / Du bist dran.

Your teacher can say ...

Turn to page ...	Schlagt Seite ... auf.
Look at the board.	Schaut an die Tafel.
Put your hands up, please!	Meldet euch, bitte!
Try again!	Versuche es noch einmal.

List of irregular verbs

Hier findest du alle unregelmäßigen Verben, die im Buch vorkommen. Die Liste enthält jeweils alle drei Formen, auch wenn sie noch nicht alle in den Units vorgekommen sind.

infinitive	simple past	past participle	German
be [bi:]	was, were [wɒz, wɜ:]	been [bi:n]	sein
beat [bi:t]	beat [bi:t]	beaten ['bi:tn]	schlagen; besiegen
become [bɪ'kʌm]	became [bɪ'keɪm]	become [bɪ'kʌm]	werden
bleed [bli:d]	bled [bled]	bled [bled]	bluten
break [breɪk]	broke [brəʊk]	broken ['brəʊkn]	brechen
bring [brɪŋ]	brought [brɔ:t]	brought [brɔ:t]	bringen; mitbringen
build [bɪld]	built [bɪlt]	built [bɪlt]	bauen
burn [bɜ:n]	burned/burnt [bɜ:nt]	burned/burnt [bɜ:nt]	brennen
buy [baɪ]	bought [bɔ:t]	bought [bɔ:t]	kaufen
choose [tʃu:z]	chose [tʃəʊz]	chosen ['tʃəʊzn]	auswählen; wählen
come [kʌm]	came [keɪm]	come [kʌm]	kommen
cost [kɒst]	cost [kɒst]	cost [kɒst]	kosten
cut [kʌt]	cut [kʌt]	cut [kʌt]	(sich) schneiden
do [du:]	did [dɪd]	done [dʌn]	machen; tun
drive [draɪv]	drove [drəʊv]	driven ['drɪvn]	fahren; treiben
draw [drɔ:]	drew [dru:]	drawn [drɔ:n]	zeichnen
dream [dri:m]	dreamed/dreamt [dremt]	dreamed/dreamt [dremt]	träumen
drink [drɪŋk]	drank [dræŋk]	drunk [drʌŋk]	trinken
eat [i:t]	ate [eɪt]	eaten ['i:tn]	essen
fall [fɔ:l]	fell [fel]	fallen ['fɔ:ln]	fallen; hinfallen
feed [fi:d]	fed [fed]	fed [fed]	füttern; ernähren
feel [fi:l]	felt [felt]	felt [felt]	(sich) fühlen
fight [faɪt]	fought [fɔ:t]	fought [fɔ:t]	kämpfen; streiten
find [faɪnd]	found [faʊnd]	found [faʊnd]	finden
fly [flaɪ]	flew [flu:]	flown [fləʊn]	fliegen
forget [fə'get]	forgot [fə'gɒt]	forgotten [fə'gɒtn]	vergessen
freeze [fri:z]	froze [frəʊz]	frozen ['frəʊzn]	frieren; gefrieren
get [get]	got [gɒt]	got [gɒt]	bekommen; werden
give [gɪv]	gave [geɪv]	given ['gɪvn]	geben
go [gəʊ]	went [went]	gone [gɒn]	gehen; fahren
grow [grəʊ]	grew [gru:]	grown [grəʊn]	anbauen; züchten; ziehen; wachsen
grow up [ˌgrəʊ‿'ʌp]	grew up [ˌgru:‿'ʌp]	grown up [ˌgrəʊn‿'ʌp]	aufwachsen
hang [hæŋ]	hung [hʌŋ]	hung [hʌŋ]	hängen
have [hæv]	had [hæd]	had [hæd]	haben; besitzen
hear [hɪə]	heard [hɜ:d]	heard [hɜ:d]	hören

infinitive	simple past	past participle	German
hide [haɪd]	hid [hɪd]	hidden ['hɪdn]	verstecken
hit [hɪt]	hit [hɪt]	hit [hɪt]	schlagen; treffen
hold [həʊld]	held [held]	held [held]	halten; festhalten
hurt [hɜ:t]	hurt [hɜ:t]	hurt [hɜ:t]	verletzen; weh tun
keep [ki:p]	kept [kept]	kept [kept]	halten
know [nəʊ]	knew [nju:]	known [nəʊn]	wissen; kennen
lay [leɪ]	laid [leɪd]	laid [leɪd]	legen; (den Tisch) decken
lead [li:d]	led [led]	led [led]	führen; anführen
leave [li:v]	left [left]	left [left]	verlassen; lassen; abfahren
lend [lend]	lent [lent]	lent [lent]	leihen; verleihen
lose [lu:z]	lost [lɒst]	lost [lɒst]	verlieren
make [meɪk]	made [meɪd]	made [meɪd]	machen; tun; bilden
mean [mi:n]	meant [ment]	meant [ment]	bedeuten; meinen
meet [mi:t]	met [met]	met [met]	kennen lernen; (sich) treffen
pay [peɪ]	paid [peɪd]	paid [peɪd]	bezahlen
put [pʊt]	put [pʊt]	put [pʊt]	setzen; legen; stellen
read [ri:d]	read [red]	read [red]	lesen
ride [raɪd]	rode [rəʊd]	ridden ['rɪdn]	fahren; reiten
ring [rɪŋ]	rang [ræŋ]	rung [rʌŋ]	klingeln; läuten
run [rʌn]	ran [ræn]	run [rʌn]	laufen; rennen
say [seɪ]	said [sed]	said [sed]	sagen; sprechen
see [si:]	saw [sɔ:]	seen [si:n]	sehen
sell [sel]	sold [səʊld]	sold [səʊld]	verkaufen
send [send]	sent [sent]	sent [sent]	schicken; senden
shine [ʃaɪn]	shone [ʃɒn]	shone [ʃɒn]	glänzen; scheinen
shoot [ʃu:t]	shot [ʃɒt]	shot [ʃɒt]	schießen
show [ʃəʊ]	showed [ʃəʊd]	shown [ʃəʊn]	zeigen
sing [sɪŋ]	sang [sæŋ]	sung [sʌŋ]	singen
sink [sɪŋk]	sank [sæŋk]	sunk [sʌŋk]	untergehen; sinken
sit [sɪt]	sat [sæt]	sat [sæt]	sitzen
sleep [sli:p]	slept [slept]	slept [slept]	schlafen
smell [smel]	smelled/smelt [smelt]	smelled/smelt [smelt]	riechen
speak [spi:k]	spoke [spəʊk]	spoken ['spəʊkn]	sprechen
spell [spel]	spelled/spelt [spelt]	spelled/spelt [spelt]	buchstabieren
spend [spend]	spent [spent]	spent [spent]	ausgeben; verbringen
stand [stænd]	stood [stʊd]	stood [stʊd]	stehen
steal [sti:l]	stole [stəʊl]	stolen ['stəʊlən]	stehlen

infinitive	simple past	past participle	German
sweep [swi:p]	**swept** [swept]	**swept** [swept]	fegen
swim [swɪm]	**swam** [swæm]	**swum** [swʌm]	schwimmen
take [teɪk]	**took** [tʊk]	**taken** ['teɪkn]	nehmen; mitnehmen
tell [tel]	**told** [təʊld]	**told** [təʊld]	erzählen; sagen
think [θɪŋk]	**thought** [θɔ:t]	**thought** [θɔ:t]	denken; glauben
throw [θrəʊ]	**threw** [θru:]	**thrown** [θrəʊn]	werfen
understand [ˌʌndə'stænd]	**understood** [ˌʌndə'stʊd]	**understood** [ˌʌndə'stʊd]	verstehen
wake up [weɪk‿'ʌp]	**woke up** [wəʊk‿'ʌp]	**woken up** [ˌwəʊkn‿'ʌp]	aufwachen
wear [weə]	**wore** [wɔ:]	**worn** [wɔ:n]	tragen
win [wɪn]	**won** [wʌn]	**won** [wʌn]	gewinnen; siegen
write [raɪt]	**wrote** [rəʊt]	**written** ['rɪtn]	schreiben

Dictionary

Im *Dictionary* sind alle wichtigen Wörter aus deinem Buch enthalten. Die Wörter stehen in alphabetischer Reihenfolge. Englische Wörter schlägst du ab S. 220 nach, deutsche Wörter ab S. 263.

Die Abkürzungen geben an, wo das Wort zum ersten Mal im Buch erscheint.

account	[ə'kaʊnt]	Konto	IV	U4	80
englisches Wort	Aussprache	deutsche Übersetzung	Band 4	Unit 4	Seite 80

Die mit einem Sternchen (*) gekennzeichneten Verben sind unregelmäßige Verben (→ *List of irregular verbs*, S. 217–219).

Manche Wörter haben verschiedene Bedeutungen. Am besten liest du alle, bevor du dich für eine entscheidest.

practice ['præktɪs] Training; Übung I[1]
addicted [ə'dɪktɪd] süchtig <IV U3, 72>[3]
*to **spend** [spend] ausgeben *(Geld)*; verbringen *(Zeit)* II[1]
accident ['æksɪdnt] Unfall III[1]
back [bæk] Hinter- IV U3, 62[2]
address [ə'dres] Adresse II[2]

1 Lernwortschatz für alle: schwarz; 2 Differenzierungswortschatz: blau; 3 kein Lernwortschatz: < >

A

a [ə] ein; eine I
a bit [ə 'bɪt] ein bisschen; ein wenig II
a few [ə 'fju:] ein paar; wenige; einige III
a five minute walk [ə 'faɪv mɪnɪt ˌwɔ:k] fünf Minuten zu Fuß III
a little [ə 'lɪtl] ein bisschen II
a lot [ə'lɒt] viel I; sehr II
a lot of [ə 'lɒt‿əv] eine Menge; viel I; viel; eine Menge III
a number of [ə 'nʌmbər‿əv] einige; mehrere IV U5, 98
a pair of [ə 'peər‿əv] ein Paar II
a/one hundred ['hʌndrəd] einhundert; hundert I
a/one thousand [ə/wʌn 'θaʊznd] eintausend; tausend II
a.m. [ˌeɪ'em] vormittags II
*to be **able** to (do sth) [bi: 'eɪbl tə] (zu etw.) fähig sein; (etw.) können; (etw.) dürfen IV U2, 34
to **abolish** [ə'bɒlɪʃ] abschaffen IV U5, 107
about [ə'baʊt] über II; ungefähr; circa; etwa II
to be about [bi: ə'baʊt] gehen um; handeln von III
out and about [ˌaʊt‿ən‿ə'baʊt] unterwegs I
absolutely [ˌæbsə'lu:tli] absolut; völlig IV U3, 59
to **accept** [ək'sept] akzeptieren; annehmen; hinnehmen IV U5, 99
accident ['æksɪdnt] Unfall III
account [ə'kaʊnt] Konto IV U4, 80
stomach **ache** ['stʌmək ˌeɪk] Bauchweh; Bauchschmerzen II
across [ə'krɒs] über; hinüber; herüber; quer durch IV U3, 54
to **act** [ækt] spielen II
acting ['æktɪŋ] Schauspielen; Schauspielerei III
acting workshop ['æktɪŋ ˌwɜ:kʃɒp] Schauspielworkshop II
action ['ækʃn] Actionfilm <IV U4, 140>; Handlung; Action IV U5, 107
Action! ['ækʃn] Achtung Aufnahme! <III>
active ['æktɪv] Aktiv <IV U3, 72>
activist ['æktɪvɪst] Aktivist; Aktivistin *(jmd. der sich für etw. engagiert)* <IV U3, 138>
activity [æk'tɪvəti] Aktivität I
activity centre [æk'tɪvəti ˌsentə] Jugendzentrum III
actor ['æktə] Schauspieler; Schauspielerin II
actually ['æktʃuəli] tatsächlich; wirklich; eigentlich III
adaptor [ə'dæptə] Adapter III
to **add** [æd] hinzufügen II
addicted [ə'dɪktɪd] süchtig <IV U3, 72>

p pen • **b** bed • **t** ten • **d** dad • **k** cat • **g** grey • **tʃ** chair • **dʒ** joke • **f** fan • **v** very • **θ** three • **ð** the

chemical additive [ˌkemɪkl ˈædətɪv] chemische Zusatzstoff <IV U3, 72>
address [əˈdres] Adresse II
to **address** [əˈdres] ansprechen; adressieren <IV U2, 46>
adjective [ˈædʒɪktɪv] Adjektiv; Eigenschaftswort I
adult [ˈædʌlt] Erwachsene; Erwachsener III
adventure [ədˈventʃə] Abenteuer III
adverb [ˈædvɜːb] Adverb <III>
ad(vert) (= advertisement) [ˈæd(vert) (ədˈvɜːtɪsmənt)] Anzeige; Annonce; Werbespot IV U2, 38
advice [ədˈvaɪs] Rat; Ratschlag III
afraid [əˈfreɪd] ängstlich II
to be afraid [biː əˈfreɪd] sich fürchten; Angst haben II
African [ˈæfrɪkən] afrikanisch; aus Afrika; Afrikaner; Afrikanerin IV U5, 97
African American [ˌæfrɪkən əˈmerɪkən] Afroamerikaner; Afroamerikanerin IV U5, 96
African-American [ˌæfrɪkənəˈmerɪkən] afroamerikanisch IV U5, 101
after [ˈɑːftə] nach I; danach; später III
after that [ˌɑːftə ˈðæt] danach I
afternoon [ˌɑːftəˈnuːn] Nachmittag I
in the afternoon [ɪn ðiˌɑːftəˈnuːn] am Nachmittag I
again [əˈgen] wieder; noch einmal II
against [əˈgenst] gegen III
age [eɪdʒ] Alter I; Zeitalter <IV U4, 140>
ago [əˈgəʊ] vor II
to **agree** [əˈgriː] zustimmen II
to agree (on) [əˈgriː (ɒn)] sich einigen (auf) <III>
right **ahead** [ˌraɪt əˈhed] geradeaus IV U1, 15
aim [eɪm] Ziel <IV U2, 50>
ain't (= isn't/aren't) [eɪnt] ist nicht; sind nicht <IV U1, 19>
air [eə] Luft IV U1, 22
airboat [ˈeəbəʊt] Propellerboot IV U5, 102
airport [ˈeəpɔːt] Flughafen II

alarm clock [əˈlɑːm ˌklɒk] Wecker I
Alaskan [əˈlæskən] Alaska-; alaskisch <IV U1, 30>
alcohol *(no pl)* [ˈælkəhɒl] Alkohol IV U3, 58
alcoholic [ˌælkəˈhɒlɪk] alkoholisch; Alkohol- <IV U3, 72>
alert [əˈlɜːt] Alarm <IV U1, 30>
alien [ˈeɪliən] Außerirdische; Außerirdischer I
alive [əˈlaɪv] am Leben III
all [ɔːl] alle I
all day [ˌɔːl ˈdeɪ] den ganzen Tag III
all right [ˌɔːl ˈraɪt] in Ordnung; alles klar II
allegiance [əˈliːdʒns] Treue IV U2, 34
pledge of allegiance [ˌpledʒ əv əˈliːdʒns] Treueeid IV U2, 34
allergic to [əˈlɜːdʒɪk tə] allergisch gegen II
allergy [ˈælədʒi] Allergie II
alley [ˈæli] Gasse; Weg IV U2, 32
alligator [ˈælɪgeɪtə] Alligator IV ZI, 9
to **allow** [əˈlaʊ] erlauben; gestatten IV U4, 84
to be allowed to (do sth) [biː əˈlaʊd tə] (etw.) dürfen IV U2, 33
allowance *(AE)* [əˈlaʊəns] Taschengeld; Unterhaltsgeld IV U2, 38
almost [ˈɔːlməʊst] fast; beinahe III
along [əˈlɒŋ] entlang I
alphabet [ˈælfəbet] Alphabet I
already [ɔːlˈredi] schon; bereits II
also [ˈɔːlsəʊ] auch III
aluminium [ˌæljəˈmɪniəm] Aluminium III
always [ˈɔːlweɪz] immer I
amazing [əˈmeɪzɪŋ] erstaunlich; unglaublich; toll III
ambulance [ˈæmbjələns] Krankenwagen III
American [əˈmerɪkən] amerikanisch; Amerikanisch; aus Amerika; Amerikaner; Amerikanerin IV ZI, 9
American Indian [əˌmerɪkən ˈɪndiən] Ureinwohner Amerikas <IV U1, 24>

Native American [ˌneɪtɪv əˈmerɪkən] Ureinwohner Amerikas; Ureinwohnerin Amerikas IV U2, 32
the **Amish** [ði ˈɑːmɪʃ] die Amischen IV U3, 53
amish [ˈɑːmɪʃ] amisch IV U3, 58
amount (of) [əˈmaʊnt (əv)] Menge; Summe <IV U1, 24>
amusement park [əˈmjuːzmənt ˌpɑːk] Freizeitpark <IV U4, 207>
an [ən] ein; eine I
and [ænd] und I
Anglo-American [ˌæŋgləʊəˈmerɪkən] anglo-amerikanisch <IV U5, 142>
angry [ˈæŋgri] wütend; zornig; verärgert; böse II
animal [ˈænɪml] Tier I
animal rescue shelter [ˌænɪml ˈreskjuː ˌʃeltə] Tierheim I
ankle [ˈæŋkl] Fußgelenk; Fußknöchel II
announcement [əˈnaʊnsmənt] Durchsage; Ankündigung II
annoyed [əˈnɔɪd] verärgert III
annoying [əˈnɔɪɪŋ] ärgerlich; lästig <IV U3, 68>
another [əˈnʌðə] ein andere; noch ein II
answer [ˈɑːnsə] Antwort I
to **answer** [ˈɑːnsə] antworten; beantworten I
to answer the phone [ˌɑːnsə ðə ˈfəʊn] ans Telefon gehen III
antenna [ænˈtenə] Antenne III
any [ˈeni] irgendwelche; irgendein II
not … any [ˌnɒt … eni] kein II
anything [ˈeniθɪŋ] irgendetwas II
Anything else? [ˌeniθɪŋ ˈels] Darf es sonst noch etwas sein? I
anything to drink [ˈeniθɪŋ tə ˈdrɪŋk] etwas zu trinken II
anyway [ˈeniweɪ] jedenfalls; trotzdem; sowieso IV U1, 14
anywhere [ˈeniweə] überall; irgendwo <IV U1, 19>
appealing [əˈpiːlɪŋ] ansprechend IV U4, 77
apple [ˈæpl] Apfel I

apple crumble [ˌæpl ˈkrʌmbl] Apfelauflauf *(mit Streuseln bedeckt)* II
to **apply** (for) [əˈplaɪ (fə)] sich bewerben (für/um) IV U2, 38
to **appreciate** [əˈpriːʃieɪt] schätzen; anerkennen; würdigen IV U5, 99
approval form [əˈpruːvl ˌfɔːm] Einverständnisformular <IV U2, 44>
April [ˈeɪprl] April I
Arabic [ˈærəbɪk] arabisch; Arabisch <IV U5, 213>
architect [ˈɑːkɪtekt] Architekt; Architektin IV U4, 75
archive [ˈɑːkaɪv] Archiv II
are [ɑː] bist; sind I
Are you serious? [ˌɑː ju ˈsɪəriəs] Im Ernst? III
area [ˈeəriə] Fläche; Gegend; Gebiet; Areal IV ZI, 9
to **argue** [ˈɑːgjuː] argumentieren; streiten <IV U4, 89>
argument [ˈɑːgjəmənt] Auseinandersetzung; Streit II; Argument <IV U3, 68>
arm [ɑːm] Arm III
armour [ˈɑːmə] Rüstung III
army [ˈɑːmi] Armee; Heer III
around [əˈraʊnd] herum; umher III; gegen; ungefähr um III; um … herum IV U1, 14
around the house [əˌraʊnd ðə ˈhaʊs] zu Hause I
to be around [biː əˈraʊnd] geben; existieren IV U4, 80
to get around [ˌget əˈraʊnd] herumkommen III
to **arrange** [əˈreɪndʒ] arrangieren <IV U3, 69>
to **arrest** [əˈrest] festnehmen; verhaften IV U5, 107
to **arrive** [əˈraɪv] ankommen II
Art [ɑːt] Kunst I
article [ˈɑːtɪkl] Artikel; Bericht *(in einer Zeitung)* <IV U1, 21>
artist [ˈɑːtɪst] Künstler; Künstlerin III
as [æz] als II; wie II
as … as [əz … əz] so … wie II
as soon as [əz ˈsuːn‿əz] sobald IV U4, 89
to **ask** [ɑːsk] fragen I
to ask about [ˈɑːsk‿əˌbaʊt] sich erkundigen nach; fragen nach II
to ask sb out [ˌɑːsk … ˈaʊt] sich mit jmdm. verabreden IV U2, 42
asking the way [ˌɑːskɪŋ ðə ˈweɪ] nach dem Weg fragen I
*to be **asleep** [biː əˈsliːp] schlafen III
to fall asleep [ˌfɔːl‿əˈsliːp] einschlafen III
to **assassinate** [əˈsæsɪneɪt] ermorden <IV U3, 138>
assistant [əˈsɪstnt] Verkäufer; Verkäuferin III
shop assistant [ˈʃɒp‿əˌsɪstnt] Verkäufer; Verkäuferin II
sales **associate** *(AE)* [ˌseɪlz əˈsəʊʃiət] Verkäufer; Verkäuferin IV U2, 38
at [æt] auf; an; in; um; bei; am I
at break [ət ˈbreɪk] in der Pause I
at home [ət ˈhəʊm] zu Hause I
at last [ət ˈlɑːst] endlich; zu guter Letzt II
at least [ət ˈliːst] mindestens; wenigstens IV U3, 64
at school [ət ˈskuːl] in der Schule I
at the back [ət ðə ˈbæk] hinten; am Ende; im hinteren Teil IV U5, 106
at the seaside [ət ðə ˈsiːsaɪd] am Meer I
at the weekend [ət ðə ˌwiːkˈend] am Wochenende I
ate [eɪt] simple past von *to eat* II
atmosphere [ˈætməsfɪə] Atmosphäre; Stimmung <IV U2, 46>
to **attach** [əˈtætʃ] verbinden III
attack [əˈtæk] Angriff; Attacke IV U1, 12
to **attack** [əˈtæk] angreifen IV U2, 42
attempt [əˈtempt] Versuch <IV U4, 88>
attic [ˈætɪk] Dachboden I
attitude [ˈætɪtjuːd] Einstellung; Haltung IV U4, 89
audition [ɔːˈdɪʃn] Vorspielen; Vorsprechen; Vorsingen; Vortanzen II
August [ˈɔːgəst] August I
in August [ɪn ˈɔːgəst] im August I
aunt [ɑːnt] Tante II
author [ˈɔːθə] Autor; Autorin <IV U3, 71>
autograph [ˈɔːtəgrɑːf] Autogramm IV U3, 53
to sign autographs [ˌsaɪn ˈɔːtəgrɑːfs] Autogramme geben IV U3, 53
avenue [ˈævənjuː] Allee; Boulevard IV U1, 14
average [ˈævrɪdʒ] durchschnittlich IV U3, 58
to **avoid** [əˈvɔɪd] vermeiden; meiden; aus dem Weg gehen; ausweichen IV U3, 62
awake [əˈweɪk] bei Bewusstsein; wach III
award [əˈwɔːd] Auszeichnung; Preis <IV U4, 140>
away [əˈweɪ] weg; entfernt II
right away [ˌraɪt‿əˈweɪ] sofort; gleich IV U4, 80
awesome [ˈɔːsəm] super; spitze IV U2, 34
awful [ˈɔːfl] schrecklich; furchtbar I

B

babysitter [ˈbeɪbiˌsɪtə] Babysitter; Babysitterin IV U2, 41
back [bæk] Rückseite <III>
at the back [ət ðə ˈbæk] hinten; am Ende; im hinteren Teil IV U5, 106
back [bæk] Hinter- IV U3, 62
back [bæk] zurück III
back home [bæk ˈhəʊm] zu Hause II
background [ˈbækgraʊnd] Hintergrund III
in the background [ɪn ðə ˈbækgraʊnd] im Hintergrund III
backpack [ˈbækpæk] Rucksack IV U3, 62
bad [bæd] schlimm; böse; schlecht III
bag [bæg] Tasche; Tüte; Sack I
baggies *(pl) (coll)* [ˈbægiz] kurze Hosen *(ugs.)* <IV U4, 77>

bagpipes *(pl)* ['bægpaɪps] Dudelsack III
pasta **bake** [ˌpæstə 'beɪk] Nudelauflauf II
baker ['beɪkə] Bäcker; Bäckerin III
baker's ['beɪkəz] Bäckerei III
bald eagle [ˌbɔ:ld 'i:gl] Weißkopfseeadler IV ZI, 8
ball [bɔ:l] Ball II
cannon ball ['kænən ˌbɔ:l] Kanonenkugel II
balloon [bə'lu:n] Luftballon I
bamboo [bæm'bu:] Bambus <IV U4, 90>
to **ban** [bæn] verbannen; verbieten; sperren IV U5, 99
banana [bə'nɑ:nə] Banane I
band [bænd] Band; Musikgruppe II
brass band [ˌbrɑ:s 'bænd] Blaskapelle; Blasensemble <IV U5, 108>
marching band ['mɑ:tʃɪŋ ˌbænd] Marschkapelle <IV U2, 194>
to start a band [ˌstɑ:t‿ə 'bænd] eine Band gründen II
bandage ['bændɪdʒ] Verband III
a **bar** of chocolate [bɑ:r‿əv 'tʃɒklət] eine Tafel Schokolade I
bar chart ['bɑ: ˌtʃɑ:t] Balkendiagramm; Säulendiagramm <IV U1, 27>
barbecue ['bɑ:bɪkju:] Grill I
bargain ['bɑ:gɪn] Schnäppchen II
barrel ['bærl] Fass; Tonne IV U3, 53
baseball ['beɪsbɔ:l] Baseball IV U1, 13
basic ['beɪsɪk] grundlegend; einfach <IV U1, 24>
basketball ['bɑ:skɪtbɔ:l] Basketball II
bat [bæt] Fledermaus I
bathroom ['bɑ:θrʊm] Bad(ezimmer) I
bathroom (AE) ['bɑ:θrʊm] Toilette; Bad(ezimmer) IV U2, 34
battle ['bætl] Schlacht; Kampf III
bay [beɪ] Bucht IV U4, 85
BC (= before Christ) [ˌbi:'si:] vor Christus <IV U2, 136>
*to **be** [bi:] sein I
to be able to (do sth) [bi: 'eɪbl tə] (zu etw.) fähig sein; (etw.) können; (etw.) dürfen IV U2, 34
to be about [bi: ə'baʊt] gehen um; handeln von III
to be afraid [bi: ə'freɪd] sich fürchten; Angst haben II
to be allowed to (do sth) [bi: ə'laʊd tə] (etw.) dürfen IV U2, 33
to be around [bi: ə'raʊnd] geben; existieren IV U4, 80
to be asleep [bi: ə'sli:p] schlafen III
to be born [bi: 'bɔ:n] geboren werden III
to be called [bi: 'kɔ:ld] heißen; genannt werden II
to be careful [bi: 'keəfl] vorsichtig sein II
to be fed up (with) [bi: fed‿'ʌp (wɪð)] die Nase voll haben (von); sauer sein III
to be good at [bi: 'gʊd‿ət] gut sein in; gut sein bei I
to be homesick [bi: 'həʊmsɪk] Heimweh haben III
to be interested in [bi: 'ɪntrəstɪd‿ɪn] sich interessieren für; interessiert sein an III
to be located [bi: ləʊ'keɪtɪd] sich befinden; liegen <IV U1, 135>
to be made of [bi: 'meɪd‿əv] hergestellt sein aus III
to be right [bi: 'raɪt] recht haben II
to be scared [bi: 'skeəd] Angst haben; erschrocken sein III
to be sick [bi: 'sɪk] sich übergeben I
to be sorry [bi: 'sɒri] leidtun III
to be up to [bi: 'ʌp tə] vorhaben III
beach [bi:tʃ] Strand I
to go beach combing [gəʊ 'bi:tʃ ˌkəʊmɪŋ] den Strand nach Strandgut absuchen II
soy **bean** ['sɔɪ ˌbi:n] Sojabohne IV ZI, 9
grizzly **bear** ['grɪzli ˌbeə] Grizzlybär <IV U1, 30>
*to **beat** [bi:t] besiegen III; schlagen; verprügeln; prügeln IV U3, 62
beat [bi:t] simple past von *to beat* III
beaten ['bi:tn] past participle von *to beat* III
beautiful ['bju:tɪfl] schön; hübsch I
became [bɪ'keɪm] simple past von *to become* II
because [bɪ'kɒz] weil; da I
because of [bɪ'kɒz‿əv] wegen III
*to **become** [bɪ'kʌm] werden; II
become [bɪ'kʌm] past participle von *to become* II
bed [bed] Bett I
bed and breakfast (B & B) [ˌbed‿ən 'brekfəst] Frühstückspension III
to go to bed [ˌgəʊ tə 'bed] ins Bett gehen I
bedroom ['bedrʊm] Schlafzimmer; Kinderzimmer I
beef [bi:f] Rindfleisch II
been [bi:n] past particple von *to be* II
before [bɪ'fɔ:] vorher; zuvor II; bevor; bis zu II; vor IV U3, 61
beginner [bɪ'gɪnə] Anfänger; Anfängerin <IV U5, 143>
beginning [bɪ'gɪnɪŋ] Anfang; Beginn III
behavior *(AE)* [bɪ'heɪvjə] Verhalten IV U2, 38
behind [bɪ'haɪnd] hinter II
to **believe** [bɪ'li:v] glauben II
bell [bel] Glocke II
to **belong** (to) [bɪ'lɒŋ (tə)] gehören (zu) IV U1, 14
belt [belt] Gürtel IV U3, 62
bench [benʃ] Bank; Sitzbank III
best [best] beste II
the best [ðə 'best] die besten II
Best wishes, [ˌbest 'wɪʃɪz] Mit den besten Wünschen, I
best-paid ['bestˌpeɪd] bestbezahlt IV U5, 97
better quality food [ˌbetə 'kwɒləti ˌfu:d] qualitativ besseres Essen <IV U3, 72>
between [bɪ'twi:n] zwischen II
big [bɪg] groß I
big wheel [ˌbɪg 'wi:l] Riesenrad II
bike [baɪk] Fahrrad I
bill [bɪl] Rechnung III

to pay the bill [ˌpeɪ ðə ˈbɪl] die Rechnung bezahlen III
billion [ˈbɪliən] Milliarde IV U1, 13
biography [baɪˈɒɡrəfi] Biografie <III>
Biology [baɪˈɒlədʒi] Biologie I
bird [bɜːd] Vogel III
bird watching [ˈbɜːd ˌwɒtʃɪŋ] Vogelbeobachtung III
birthday [ˈbɜːθdeɪ] Geburtstag I
Happy birthday! [ˌhæpi ˈbɜːθdeɪ] Alles Gute zum Geburtstag! I
biscuit [ˈbɪskɪt] Keks II
dog biscuit [ˈdɒɡ ˌbɪskɪt] Hundekeks II
a **bit** [ə ˈbɪt] ein bisschen; ein wenig II
black [blæk] schwarz I
blanket [ˈblæŋkɪt] Decke; Bettdecke; Wolldecke IV U3, 62
blast [blɑːst] Wahnsinnsspaß IV U2, 34
bled [bled] simple past, past participle von *to bleed* III
*to **bleed** [bliːd] bluten III
blew [bluː] simple past von *to blow* <IV U2, 136>
blockbuster [ˈblɒkˌbʌstə] Kassenschlager; Bestseller <IV U4, 140>
blog [blɒɡ] Blog; Internettagebuch II
blond [blɒnd] blond <IV U4, 77>
bloody [ˈblʌdi] blutig <IV U2, 136>
blouse [blaʊz] Bluse I
*to **blow** [bləʊ] wehen; blasen; pusten <IV U2, 136>
blue [bluː] blau I
blues [bluːz] Blues *(Musikrichtung)* IV U5, 97
board [bɔːd] Tafel I; Brett <IV U3, 72>
on board [ˈɒn bɔːd] an Bord III
boarding school [ˈbɔːdɪŋ ˌskuːl] Internat <IV U2, 137>
boat [bəʊt] Boot II
boat trip [ˈbəʊt ˌtrɪp] Bootsfahrt; Schiffsfahrt II
body [ˈbɒdi] Körper III; Leiche IV U3, 62
body lotion [ˈbɒdi ˌləʊʃn] Körperlotion III
bonus [ˈbəʊnəs] Bonus; Prämie IV U2, 39
book [bʊk] Buch; Heft I
exercise book [ˈeksəsaɪz ˌbʊk] Übungsheft I
to **book** [bʊk] buchen; reservieren IV U4, 76
booklet [ˈbʊklət] Broschüre; Heft IV U5, 102
to **bookmark** [ˈbʊkmɑːk] zu … hinfügen II
boot [buːt] Stiefel II
border [ˈbɔːdə] Grenze IV U1, 19
to cross the border [ˌkrɒs ðə ˈbɔːdə] über die Grenze gehen; die Grenze überschreiten IV U1, 19
bored [bɔːd] gelangweilt IV U3, 57
boring [ˈbɔːrɪŋ] langweilig I
*to be **born** [biː ˈbɔːn] geboren werden III
borough [ˈbʌrə] Stadtteil; Bezirk IV U1, 12
to **borrow** [ˈbɒrəʊ] ausleihen II
boss [bɒs] Boss; Chef; Chefin II
bossy [ˈbɒsi] rechthaberisch IV U2, 39
a **bottle** of [ˈbɒtl] eine Flasche … I
bottle bank [ˈbɒtl bæŋk] Altglascontainer II
bought [bɔːt] simple past von *to buy* I; past participle von *to buy* II
boulevard [ˈbuːləvɑːd] Boulevard <IV U4, 141>
bow [bəʊ] Bogen <IV U2, 136>
bowl [bəʊl] Schale; Schälchen; Schüssel II
bowling [ˈbəʊlɪŋ] Bowlen IV U3, 58
box [bɒks] Box; Kiste I
a box of [bɒks] eine Schachtel … I
telephone box [ˈtelɪfəʊn ˌbɒks] Telefonzelle II
boy [bɔɪ] Junge I
boyfriend [ˈbɔɪfrend] Freund *(in einer Paarbeziehung)* IV U3, 54
brand [brænd] Marke III
brass band [ˌbrɑːs ˈbænd] Blaskapelle; Blasensemble <IV U5, 108>
brave [breɪv] tapfer; mutig III
bread [bred] Brot II
sliced bread [ˌslaɪst ˈbred] in Scheiben geschnittenes Brot III
break [breɪk] Pause IV U2, 39
at break [ət ˈbreɪk] in der Pause I
to take a break [ˌteɪk‿ə ˈbreɪk] Pause machen II
*to **break** [breɪk] brechen; kaputt machen II
breakdancing [ˈbreɪkdɑːnsɪŋ] Breakdance <IV U1, 136>
breakfast [ˈbrekfəst] Frühstück I
bed and breakfast (B & B) [ˌbed‿ən ˈbrekfəst] Frühstückspension III
to have breakfast [ˌhæv ˈbrekfəst] frühstücken I
breast [brest] Brust <IV U3, 72>
to **breathe** [briːð] atmen III; <IV U4, 88>
bridge [brɪdʒ] Brücke II
briefcase [ˈbriːfkeɪs] Aktenkoffer; Aktentasche III
bright [braɪt] hell; leuchtend; strahlend IV ZI, 8
brilliant [ˈbrɪliənt] toll I
*to **bring** [brɪŋ] bringen; mitbringen II
to bring down [ˌbrɪŋ ˈdaʊn] herunterbringen <IV U2, 35>
British [ˈbrɪtɪʃ] britisch II
broadcast [ˈbrɔːdkɑːst] Sendung; Ausstrahlung; Übertragung <IV U5, 97>
brochure [ˈbrəʊʃə] Broschüre; Prospekt III
broke [brəʊk] simple past von *to break* II
broken [ˈbrəʊkn] past participle von *to break* II
brother [ˈbrʌðə] Bruder I
brought [brɔːt] simple past von *to bring* II
brown [braʊn] braun I
speech **bubble** [ˈspiːtʃ ˌbʌbl] Sprechblase <III>
buddy *(infml)* [ˈbʌdi] Kumpel IV U2, 45
buffalo [ˈbʌfləʊ] Büffel <IV U2, 136>
buffet [ˈbʊfeɪ] Büfett III
*to **build** [bɪld] bauen II

builder [ˈbɪldə] Bauarbeiter; Bauarbeiterin II
ship builder [ˈʃɪp ˌbɪldə] Schiffsbauer; Schiffsbauerin III
building [ˈbɪldɪŋ] Gebäude II
built [bɪlt] simple past, past participle von *to build* II
light **bulb** [ˈlaɪt ˌbʌlb] Glühbirne III
bullet [ˈbʊlɪt] Kugel; Geschoss IV U3, 63
burger [ˈbɜːgə] Hamburger II
*to **burn** [bɜːn] verbrennen; brennen III
burnt [bɜːnt] simple past, past participle von *to burn* III
bus [bʌs] Bus I
bus stop [ˈbʌs ˌstɒp] Bushaltestelle II
on the bus [ˌɒn ðə ˈbʌs] im Bus II
bushy [ˈbʊʃi] buschig <IV U4, 77>
business [ˈbɪznɪs] Geschäft; Branche <IV U2, 137>
businessman [ˈbɪznɪsmæn] Geschäftsmann IV U4, 84
busy [ˈbɪzi] beschäftigt I
a busy day [ə ˌbɪzi ˈdeɪ] ein ausgefüllter Tag I
but [bʌt] aber I
butcher's [ˈbʊtʃəz] Metzgerei III
butter [ˈbʌtə] Butter I
peanut butter [ˌpiːnʌt ˈbʌtə] Erdnussbutter III
*to **buy** [baɪ] kaufen I
by [baɪ] von II; bis (spätestens) III
to go by (train) [ˌgəʊ baɪ (ˈtreɪn)] mit (dem Zug) fahren I
Bye! [baɪ] Tschüss! I

C

cabbage [ˈkæbɪdʒ] Kohl; Kraut II
cable **car** [ˈkeɪbl ˌkɑː] Seilbahn IV U4, 74
café [ˈkæfeɪ] Café I
cafeteria [kæfəˈtɪəriə] Cafeteria; Mensa I
cage [keɪdʒ] Käfig I
cake [keɪk] Kuchen I
piece of cake [ˈpiːs‿əv keɪk] einfach <IV U3, 68>
calculator [ˈkælkjəleɪtə] (Taschen-)Rechner I
call [kɔːl] Anruf; Ruf III
phone call [ˈfəʊn ˌkɔːl] Telefonanruf I
call-and-response [ˌkɔːlənrɪˈspɒns] Ruf-Antwort <IV U5, 108>
to **call** [kɔːl] rufen; anrufen II
to be called [biː ˈkɔːld] heißen; genannt werden II
caller [ˈkɔːlə] Anrufer; Anruferin III
calorie [ˈkælri] Kalorie <IV U3, 72>
came [keɪm] simple past von *to come* I
camel [ˈkæml] Kamel III
camera [ˈkæmrə] Fotoapparat; Kamera <III>
camp [kæmp] Camp; Lager II
camper [ˈkæmpə] Camper; Camperin <IV U1, 30>
camping [ˈkæmpɪŋ] Camping; Zelten III
to go camping [ˌgəʊ ˈkæmpɪŋ] campen gehen; zelten II
campsite [ˈkæmpsaɪt] Campingplatz; Zeltplatz III
campus [ˈkæmpəs] Campus; Schulgelände IV U2, 35
a **can** of [kæn] eine Dose … I
can [kæn; kən] können I
Can I come back for it later? [kæn aɪ kʌm ˌbæk fər‿ɪt ˈleɪtə] Kann ich später nochmal wiederkommen? I
can't [kɑːnt] nicht können I
canary [kəˈneəri] Kanarienvogel III
candle [ˈkændl] Kerze I
cannon [ˈkænən] Kanone II
cannon ball [ˈkænən ˌbɔːl] Kanonenkugel II
cannot [ˈkænɒt] nicht können III
canoe [kəˈnuː] Kanu <IV U2, 136>
canoeing [kəˈnuːɪŋ] Kanufahren I
canvas [ˈkænvəs] Leinwand <IV U1, 134>
cap [kæp] Kappe; Mütze I
capital (city) [ˈkæpɪtl (ˌsɪti)] Hauptstadt III
captain [ˈkæptɪn] Kapitän; Kapitänin I
caption [ˈkæpʃn] Untertitel; Bildunterschrift <II>
car [kɑː] Auto I
car park [ˈkɑː ˌpɑːk] Parkplatz <IV U1, 15>
caravan [ˈkærəvæn] Wohnwagen III
card [kɑːd] Karte; Spielkarte II
prompt card [ˈprɒmt ˌkɑːd] Stichwortkarte <II>
cardboard [ˈkɑːdbɔːd] Pappe; Karton III
to **care** (for) [ˈkeə (fɔː)] sich kümmern (um) III
to take care of sb [ˌteɪk ˈkeər‿əv] sich um jmdn. kümmern; für jmdn. sorgen IV U2, 41
career [kəˈrɪə] Beruf; Laufbahn; Karriere IV U1, 18
*to be **careful** [biː ˈkeəfl] vorsichtig sein II
caretaker [ˈkeəˌteɪkə] Hausmeister; Hausmeisterin I
carnival [ˈkɑːnɪvl] Karneval; Fasching I
carpenter [ˈkɑːpəntə] Zimmermann; Zimmerin; Tischler; Tischlerin II
carpet [ˈkɑːpɪt] Teppich I; <IV U4, 140>
carrot [ˈkærət] Karotte II
to **carry** [ˈkæri] tragen III
cart [kɑːt] Stand IV U1, 14
cartoon [kɑːˈtuːn] Cartoon; Zeichentrickfilm <IV U4, 81>
court **case** [ˈkɔːt ˌkeɪs] Gerichtsverhandlung; Rechtsfall IV U5, 107
pencil **case** [ˈpensl ˌkeɪs] Federmäppchen I
casino [kəˈsiːnəʊ] Kasino; Spielkasino <IV U2, 137>
cast [kɑːst] Gips III
castle [ˈkɑːsl] Schloss; Burg II
cat [kæt] Katze I
*to **catch** [kætʃ] finden <IV U4, 77>
to catch up with [ˌkætʃ‿ˈʌp wɪð] einholen IV U3, 62

I didn't catch that. [aɪ ˌdɪdnt 'kætʃ ðæt] Das habe ich nicht verstanden.; Das habe ich nicht gehört. IV U5, 102

catchy ['kætʃi] eingängig; einprägsam IV U4, 77

category ['kætəgri] Kategorie <IV U4, 140>

catering college ['keɪtərɪŋ ˌkɒlɪdʒ] Hotelfachschule II

cathedral [kə'θi:drl] Dom; Kathedrale <IV U1, 187>

Catholic ['kæθlɪk] Katholik; Katholikin; katholisch III

to **cause** [kɔ:z] verursachen IV U4, 86

'cause (= because) [kɒz] weil <IV U2, 35>

cave [keɪv] Höhle II

ceiling ['si:lɪŋ] Zimmerdecke IV U1, 14

to **celebrate** ['seləbreɪt] feiern I

celebration [ˌselə'breɪʃn] Feier IV U3, 52

celebrity [sə'lebrəti] Prominenter; Prominente; berühmte Person IV U5, 97

cemetery ['semətri] Friedhof <IV U3, 138>

center *(AE)* ['sentə] Zentrum; Mitte; Center IV U1, 13

centimetre (cm) ['sentɪˌmi:tə] Zentimeter (cm) I

centre ['sentə] Zentrum; Mitte; Center III

activity centre [æk'tɪvəti ˌsentə] Jugendzentrum III

city centre [ˌsɪti 'sentə] Stadtzentrum; Stadtmitte III

shopping centre ['ʃɒpɪŋ ˌsentə] Einkaufszentrum I

in the centre of [ˌɪn ðə 'sentər‿əv] in der Mitte von III

century ['senʃri] Jahrhundert III

cereal ['sɪəriəl] Müsli; Cornflakes III

ceremony ['serɪməni] Zeremonie <IV U4, 140>

certain ['sɜ:tn] bestimmt; sicher <IV U1, 24>

cevapcici [səvæp'tʃətʃi] Cevapcici <IV U5, 213>

chair [tʃeə] Stuhl I

chance [tʃɑ:ns] Chance; Gelegenheit; Möglichkeit II

change [tʃeɪndʒ] Münzgeld; Wechselgeld II

to **change** [tʃeɪndʒ] wechseln II; verändern; (sich) ändern; umsteigen III

to change one's mind [ˌtʃeɪndʒ wʌnz 'maɪnd] seine Meinung ändern III

character ['kærəktə] Charakter <IV U1, 24>

charades [ʃə'rɑ:dz] Scharaden <II>

charger ['tʃɑ:dʒə] Ladegerät III

chart [tʃɑ:t] Tabelle; Diagramm <II>

bar chart ['bɑ: ˌtʃɑ:t] Balkendiagramm; Säulendiagramm <IV U1, 27>

pie chart ['paɪ ˌtʃɑ:t] Kuchendiagramm; Tortendiagramm <IV U1, 27>

chaser ['tʃeɪsə] Jäger; Jägerin; Verfolger; Verfolgerin IV U2, 33

video **chat** ['vɪdiəʊ ˌtʃæt] Video-Chat III

to **chat** [tʃæt] chatten; plaudern II

cheap [tʃi:p] billig II

check [tʃek] Kontrolle IV U1, 22

to **check** [tʃek] überprüfen; kontrollieren III

to check in [ˌtʃek‿'ɪn] einchecken III

to check out [ˌtʃek‿'aʊt] auschecken III

checklist ['tʃeklɪst] Checkliste <I>

cheeky ['tʃi:ki] frech III

to **cheer** sb up [ˌtʃɪər‿'ʌp] jmdn. aufheitern; jmdn. aufmuntern III

cheerleader ['tʃɪəˌli:də] Cheerleader *(Mädchen, das in einer Gruppe eine Sportmannschaft anfeuert)* IV U2, 34

cheese [tʃi:z] Käse I

cheesecake ['tʃi:skeɪk] Käsekuchen II

chef [ʃef] Koch; Köchin II

head chef ['hed ʃef] Chefkoch II

chemical additive [ˌkemɪkl 'ædətɪv] chemische Zusatzstoff <IV U3, 72>

chewing gum ['tʃu:ɪŋ ˌgʌm] Kaugummi I

chic [ʃɪk] schick; elegant I

chicken ['tʃɪkɪn] Huhn I; Hühnchen II

children *(pl)* ['tʃɪldrən] Kinder II

to **chill** out [ˌtʃɪl‿'aʊt] chillen; sich entspannen IV U4, 76

chilli ['tʃɪli] Chili II

chilli con carne ['tʃɪli kɒn ˌkɑ:ni] Chili con carne II

Chinese [tʃaɪ'ni:z] chinesisch; Chinesich; aus China; Chinese; Chinesin IV U5, 99

chips *(pl)* [tʃɪps] Pommes I

fish and chips [ˌfɪʃ‿ən 'tʃɪps] Pommes mit Fisch I

chocolate ['tʃɒklət] Schokolade I; Praline IV U3, 54

choice [tʃɔɪs] Auswahl; Wahl IV U5, 102

*to **choose** [tʃu:z] wählen; auswählen II

choreography [ˌkɒri'ɒgrəfi] Choreografie <IV U5, 143>

chorus ['kɔ:rəs] Refrain <I>

chose [tʃəʊz] simple past von *to choose* II

chosen ['tʃəʊzn] past participle von *to choose* II

Christian ['krɪstʃn] christlich IV U3, 53

Christmas ['krɪsməs] Weihnachten I

church [tʃɜ:tʃ] Kirche II

cinema ['sɪnəmə] Kino I

circle ['sɜ:kl] Kreis; Ring III

to **cite** [saɪt] zitieren; anführen <IV U1, 27>

citizen ['sɪtɪzn] Staatsbürger; Staatsbürgerin; Staatsangehöriger; Staatsangehörige IV U1, 18

city ['sɪti] Stadt; Großstadt II

city centre [ˌsɪti 'sentə] Stadtzentrum; Stadtmitte III

civil rights *(pl)* [ˌsɪvl 'raɪts] Bürgerrechte IV U5, 96

Civil War [ˌsɪvl 'wɔ:] Bürgerkrieg <IV U3, 138>

class [klɑ:s] Klasse; Unterricht III; Unterrichtsstunde; Kurs IV U2, 34
classic ['klæsɪk] Klassiker <IV U4, 140>
classmate ['klɑ:smeɪt] Klassenkamerad; Klassenkameradin; Mitschüler; Mitschülerin <II>
classroom ['klɑ:srʊm] Klassenzimmer I
to **clean** [kli:n] sauber machen; putzen I
clean [kli:n] sauber III
vacuum **cleaner** ['vækju:m ˌkli:nə] Staubsauger IV U3, 59
to **clear** the table [ˌklɪə ðə 'teɪbl] den Tisch abräumen II
clear [klɪə] klar; eindeutig; deutlich IV U4, 77
clever ['klevə] schlau; klug; intelligent II
to **click** [klɪk] klicken I
to **climb** [klaɪm] besteigen; steigen; klettern III
climbing ['klaɪmɪŋ] Kletter- IV U4, 78
clip [klɪp] Clip; Ausschnitt; Kurzfilm IV U4, 80
clock [klɒk] Uhr II
alarm clock [ə'lɑ:m ˌklɒk] Wecker I
clock tower ['klɒk ˌtaʊə] Uhrenturm II
o'clock [ə'klɒk] Uhr *(Zeitangabe bei vollen Stunden)* I
to **close** [kləʊz] schließen; zumachen I
close [kləʊs] in der Nähe; nahe III
clothes *(pl)* [kləʊðz] Kleider *(Pl.)*; Kleidung I
cloud [klaʊd] Wolke IV U2, 33
cloudy ['klaʊdi] wolkig I
club [klʌb] Klub; Verein II
clubhouse ['klʌbhaʊs] Klubhaus; Vereinsheim IV U3, 62
clue [klu:] Hinweis; Spur I
coach [kəʊtʃ] Trainer; Trainerin <III>; Reisebus <IV U5, 214>
coal [kəʊl] Kohle III
coast [kəʊst] Küste III
on the coast [ˌɒn ðə 'kəʊst] an der Küste III
coastline ['kəʊstlaɪn] Küste <IV U4, 207>
coat [kəʊt] Jacke I
dress **code** ['dres ˌkəʊd] Kleiderordnung; Bekleidungsvorschriften IV U2, 36
coin [kɔɪn] Münze III
coke [kəʊk] Cola I
cold [kəʊld] kalt I
to get cold [ˌget 'kəʊld] frieren III
collar ['kɒlə] Halsband I
to **collect** [kə'lekt] sammeln I
college ['kɒlɪdʒ] College; Institut IV U1, 19
catering college ['keɪtərɪŋ ˌkɒlɪdʒ] Hotelfachschule II
colonist ['kɒlənɪst] Kolonist; Kolonistin; Siedler; Siedlerin <IV U1, 24>
color *(AE)* ['kʌlə] Farbe IV ZI, 8
colour ['kʌlə] Farbe I
colourful ['kʌləfl] bunt II
comb [kəʊm] Kamm III
combination [ˌkɒmbɪ'neɪʃn] Kombination II
*to **come** [kʌm] kommen I
to come out [kʌm‿'aʊt] hervorkommen II
Come on! [ˌkʌm‿'ɒn] Komm jetzt! I
comedy ['kɒmədi] Komödie III
comfortable ['kʌmftəbl] bequem; angenehm II
comic ['kɒmɪk] Comic(heft) II
comment ['kɒment] Kommentar IV U4, 82
to **communicate** [kə'mju:nɪkeɪt] kommunizieren; sich verständigen IV U4, 80
community [kə'mju:nəti] Gemeinde; Gemeinschaft IV U1, 18
commuter [kə'mju:tə] Pendler; Pendlerin IV U1, 15
company ['kʌmpəni] Firma; Gesellschaft II
to **compare** [kəm'peə] vergleichen I
comparison [kəm'pærɪsn] Vergleich <IV U2, 37>
competition [ˌkɒmpə'tɪʃn] Wettbewerb; Turnier III; Konkurrenz IV U2, 34
to **complete** [kəm'pli:t] vervollständigen I; absolvieren; abschließen <IV U2, 44>; fertigstellen IV U5, 101
computer [ˌkəm'pju:tə] Computer I
computer game [ˌkəm'pju:tə geɪm] Computerspiel I
to **concentrate** ['kɒnsntreɪt] (sich) konzentrieren IV U3, 58
concert ['kɒnsət] Konzert II
to **conclude** [kən'klu:d] schließen; zusammenfassen <IV U3, 201>
conclusion [kən'klu:ʒn] Schlussfolgerung; Schluss III
condition [kən'dɪʃn] Bedingung; Zustand IV U1, 22
confident ['kɒnfɪdnt] selbstsicher; selbstbewusst III
to **confirm** [kən'fɜ:m] bestätigen; bekräftigen IV U4, 84
conflict ['kɒnflɪkt] Konflikt; Auseinandersetzung <IV U5, 99>
confused [kən'fju:zd] verwirrt; wirr III
Congratulations! [kənˌgrætʃu'leɪʃnz] Glückwunsch! II
to **connect** [kə'nekt] verbinden III
connecting [kə'nektɪŋ] verbindend <II>
consent [kən'sent] Zustimmung; Einwilligung <IV U4, 88>
constant ['kɒnstənt] ständig; konstant; stetig; permanent <IV U4, 88>
construction site [kən'strʌkʃn ˌsaɪt] Baustelle IV U1, 15
contact ['kɒntækt] Kontakt IV U3, 58
eye contact [aɪ 'kɒntækt] Augenkontakt <IV U2, 47>
to **contact** ['kɒntækt] sich in Verbindung setzen; kontaktieren <IV U1, 30>
container [kən'teɪnə] Container; Behälter; Behältnis <IV U1, 30>
content ['kɒntent] Inhalt III
to **control** [kən'trəʊl] kontrollieren <IV U3, 68>
convenience food [kən'vi:niəns ˌfu:d] Fertignahrung <IV U3, 72>

conversation [ˌkɒnvə'seɪʃn] Konversation; Gespräch; Unterhaltung <IV U4, 76>
convinced [kən'vɪnst] überzeugt IV U3, 59
to **cook** [kʊk] kochen II
to **cool** [ku:l] kühlen III
cool [ku:l] cool; super; kühl I
to keep cool [ˌki:p 'ku:l] Ruhe bewahren <III>
cooperative [kəʊ'ɒprətɪv] kooperativ; hilfsbereit IV U2, 38
copy ['kɒpi] Kopie II; Abschrift <III>; Exemplar IV U5, 97
to **copy** ['kɒpi] kopieren II; abschreiben <III>
corn [kɔ:n] Korn; Mais; Getreide IV ZI, 9
corner ['kɔ:nə] Ecke III
corner shop ['kɔ:nə ˌʃɒp] Tante-Emma-Laden I
Cornish ['kɔ:nɪʃ] Cornish; aus Cornwall II
to **correct** [kə'rekt] verbessern I
correct [kə'rekt] richtig; korrekt <III>
corridor ['kɒrɪdɔ:] Gang; Flur; Korridor III
*to **cost** [kɒst] kosten III
cost [kɒst] simple past, past participle von *to cost* III
costume ['kɒstju:m] Kostüm I
cosy ['kəʊzi] gemütlich III
cottage ['kɒtɪdʒ] Häuschen III
cotton ['kɒtn] Baumwolle III
to **cough** [kɒf] husten III
could [kʊd] konnte; könnte III
to **count** [kaʊnt] zählen IV U5, 105
country ['kʌntri] ländliche Gegend; Land I; Country *(Musikrichtung)* IV U5, 97
country and western music [ˌkʌntri ənd 'westən ˌmju:zɪk] Countrymusik <IV U5, 143>
countryside ['kʌntrɪsaɪd] Landschaft; Land III
couple of [kʌpl‿əv] paar <IV U3, 72>
courage ['kʌrɪdʒ] Mut; Tapferkeit; Courage IV U5, 107
course [kɔ:s] Kurs III
main course [ˌmeɪn 'kɔ:s] Hauptgericht II
of course [əv 'kɔ:s] natürlich; selbstverständlich II
court [kɔ:t] Spielfeld III; Gericht IV U5, 107
court case ['kɔ:t ˌkeɪs] Gerichtsverhandlung; Rechtsfall IV U5, 107
cousin ['kʌzn] Cousin; Cousine II
to **cover** ['kʌvə] bedecken; abdecken IV U3, 58
to cover in flour [ˌkʌvər‿ɪn 'flaʊə] in Mehl wenden IV U5, 98
cow [kaʊ] Kuh III
co-worker ['kəʊˌwɜ:kə] Arbeitskollege; Arbeitskollegin IV U2, 38
cranberry ['krænbri] Cranberry; Preiselbeer- <IV U3, 72>
crazy ['kreɪzi] verrückt I
to drive sb crazy [ˌdraɪv … 'kreɪzi] jmdn. verrückt machen III
creative [kri'eɪtɪv] kreativ <IV U4, 90>
creepy ['kri:pi] gruselig IV U3, 53
crew [kru:] Crew; Besatzung; Mannschaft III
cricket ['krɪkɪt] Kricket II
crisp [krɪsp] Kartoffelchip I
Croatian [krəʊ'eɪʃn] kroatisch; Kroatisch; aus Kroatien; Kroate; Kroatin <IV U5, 213>
crocodile ['krɒkədaɪl] Krokodil I
to **cross** [krɒs] überqueren III
to cross the border [ˌkrɒs ðə 'bɔ:də] über die Grenze gehen; die Grenze überschreiten IV U1, 19
crowd [kraʊd] Menschenmenge II
crowded ['kraʊdɪd] überfüllt IV U1, 22
Cuban ['kju:bən] kubanisch; aus Kuba; Kubaner; Kubanerin IV U1, 21
cuddly ['kʌdli] knuddelig III
cuddly toy ['kʌdli ˌtɔɪ] Kuscheltier III
cultural ['kʌltʃrl] kulturell IV U1, 13
cultural movement [ˌkʌltʃrl 'mu:vmənt] Kulturbewegung IV U1, 13
culture ['kʌltʃə] Kultur IV U5, 97
cup [kʌp] Tasse II
cupboard ['kʌbəd] Schrank III
currency ['kʌrnsi] Währung IV ZI, 8
curry ['kʌri] Curry II
custard ['kʌstəd] Vanillesauce II
custom ['kʌstəm] Brauch; Sitte IV U5, 97
customer ['kʌstəmə] Kunde; Kundin III
*to **cut** [kʌt] schneiden III
cut [kʌt] simple past, past participle von *to cut* III
cute [kju:t] niedlich; süß II
cyberbullying ['saɪbəˌbʊliɪŋ] Cyber-Mobbing IV U4, 80
cycling ['saɪklɪŋ] Radfahren III

D

dad [dæd] Papa; Vati I
daily ['deɪli] täglich III
dairy product ['deəri ˌprɒdʌkt] Milchprodukt; Milcherzeugnis <IV U3, 72>
dance [dɑ:ns] Tanz III
folk dance ['fəʊk ˌdɑ:ns] Volkstanz <IV U5, 143>
line dance ['laɪn ˌdɑ:ns] Line Dance *(alle tanzen zusammen in einer Reihe)* <IV U5, 143>
to **dance** [dɑ:ns] tanzen I
dancer ['dɑ:nsə] Tänzer; Tänzerin I
dancing ['dɑ:nsɪŋ] Tanzen; Tanz- IV U2, 43
dangerous ['deɪndʒrəs] gefährlich III
daredevil ['deəˌdevl] Draufgänger; Draufgängerin IV U3, 53
the **dark** [ðə 'dɑ:k] Dunkelheit III
dark [dɑ:k] dunkel I
data ['deɪtə] Daten; Angaben <IV U1, 26>
date [deɪt] Zeitpunkt; Datum I; Verabredung; Date IV U2, 42
daughter ['dɔ:tə] Tochter I
day [deɪ] Tag I
a busy day [ə ˌbɪzi 'deɪ] ein ausgefüllter Tag I
all day [ˌɔ:l 'deɪ] den ganzen Tag III

lucky day [ˌlʌki ˈdeɪ] Glückstag II
one day [wʌn ˈdeɪ] eines Tages III
four hours a day [ˌfɔːr aʊəz‿ə ˈdeɪ] vier Stunden täglich I
dead [ded] tot III
deadly [ˈdedli] tod-; tödlich III
deaf [def] gehörlos; schwerhörig; taub III
*to **deal** (with) [diːl (wɪð)] sich befassen mit; umgehen mit IV U3, 73
dealt (with) [delt (wɪð)] simple past, past participle von *to deal (with)* IV U3, 73
Dear …, [dɪə] Liebe(r) …, *(Anrede in Briefen)* I
death [deθ] Tod <IV U5, 108>
December [dɪˈsembə] Dezember I
to **decide** [dɪˈsaɪd] (sich) entscheiden III
decision [dɪˈsɪʒn] Entscheidung IV U1, 18
to **defeat** [dɪˈfiːt] besiegen <IV U3, 138>
definition [ˌdefɪˈnɪʃn] Definition <III>
degree [dɪˈgriː] Grad IV U5, 102
delicious [dɪˈlɪʃəs] köstlich II
department [dɪˈpɑːtmənt] Abteilung II
department store [dɪˈpɑːtmənt ˌstɔː] Kaufhaus II
to **describe** [dɪˈskraɪb] beschreiben IV U3, 73
design [dɪˈzaɪn] Design; Gestaltung IV U4, 77
Design Technology (DT) [dɪˌzaɪn tekˈnɒlədʒi, ˌdiːˈtiː] Technik I
to **design** [dɪˈzaɪn] entwerfen; gestalten <III>
desk [desk] Schreibtisch IV U3, 62
information desk [ɪnfəˈmeɪʃn ˌdesk] Information II
dessert [dɪˈzɜːt] Nachspeise II
to **destroy** [dɪˈstrɔɪ] zerstören <IV U5, 142>
detail [ˈdiːteɪl] Detail; Einzelheit IV U5, 102
detective [dɪˈtektɪv] Detektiv; Detektivin <I>
detention [dɪˈtenʃn] Nachsitzen IV U2, 35
to **develop** [dɪˈveləp] entwickeln IV U4, 75
device [dɪˈvaɪs] Gerät; Vorrichtung IV U3, 58
dialogue [ˈdaɪəlɒg] Dialog; Gespräch <I>
diamond [ˈdaɪəmənd] Diamant <II>
diary [ˈdaɪəri] Tagebuch I
dictionary [ˈdɪkʃnri] Wörterbuch <III>
did [dɪd] simple past von *to do* I
to **die** [daɪ] sterben III
difficult [ˈdɪfɪklt] schwierig II
difficulty [ˈdɪfɪklti] Schwierigkeit <IV U4, 88>
dining room [ˈdaɪnɪŋ ˌrʊm] Esszimmer I
dinner [ˈdɪnə] Mittagessen; Abendessen II
direct speech [dɪˌrekt ˈspiːtʃ] direkte Rede <IV U5, 110>
direction [dɪˈrekʃn] Richtung IV U2, 33
directions [dɪˈrekʃnz] Anweisungen; Wegbeschreibung <III>
director [dɪˈrektə] Regisseur; Regisseurin II
dirty [ˈdɜːti] dreckig; schmutzig I
to **disagree** [ˌdɪsəˈgriː] anderer Meinung sein; nicht einverstanden sein II
to **disappear** [ˌdɪsəˈpɪə] verschwinden IV U3, 62
disaster [dɪˈzɑːstə] Katastrophe; Desaster; Unglück III
to **discover** [dɪˈskʌvə] entdecken <IV U2, 136>
discovery [dɪˈskʌvri] Entdeckung IV U4, 84
discrimination [dɪˌskrɪmɪˈneɪʃn] Diskriminierung IV U5, 96
to **discuss** [dɪˈskʌs] diskutieren <IV U3, 59>
disease [dɪˈziːz] Krankheit IV U1, 22
dish [dɪʃ] Gericht; Speise II
dishwasher [ˈdɪʃˌwɒʃə] Spülmaschine IV U3, 59
to **dislike** [dɪˈslaɪk] nicht mögen IV U4, 81
distance [ˈdɪstns] Entfernung; Distanz IV ZI, 9
in the distance [ˌɪn ðə ˈdɪstns] in der Ferne IV U1, 15
to **distract** sb (from sth) [dɪˈstrækt (frəm)] jmdn. (von etw.) ablenken <IV U2, 47>
to **divide** (up) [dɪˈvaɪd (ʌp)] teilen; aufteilen; unterteilen <IV U4, 79>
DJing [ˌdiːˈdʒeɪɪŋ] Musikauflegen <IV U1, 134>
*to **do** [duː] machen; tun I
to do homework [ˌduː ˈhəʊmwɜːk] Hausaufgabe(n) machen I
to do the right thing [ˌduː ðə ˈraɪt θɪŋ] das Richtige tun III
to do the shopping [ˌduː ðə ˈʃɒpɪŋ] Einkäufe machen; Besorgungen machen II
to do the washing up [ˌduː ðə ˈwɒʃɪŋ‿ʌp] abspülen II
doctor [ˈdɒktə] Arzt; Ärztin II
document [ˈdɒkjəmənt] Dokument <IV U3, 139>
documentary [ˌdɒkjəˈmentri] Dokumentarfilm <IV U4, 140>
dog [dɒg] Hund I
dog biscuit [ˈdɒg ˌbɪskɪt] Hundekeks II
dog walker [ˈdɒg ˌwɔːkə] Hundeausführer; Hundeausführerin IV U2, 41
to take the dog for a walk [ˌteɪk ðə dɒg fɔːr‿ə ˈwɔːk] den Hund ausführen I
dollar [ˈdɒlə] Dollar *(amer. Währungseinheit)* IV ZI, 8
dome [dəʊm] Kuppel II
done [dʌn] past participle von *to do* II
door [dɔː] Tür II
doorbell [ˈdɔːbel] Türklingel IV U3, 54
to **doubt** [daʊt] bezweifeln IV U3, 59
down [daʊn] entlang; herunter; hinunter III; traurig III

down there [ˌdaʊn 'ðeə] dahin; da unten IV U5, 98
to **download** [ˌdaʊn'ləʊd] herunterladen II
downtown *(AE)* [ˌdaʊn'taʊn] im Stadtzentrum <IV U1, 15>
Dr ['dɒktə] Dr. *(Anrede)* III
draft [drɑ:ft] Entwurf <II>
to **drag** [dræg] schleppen; schleifen; ziehen IV U5, 107
drama ['drɑ:mə] Theater II; Drama III
drank [dræŋk] simple past von *to drink* II
*to **draw** [drɔ:] zeichnen II
drawn [drɔ:n] past participle von *to draw* II
dreadful ['dredfl] furchtbar III
dream [dri:m] Traum II
*to **dream** [dri:m] träumen III
dreamt [dremt] simple past, past participle von *to dream* III
dress [dres] Kleid II
dress code ['dres ˌkəʊd] Kleiderordnung; Bekleidungsvorschriften IV U2, 36
fancy dress [ˌfænsi 'dres] Verkleidung; Kostüm I
dressed (as) [drest] angezogen (wie); verkleidet (als) III
to get dressed [ˌget 'drest] sich anziehen II
drew [dru:] simple past von *to draw* II
drink [drɪŋk] Getränk II
*to **drink** [drɪŋk] trinken II
anything to drink ['eniθɪŋ tə 'drɪŋk] etwas zu trinken II
drive [draɪv] Fahrt; Autofahrt III
*to **drive** [draɪv] fahren; treiben IV U2, 33
to drive sb crazy [ˌdraɪv … 'kreɪzi] jmdn. verrückt machen III
driven ['drɪvn] past participle von *to drive* IV U2, 33
driver ['draɪvə] Fahrer; Fahrerin III
driver's license *(AE)* ['draɪvəz ˌlaɪsns] Führerschein <IV U2, 44>
lorry driver ['lɒri ˌdraɪvə] LKW-Fahrer; LKW-Fahrerin II
driving ['draɪvɪŋ] Fahren; Fahr- <IV U2, 44>
driving school ['draɪvɪŋ ˌsku:l] Fahrschule <IV U2, 44>
drove [drəʊv] *simple past von to drive* IV U2, 33
drug [drʌg] Droge <IV U3, 72>
drumming ['drʌmɪŋ] Trommel- III
drunk [drʌŋk] past participle von *to drink* II; betrunken IV U3, 63
dry [draɪ] trocken III
dull [dʌl] langweilig; matt IV U4, 77
dumpling ['dʌmplɪŋ] Kloß II
during ['djʊərɪŋ] während III

E

each [i:tʃ] jede <III>
each other [ˌi:tʃ‿'ʌðə] einander; sich; sich gegenseitig III
each [i:tʃ] pro Stück II
bald **eagle** [ˌbɔ:ld 'i:gl] Weißkopfseeadler IV ZI, 8
ear [ɪə] Ohr II
early ['ɜ:li] früh III
to **earn** [ɜ:n] verdienen IV U2, 38
east [i:st] Osten III
east of ['i:st‿əv] östlich von IV ZI, 9
Easter ['i:stə] Ostern IV U3, 56
easy ['i:zi] einfach; leicht I
*to **eat** [i:t] essen I
eaten ['i:tn] past participle von *to eat* II
edition [ɪ'dɪʃn] Ausgabe; Auflage; Edition IV U4, 84
education [ˌedʒʊ'keɪʃn] Ausbildung; Erziehung; Bildung IV U2, 38
effect [ɪ'fekt] Effekt; Wirkung <IV U3, 72>
special effect [ˌspeʃl ɪ'fekt] Spezialeffekt <IV U4, 140>
egg [eg] Ei II
scrambled egg [ˌskræmbld‿'eg] Rührei II
eight [eɪt] acht I
eighteen [ˌeɪ'ti:n] achtzehn I
eighty ['eɪti] achtzig I
not … **either** [nɒt … 'aɪðə] auch nicht III
elective [ɪ'lektɪv] Wahlfach IV U2, 34
electric [ɪ'lektrɪk] elektrisch IV U3, 59
electricity [ˌelɪk'trɪsəti] Strom; Elektrizität III
element ['elɪmənt] Element <IV U5, 143>
elephant ['elɪfənt] Elefant I
elevator *(AE)* ['elɪveɪtə] Aufzug; Lift IV U1, 13
eleven [ɪ'levn] elf I
e-mail ['i:meɪl] E-Mail II
embarrassed [ɪm'bærəst] verlegen II
embarrassing [ɪm'bærəsɪŋ] peinlich IV U2, 42
emergency [ɪ'mɜ:dʒnsi] Notfall III
emergency call [ɪ'mɜ:dʒnsi ˌkɔ:l] Notruf III
emergency service [ɪ'mɜ:dʒnsi ˌsɜ:vɪs] Notdienst; Rettungsdienst III
to **emigrate** ['emɪgreɪt] auswandern; emigrieren IV U1, 18
emotion [ɪ'məʊʃn] Gefühl; Emotion <IV U5, 110>
to **emphasize** ['emfəsaɪz] betonen <IV U2, 51>
to **employ** [ɪm'plɔɪ] einstellen; anstellen; beschäftigen <IV U4, 88>
encyclopedia [ɪnˌsaɪklə'pi:diə] Enzyklopädie; Lexikon IV U4, 86
end [end] Ende; Schluss II
in the end [ɪn ði 'end] schließlich; zum Schluss II
to **end** [end] enden; beenden; aufhören IV U2, 34
ending ['endɪŋ] Schluss; Ende III
enemy ['enəmi] Feind; Feindin III
energetic [ˌenə'dʒetɪk] tatkräftig IV U4, 89
engine ['endʒɪn] Motor IV U3, 54
steam engine ['sti:m‿endʒɪn] Dampfmaschine III
engineer [ˌendʒɪ'nɪə] Ingenieur; Ingenieurin; Techniker; Technikerin II
English ['ɪŋglɪʃ] Englisch I

the English [ði 'ɪŋglɪʃ] die Engländer III
to enjoy [ɪn'dʒɔɪ] mögen; genießen III
enough [ɪ'nʌf] genug; genügend III
to enter ['entə] hineingehen; hereinkommen; betreten; eintreten IV U3, 54
entertainment *(no pl)* [ˌentə'teɪnmənt] Unterhaltung <IV U4, 90>
entry ['entri] Eintrag IV U4, 86; Einfluss <IV U5, 214>
entry form ['entri ˌfɔ:m] Anmeldeformular II
equipment [ɪ'kwɪpmənt] Ausrüstung III
Victorian **era** [vɪkˌtɔ:riən 'ɪərə] viktorianisches Zeitalter III
eraser [ɪ'reɪzə] Radiergummi I
escalator ['eskəleɪtə] Rolltreppe II
to escape [ɪ'skeɪp] entkommen; fliehen; entfliehen; flüchten IV U1, 23
estimate ['estɪmeɪt] Schätzung <IV U4, 88>
ethnic ['eθnɪk] ethnisch; Volks- <IV U1, 26>
euro ['jʊərəʊ] Euro *(Währung)* III
European [ˌjʊərə'pi:ən] europäisch; Europäisch; aus Europa; Europäer; Europäerin IV U2, 32
even ['i:vn] noch; sogar II
evening ['i:vnɪŋ] Abend I
in the evenings [ɪn ði 'i:vnɪŋz] abends III
event [ɪ'vent] Ereignis; Veranstaltung IV U1, 13
sporting event ['spɔ:tɪŋ ɪˌvent] Sportereignis; Sportveranstaltung <IV U2, 50>
ever ['evə] jemals II
every ['evri] jede I; alle III
everybody ['evribɒdi] jeder; alle IV U3, 53
everyone ['evriwʌn] jeder I; zusammen; alle II
everything ['evriθɪŋ] alles II
exact [ɪg'zækt] exakt; genau III
exactly [ɪg'zæktli] genau IV U3, 59
example [ɪg'zɑ:mpl] Beispiel IV U1, 18
for example [fər‿ɪg'zɑ:mpl] zum Beispiel IV U2, 34
excellent ['ekslnt] exzellent; hervorragend IV U5, 102
except [ɪk'sept] außer III
exchange [ɪks'tʃeɪndʒ] Austausch IV U2, 34
to exchange [ɪks'tʃeɪndʒ] tauschen; austauschen <III>
excited [ɪk'saɪtɪd] aufgeregt; begeistert II
excitement [ɪk'saɪtmənt] Aufregung IV U4, 86
exciting [ɪk'saɪtɪŋ] spannend; aufregend I
Excuse me. [ɪk'skju:z mi] Entschuldigung. I
exercise book ['eksəsaɪz ˌbʊk] Übungsheft I
exhausted [ɪg'zɔ:stɪd] erschöpft III
to expect [ɪk'spekt] erwarten III
expensive [ɪk'spensɪv] teuer II
experience [ɪk'spɪəriəns] Erfahrung IV U5, 109
to experience [ɪk'spɪəriəns] erleben; erfahren <IV U1, 134>
experiment [ɪk'sperɪmənt] Versuch II
expert ['ekspɜ:t] Experte; Expertin IV U4, 77
to explain [ɪk'spleɪn] erklären III
to explode [ɪk'spləʊd] explodieren III
to explore [ɪk'splɔ:] erkunden; erforschen II
explosion [ɪk'spləʊʒn] Explosion III
extra ['ekstrə] zusätzlich; Zusatz- II
extra practice [ˌekstrə 'præktɪs] Zusatzübungen <I>
extracurricular [ˌekstrəkə'rɪkjələ] außerhalb des Lehrplans; außerunterrichtlich *(Zusatzangebot)* IV U2, 34
extreme [ɪk'stri:m] Extreme <IV U1, 30>
extremely [ɪk'stri:mli] äußerst; sehr IV U4, 80
eye [aɪ] Auge II
eye contact [aɪ 'kɒntækt] Augenkontakt <IV U2, 47>

F

fable ['feɪbl] Fabel; Märchen III
face [feɪs] Gesicht I
to face [feɪs] schauen <IV U5, 143>
fact [fækt] Fakt; Tatsache II
factory ['fæktri] Fabrik; Werk III
to fail (at) [feɪl (ət)] versagen (in/bei); ausfallen; fehlschlagen IV U1, 19
failed [feɪld] fehlgeschlagen; gescheitert; erfolglos <IV U4, 88>
fall *(AE)* [fɔ:l] Herbst IV ZI, 8
*to **fall** [fɔ:l] fallen; hinfallen I
to fall (over) [ˌfɔ:l‿'əʊvə] fallen; hinfallen; umfallen III
to fall asleep [ˌfɔ:l‿ə'sli:p] einschlafen III
to fall behind [ˌfɔ:l bɪ'haɪnd] zurückfallen <IV U2, 35>
to fall in love (with) [ˌfɔ:l‿ɪn 'lʌv] sich verlieben (in) III
to fall out of [ˌfɔ:l‿'aʊt‿əv] herausfallen aus IV U2, 42
false [fɔ:ls] falsch <IV U3, 201>
familiar [fə'mɪliə] vertraut; bekannt IV U2, 34
family ['fæmli] Familie I
host family ['həʊst ˌfæmli] Gastfamilie IV U2, 34
famine ['fæmɪn] Hungersnot <IV U1, 188>
famous ['feɪməs] berühmt I
fan [fæn] Fan I; Ventilator IV U3, 59
fancy dress [ˌfænsi 'dres] Verkleidung; Kostüm I
fantastic [fæn'tæstɪk] fantastisch; großartig II
fantasy ['fæntəsi] Fantasie; Fantasy II
fantasy trip ['fæntəsi ˌtrɪp] Fantasieausflug I
FAQ (= frequently asked questions) [ˌefeɪ'kju: (ˌfri:kwəntli ˌɑ:skt 'kwestʃənz)] häufig gestellte Fragen <IV U1, 30>

far [fɑː] weit III
fare [feə] Fahrpreis III
farewell speech [feə'wel spiːtʃ] Abschiedsrede II
farm [fɑːm] Bauernhof I
wind farm ['wɪnd fɑːm] Windpark III
farmer ['fɑːmə] Bauer; Bäuerin; Landwirt; Landwirtin I
farmers' market [ˌfɑːməz 'mɑːkɪt] Bauernmarkt <IV U3, 72>
farming ['fɑːmɪŋ] Landwirtschaft; Ackerbau IV U4, 84
farmland ['fɑːmlænd] Ackerland; Ackerboden; Landwirtschaftsflächen IV U2, 32
fascinating ['fæsɪneɪtɪŋ] faszinierend IV U4, 77
fashion *(no pl)* ['fæʃn] Mode IV U3, 58
out of fashion [ˌaʊt‿əv 'fæʃn] altmodisch; nicht mehr aktuell IV U4, 81
fashionable ['fæʃnəbl] modisch II
fast [fɑːst] schnell II
fast food restaurant [ˌfɑːst fuːd 'restrɒnt] Fastfood-Restaurant I
the fastest [ðə 'fɑːstɪst] der/die/das schnellste I
father ['fɑːðə] Vater I
favorite *(AE)* ['feɪvrɪt] Lieblings- IV U4, 80
favourite ['feɪvrɪt] Lieblings- I
feature ['fiːtʃə] Merkmal <III>
feature story ['fiːtʃə ˌstɔːri] Leitartikel; Sonderbericht <IV U5, 110>
February ['februri] Februar I
fed [fed] simple past von *to feed* I; past participle von *to feed* II
*to be **fed** up (with) [biː fed‿'ʌp (wɪð)] die Nase voll haben (von); sauer sein III
federal ['fedrl] Bundes-; föderalistisch <IV U4, 88>
fee [fiː] Gebühr <IV U3, 66>
*to **feed** [fiːd] füttern I
feedback ['fiːdbæk] Feedback; Rückmeldung IV U2, 39
*to **feel** [fiːl] (sich) fühlen II
to feel sick [ˌfiːl 'sɪk] Übelkeit verspüren; sich schlecht fühlen IV U5, 103
to feel sorry [ˌfiːl 'sɒri fə] Mitleid haben mit; bedauern III
to make sb feel like sth [ˌmeɪk … 'fiːl laɪk] jmdm. das Gefühl geben, etw. zu sein III
feeling ['fiːlɪŋ] Gefühl <III>
foot *(sg)* [fʊt], **feet** *(pl)* [fiːt] Fuß I
fell [fel] simple past von *to fall* I
felt-tip [ˌfelt'tɪp] Filzstift I
felt [felt] simple past von *to feel* II
fever ['fiːvə] Fieber IV U4, 84
few [fjuː] wenige IV U1, 23
a few [ə 'fjuː] ein paar; wenige; einige III
science **fiction** [ˌsaɪəns 'fɪkʃn] Science-Fiction I
fictional ['fɪkʃnl] fiktiv <IV U1, 135>
field [fiːld] Feld; Wiese; Weide IV ZI, 9
field goal ['fiːld ˌgəʊl] Feldtor <IV U2, 50>
field trip ['fiːld ˌtrɪp] Schulausflug <IV U2, 46>
fifteen [ˌfɪf'tiːn] fünfzehn I
fifty ['fɪfti] fünfzig I
fight [faɪt] Kampf; Streit III
*to **fight** [faɪt] kämpfen; (sich) streiten III
file [faɪl] Datei II
filled with ['fɪld ˌwɪð] gefüllt mit <IV U3, 72>
film [fɪlm] Film I
film maker ['fɪlm ˌmeɪkə] Filmemacher; Filmemacherin <III>
to **film** [fɪlm] filmen; drehen <III>
filming ['fɪlmɪŋ] Filmen; Drehen <IV U3, 54>
final match [ˌfaɪnl 'mætʃ] Endspiel <IV U2, 50>
finally ['faɪnli] schließlich; zum Schluss II
financial [faɪ'nænʃl] finanziell; Finanz- IV U1, 14
*to **find** [faɪnd] finden; herausfinden I
to find out [ˌfaɪnd‿'aʊt] herausfinden I
fine [faɪn] gut; in Ordnung; schön II
finger ['fɪŋgə] Finger III
fingerprint ['fɪŋgəprɪnt] Fingerabdruck II
to **finish** ['fɪnɪʃ] beenden; enden; aufhören; fertigstellen; vervollständigen II
fire [faɪə] Feuer II
fire engine ['faɪər‿ˌendʒɪn] Feuerwehrauto II
firework ['faɪəwɜːk] Feuerwerk <IV U3, 139>
first [fɜːst] zuerst; als Erstes; erste I
the first time [ðə ˌfɜːst 'taɪm] das erste Mal I
fish *(sg)* [fɪʃ], **fish** *(pl)* [fɪʃ] Fisch I
fish and chips [ˌfɪʃ‿ən 'tʃɪps] Pommes mit Fisch I
fisherman ['fɪʃəmən] Fischer <IV U2, 136>
fishing ['fɪʃɪŋ] Angeln; Fischen IV U5, 104
to **fit** [fɪt] passen II
to fit (in) [fɪt (ɪn)] hineinpassen (in) <IV U2, 35>
fit [fɪt] fit; in Form III
fitness ['fɪtnəs] Fitness <IV U3, 72>
fitness instructor ['fɪtnəs ɪnˌstrʌktə] Fitnesstrainer; Fitnesstrainerin <IV U3, 72>
jumping fitness ['dʒʌmpɪŋ ˌfɪtnəs] Jumping Fitness *(Trendsportart)* IV U4, 81
five [faɪv] fünf I
flag [flæg] Flagge; Fahne II
flamingo [flə'mɪŋgəʊ] Flamingo I
flat [flæt] Wohnung I
flat [flæt] flach; platt IV U2, 32
flew [fluː] simple past von *to fly* II
flexible ['fleksɪbl] flexibel <IV U3, 68>
flight [flaɪt] Flug IV U3, 52
floor [flɔː] Stockwerk; Etage IV U3, 62
flour [flaʊə] Mehl IV U5, 98
to cover in flour [ˌkʌvər‿ɪn 'flaʊə] in Mehl wenden IV U5, 98
flower ['flaʊə] Blume III

flown [fləʊn] past participle von *to fly* II
fluent ['flu:ənt] fließend; flüssig III
*__to fly__ [flaɪ] fliegen II
flyer ['flaɪə] Flyer; Faltblatt II
foggy ['fɒgi] neblig IV U4, 75
folk dance ['fəʊk ˌdɑ:ns] Volkstanz <IV U5, 143>
to **follow** ['fɒləʊ] befolgen; folgen III
follower ['fɒləʊə] Follower; Followerin; Anhänger; Anhängerin IV U4, 81
food [fu:d] Essen; Lebensmittel I
  convenience food [kən'vi:niəns ˌfu:d] Fertignahrung <IV U3, 72>
  food stall ['fu:d ˌstɔ:l] Essensstand II
  better quality food [ˌbetə 'kwɒləti ˌfu:d] qualitativ besseres Essen <IV U3, 72>
  frozen food ['frəʊzn ˌfu:d] Tiefkühlkost; Tiefkühlprodukte <IV U3, 72>
foot *(sg)* [fʊt], **feet** *(pl)* [fi:t] Fuß I
  to go on foot [ˌgəʊ‿ɒn 'fʊt] zu Fuß gehen I
football ['fʊtbɔ:l] Fußball I
for [fɔ:] für I; seit IV U4, 80
  for five months [fə ˌfaɪv 'mʌnθs] fünf Monate lang I
  for fun [fə 'fʌn] zum Spaß III
forbidden [fə'bɪdn] verboten IV U3, 58
to **force** [fɔ:s] zwingen IV U5, 96
foreground ['fɔ:graʊnd] Vordergrund III
  in the foreground [ɪn ðə 'fɔ:graʊnd] im Vordergrund III
foreign ['fɒrɪn] fremd; ausländisch IV U1, 18
forest ['fɒrɪst] Wald IV U3, 52
to **foretell** [fɔ:'tel] vorhersagen III
forever [fə'revə] für immer; ewig II
*__to forget__ [fə'get] vergessen I
forgot [fə'gɒt] simple past von *to forget* II
forgotten [fə'gɒtn] past participle von *to forget* II
fork [fɔ:k] Gabel II
form [fɔ:m] Form <III>
  approval form [ə'pru:vl ˌfɔ:m] Einverständnisformular <IV U2, 44>
  entry form ['entri ˌfɔ:m] Anmeldeformular II
forty ['fɔ:ti] vierzig I
forward ['fɔ:wəd] vorwärts <IV U2, 137>
fought [fɔ:t] simple past, past participle von *to fight* III
to **found** [faʊnd] gründen IV U5, 98
found [faʊnd] simple past von *to find* II
four [fɔ:] vier I
fourteen [ˌfɔ:'ti:n] vierzehn I
fourth [fɔ:θ] vierte I
land of the **free** [ˌlænd‿əv ðə 'fri:] Land der Freien IV U3, 53
free [fri:] kostenlos III
  free range [ˌfri: 'reɪndʒ] Freiland- II
  free time [ˌfri: 'taɪm] Freizeit I
freedom *(no pl)* ['fri:dəm] Freiheit; Unabhängigkeit IV U1, 23
*__to freeze__ [fri:z] frieren; gefrieren III
freeze frame ['fri:z ˌfreɪm] Standbild <II>
freezing ['fri:zɪŋ] eiskalt; gefrierend IV U3, 54
French [frentʃ] Französisch I
the **French** [ðə 'frenʃ] die Franzosen IV U5, 98
fresh [freʃ] frisch II
Friday ['fraɪdeɪ] Freitag I
fridge [frɪdʒ] Kühlschrank III
fried [fraɪd] (in der Pfanne) gebraten II
friend [frend] Freund; Freundin I
  to make friends [ˌmeɪk 'frendz] Freundschaften schließen I
to **friend** [frend] befreunden *(jmdn. zu seiner Freundesliste hinzufügen)* IV U4, 81
friendly ['frendli] freundlich; nett III
frisbee ['frɪzbi] Frisbeescheibe I
from [frɒm] aus; von I
in **front** of [ɪn 'frʌnt‿əv] vor; davor <III>
froze [frəʊz] simple past von *to freeze* III
frozen ['frəʊzn] past participle von *to freeze* III
  frozen food ['frəʊzn ˌfu:d] Tiefkühlkost; Tiefkühlprodukte <IV U3, 72>
fruit [fru:t] Frucht; Obst I
to **fry** [fraɪ] braten; frittieren IV U5, 98
full [fʊl] vollwertig <IV U2, 136>; voll IV U5, 106
fun [fʌn] Freude; Spaß I
  for fun [fə 'fʌn] zum Spaß III
funeral ['fju:nrəl] Beerdigung; Begräbnis <IV U5, 108>
funny ['fʌni] merkwürdig; komisch; lustig; witzig I
furious ['fjʊəriəs] wütend III
further ['fɜ:ðə] weiter <IV U2, 136>
future ['fju:tʃə] Zukunft IV U1, 18
future ['fju:tʃə] zukünftig IV U1, 22

G

game [geɪm] Spiel I
  computer game [ˌkəm'pju:tə geɪm] Computerspiel I
gamer ['geɪmə] Spieler *(Computer)*; Spielerin *(Computer)* II
street **gang** ['stri:t ˌgæŋ] Straßengang <IV U1, 134>
garbage *(AE)* ['gɑ:bɪdʒ] Müll; Abfall <IV U1, 30>
garden ['gɑ:dn] Garten I
garlic ['gɑ:lɪk] Knoblauch II
gas [gæs] Gas III
gas *(AE)* [gæs] Benzin <IV U3, 66>
gateway ['geɪtweɪ] Tor; Eingangstor IV U1, 12
to **gather** ['gæðə] (sich) sammeln IV U3, 64
gave [geɪv] simple past von *to give* II
gel [dʒel] Gel III
  hair gel ['heə ˌdʒel] Haargel III
  shower gel ['ʃaʊə ˌdʒel] Duschgel III
in **general** [ɪn 'dʒenrl] allgemein; generell IV U3, 73
generation [ˌdʒenə'reɪʃn] Generation <IV U2, 137>
generous ['dʒenrəs] großzügig IV U2, 39

geocaching ['dʒiəʊkæʃɪŋ] Geocaching *(eine Art elektronische Schatzsuche)* I
Geography [dʒi'ɒgrəfi] Geografie; Erdkunde I
German ['dʒɜ:mən] Deutsch I; deutsch; aus Deutschland III
*to **get** [get] bekommen I; verstehen III
to get around [ˌget ə'raʊnd] herumkommen III
to get cold [ˌget 'kəʊld] frieren III
to get dressed [ˌget 'drest] sich anziehen II
to get in ['get‿ɪn] hereinkommen I
to get into [ˌget‿'ɪntə] hineinkommen; hineingelangen IV U1, 14
to get married [ˌget 'mærɪd] heiraten II
to get off [ˌget‿'ɒf] aussteigen II
to get out [ˌget 'aʊt] herauskommen III
to get ready [ˌget 'redi] sich vorbereiten; sich fertig machen IV U3, 54
to get sth [get] etw. verstehen IV U5, 102
to get stuck [ˌget 'stʌk] stecken bleiben IV U3, 54
to get to ['get tə] hinkommen zu; gelangen <IV U1, 14>
to get to know [ˌget tə 'nəʊ] kennen lernen II
to get up [ˌget‿'ʌp] aufstehen I
to get used to (sth) [ˌget 'ju:zd tə] sich an (etw.) gewöhnen IV U1, 18
ghost [gəʊst] Geist II
giant [dʒaɪənt] Riese III
giant [dʒaɪənt] Riesen-; riesig IV U4, 74
giraffe [dʒɪ'rɑ:f] Giraffe I
girl [gɜ:l] Mädchen I
girlfriend ['gɜ:lfrend] Freundin *(in einer Paarbeziehung)* IV U2, 38
*to **give** [gɪv] geben I
to give a talk [ˌgɪv‿ə 'tɔ:k] einen Vortrag halten <III>
to give reasons [ˌgɪv 'ri:znz] Gründe nennen; Gründe angeben III
to give sth a miss [ˌgɪv sʌmθɪŋ‿ə 'mɪs] auf etw. verzichten; etw. bleiben lassen III
to give up [ˌgɪv‿'ʌp] aufgeben IV U4, 84
glad [glæd] froh IV U3, 54
glass [glɑ:s] Glas II
global ['gləʊbl] global; weltweit <IV U1, 134>
glue [glu:] Klebstoff I
*to **go** [gəʊ] gehen; fahren I
to go beach combing [gəʊ 'bi:tʃ ˌkəʊmɪŋ] den Strand nach Strandgut absuchen II
to go by (train) [ˌgəʊ baɪ ('treɪn)] mit (dem Zug) fahren I
to go camping [ˌgəʊ 'kæmpɪŋ] campen gehen; zelten II
to go for a walk [ˌgəʊ fər‿ə 'wɔ:k] spazieren gehen I
to go on foot [ˌgəʊ‿ɒn 'fʊt] zu Fuß gehen I
to go out with [ˌgəʊ‿'aʊt wɪð] gehen mit IV U3, 58
to go shopping [ˌgəʊ 'ʃɒpɪŋ] einkaufen gehen II
to go sightseeing [gəʊ 'saɪtsi:ɪŋ] eine Besichtigungstour machen II
to go swimming [ˌgəʊ 'swɪmɪŋ] schwimmen gehen I
to go to bed [ˌgəʊ tə 'bed] ins Bett gehen I
field **goal** ['fi:ld ˌgəʊl] Feldtor <IV U2, 50>
goat [gəʊt] Ziege III
gold [gəʊld] Gold III
gold [gəʊld] golden; Gold- III
gold rush ['gəʊld ˌrʌʃ] Goldrausch IV U4, 84
golden ['gəʊldn] golden; Gold- IV U4, 75
gone [gɒn] past participle von *to go* II
good [gʊd] gut I
to be good at [bi: 'gʊd‿ət] gut sein in; gut sein bei I
good luck [ˌgʊd 'lʌk] viel Glück II
Good morning. [ˌgʊd 'mɔ:nɪŋ] Guten Morgen. II
Goodbye. [gʊd'baɪ] Auf Wiedersehen. I
gospel ['gɒspl] Gospel *(Musikrichtung)* IV U5, 97
gossip ['gɒsɪp] Klatsch; Tratsch; Gerede IV U3, 58
got [gɒt] simple past von *to get* I
government ['gʌvnmənt] Regierung IV U5, 96
state government ['steɪt ˌgʌvnmənt] Landesregierung IV U5, 98
GPS *(Global Positioning System)* [ˌdʒi:pi:'es] GPS *(ein satellitengestütztes System zur weltweiten Positionsbestimmung)* I
to **grab** [græb] schnappen; greifen; ergreifen III
grade *(AE)* [greɪd] Note; Klasse IV U2, 32
graffiti [grə'fi:ti] Graffiti <IV U1, 134>
grammar ['græmə] Grammatik <I>
grandad ['grændæd] Opa III
great-great-grandad [ˌgreɪtgreɪt 'grændæd] Ururopa I
grandfather ['grænˌfɑ:ðə] Großvater II
grandma ['grænmɑ:] Oma II
grandmother ['grænˌmʌðə] Großmutter II
grandparents *(pl)* ['grænˌpeərənts] Großeltern II
grave [greɪv] Grab III
great [greɪt] großartig; toll I
great-grandparents [ˌgreɪt'grænˌpeərənts] Urgroßeltern IV U1, 25
Greek [gri:k] griechisch; Griechisch; aus Griechenland IV U5, 99
green [gri:n] grün I
greengrocer's ['gri:nˌgrəʊsəz] Obst- und Gemüseladen III
grew [gru:] simple past von *to grow* IV U3, 58
grey [greɪ] grau I
grid [grɪd] Gitter; Raster IV U5, 101

to **grin** [grɪn] grinsen IV U3, 64
grizzly bear ['grɪzli ˌbeə] Grizzlybär <IV U1, 30>
groceries *(pl)* ['grəʊsriz] Lebensmittel IV U4, 89
ground [graʊnd] Boden; Erdboden III
grounds *(pl)* [graʊndz] Gebiet; Gelände IV U1, 13
group [gru:p] Gruppe I
group skills ['gru:p ˌskɪlz] Fertigkeit Kooperatives Lernen <I>
tutor group ['tju:tə ˌgru:p] Klasse I
*to **grow** [grəʊ] anbauen; züchten; ziehen; wachsen IV U3, 58
to grow up [ˌgrəʊ‿'ʌp] aufwachsen III
grown [grəʊn] past participle von *to grow* IV U3, 58
to **guess** [ges] erraten; raten; überlegen II; annehmen; vermuten; schätzen IV U3, 59
guest [gest] Gast III
guide [gaɪd] Führer; Führerin <IV U1, 15>
guided tour ['gaɪdɪd ˌtɔ:] Führung <IV U1, 13>
guinea pig ['gɪni: pɪg] Meerschweinchen II
guitar [gɪ'tɑ:] Gitarre III
gun [gʌn] Schusswaffe IV U3, 62
guys *(pl)* [gaɪz] Leute II
gym(nasium) [dʒɪm (dʒɪm'neɪziəm)] Turnhalle IV U2, 42
gymnasium [dʒɪm'neɪziəm] Fitnessraum III

H

had [hæd] simple past von *to have* I; past participle von *to have* II
haggis ['hægɪs] Haggis *(schottisches Gericht aus Schafsinnereien)* III
hair [heə] Haar; Haare III
hair straightener ['heə ˌstreɪtnə] Haarglätter IV U3, 59
hair gel ['heə ˌdʒel] Haargel III
hairbrush ['heəbrʌʃ] Haarbürste III
haircut ['heəkʌt] Haarschnitt II
to have a haircut ['heəkʌt] sich die Haare schneiden lassen II
hairdo ['heədu:] Frisur <IV U4, 77>
hairdresser ['heəˌdresə] Friseur; Friseurin II
hairdryer ['heəˌdraɪə] Fön III
half *(sg)* [hɑ:f], **halves** *(pl)* [hɑ:vz] (die) Hälfte IV U4, 80
half [hɑ:f] halb III
half a million [ˌhɑ:f‿ə 'mɪljən] eine halbe Million III
half past (two) [ˌhɑ:f 'pɑ:st] halb (drei) I
half-mast [ˌhɑ:f'mɑ:st] halbmast <IV U3, 138>
hall [hɔ:l] Flur; Korridor; Diele IV U2, 34
Halloween [ˌhæləʊ'i:n] Halloween I
ham [hæm] Schinken II
hand [hænd] Hand III
*to **hang** [hæŋ] hängen II
to hang out (with) [ˌhæŋ‿'aʊt (wɪð)] rumhängen (mit); sich treffen (mit); sich herumtreiben (mit) IV U3, 58
to **happen** ['hæpn] geschehen; passieren II
happy ['hæpi] glücklich; froh I
Happy birthday! [ˌhæpi 'bɜ:θdeɪ] Alles Gute zum Geburtstag! I
harbor *(AE)* ['hɑ:bə] Hafen IV U1, 22
harbour ['hɑ:bə] Hafen II
hard [hɑ:d] hart; schwer; schwierig II
hard-working [ˌhɑ:d'wɜ:kɪŋ] fleißig IV U2, 39
hat [hæt] Hut II
to **hate** [heɪt] hassen; nicht mögen III
*to **have** [hæv] haben; besitzen I
to have a haircut ['heəkʌt] sich die Haare schneiden lassen II
to have a look [ˌhæv‿ə 'lʊk] anschauen II
to have breakfast [ˌhæv 'brekfəst] frühstücken I
to have to ['hæv tə] müssen II
have you got [ˌhæv ju: 'gɒt] hast du II
Have a seat. [ˌhæv‿ə 'si:t] Setzen Sie sich.; Setz dich. IV U3, 54
he [hi:] er I
head [hed] Kopf II
head chef ['hed ˌʃef] Chefkoch II
head first ['hed fɜ:st] kopfüber III
headache ['hedeɪk] Kopfschmerzen; Kopfweh II
heading ['hedɪŋ] Überschrift; Titel <III>
headline ['hedlaɪn] Schlagzeile; Überschrift IV U4, 77
healthy ['helθi] gesund <IV U3, 72>
*to **hear** [hɪə] hören I
heard [hɜ:d] simple past von *to hear* I; past participle von *to hear* II
heart [hɑ:t] Herz IV U3, 63
heartbeat ['hɑ:tbi:t] Herzschlag <IV U2, 35>
heat [hi:t] Hitze IV U5, 102
heaven ['hevn] Himmel <IV U5, 108>
heavy ['hevi] schwer; stark II
hectic ['hektɪk] hektisch <IV U2, 47>
height [haɪt] Höhe II
held [held] simple past, past participle von *to hold* III
helicopter ['helɪkɒptə] Helikopter; Hubschrauber IV U4, 79
Hello. [hə'ləʊ] Hallo. I
helmet ['helmət] Helm I
help [help] Hilfe II
to **help** [help] helfen I
to help oneself [ˌhelp wʌn'self] sich bedienen III
I couldn't help but … [ˌaɪ kʊdnt 'help bʌt] Ich konnte nicht anders als … III
helper ['helpə] Helfer; Helferin IV U4, 89
helpful ['helpfl] hilfsbereit; hilfreich; nützlich IV U2, 38
her [hɜ:] ihr I
here [hɪə] hier I
Here you are. [ˌhɪə ju‿'ɑ:] Bitte schön. I
hero *(sg)* ['hɪərəʊ], **heroes** *(pl)* ['hɪərəʊz] Held III
hers [hɜ:z] ihre II

herself [hɜ:'self] sie selbst; sich selbst III
Hi. [haɪ] Hi.; Hallo. I
Say hi to … [seɪ 'haɪ tə] Grüße … von mir. I
hid [hɪd] simple past von *to hide* III
hidden ['hɪdn] past participle von *to hide* III
*to **hide** [haɪd] (sich) verstecken III
high [haɪ] hoch; groß I
high school ['haɪ ˌsku:l] Highschool *(weiterführende Schule, Oberstufe)* IV U1, 18
high-action [ˌhaɪ'ækʃn] mit Action vollgepackt <IV U4, 140>
highlighted ['haɪlaɪtɪd] markiert <III>
high-tech [ˌhaɪ'tek] Hightech- IV U4, 75
to **hike** [haɪk] wandern II
hiking ['haɪkɪŋ] Wandern III
hill [hɪl] Berg; Hügel IV U4, 74
him [hɪm] ihn; ihm I
himself [hɪm'self] er selbst; sich (selbst) III
hip hop ['hɪphɒp] Hip-Hop *(Musik)* III
his [hɪz] sein I; seins; seiner II
historic [hɪ'stɒrɪk] historisch IV U5, 98
History ['hɪstri] Geschichte I
history ['hɪstri] Geschichte III
*to **hit** [hɪt] treffen; schlagen II; (sich) stoßen; anstoßen; gegen etw. fahren III
hit [hɪt] simple past, past participle von to *hit* II
hobby ['hɒbi] Hobby III
*to **hold** [həʊld] halten; festhalten III
hole [həʊl] Loch I
holiday ['hɒlədeɪ] Ferien; Urlaub II; Feiertag <IV U1, 24>
national holiday [ˌnæʃnl 'hɒlədeɪ] Nationalfeiertag <IV U2, 50>
home [həʊm] Zuhause; Heim I
at home [ət 'həʊm] zu Hause I
back home [bæk 'həʊm] zu Hause II
Homecoming *(AE)* ['həʊmˌkʌmɪŋ] Ehemaligentreffen IV U2, 33
home-packed [ˌhəʊm'pækt] zu Hause gemacht <IV U4, 90>
homeroom ['həʊmru:m] erste Stunde *(in der Schule)* IV U2, 45
*to be **homesick** [bi: 'həʊmsɪk] Heimweh haben III
*to do **homework** [ˌdu: 'həʊmwɜ:k] Hausaufgabe(n) machen I
honestly ['ɒnɪstli] ehrlich IV U3, 63
honor *(AE)* ['ɒnə] Ehre IV U1, 25
to **hoover** ['hu:və] staubsaugen II
hope [həʊp] Hoffnung IV U1, 13
to **hope** [həʊp] hoffen II
hopeful ['həʊpfl] hoffnungsvoll III
horrible ['hɒrəbl] schrecklich; furchtbar III
horror ['hɒrə] Horrorfilm <IV U4, 140>
horse [hɔ:s] Pferd I
horse riding ['hɔ:s ˌraɪdɪŋ] Reiten I
hospital ['hɒspɪtl] Krankenhaus I
hospitality [ˌhɒspɪ'tæləti] Gastfreundschaft; Gastfreundlichkeit <IV U5, 142>
host [həʊst] Talkmaster; Gastgeber; Gastgeberin <IV U3, 68>
host family ['həʊst ˌfæmli] Gastfamilie IV U2, 34
hostel ['hɒstl] Herberge III
hot [hɒt] heiß I
hot dog ['hɒt ˌdɒg] Hot Dog *(Würstchen im Brötchen)* IV U1, 14
hotel [həʊ'tel] Hotel II
40 kilometres an **hour** [kɪ'lɒmi:təz‿ən‿'aʊə] 40 Kilometer pro Stunde I
rush **hour** ['rʌʃ ˌaʊə] Hauptverkehrszeit IV U1, 14
working **hours** *(pl)* ['wɜ:kɪŋ ˌaʊəz] Arbeitszeit IV U2, 39
house [haʊs] Haus I
around the house [əˌraʊnd ðə 'haʊs] zu Hause I
State House *(AE)* ['steɪt ˌhaʊs] Regierungsgebäude IV U5, 98
tree house ['tri: ˌhaʊs] Baumhaus I
how [haʊ] wie I
How are you? [ˌhaʊ‿'ɑ: jə] Wie geht es dir? I
How are you doing? [ˌhaʊ‿ə jə 'du:ɪŋ] Wie geht's dir? IV U3, 55
How do I get there? [ˌhaʊ du aɪ 'get ðeə] Wie komme ich dahin? III
how many [ˌhaʊ 'meni] wie viele II
How much (is/are) …? [ˌhaʊ 'mʌtʃ‿ɪz/ɑ:] Wie viel (kostet/kosten) …? I
How old are you? [haʊ‿'əʊld‿ə ˌju:] Wie alt bist du? I
How to … ['haʊ tə] Wie man … II
How's it going? [ˌhaʊz‿ɪt 'gəʊɪŋ] Wie geht's?; Wie läuft's? IV U3, 54
however [haʊ'evə] jedoch III
huge [hju:dʒ] riesig; riesengroß; gewaltig IV U4, 75
a/one **hundred** ['hʌndrəd] einhundert; hundert I
hung [hʌŋ] simple past von *to hang* II
hunger ['hʌŋgə] Hunger <IV U2, 136>
hungry ['hʌŋgri] hungrig I
to **hunt** [hʌnt] jagen <IV U2, 136>
hunter ['hʌntə] Jäger; Jägerin IV U4, 85
to **hurry** ['hʌri] sich beeilen III
*to **hurt** [hɜ:t] weh tun; verletzen II
hurt [hɜ:t] simple past, past participle von *to hurt* II
husband ['hʌzbənd] Ehemann IV U3, 54
husky ['hʌski] Husky *(Schlittenhunderasse)* <IV U1, 30>

I

I [aɪ] ich I
I didn't catch that. [aɪ ˌdɪdnt 'kætʃ ðæt] Das habe ich nicht verstanden.; Das habe ich nicht gehört. IV U5, 102
I don't know! [ˌaɪ dəʊnt 'nəʊ] Ich weiß (es) nicht! I
I see. [aɪ 'si:] Ich verstehe. IV U5, 103
I wouldn't like (to) … [aɪ 'wʊdnt laɪk (tə)] ich möchte nicht …; ich würde nicht gerne … I
I'd like (to) … (= I would like to) [aɪd 'laɪk (tə)] ich möchte …; ich würde gerne … I
I'd rather [aɪd 'rɑ:ðə] ich würde lieber III

I'm from … ['aɪm ˌfrɒm] ich komme aus … I
ice cream [ˌaɪs 'kri:m] Eiscreme; Eis II
iceberg ['aɪsbɜ:g] Eisberg III
ID [ˌaɪ'di:] Ausweis; Personalausweis III
idea [aɪ'dɪə] Idee I
ideal [aɪ'dɪəl] ideal; optimal <IV U3, 72>
if [ɪf] wenn II
ill [ɪl] krank; schlecht II
illegally [ɪ'li:gli] illegal; unrechtmäßig; rechtswidrig <IV U4, 88>
illness ['ɪlnəs] Krankheit <IV U2, 136>
to **imagine** [ɪ'mædʒɪn] sich vorstellen <IV U1, 19>
immigrant ['ɪmɪgrənt] Immigrant; Immigrantin; Einwanderer; Einwandererin IV U1, 13
to **immigrate** ['ɪmɪgreɪt] einwandern; immigrieren IV U1, 18
immigration [ˌɪmɪ'greɪʃn] Immigration; Zuwanderung IV U1, 22
impact ['ɪmpækt] Einfluss; Auswirkung IV U4, 80
speech **impaired** ['spi:tʃ ɪmˌpeərd] sprachbehindert IV U5, 102
important [ɪm'pɔ:tnt] wichtig; einflussreich III
impossible [ɪm'pɒsəbl] unmöglich III
to **impress** [ɪm'pres] beeindrucken III
in [ɪn] in; im I
in August [ɪn 'ɔ:gəst] im August I
in front of [ɪn 'frʌnt‿əv] vor; davor <III>
in the background [ɪn ðə 'bækgraʊnd] im Hintergrund III
in the centre of [ˌɪn ðə 'sentər‿əv] in der Mitte von III
in the distance [ˌɪn ðə 'dɪstns] in der Ferne IV U1, 15
in the end [ɪn ði 'end] schließlich; zum Schluss II
in the evenings [ɪn ði 'i:vnɪŋz] abends III
in the foreground [ɪn ðə 'fɔ:graʊnd] im Vordergrund III
in the middle [ɪn ðə 'mɪdl] in der Mitte III
in the south of [ˌɪn ðə 'saʊθ‿əv] im Süden von III
in the world [ɪn ðə 'wɜ:ld] auf der Welt II
in tow [ɪn 'təʊ] im Schlepptau IV U2, 42
income ['ɪnkʌm] Einkommen <IV U4, 88>
to **increase** [ɪn'kri:s] zunehmen; vergrößern IV U4, 84
independence [ˌɪndɪ'pendəns] Unabhängigkeit IV U1, 13
Indian ['ɪndiən] indisch II
indoor [ˌɪn'dɔ:] Hallen-; Innen- III
Industrial Revolution [ɪnˌdʌstriəl revl'u:ʃn] industrielle Revolution III
industry ['ɪndəstri] Industrie III
influence ['ɪnfluəns] Einfluss IV U5, 98
to **influence** ['ɪnfluəns] beeinflussen IV U4, 80
information desk [ɪnfə'meɪʃn ˌdesk] Information II
informative [ɪn'fɔ:mətɪv] informativ IV U4, 77
informed [ɪn'fɔ:md] informiert <IV U3, 68>
ingredient [ɪn'gri:diənt] Zutat II
inhabitant [ɪn'hæbɪtnt] Einwohner; Einwohnerin; Bewohner; Bewohnerin III
injection [ɪn'dʒekʃn] Spritze III
innocent ['ɪnəsnt] unschuldig IV U3, 63
insect ['ɪnsekt] Insekt III
inside [ˌɪn'saɪd] in … hinein II; in; innen in; im Innern III; innen; drinnen IV U1, 25
instead [ɪn'sted] stattdessen; anstelle von IV U4, 80
instruction [ɪn'strʌkʃn] Unterricht; Anweisung <IV U2, 44>
instructor [ɪn'strʌktə] Lehrer; Lehrerin III
fitness instructor ['fɪtnəs ɪnˌstrʌktə] Fitnesstrainer; Fitnesstrainerin <IV U3, 72>
intelligent [ɪn'telɪdʒnt] intelligent; klug; vernünftig III
to **interest** ['ɪntrəst] interessieren <IV U4, 89>
*to be **interested** in [bi: 'ɪntrəstɪd‿ɪn] sich interessieren für; interessiert sein an III
interesting ['ɪntrəstɪŋ] interessant I
internet ['ɪntənet] Internet II
to surf the internet [ˌsɜ:f ði 'ɪntənet] im Internet surfen II
to **interrupt** [ˌɪntə'rʌpt] unterbrechen IV U4, 94
interview ['ɪntəvju:] Interview; Befragung II; Vorstellungsgespräch IV U2, 38
to **interview** ['ɪntəvju:] interviewen; befragen I
interviewer ['ɪntəvju:ə] Interviewer; Interviewerin; Befrager; Befragerin IV U1, 18
to **introduce** [ˌɪntrə'dju:s] einführen; einleiten; zeigen <IV U4, 90>; vorstellen IV U5, 98
introduction [ˌɪntrə'dʌkʃn] Einleitung; Einführung III
to **invade** [ɪn'veɪd] einmarschieren (in); eindringen (in) III
to **invent** [ɪn'vent] erfinden III
invention [ɪn'venʃn] Erfindung III
inventor [ɪn'ventə] Erfinder; Erfinderin III
invincible [ɪn'vɪnsəbl] unschlagbar; unsbesiegbar <IV U2, 35>
invitation [ˌɪnvɪ'teɪʃn] Einladung I
to **invite** [ɪn'vaɪt] einladen I
Irish ['aɪrɪʃ] irisch; Irisch III
is [ɪz] ist I
… is 99p [ɪz ˌnaɪntinaɪn 'pens] … kostet 99 Pence I
Islam ['ɪzlɑ:m] Islam <IV U5, 213>
island ['aɪlənd] Insel II
isn't it? ['ɪznt‿ɪt] nicht wahr?; stimmt's? II
it [ɪt] es I
IT (Information Technology) [ˌaɪ'ti:] Informatik; Informationstechnik I

Italian [ɪ'tæliən] italienisch; Italienisch; aus Italien; Italiener; Italienerin IV U5, 99
its [ɪts] sein; ihr III
itself [ɪt'self] (sich) selbst III

J

jacket ['dʒækɪt] Jacke II
jacket potato [ˌdʒækɪt pə'teɪtəʊ] Ofenkartoffel II
jam [dʒæm] Marmelade; Konfitüre III
traffic jam ['træfɪk ˌdʒæm] Stau IV U1, 14
Jamaican [dʒə'meɪkən] jamaikanisch II
January ['dʒænjuri] Januar I
Japanese [ˌdʒæpən'i:z] japanisch; Japanisch; aus Japan; Japaner; Japanerin IV U5, 99
jar [dʒɑ:] Glas III
jazz [dʒæz] Jazz *(Musikrichtung)* IV U5, 97
jealous ['dʒeləs] eifersüchtig; neidisch II
jeans *(pl)* [dʒi:nz] Jeans I
jeweller's ['dʒu:ələz] Juwelierladen III
jewellery ['dʒu:əlri] Schmuck II
Jewish ['dʒu:ɪʃ] jüdisch <IV U5, 213>
job [dʒɒb] Job; Aufgabe; Tätigkeit; Arbeit; Beruf II
job title ['dʒɒb ˌtaɪtl] Stellenbezeichnung; Berufsbezeichnung IV U2, 38
to **join** [dʒɔɪn] sich anschließen III
joke [dʒəʊk] Witz I
journalism ['dʒɜ:nlɪzm] Journalistik; Journalismus IV U2, 34
journey ['dʒɜ:ni] Fahrt; Reise III
to **joust** [dʒaʊst] einen Turnierzweikampf austragen; turnieren III
jousting ['dʒaʊstɪŋ] Turnierzweikampf III
judge [dʒʌdʒ] Juror; Jurorin II
juice [dʒu:s] Saft II
orange juice ['ɒrɪndʒ ˌdʒu:s] Orangensaft IV U4, 82
July [dʒʊ'laɪ] Juli I
jumble sale ['dʒʌmbl ˌseɪl] Flohmarkt II
to **jump** [dʒʌmp] zusammenzucken; erschrecken III; springen IV U3, 63
jumping fitness ['dʒʌmpɪŋ ˌfɪtnəs] Jumping Fitness *(Trendsportart)* IV U4, 81
June [dʒu:n] Juni I
jungle ['dʒʌŋgl] Dschungel IV U5, 102
junior ['dʒu:niə] Nachwuchs- <IV U2, 137>
just [dʒʌst] gerade (eben); soeben; nur II

K

kebab [kɪ'bæb] Döner <IV U5, 213>
*to **keep** [ki:p] halten II; aufbewahren; behalten IV U2, 34
to keep cool [ˌki:p 'ku:l] Ruhe bewahren <III>
to keep going [ki:p 'gəʊɪŋ] weitergehen; weitermachen IV U4, 85
to keep in touch [ˌki:p ɪn 'tʌtʃ] in Verbindung bleiben II
to keep out [ˌki:p‿'aʊt] draußen halten III
keep running ['ki:p rʌnɪŋ] am Laufen halten <IV U3, 68>
kennel ['kenl] Hundezwinger <IV U1, 30>
kept [kept] simple past, past participle von *to keep* II
ketchup ['ketʃʌp] Ketchup II
key [ki:] Legende <IV U1, 27>
keyword ['ki:wɜ:d] Schlüsselwort <IV U1, 31>
to **kick** [kɪk] schießen; treten <IV U2, 50>
kid [kɪd] Kind II
to **kill** [kɪl] töten III
killing ['kɪlɪŋ] Tötung; Ermordung IV U5, 98
7 **kilograms** a day [ˌkɪləgræmz ə 'deɪ] sieben Kilogramm täglich I
40 **kilometres** an hour [kɪ'lɒmi:təz‿ən‿'aʊə] 40 Kilometer pro Stunde I
kilt [kɪlt] Schottenrock; Kilt III
kind [kaɪnd] Art; Sorte <IV U3, 72>
king [kɪŋ] König III
kiss [kɪs] Kuss II
kitchen ['kɪtʃɪn] Küche I
knee [ni:] Knie III
knife *(sg)* [naɪf], **knives** *(pl)* [naɪvz] Messer II
knight [naɪt] Ritter III
*to **know** [nəʊ] kennen; wissen I; verstehen IV U5, 103
to get to know [ˌget tə 'nəʊ] kennen lernen II
I don't know! [ˌaɪ dəʊnt 'nəʊ] Ich weiß (es) nicht! I
knowledge *(no pl)* ['nɒlɪdʒ] Wissen; Kenntnisse <IV U1, 24>

L

label ['leɪbl] Etikett; Beschriftung <IV U1, 27>
to **label** ['leɪbl] beschriften <III>
laborer *(AE)* ['leɪbərə] Arbeiter; Arbeiterin; Arbeitskraft <IV U4, 88>
ladder ['lædə] Leiter I
laid [leɪd] simple past, past participle von *to lay* II
lake [leɪk] See III
lamb [læm] Lamm II
lamp [læmp] Lampe I
land [lænd] Land II
land of the free [ˌlænd‿əv ðə 'fri:] Land der Freien IV U3, 53
to **land** [lænd] landen IV U3, 54
landlord ['lændlɔ:d] Eigentümer II
landmark ['lænmɑ:k] Wahrzeichen IV U1, 14
landowner ['lændˌəʊnə] Grundbesitzer; Grundbesitzerin IV U4, 84
landscape ['lændskeɪp] Landschaft IV ZI, 9
language ['læŋgwɪdʒ] Sprache II
language tip [ˌlæŋgwɪdʒ 'tɪp] Grammatikhinweis <I>
sign language ['saɪn ˌlæŋgwɪdʒ] Gebärdensprache; Zeichensprache III
large [lɑ:dʒ] groß II

lasagne [lə'zænjə] Lasagne II
last [lɑ:st] letzte I
at last [ət 'lɑ:st] endlich; zu guter Letzt II
late [leɪt] (zu) spät II
later ['leɪtə] später I
laugh [lɑ:f] Lachen IV U3, 63
to **laugh** [lɑ:f] lachen II
law [lɔ:] Gesetz; Recht IV U5, 96
to mow the **lawn** [ˌməʊ ðə 'lɔ:n] den Rasen mähen <IV U2, 195>
*to **lay** [leɪ] decken; legen II
to lay the table [ˌleɪ ðə 'teɪbl] den Tisch decken II
layout ['leɪaʊt] Layout; Anordnung IV U4, 77
lazy ['leɪzi] faul IV U2, 39
*to **lead** [li:d] führen; anführen IV U3, 58
leader ['li:də] Führer; Führerin; Anführer; Anführerin III
to **learn** [lɜ:n] lernen II
to learn about sth [ˌlɜ:n ə'baʊt] etwas erfahren über III
least [li:st] geringste; am wenigsten <IV U3, 59>
at **least** [ət 'li:st] mindestens; wenigstens IV U3, 64
leather ['leðə] Leder III
leave [li:v] abfahren; verlassen; lassen II
leaving ['li:vɪŋ] Abschieds- II
led [led] simple past, past participle von *to lead* IV U3, 58
left [left] simple past, past participle von *to leave* II
left [left] links III
to turn left (into …) [ˌtɜ:n 'left] (nach) links abbiegen I
on the left [ɒn ðə 'left] auf der linken Seite; links I
leg [leg] Bein II
legal ['li:gl] legal; rechtlich; Rechts- <IV U4, 88>
lemon ['lemən] Zitrone II
lemonade [ˌlemə'neɪd] Limonade II
*to **lend** [lend] leihen; verleihen II
length *(no pl)* [leŋθ] Dauer; Länge <IV U2, 44>
lent [lent] simple past von *to lend* II
less [les] weniger III
lesson ['lesn] Schulstunde; Unterricht I
let's (= let us) [lets] lass(t) uns I
letter ['letə] Buchstabe; Brief III
lettuce ['letɪs] Kopfsalat II
water **level** ['wɔ:tə ˌlevl] Wasserpegel; Wasserstand <IV U5, 142>
library ['laɪbri] Bibliothek; Bücherei III
driver's **license** *(AE)* ['draɪvəz ˌlaɪsns] Führerschein <IV U2, 44>
*to **lie** [laɪ] liegen <IV U5, 143>
life *(sg)* [laɪf], **lives** *(pl)* [laɪvz] Leben I
school life ['sku:ˌlaɪf] Schulalltag <I>
lifeboat ['laɪfbəʊt] Rettungsboot III
lifestyle ['laɪfstaɪl] Lebensart; Lifestyle IV U4, 74
lifetime ['laɪftaɪm] Leben; Lebenszeit IV U4, 76
lift [lɪft] Aufzug <IV U1, 15>
light [laɪt] Licht IV U1, 13
light bulb ['laɪt ˌbʌlb] Glühbirne III
lights [laɪts] Ampel IV U1, 14
to **like** [laɪk] mögen; gern haben I
would like [wʊd 'laɪk] würde(n) gern; hätte(n) gern II
I wouldn't like (to) … [aɪ 'wʊdnt laɪk (tə)] ich möchte nicht …; ich würde nicht gerne … I
I'd like (to) … (= I would like to) [aɪd 'laɪk (tə)] ich möchte …; ich würde gerne … I
Would you like (to)…? [ˌwʊd jə 'laɪk (tə)] Möchtest du? I
like [laɪk] wie II
like that [laɪk 'ðæt] so I
like this [laɪk 'ðɪs] so; auf diese Weise III
line [laɪn] Zeile <I>; Linie III; Schlange <IV U5, 110>
line dance ['laɪn ˌdɑ:ns] Line Dance *(alle tanzen zusammen in einer Reihe)* <IV U5, 143>
lines *(pl)* [laɪnz] Text II
to **link** [lɪŋk] verbinden IV U5, 107
linking word [ˌlɪŋkɪŋ 'wɜ:d] Verbindungswort <IV U3, 73>
lion ['laɪən] Löwe I
list [lɪst] Liste II
ranking list ['ræŋkɪŋ lɪst] Rangliste; Rangfolge <IV U3, 59>
shopping list ['ʃɒpɪŋ ˌlɪst] Einkaufszettel I
to **listen** (to) ['lɪsn (tə)] hören; anhören; zuhören I
listener ['lɪsenə] Zuhörer; Zuhörerin <IV U2, 46>
listening ['lɪsnɪŋ] Hörverstehen <I>
little ['lɪtl] klein II; wenig; kaum IV U1, 22
a little [ə 'lɪtl] ein bisschen II
to **live** [lɪv] wohnen; leben I
to live off ['lɪvˌɒf] von leben <IV U3, 72>
living room ['lɪvɪŋ ˌrʊm] Wohnzimmer I
loaf *(sg)* [ləʊf], **loaves** *(pl)* [ləʊvz] Brotlaib III
local ['ləʊkl] hiesig; örtlich; lokal III
*to be **located** [bi: ləʊ'keɪtɪd] sich befinden; liegen <IV U1, 135>
location [ləʊ'keɪʃn] Drehort; Lage III; Aufenthaltsort <IV U5, 111>
locker ['lɒkə] Schließfach; Spind IV U2, 34
lonely ['ləʊnli] einsam III
long [lɒŋ] lang I
look [lʊk] Blick; Anblick; Sicht IV U1, 14
to have a look [ˌhævˌə 'lʊk] anschauen II
to **look** [lʊk] (nach)schauen I; aussehen; sehen II
to look after [ˌlʊkˌ'ɑ:ftə] aufpassen; hüten II
to look at ['lʊkˌət] anschauen I
to look for ['lʊk ˌfə] suchen I
Well, look … [wel 'lʊk] Na ja, schau mal … nach. I
lookout point ['lʊkaʊt ˌpɔɪnt] Aussichtspunkt II
loose [lu:s] locker; lose II

lorry driver ['lɒri ˌdraɪvə] LKW-Fahrer; LKW-Fahrerin II
*to **lose** [lu:z] verlieren II
lost [lɒst] simple past von *to lose* II; past participle von *to lose* III
parking **lot** *(AE)* ['pɑ:kɪŋ ˌlɒt] Parkplatz IV U1, 15
a **lot** [ə'lɒt] viel I; sehr II
a lot of [ə 'lɒt‿əv] eine Menge; viel I
body **lotion** ['bɒdi ˌləʊʃn] Körperlotion III
lots [lɒts] viel; jede Menge III
lots of ['lɒts‿əv] viel; jede Menge I
loud [laʊd] laut III
*to fall in **love** (with) [ˌfɔ:l‿ɪn 'lʌv] sich verlieben (in) III
to **love** [lʌv] lieben; gern mögen I
lovely ['lʌvli] schön; herrlich; hübsch II
low [ləʊ] niedrig II
lower ['ləʊə] untere III
lucky day [ˌlʌki 'deɪ] Glückstag II
lunch [lʌnʃ] Mittagessen I
packed lunch [ˌpækt 'lʌnʃ] Lunchpaket; Vesper II
lunchtime ['lʌnʃtaɪm] Mittagszeit; Mittagspause I
lyrics ['lɪrɪks] Liedtext <II>

M

machine [mə'ʃi:n] Automat; Maschine II
payment machine ['peɪmənt ˌməʃi:n] Bezahlautomat II
made [meɪd] past participle von *to make* II
to be made of [bi: 'meɪd‿əv] hergestellt sein aus III
magazine [ˌmægə'zi:n] Zeitschrift I
magic ['mædʒɪk] Magie; Zauberei II
main course [ˌmeɪn 'kɔ:s] Hauptgericht II
mainly ['meɪnli] hauptsächlich; in erster Linie; vorwiegend <IV U5, 108>
major ['meɪdʒə] Haupt-; wichtig; bedeutend IV ZI, 8
majority [mə'dʒɒrəti] Mehrheit; Mehrzahl IV U1, 22
*to **make** [meɪk] erstellen; machen; tun I
to make a reservation [ˌmeɪk‿ə 'rezəveɪʃn] reservieren III
to make friends [ˌmeɪk 'frendz] Freundschaften schließen I
to make it ['meɪk‿ɪt] es schaffen IV U3, 54
to make sb feel like sth [ˌmeɪk … 'fi:l laɪk] jmdm. das Gefühl geben, etw. zu sein III
to make sure [ˌmeɪk 'ʃɔ:] sich versichern IV U1, 14
maker ['meɪkə] Macher; Macherin <IV U4, 79>
film maker ['fɪlm ˌmeɪkə] Filmemacher; Filmemacherin <III>
make-up ['meɪkʌp] Make-up; Schminke IV U3, 58
mama ['mæmə] Mama II
man *(sg)* [mæn], **men** *(pl)* [men] Mann I
manager ['mænɪdʒə] Manager; Managerin; Geschäftsführer; Geschäftsführerin IV U2, 38
many ['meni] viele II
how many [ˌhaʊ 'meni] wie viele II
map [mæp] Stadtplan; Landkarte I
March [mɑ:tʃ] März I
to **march** [mɑ:tʃ] marschieren <IV U5, 108>
marching band ['mɑ:tʃɪŋ ˌbænd] Marschkapelle <IV U2, 194>
market ['mɑ:kɪt] Markt II
farmers' market [ˌfɑ:məz 'mɑ:kɪt] Bauernmarkt <IV U3, 72>
market stall ['mɑ:kɪt ˌstɔ:l] Marktstand; Marktbude <IV U2, 195>
marquee [mɑ:'ki:] Partyzelt; Festzelt <IV U1, 19>
*to get **married** [ˌget 'mærɪd] heiraten II
mashed potatoes [ˌmæʃt pə'teɪtəʊz] Kartoffelbrei II
final **match** [ˌfaɪnl 'mætʃ] Endspiel <IV U2, 50>
to **match** [mætʃ] zuordnen I; zusammenpassen <IV U4, 95>
material [mə'tɪəriəl] Material; Stoff <III>
Math *(AE)* [mæθ] Mathematik; Mathe IV U2, 34
Maths [mæθs] Mathematik; Mathe I
It doesn't **matter**. [ɪt ˌdʌznt 'mætə] Es ist egal. II
May [meɪ] Mai I
may [meɪ] vielleicht; dürfen; können II
maybe ['meɪbi] vielleicht II
mayonnaise [ˌmeɪə'neɪz] Mayonnaise II
me [mi:] ich; mich; mir I
Excuse me. [ɪk'skju:z mi] Entschuldigung. I
meal [mi:l] Essen; Mahlzeit II
*to **mean** [mi:n] bedeuten; meinen III
mean [mi:n] gemein <IV U1, 19>
meaning ['mi:nɪŋ] Bedeutung; Sinn <III>
meant [ment] simple past, past participle von *to mean* III
meat [mi:t] Fleisch I
social **media** [ˌsəʊʃl 'mi:diə] soziale Medien IV U4, 80
mediation [ˌmi:'di'eɪʃn] Sprachmittlung <I>
mediation skills [ˌmi:di'eɪʃn ˌskɪlz] Fertigkeit Sprachmitteln <I>
medicine ['medsn] Medikamente; Medizin III
*to **meet** [mi:t] kennen lernen I; (sich) treffen II
member ['membə] Mitglied <IV U4, 84>
in **memory** of [ɪn 'memri əv] in Erinnerung an <IV U3, 139>
menu ['menju:] Speisekarte II
mess [mes] Unordnung; Durcheinander I
message ['mesɪdʒ] Nachricht; SMS II; Botschaft IV U4, 77
morning message ['mɔ:nɪŋ ˌmesɪdʒ] morgendliche Ansprache IV U2, 34

p pen • b bed • t ten • d dad • k cat • g grey • tʃ chair • dʒ joke • f fan • v very • θ three • ð the

text message ['tekst ˌmesɪdʒ] Textnachricht (SMS) I
met [met] simple past von *to meet* I
metal ['metl] Metall III
metre ['mi:tə] Meter I
microwave ['maɪkrəweɪv] Mikrowelle II
mid [mɪd] mittel <IV U5, 108>
middle ['mɪdl] Mitte III
in the middle [ɪn ðə 'mɪdl] in der Mitte III
midnight ['mɪdnaɪt] Mitternacht III
migrant ['maɪgrnt] Migrant; Migrantin <IV U4, 88>
to **migrate** [maɪ'greɪt] wandern; umherziehen <IV U2, 136>
mild [maɪld] mild I
mile [maɪl] Meile II
square mile (= sq. mi.) [ˌskweə 'maɪl] Quadratmeile IV ZI, 8
milk [mɪlk] Milch II
milkshake ['mɪlkˌʃeɪk] Milchmischgetränk; Milchshake III
million ['mɪljən] Million III
half a million [ˌhɑ:f‿ə 'mɪljən] eine halbe Million III
mind map ['maɪnd ˌmæp] Wörternetz <III>
Never **mind.** [ˌnevə 'maɪnd] Macht nichts.; Schon gut.; Mach dir nichts draus. II
mine [maɪn] Bergwerk III
mine [maɪn] meins; meine II
of mine [əv 'maɪn] von mir II
miner ['maɪnə] Bergarbeiter; Bergarbeiterin III
mineral water ['mɪnrl ˌwɔ:tə] Mineralwasser III
minimum ['mɪnɪməm] Minimum; minimal; Mindest- IV U2, 38
minority [maɪ'nɒrəti] Minderheit IV U1, 23
minute ['mɪnɪt] Minute II
mirror ['mɪrə] Spiegel III
miserable ['mɪzrəbl] elend; armselig; jämmerlich III
*to give sth a **miss** [ˌgɪv sʌmθɪŋ‿ə 'mɪs] auf etw. verzichten; etw. bleiben lassen III
to **miss** [mɪs] vermissen II; verpassen; verfehlen <IV U1, 187>
missing ['mɪsɪŋ] fehlend <IV U4, 76>
to **mix** [mɪks] mischen; vermischen; mixen IV U5, 98
mobile (phone) ['məʊbaɪl (ˌfəʊn)] Handy I
modern ['mɒdn] modern I
moment ['məʊmənt] Moment; Augenblick II
Monday ['mʌndeɪ] Montag I
money ['mʌni] Geld I
monkey ['mʌŋki] Affe I
monster ['mɒnstə] Ungeheuer; Monster III
month [mʌnθ] Monat I
monthly ['mʌnθli] monatlich III
monument ['mɒnjəmənt] Denkmal II
moral ['mɒrl] moralisch <IV U1, 24>
more [mɔ:] mehr II
once more ['wʌns ˌmɔ:] noch einmal II
morning ['mɔ:nɪŋ] Morgen; Vormittag I
Good morning. [ˌgʊd 'mɔ:nɪŋ] Guten Morgen. II
morning message ['mɔ:nɪŋ ˌmesɪdʒ] morgendliche Ansprache IV U2, 34
mosque [mɒsk] Moschee II
the **most** famous [ðə 'məʊst ˌfeɪməs] der berühmteste II
mostly ['məʊstli] meistens; hauptsächlich IV U3, 58
mother ['mʌðə] Mutter I
to **motivate** ['məʊtɪveɪt] motivieren <IV U2, 50>
motivated ['məʊtɪveɪtɪd] motiviert IV U1, 18
motorbike ['məʊtəbaɪk] Motorrad I
mountain ['maʊntɪn] Berg III
mouse *(sg)* [maʊs], **mice** *(pl)* [maɪs] Maus I
moussaka [mu'sɑ:kə] Moussaka II
mouth [maʊθ] Mund II
move [mu:v] Bewegung III
to **move** [mu:v] (sich) bewegen III
to move (house) [mu:v] umziehen II
movement ['mu:vmənt] Bewegung IV U1, 13
cultural movement [ˌkʌltʃrl 'mu:vmənt] Kulturbewegung IV U1, 13
movie ['mu:vi] Film I
movie theater *(AE)* ['mu:vi ˌθi:ətə] Kino IV U5, 106
to **mow** the lawn [ˌməʊ ðə 'lɔ:n] den Rasen mähen <IV U2, 195>
Mr ['mɪstə] Herr *(Anrede)* I
Mrs ['mɪsɪz] Frau *(Anrede)* I
Ms [mɪz] Frau *(Anrede)* I
much [mʌtʃ] viel I
so much [ˌsəʊ 'mʌtʃ] so sehr III
too much [ˌtu: 'mʌtʃ] zu sehr II
mud [mʌd] Schlamm; Matsch I
stuck in the mud [ˌstʌk‿ɪn ðə 'mʌd] im Schlamm festgesteckt I
multicultural [ˌmʌlti'kʌltʃrl] multikulturell IV U5, 98
mum [mʌm] Mama; Mutti I
mural ['mjʊərəl] Wandgemälde III
murderer ['mɜ:drə] Mörder; Mörderin III
museum [mju:'zi:əm] Museum II
music ['mju:zɪk] Musik I
country and western music [ˌkʌntri ənd 'westən ˌmju:zɪk] Countrymusik <IV U5, 143>
musical ['mju:zɪkl] Musical <IV U1, 134>
musical ['mju:zɪkl] Musik-; musikalisch III
musician [mju:'zɪʃn] Musiker; Musikerin <IV U4, 141>
Muslim ['mʊzlɪm] Muslim; Muslimin I; muslimisch <IV U5, 213>
must [mʌst] müssen I
must not/never [ˌmʌst 'nɒt/'nevə] nicht/nie dürfen III
mustn't ['mʌsnt] nicht dürfen III
mustard ['mʌstəd] Senf II

my [maɪ] mein I
My name is … [maɪ 'neɪm‿ɪz] Ich heiße … I
myself [maɪ'self] selbst; selber III
mystery ['mɪstri] Rätsel; Geheimnis I
mystery story ['mɪstri ˌstɔ:ri] Krimi (= Kriminalgeschichte); Detektivgeschichte IV U3, 53

N

to **nag** [næg] nörgeln; meckern III
nail [neɪl] Nagel III
nail scissors ['neɪl ˌsɪzəz] Nagelschere III
name [neɪm] Name I
My name is … [maɪ 'neɪm‿ɪz] Ich heiße … I
to **name** [neɪm] benennen IV ZI, 9
napkin ['næpkɪn] Serviette II
narrator [nə'reɪtə] Erzähler; Erzählerin I
national ['næʃnl] National-; national III
national holiday [ˌnæʃnl 'hɒlədeɪ] Nationalfeiertag <IV U2, 50>
national park [ˌnæʃnl 'pɑ:k] Nationalpark; Naturpark <IV U1, 30>
nationality [ˌnæʃn'æləti] Nationalität; Staatsangehörigkeit <IV U5, 99>
Native American [ˌneɪtɪv‿ə'merɪkən] Ureinwohner Amerikas; Ureinwohnerin Amerikas IV U2, 32
nature ['neɪtʃə] Natur III
naughty ['nɔ:ti] frech; böse III
near [nɪə] in der Nähe von I; nah III
to **need** [ni:d] brauchen II
needn't ['ni:dnt] nicht brauchen; nicht müssen I
with special **needs** [wɪθ ˌspeʃl 'ni:dz] mit Behinderung; mit besonderen Bedürfnissen III
neighbor *(AE)* ['neɪbə] Nachbar; Nachbarin IV U3, 54
neighbour ['neɪbə] Nachbar; Nachbarin III
nervous ['nɜ:vəs] nervös; aufgeregt II
net [net] Netz IV U4, 75
safety net ['seɪfti ˌnet] Sicherheitsnetz IV U4, 75
netball ['netbɔ:l] Korbball I
never ['nevə] nie; niemals I
Never mind. [ˌnevə 'maɪnd] Macht nichts.; Schon gut.; Mach dir nichts draus. II
new [nju:] neu I
New Yorker [ˌnju: 'jɔ:kə] New Yorker; New Yorkerin IV U1, 13
news [nju:z] Neuigkeit(en); Nachricht(en) II
newsagent's ['nju:zˌeɪdʒnts] Zeitschriftenladen III
newspaper ['nju:sˌpeɪpə] Zeitung <I>
next [nekst] nächste I; als Nächstes II
next to ['nekst tə] neben I
nice [naɪs] nett; schön I; lecker; gut III
Nice to meet you. [ˌnaɪs tə 'mi:t ju:] Nett, dich kennen zu lernen. I
nickname ['nɪkneɪm] Spitzname IV U4, 75
niece [ni:s] Nichte III
night [naɪt] Nacht I
night walk ['naɪt wɔ:k] Nachtwanderung I
nightmare ['naɪtmeə] Alptraum <IV U3, 68>
nine [naɪn] neun I
nineteen [ˌnaɪn'ti:n] neunzehn I
ninety ['naɪnti] neunzig I
no [nəʊ] kein; keine; nein I
no one ['nəʊ wʌn] niemand I
No way! [ˌnəʊ 'weɪ] Auf keinen Fall!; Was?!; Echt?! III
nobody ['nəʊbədi] niemand III
noise [nɔɪz] Geräusch I
noisy ['nɔɪzi] laut III
Norman ['nɔ:mən] Normanne; Normannin III
the **Normans** [ðə 'nɔ:mənz] die Normannen III
north [nɔ:θ] Norden III
north of ['nɔ:θ‿əv] nördlich von IV ZI, 9
northwest [ˌnɔ:θ'west] Nordwesten III
northwest of [ˌnɔ:θ'west‿əv] nordwestlich III
nose [nəʊz] Nase I
not [nɒt] nicht I
not … any [ˌnɒt … eni] kein II
not … any more [ˌnɒt … eni 'mɔ:] nicht mehr III
not … either [nɒt … 'aɪðə] auch nicht III
not … yet [nɒt … 'jet] noch nicht II
note [nəʊt] Geldschein II
sticky note [ˌstɪki 'nəʊt] Haftnotizzettel <IV U3, 65>
*to take **notes** [ˌteɪk 'nəʊts] sich Notizen machen I
nothing ['nʌθɪŋ] nichts IV U5, 99
to **notice** ['nəʊtɪs] bemerken; wahrnehmen IV U2, 42
noun [naʊn] Nomen; Hauptwort <I>
November [nə'vembə] November I
now [naʊ] jetzt; nun I; heutzutage II
right now [ˌraɪt 'naʊ] gerade; jetzt gleich; sofort III
nowhere ['nəʊweə] nirgendwo; nirgendwohin IV U2, 34
number ['nʌmbə] Nummer; Zahl I
a number of [ə 'nʌmbər‿əv] einige; mehrere IV U5, 98
phone number ['fəʊn ˌnʌmbə] Telefonnummer III
nurse [nɜ:s] Krankenschwester; Krankenpfleger II
nut [nʌt] Nuss I

O

o'clock [ə'klɒk] Uhr *(Zeitangabe bei vollen Stunden)* I
oak [əʊk] Eiche <IV U5, 142>
OAP [ˌəʊeɪ'pi:] Rentner; Rentnerin <IV U5, 214>
oat [əʊt] Hafer III
object ['ɒbdʒɪkt] Objekt; Gegenstand <III>
ocean ['əʊʃn] Ozean; Meer IV ZI, 9
October [ɒk'təʊbə] Oktober I
the **odd** one out [ˌɒd wʌn‿'aʊt] das Wort, das nicht in die Gruppe passt <III>

of course [əv 'kɔ:s] natürlich; selbstverständlich II
of mine [əv 'maɪn] von mir II
a photo **of** [ə 'fəʊtəʊ‿əv] ein Foto von I
*to be made **of** [bi: 'meɪd‿əv] hergestellt sein aus III
couple **of** [kʌpl‿əv] paar <IV U3, 72>
off [ɒf] von … weg IV U5, 107
special **offer** [ˌspeʃl‿'ɒfə] Sonderangebot III
office ['ɒfɪs] Büro II
post office ['pəʊst‿ˌɒfɪs] Postamt I
police **officer** [pə'li:s‿ˌɒfɪsə] Polizeibeamter; Polizeibeamtin I
official [ə'fɪʃl] offiziell <IV U4, 88>
often ['ɒfn] oft; häufig I
oh [əʊ] null *(bei Uhrzeiten und Telefonnummern)* I
oh dear [ˌəʊ 'dɪə] oje III
oil [ɔɪl] Öl IV U5, 98
OK [əʊ'keɪ] okay I
old [əʊld] alt I
on [ɒn] auf; an; am I
on board ['ɒn bɔ:d] an Bord III
on purpose [ɒn 'pɜ:pəs] absichtlich II
on Saturdays [ɒn 'sætədeɪz] samstags I
on 7th July [ɒn ðə ˌsevnθ əv 'dʒʊlaɪ] am 7. Juli I
on the bus [ˌɒn ðə 'bʌs] im Bus II
on the left [ɒn ðə 'left] auf der linken Seite; links I
on the right [ɒn ðə 'raɪt] auf der rechten Seite; rechts I
on time [ɒn 'taɪm] pünktlich III
on Tuesday [ˌɒn 'tju:zdeɪ] am Dienstag I
on TV [ɒn ˌti:'vi:] im Fernsehen IV U1, 13
on weekdays [ɒn 'wi:kdeɪz] unter der Woche; an Werktagen III
to try on [ˌtraɪ 'ɒn] anprobieren II
once [wʌns] einst; einmal IV U1, 25
once more ['wʌns ˌmɔ:] noch einmal II
one [wʌn] eins I
a/one hundred ['hʌndrəd] einhundert; hundert I
no one ['nəʊ wʌn] niemand I
one day [wʌn 'deɪ] eines Tages III
one stop [ˌwʌn 'stɒp] einmal Umsteigen <IV U3, 66>
one(s) [wʌn(z)] *Platzhalter für ein Nomen* III
to help **oneself** [ˌhelp wʌn'self] sich bedienen III
one-way ['wʌnweɪ] einfach <IV U3, 66>
onion ['ʌnjən] Zwiebel II
online [ˌɒn'laɪn] online II
only ['əʊnli] einzige II; nur; bloß; erst III
to **open** ['əʊpn] öffnen; aufmachen I
opening ['əʊpnɪŋ] Anfang; Eröffnung <IV U5, 111>
opening times ['əʊpənɪŋ ˌtaɪmz] Öffnungszeiten IV U5, 105
operation [ˌɒpr'eɪʃn] Operation III
operator ['ɒpreɪtə] Vermittlung III
opinion [ə'pɪnjən] Meinung III
opportunity [ˌɒpə'tju:nəti] Gelegenheit; Chance IV U1, 18
opposite ['ɒpəzɪt] Gegenteil <II>
opposite ['ɒpəzɪt] gegenüber I
optimistic [ˌɒptɪ'mɪstɪk] optimistisch III
or [ɔ:] oder I
orange ['ɒrɪndʒ] orange; Orange I
orange juice ['ɒrɪndʒ ˌdʒu:s] Orangensaft IV U4, 82
orchestra ['ɔ:kɪstrə] Orchester III
order ['ɔ:də] Reihenfolge <III>
to **order** ['ɔ:də] bestellen II
ordinal number [ˌɔ:dɪnəl 'nʌmbə] Ordinalzahl I
organic [ɔ:'gænɪk] Bio-; organisch <IV U3, 72>
to **organize** ['ɔ:gənaɪz] organisieren II
origin ['ɒrɪdʒɪn] Ursprung <IV U5, 143>
original [ə'rɪdʒnl] original; ursprünglich <IV U1, 24>
other ['ʌðə] andere I
each other [i:tʃ‿'ʌðə] einander; sich; sich gegenseitig III
others ['ʌðəz] andere II
our [aʊə] unser I
ours [aʊəz] unsere III
ourselves [ˌaʊə'selvz] selber; selbst III
out [aʊt] heraus II; aus; draußen; außerhalb <IV U3, 68>
to ask sb out [ˌɑ:sk … 'aʊt] sich mit jmdm. verabreden IV U2, 42
to fall out of [ˌfɔ:l‿'aʊt‿əv] herausfallen aus IV U2, 42
to go out with [ˌgəʊ‿'aʊt wɪð] gehen mit IV U3, 58
to keep out [ˌki:p‿'aʊt] draußen halten III
to point out [ˌpɔɪnt‿'aʊt] hinweisen auf <IV U1, 187>
out and about [ˌaʊt‿ən‿ə'baʊt] unterwegs I
out of ['aʊt‿əv] aus … heraus I; von <IV U2, 44>
out of fashion [ˌaʊt‿əv 'fæʃn] altmodisch; nicht mehr aktuell IV U4, 81
outdated [ˌaʊt'deɪtɪd] veraltet IV U4, 81
outdoor [ˌaʊt'dɔ:] Freiluft-; Outdoor- III
the **outdoors** [ˌði 'aʊtdɔ:z] die freie Natur IV U5, 96
outfit ['aʊtfɪt] Outfit; Kleidung III
outline ['aʊtlaɪn] Skizze; Kontur; Überblick <III>
outnumbered [ˌaʊt'nʌmbəd] in der Unterzahl IV U5, 102
outside [ˌaʊt'saɪd] draußen; im Freien III; außerhalb IV U2, 38
over ['əʊvə] über IV U1, 12
over there [ˌəʊvə 'ðeə] da drüben; dort drüben II
to **own** [əʊn] besitzen II
own [əʊn] eigene II
owner ['əʊnə] Besitzer; Besitzerin <IV U4, 88>

P

p.m. [ˌpi:'em] nachmittags II
to **pack** [pæk] packen; einpacken II
to pack up [ˌpæk‿ʌp] packen; einpacken II

package ['pækɪdʒ] Paket IV U5, 102
packed lunch [ˌpækt 'lʌnʃ] Lunchpaket; Vesper II
a **packet** of ['pækɪt] eine Packung …; eine Tüte … I
paddle ['pædl] Paddel <IV U3, 72>
paddle steamer ['pædl ˌsti:mə] Raddampfer <IV U5, 142>
standup **paddleboarding** ['stændʌp ˌpædlbɔ:dɪŋ] Stehpaddeln <IV U3, 72>
paddlewheel ['pædlˌwi:l] Schaufelrad <IV U5, 142>
paella [paɪ'elə] Paella IV U5, 99
paid [peɪd] simple past, past participle von *to pay* II
to **paint** [peɪnt] streichen; anmalen; malen IV U4, 75
pair [peə] Paar IV U2, 41
a pair of [ə 'peər‿əv] ein Paar II
pancake ['pænkeɪk] Pfannkuchen II
to **panic** ['pænɪk] panisch werden II
pantomime ['pæntəmaɪm] Weihnachtstheaterstück II
paper ['peɪpə] Papier III
paperboy ['peɪpəˌbɔɪ] Zeitungsausträger IV U2, 41
papergirl ['peɪpəˌgɜ:l] Zeitungsausträgerin IV U2, 41
papers ['peɪpəz] Unterlagen; Papiere IV U1, 19
parade [pə'reɪd] Parade; Umzug III
paradise ['pærədaɪs] Paradies IV ZI, 9
paragraph ['pærəgrɑ:f] Paragraph; Absatz <III>
pardon ['pɑ:dn] Begnadigung; Entschuldigung; Verzeihung IV U3, 67
to **pardon** ['pɑ:dn] begnadigen; entschuldigen; verzeihen IV U3, 53
Pardon? ['pɑ:dn] Wie bitte? I
parent ['peərnt] Elternteil <IV U1, 188>
parents *(pl)* ['peərnts] Eltern II
park [pɑ:k] Park I
amusement park [ə'mju:zmənt ˌpɑ:k] Freizeitpark <IV U4, 207>
national park [ˌnæʃnl 'pɑ:k] Nationalpark; Naturpark <IV U1, 30>
theme park ['θi:m ˌpɑ:k] Freizeitpark I
parking lot *(AE)* ['pɑ:kɪŋ ˌlɒt] Parkplatz IV U1, 15
part [pɑ:t] Rolle; Teil II
to take part (in) [ˌteɪk 'pɑ:t] teilnehmen (an) III
partner ['pɑ:tnə] Partner; Partnerin III
part-time [ˌpɑ:t'taɪm] Teilzeit-; Halbtags- IV U2, 38
party ['pɑ:ti] Party; Feier I
pass [pɑ:s] Ausweis; Pass IV U2, 34
to **pass** [pɑ:s] reichen II
passenger ['pæsndʒə] Passagier; Passagierin II
passive ['pæsɪv] Passiv; Passiv- <IV U5, 101>
past [pɑ:st] Vergangenheit III
past perfect [ˌpɑ:st 'pɜ:fɪkt] Plusquamperfekt <IV U1, 20>
simple past [ˌsɪmpl 'pɑ:st] einfache Vergangenheit <III>
past [pɑ:st] nach *(bei Uhrzeitangaben)* I; vorbei (an) III
half past (two) [ˌhɑ:f 'pɑ:st] halb (drei) I
pasta ['pæstə] Pasta; Nudeln II
pasta bake [ˌpæstə 'beɪk] Nudelauflauf II
to **paste** [peɪst] einfügen II
pasty ['pæsti] Pastete II
path [pɑ:θ] Pfad; Weg <IV U1, 30>
patient ['peɪʃnt] Patient; Patientin II
patient ['peɪʃnt] geduldig III
to **patrol** [pə'trəʊl] patrouillieren; Streife gehen <IV U1, 30>
patterned ['pætənd] gemustert II
*to **pay** [peɪ] bezahlen II
to pay back [ˌpeɪ 'bæk] zurückzahlen II
to pay the bill [ˌpeɪ ðə 'bɪl] die Rechnung bezahlen III
pay phone ['peɪ fəʊn] Münztelefon III
payment machine ['peɪmənt ˌməʃi:n] Bezahlautomat II
PE (Physical Education) [ˌpi:'i:, ˌfɪzɪkl edʒʊ'keɪʃn] Sportunterricht I
peace [pi:s] Frieden III
peaceful ['pi:sfl] friedlich IV U5, 96
peach [pi:tʃ] Pfirsich I
peanut butter [ˌpi:nʌt 'bʌtə] Erdnussbutter III
pecan ['pi:kæn] Pekannuss IV U3, 67
pen [pen] Füller; Stift I
pence *(pl)* [pens], **penny** *(sg)* ['peni] Pence *(brit. Währungseinheit)* I
… is 99p [ɪz ˌnaɪntinaɪn 'pens] … kostet 99 Pence I
pencil ['pensl] Bleistift I
pencil case ['pensl ˌkeɪs] Federmäppchen I
pencil sharpener ['pensl ˌʃɑ:pnə] Anspitzer I
penguin ['peŋgwɪn] Pinguin I
people ['pi:pl] Leute; Menschen I
pepper ['pepə] Pfeffer II
per [pɜ:] pro IV U2, 41
percent (%) [pə'sent] Prozent IV U1, 23
present **perfect** [ˌpreznt 'pɜ:fɪkt] das Perfekt <III>
past **perfect** [ˌpɑ:st 'pɜ:fɪkt] Plusquamperfekt <IV U1, 20>
perfect ['pɜ:fɪkt] perfekt; vollkommen IV ZI, 9
performance [pə'fɔ:məns] Aufführung; Vorstellung <IV U2, 50>
perfume ['pɜ:fju:m] Parfüm III
period ['pɪəriəd] Stunde; Unterrichtsstunde IV U2, 34
study hall period ['stʌdi hɔ:l ˌpɪəriəd] Freistunde IV U2, 34
permanent ['pɜ:mnənt] permanent; dauerhaft <IV U1, 24>
person ['pɜ:sn] Person; Mensch II
personal ['pɜ:snl] persönlich III
perspective [pə'spektɪv] Perspektive; Blickwinkel <IV U3, 68>
pet [pet] Haustier I
pet shop ['pet ʃɒp] Tierhandlung III
phone [fəʊn] Telefon II
to answer the phone [ˌɑ:nsə ðə 'fəʊn] ans Telefon gehen III
mobile (phone) ['məʊbaɪl (ˌfəʊn)] Handy I

pay phone ['peɪ fəʊn] Münztelefon III
phone call ['fəʊn ˌkɔ:l] Telefonanruf I
phone number ['fəʊn ˌnʌmbə] Telefonnummer III
to **phone** [fəʊn] anrufen; telefonieren I
photo ['fəʊtəʊ] Foto I
to take a photo [ˌteɪk‿ə 'fəʊtəʊ] ein Foto machen I
phrase [freɪz] Ausdruck; Redewendung; Satz <III>
to **pick** [pɪk] pflücken; herauslesen <IV U4, 88>
to pick up [ˌpɪk‿'ʌp] aufheben III; abholen IV U2, 43
to pick up the pieces [ˌpɪk ˌʌp ðə 'pi:si:z] etw. wieder in den Griff bekommen <IV U2, 137>
pick-up ['pɪkʌp] Abholung; Pick-up IV U5, 102
picnic ['pɪknɪk] Picknick I
picture ['pɪktʃə] Bild I
pie [paɪ] Kuchen; Pastete II
pie chart ['paɪ ˌtʃɑ:t] Kuchendiagramm; Tortendiagramm <IV U1, 27>
piece [pi:s] Stück II
piece of cake ['pi:s‿əv keɪk] einfach <IV U3, 68>
pierogi [pjɜ'rɔgi] Pirogge II
pilgrim ['pɪlgrɪm] Pilger- <IV U3, 139>
pilot ['paɪlət] Pilot; Pilotin IV U4, 79
pinch [pɪntʃ] Prise II
pineapple ['paɪnæpl] Ananas III
pink [pɪŋk] pink; rosa I
pipe [paɪp] Rohr III
pirate ['paɪrət] Pirat; Piratin I
it's a **pity** [ˌɪts‿ə 'pɪti] (es ist) schade IV U3, 63
pizza ['pi:tsə] Pizza I
place [pleɪs] Platz; Stelle; Ort I
to take place [ˌteɪk 'pleɪs] stattfinden <IV U4, 140>
plain [pleɪn] Ebene <IV U2, 136>
plain [pleɪn] schlicht; einfach II
plan [plæn] Plan II
to **plan** [plæn] planen II
plane [pleɪn] Flugzeug II
plant [plɑ:nt] Pflanze III
plantain ['plænteɪn] Kochbanane II
plantation [plæn'teɪʃn] Plantage IV U5, 97
plaster ['plɑ:stə] Pflaster III
plastic ['plæstɪk] Plastik; Kunststoff III
plate [pleɪt] Teller II
play [pleɪ] Theaterstück II
to **play** [pleɪ] spielen I
player ['pleɪə] Spieler; Spielerin II
playground ['pleɪgraʊnd] Schulhof; Pausenhof; Spielplatz I
please [pli:z] bitte I
pledge [pledʒ] Versprechen IV U2, 34
pledge of allegiance [ˌpledʒ‿əv‿ə'li:dʒns] Treueeid IV U2, 34
plus [plʌs] plus <IV U2, 50>
pocketful ['pɒkɪtfʊl] Tasche voll <IV U1, 19>
podcast ['pɒdkɑ:st] Podcast IV U4, 94
poem ['pəʊɪm] Gedicht III
lookout **point** ['lʊkaʊt ˌpɔɪnt] Aussichtspunkt II
starting **point** ['stɑ:tɪŋ ˌpɔɪnt] Ausgangspunkt <III>
to **point** [pɔɪnt] zeigen IV U3, 62
to point out [ˌpɔɪnt‿'aʊt] hinweisen auf <IV U1, 187>
pointless ['pɔɪntləs] sinnlos IV U4, 77
police [pə'li:s] Polizei III
police officer [pə'li:s‿ɒfɪsə] Polizeibeamter; Polizeibeamtin I
Polish ['pəʊlɪʃ] polnisch; Polnisch; aus Polen IV U5, 99
polite [pə'laɪt] höflich II
political [pə'lɪtɪkl] politisch IV U1, 23
swimming **pool** ['swɪmɪŋ ˌpu:l] Schwimmbad I
poor [pɔ:] arm IV U1, 18
popcorn ['pɒpkɔ:n] Popcorn I
popular ['pɒpjələ] beliebt III
population [ˌpɒpjə'leɪʃn] Einwohner; Einwohnerzahl; Bevölkerung IV ZI, 8
pork [pɔ:k] Schweinefleisch II
porridge ['pɒrɪdʒ] Haferbrei III
positive ['pɒzətɪv] positiv III
possessive pronoun [pə'sesɪv ˌprəʊnaʊn] Possessivpronomen <III>
possible ['pɒsəbl] möglich <IV U2, 50>
post office ['pəʊst‿ɒfɪs] Postamt I
to **post** [pəʊst] aufgeben *(einen Brief)*; abschicken *(einen Brief)* III; online stellen; posten IV U4, 80
postcard ['pəʊstkɑ:d] Postkarte I
poster ['pəʊstə] Poster I
pot [pɒt] Topf III
potato *(sg)* [pə'teɪtəʊ], **potatoes** *(pl)* [pə'teɪtəʊz] Kartoffel II
jacket potato [ˌdʒækɪt pə'teɪtəʊ] Ofenkartoffel II
mashed potatoes [ˌmæʃt pə'teɪtəʊz] Kartoffelbrei II
pound [paʊnd] Pfund *(brit. Währungseinheit)* I
poverty ['pɒvəti] Armut IV U1, 23
powerful ['paʊəfl] stark; mächtig; bedeutend; beeindruckend IV U1, 22
practical ['præktɪkl] praktisch IV U4, 89
practice ['præktɪs] Training; Übung I
to **practise** ['præktɪs] üben; trainieren III
prairie ['preəri] Prärie <IV U2, 136>
to **prefer** [prɪ'fɜ:] vorziehen II
to **prepare** [prɪ'peə] zubereiten; vorbereiten III
present ['preznt] Geschenk I
present perfect [ˌpreznt 'pɜ:fɪkt] das Perfekt <III>
present progressive [ˌpreznt prə'gresɪv] Verlaufsform der Gegenwart <III>
simple present [ˌsɪmpl 'preznt] Gegenwart; Präsens <III>
to **present** [prɪ'zent] präsentieren I
presentation [ˌprezn'teɪʃn] Präsentation; Vortrag IV U2, 51
president ['prezɪdnt] Präsident; Präsidentin <IV U2, 46>
pretty ['prɪti] hübsch II

pretty ['prɪti] ziemlich IV U3, 58
price [praɪs] Preis II
principal *(AE)* ['prɪnsɪpl] Schulleiter; Schulleiterin IV U2, 34
prison ['prɪzn] Gefängnis II
prize [praɪz] Preis II
probably ['prɒbəbli] wahrscheinlich III
problem ['prɒbləm] Problem I
to **produce** [prə'dju:s] herstellen; produzieren; anbauen; erzeugen; verursachen IV U1, 13
product ['prɒdʌkt] Produkt <III>
dairy product ['deəri ˌprɒdʌkt] Milchprodukt; Milcherzeugnis <IV U3, 72>
profile ['prəʊfaɪl] Profil; Steckbrief <I>
present **progressive** [ˌpreznt prə'gresɪv] Verlaufsform der Gegenwart <III>
project ['prɒdʒekt] Projekt III
to **promise** ['prɒmɪs] versprechen IV U2, 34
prompt card ['prɒmt ˌkɑ:d] Stichwortkarte <II>
possessive **pronoun** [pə'sesɪv ˌprəʊnaʊn] Possessivpronomen <III>
prop [prɒp] Requisit III
to **protect** [prə'tekt] schützen III
protest ['prəʊtest] Protest; Demonstration IV U5, 96
to **protest** [prə'test] protestieren <IV U3, 138>
Protestant ['prɒtɪstnt] Protestant; Protestantin; protestantisch III
proud (of) [praʊd (əv)] stolz (auf) III
to **prove** [pru:v] beweisen IV U4, 84
pub [pʌb] Kneipe; Gasthaus III
the **public** [ðə 'pʌblɪk] die Öffentlichkeit <IV U5, 142>
public ['pʌblɪk] öffentlich <IV U3, 138>
public transport [ˌpʌblɪk 'trænspɔ:t] öffentliche Verkehrsmittel III
published ['pʌblɪʃt] veröffentlicht <IV U3, 72>
pudding ['pʊdɪŋ] Nachspeise; Pudding II

Puerto Rican [ˌpwɜ:tə‿'ri:kən] puerto-rikanisch; aus Puerto Rico; Puertorikaner; Puertorikanerin <IV U1, 134>
to **puke** [pju:k] erbrechen; sich übergeben IV U3, 62
to **pull** [pʊl] ziehen I
pumpkin ['pʌmpkɪn] Kürbis; Kürbis- <IV U3, 72>
purple ['pɜ:pl] lila; violett I
on **purpose** [ɒn 'pɜ:pəs] absichtlich II
to **push** [pʊʃ] schieben I; schubsen; drängeln III
*to **put** [pʊt] setzen; legen; stellen II
to put in [ˌpʊt‿'ɪn] einsetzen I
to put in the right order [ˌpʊt‿ɪn ðə 'raɪt ɔ:də] in die richtige Reihenfolge bringen I
to put on [ˌpʊt‿'ɒn] anlegen; anziehen III
to put up [ˌpʊt‿'ʌp] aufstellen; errichten IV U3, 64
put [pʊt] simple past von *to put* II

Q

qualification [ˌkwɒlɪfɪ'keɪʃn] Qualifikation; Abschluss; Schulabschluss <IV U4, 88>
better **quality** food [ˌbetə 'kwɒləti ˌfu:d] qualitativ besseres Essen <IV U3, 72>
quarter ['kwɔ:tə] Viertel <IV U2, 50>
quarter past ['kwɔ:tə pɑ:st] Viertel nach I
quarter to ['kwɔ:tə tə] Viertel vor I
queen [kwi:n] Königin III
question ['kwestʃən] Frage I
queue [kju:] Warteschlange II
quick [kwɪk] schnell III
quickly ['kwɪkli] schnell II
quiet ['kwaɪət] ruhig; leise; still III
quite [kwaɪt] ziemlich; ganz; völlig III
quote [kwəʊt] Zitat <IV U5, 107>

R

raccoon [rə'ku:n] Waschbär I
race [reɪs] Wettrennen; Rennen I

racism ['reɪsɪzm] Rassismus IV U5, 98
radio ['reɪdiəʊ] Radio III
rafting ['rɑ:ftɪŋ] Rafting III
railway ['reɪlweɪ] Eisenbahn IV U4, 86
railway track ['reɪlweɪ ˌtræk] Gleis IV U3, 64
to **rain** [reɪn] regnen I
rainbow ['reɪnbəʊ] Regenbogen III
raincoat ['reɪnkəʊt] Regenmantel III
ran [ræn] simple past von *to run* III
rang [ræŋ] simple past von *to ring* II
ranger *(AE)* [reɪndʒə] Ranger; **Rangerin** <IV U1, 30>
to **rank** [ræŋk] einstufen <IV U3, 59>
ranking list ['ræŋkɪŋ lɪst] Rangliste; Rangfolge <IV U3, 59>
rap [ræp] Rap <I>
to **rap** [ræp] rappen II
rapper ['ræpə] Rapper; Rapperin III
raspberry ['rɑ:zbri] Himbeere III
to **rate** [reɪt] bewerten; einstufen III
I'd **rather** [aɪd 'rɑ:ðə] ich würde lieber III
rating ['reɪtɪŋ] Bewertung <III>
razor ['reɪzə] Rasierer; Rasierapparat IV U3, 59
to **reach** [ri:tʃ] erreichen IV U3, 63
to **react** [ri'ækt] reagieren <IV U3, 69>
*to **read** [ri:d] lesen I
reader ['ri:də] Leser; Leserin IV U1, 21
reading ['ri:dɪŋ] Lesen <I>
ready ['redi] fertig; bereit I
to get ready [ˌget 'redi] sich vorbereiten; sich fertig machen IV U3, 54
real [rɪəl] echt; richtig; wirklich II
reality [ri'æləti] Realität; Wirklichkeit <IV U4, 88>
really ['rɪəli] echt II; wirklich IV U3, 58
Really? ['rɪəli] Wirklich? I
reason ['ri:zn] Grund III
to give reasons [ˌgɪv 'ri:znz] Gründe nennen; Gründe angeben III
*to **rebuild** [ˌri:'bɪld] wiederaufbauen <IV U2, 137>
receipt [ri'si:t] Quittung II
recent ['ri:snt] kürzlich; neueste; letzte <IV U4, 88>

recipe ['resɪpi] Rezept II
to **record** [rɪ'kɔ:d] aufnehmen <III>
recording [rɪ'kɔ:dɪŋ] Aufnahme <III>
red [red] rot I
redwood (tree) ['redwʊd (tri:)] Mammutbaum IV U4, 74
to **refuse** [rɪ'fju:z] sich weigern; ablehnen IV U5, 107
region ['ri:dʒn] Region; Gegend IV U5, 97
registration [ˌredʒɪ'streɪʃn] Überprüfung der Anwesenheit I; Anmeldung II
to **regret** [rɪ'gret] bedauern IV U3, 58
regular ['regjələ] regelmäßig; normal; üblich; gleichmäßig IV U4, 89
to **reject** [rɪ'dʒekt] zurückweisen; ablehnen IV U5, 99
relationship [rɪ'leɪʃnʃɪp] Beziehung <IV U2, 46>
relaxed [rɪ'lækst] entspannt; locker; gelassen IV U4, 74
to **release** [rɪ'li:s] veröffentlichen; herausgeben; freigeben; freisetzen; loslassen IV U5, 97
relevant ['reləvənt] relevant <IV U5, 110>
reliable [rɪ'laɪəbl] verlässlich; zuverlässig; vertrauenswürdig IV U5, 109
religious [rɪ'lɪdʒəs] religiös; gläubig IV U1, 23
RE (Religious Education) [ˌɑ:ˈri:, rɪˌlɪdʒəsˌedʒʊ'keɪʃn] Religionsunterricht I
to **remain** [rɪ'meɪn] übrig bleiben <IV U5, 142>
to **remember** [rɪ'membə] sich merken; sich erinnern (an) II
rent [rent] Miete II
to **rent** [rent] mieten III
to **repair** [rɪ'peə] reparieren III
to **repeat** [rɪ'pi:t] wiederholen III
to **replace** [rɪ'pleɪs] ersetzen IV U1, 12
report [rɪ'pɔ:t] Bericht IV U4, 84
to **report** (on) [rɪ'pɔ:t (ɒn)] berichten (über) IV U2, 33
reporter [rɪ'pɔ:tə] Reporter; Reporterin III
republic [rɪ'pʌblɪk] Republik III
request [rɪ'kwest] Anfrage IV U4, 81
animal **rescue** shelter [ˌænɪml 'reskju: ˌʃeltə] Tierheim I
to **resent** [rɪ'zent] übelnehmen; verübeln IV U5, 99
reservation [ˌrezə'veɪʃn] Reservierung IV U4, 76; Reservat IV U2, 32
to make a reservation [ˌmeɪkˌə 'rezəveɪʃn] reservieren III
resident ['rezɪdnt] Bewohner; Bewohnerin; Anwohner; Anwohnerin; Einwohner; Einwohnerin <IV U1, 24>
to **respect** [rɪ'spekt] respektieren IV U4, 89
responsible [rɪs'pɒnsəbl] verantwortlich; verantwortungsvoll IV U2, 38
the **rest** [ðə 'rest] der Rest IV U1, 22
to **rest** [rest] rasten; ausruhen; liegen II
restaurant ['restrɒnt] Restaurant II
result [rɪ'zʌlt] Ergebnis II
*to **retell** [ˌri:'tel] nacherzählen; nochmals erzählen <IV U2, 42>
return ticket [rɪ'tɜ:n ˌtɪkɪt] Hin- und Rückfahrkarte III
to **return** [rɪ'tɜ:n] zurückkehren; zurückgeben IV U1, 23
review [rɪ'vju:] Kritik III
Industrial **Revolution** [ɪnˌdʌstriəl revl'u:ʃn] industrielle Revolution III
rice [raɪs] Reis II
rich [rɪtʃ] reich III
ridden ['rɪdn] past participle von *to ride* II
ride [raɪd] Fahrt; Ritt IV U1, 14
*to **ride** [raɪd] fahren; reiten II
horse **riding** ['hɔ:s ˌraɪdɪŋ] Reiten I
right [raɪt] Recht IV U5, 96
civil rights *(pl)* [ˌsɪvl 'raɪts] Bürgerrechte IV U5, 96
right [raɪt] richtig; korrekt I; rechts III; gerade; genau; in dem Moment als IV U2, 42
right ahead [ˌraɪtˌə'hed] geradeaus IV U1, 15
right away [ˌraɪtˌə'weɪ] sofort; gleich IV U4, 80
right now [ˌraɪt 'naʊ] gerade; jetzt gleich; sofort III
all right [ˌɔ:l 'raɪt] in Ordnung; alles klar II
to be right [bi: 'raɪt] recht haben II
to do the right thing [ˌdu: ðə 'raɪt θɪŋ] das Richtige tun III
to turn right (into …) [ˌtɜ:n 'raɪt] rechts abbiegen I
on the right [ɒn ðə 'raɪt] auf der rechten Seite; rechts I
You're right. [jɔ:ˈraɪt] Du hast recht. I
*to **ring** [rɪŋ] läuten; klingeln II
river ['rɪvə] Fluss I
road [rəʊd] Straße I
roadwork *(AE)* ['rəʊdwɜ:k] Straßenbauarbeiten IV U1, 14
roast [rəʊst] gebraten <IV U3, 72>
robotic [rə'bɒtɪk] roboterhaft <IV U1, 134>
rock [rɒk] Fels; Stein III
rock climbing ['rɒk ˌklaɪmɪŋ] Klettern I
rock'n'roll [ˌrɒkˌən 'rəʊl] Rock 'n' Roll *(Musikrichtung)* IV U5, 97
rode [rəʊd] simple past von *to ride* II
role [rəʊl] Rolle IV U5, 107
role play ['rəʊl ˌpleɪ] Rollenspiel <II>
to **roll up** [ˌrəʊlˈʌp] zusammenrollen; aufrollen; aufkrempeln IV U3, 62
roller coaster ['rəʊlə ˌkəʊstə] Achterbahn II
the **Romans** [ðə 'rəʊmənz] die Römer III
romance ['rəʊmæns] Liebesgeschichte III
Romanian [rʊ'meɪniən] rumänisch; Rumänisch; aus Rumänien; Rumäne; Rumänin <IV U5, 213>
roof [ru:f] Dach II
room [ru:m] Zimmer; Raum I
dining room ['daɪnɪŋ ˌrʊm] Esszimmer I
rope [rəʊp] Seil I
rose [rəʊz] Rose IV ZI, 8
roulade [rʊ:'lɑ:d] Roulade <IV U3, 72>

round trip [ˌraʊnd ˈtrɪp] Hin- und Rückflug; Hin- und Rückfahrt <IV U3, 66>
routine [ruːˈtiːn] Routine; Ablauf <IV U2, 50>
royal [ˈrɔɪəl] königlich II
rubber [ˈrʌbə] Gummi III
rubbish [ˈrʌbɪʃ] Müll; Abfall II
rude [ruːd] unhöflich; unverschämt IV U2, 39
rugby [ˈrʌgbi] Rugby III
to **ruin** [ˈruːɪn] ruinieren; zerstören II
rule [ruːl] Regel III
ruler [ˈruːlə] Lineal I
*to **run** [rʌn] rennen; laufen I; betreiben; leiten; führen III
to run away [ˌrʌn‿əˈweɪ] weglaufen III
to run out of [ˌrʌn‿ˈaʊt‿əv] ausgehen *(Ware)* III
run [rʌn] past participle von to run III
rung [rʌŋ] past participle von *to ring* III
keep **running** [ˈkiːp rʌnɪŋ] am Laufen halten <IV U3, 68>
gold **rush** [ˈgəʊld ˌrʌʃ] Goldrausch IV U4, 84
to **rush** [rʌʃ] eilen; sich beeilen; stürzen III
rush hour [ˈrʌʃ ˌaʊə] Hauptverkehrszeit IV U1, 14
Russian [ˈrʌʃn] russisch; Russisch; aus Russland; Russe; Russin IV U5, 99

S

sad [sæd] traurig III
safe [seɪf] sicher; ungefährlich III
safety [ˈseɪfti] Sicherheit IV U4, 75
safety net [ˈseɪfti ˌnet] Sicherheitsnetz IV U4, 75
said [sed] simple past von *to say* I
saint [seɪnt] Heilige; Heiliger <IV U5, 108>
salad [ˈsæləd] Salat II
sale [seɪl] Schlussverkauf; Ausverkauf II
jumble sale [ˈdʒʌmbl ˌseɪl] Flohmarkt II
sales associate *(AE)* [ˌseɪlz əˈsəʊʃiət] Verkäufer; Verkäuferin IV U2, 38
saleswoman [ˈseɪlzˌwʊmən] Verkäuferin <IV U5, 110>
salt [sɔːlt] Salz II
the **same** [ðə ˈseɪm] derselbe; gleich II
sand [sænd] Sand II
sandal [ˈsændl] Sandale <IV U4, 77>
sandwich [ˈsænwɪdʒ] Sandwich; belegtes Brot I
sang [sæŋ] simple past von *to sing* II
sank [sæŋk] simple past von *to sink* III
sat [sæt] simple past, past participle von *to sit* IV U3, 63
Saturday [ˈsætədeɪ] Samstag I
on Saturdays [ɒn ˈsætədeɪz] samstags I
sauce [sɔːs] Soße II
sausage [ˈsɒsɪdʒ] Wurst; Bratwurst II
sausage roll [ˌsɒsɪdʒ ˈrəʊl] *Blätterteig mit Wurstfüllung* II
to **save** [seɪv] speichern II; retten; bergen III; sparen IV U1, 22
saw [sɔː] simple past von *to see* I
saxophone [ˈsæksəfəʊn] Saxofon I
*to **say** [seɪ] nachsprechen; nennen; sagen; sprechen I
to say sorry [ˌseɪ ˈsɒri] sich entschuldigen II
Say hi to ... [seɪ ˈhaɪ tə] Grüße ... von mir. I
to **scan** [skæn] scannen; nach Details durchsuchen <III>
to **scare** [skeə] erschrecken II
scared [skeəd] verängstigt I
to be **scared** [biː ˈskeəd] Angst haben; erschrocken sein III
scarf *(sg)* [skɑːf], **scarves** *(pl)* [skɑːvz] Schal; Tuch II
scary [ˈskeəri] gruselig; beängstigend I
scene [siːn] Szene II
to set the scene [ˌset ðə ˈsiːn] beste Voraussetzungen schaffen <IV U3, 69>
schedule *(AE)* [ˈskedʒuːl] Stundenplan; Fahrplan IV U2, 32
school [skuːl] Schule I
at school [ət ˈskuːl] in der Schule I
boarding school [ˈbɔːdɪŋ ˌskuːl] Internat <IV U2, 137>
driving school [ˈdraɪvɪŋ ˌskuːl] Fahrschule <IV U2, 44>
high school [ˈhaɪ ˌskuːl] Highschool *(weiterführende Schule, Oberstufe)* IV U1, 18
school life [ˈskuː‿ˌlaɪf] Schulalltag <I>
Science [saɪəns] Wissenschaft; Naturwissenschaft I
science fiction [ˌsaɪəns ˈfɪkʃn] Science-Fiction I
scissors *(pl)* [ˈsɪzəz] Schere III
nail scissors [ˈneɪl ˌsɪzəz] Nagelschere III
scone [skɒn] Scone *(eine Art süßes Brötchen)* II
score [skɔː] Punktestand <IV U2, 50>
Scot [skɒt] Schotte; Schottin III
Scottish [ˈskɒtɪʃ] schottisch III
scrambled egg [skræmbld‿ˈeg] Rührei II
to **scream** [skriːm] schreien; kreischen IV U3, 63
script [skrɪpt] Drehbuch; Skript <III>
sea [siː] Meer I
to **search** [sɜːtʃ] durchsuchen <III>
at the **seaside** [ət ðə ˈsiːsaɪd] am Meer I
season [ˈsiːzn] Saison; Jahreszeit <IV U2, 50>
seat [siːt] Sitzplatz; Platz IV U5, 102
Have a seat. [ˌhæv‿ə ˈsiːt] Setzen Sie sich.; Setz dich. IV U3, 54
second [ˈseknd] Sekunde II
second [ˈseknd] zweite I; zweitens IV U2, 51
secret [ˈsiːkrət] Geheimnis II
secret [ˈsiːkrət] geheim II
section [ˈsekʃn] Abschnitt <III>

security [sɪ'kjʊərəti] Sicherheit <IV U1, 30>
*__to see__ [siː] sehen I
I see. [aɪ 'siː] Ich verstehe. IV U5, 103
See you! ['siː ˌjuː] Tschüss!; Bis bald! I
See you soon! [ˌsiː juː 'suːn] Bis bald! I
to **seem** [siːm] scheinen IV U3, 64
seen [siːn] past participle von *to see* II
segregated ['segrɪgeɪtɪd] getrennt IV U5, 106
segregation [ˌsegrɪ'geɪʃn] Rassentrennung; Trennung IV U5, 106
self [self] selbst; sich III
selfie ['selfi] Selfie *(Schnappschuss von sich selbst)* IV U4, 83
selfish ['selfɪʃ] selbstsüchtig IV U2, 39
*__to sell__ [sel] verkaufen III
*__to send__ [send] schicken; senden I
senior citizen [ˌsiːnjə 'sɪtɪzn] Rentner; Rentnerin <IV U5, 214>
sensation [sen'seɪʃn] Sensation <IV U5, 143>
sense of smell [ˌsens‿əv 'smel] Geruchssinn <IV U1, 30>
sent [sent] simple past von *to send* I; past participle von *to send* II
sentence ['sentəns] Satz <I>
separate ['seprət] getrennt; separat; verschieden IV U5, 106
September [sep'tembə] September I
Serbian ['sɜːbiən] serbisch; Serbisch; aus Serbien; Serbe; Serbin <IV U5, 213>
serious ['sɪəriəs] ernst III
Are you serious? [ˌɑː ju 'sɪəriəs] Im Ernst? III
to take sth seriously [ˌteɪk 'sɪəriəsli] etw. ernst nehmen IV U1, 18
to **serve** [sɜːv] servieren IV U2, 33
service ['sɜːvɪs] Dienst III
emergency service [ɪ'mɜːdʒnsi ˌsɜːvɪs] Notdienst; Rettungsdienst III

*to **set** the scene [ˌset ðə 'siːn] beste Voraussetzungen schaffen <IV U3, 69>
to **settle** ['setl] besiedeln; sich niederlassen IV U4, 75
settler ['setlə] Siedler; Siedlerin IV U2, 32
seven ['sevn] sieben I
seventeen [ˌsevn'tiːn] siebzehn I
seventy ['sevnti] siebzig I
shampoo [ʃæm'puː] Shampoo III
shamrock ['ʃæmrɒk] Kleeblatt III
shape [ʃeɪp] Form <III>
to **share** [ʃeə] teilen III
shark [ʃɑːk] Hai I
pencil **sharpener** ['pensl ˌʃɑːpnə] Anspitzer I
she [ʃiː] sie I
sheep *(sg)* [ʃiːp], **sheep** *(pl)* [ʃiːp] Schaf I
shelf *(sg)* [ʃelf], **shelves** *(pl)* [ʃelvz] Regal; Regalbrett I
animal rescue **shelter** [ˌænɪml 'reskjuː ˌʃeltə] Tierheim I
*__to shine__ [ʃaɪn] scheinen; glänzen IV ZI, 8
ship [ʃɪp] Schiff I
ship builder ['ʃɪp ˌbɪldə] Schiffsbauer; Schiffsbauerin III
shipyard ['ʃɪpjɑːd] Werft III
shirt [ʃɜːt] Hemd; Shirt II
shoe [ʃuː] Schuh II
shone [ʃɒn] simple past, past participle von *to shine* IV ZI, 8
*__to shoot__ (a film) [ˌʃuːt (ə 'fɪlm)] (einen Film) drehen <III>
to shoot (at) [ʃuːt (ət)] schießen (auf) IV U3, 63
shop [ʃɒp] Geschäft; Laden I
corner shop ['kɔːnə ˌʃɒp] Tante-Emma-Laden I
shop assistant ['ʃɒp‿əˌsɪstnt] Verkäufer; Verkäuferin II
sports shop ['spɔːts ˌʃɒp] Sportgeschäft I
shopping ['ʃɒpɪŋ] Einkaufen I

to do the shopping [ˌduː ðə 'ʃɒpɪŋ] Einkäufe machen; Besorgungen machen II
to go shopping [ˌgəʊ 'ʃɒpɪŋ] einkaufen gehen II
shopping centre ['ʃɒpɪŋ ˌsentə] Einkaufszentrum I
shopping list ['ʃɒpɪŋ ˌlɪst] Einkaufszettel I
short [ʃɔːt] kurz II
shortly ['ʃɔːtli] kurz III
shorts *(pl)* [ʃɔːts] Shorts; kurze Hose I
shot [ʃɒt] simple past, past participle von *to shoot* IV U3, 63
should [ʃʊd] sollte III
shout [ʃaʊt] Schrei I
to **shout** [ʃaʊt] schreien; rufen II
show [ʃəʊ] Show; Schau; Aufführung IV U5, 102
talent show ['tælənt ˌʃəʊ] Talentwettbewerb I
talk show ['tɔːk ˌʃəʊ] Talkshow <IV U3, 68>
TV show [ˌtiː'viː ˌʃəʊ] Fernsehsendung II
*__to show__ [ʃəʊ] zeigen II
to show off ['ʃəʊ‿ɒf] angeben <IV U5, 142>
to show up [ˌʃəʊ‿'ʌp] auftauchen; erscheinen IV U2, 42
showboat ['ʃəʊˌbəʊt] Theaterschiff <IV U5, 142>
shower ['ʃaʊə] Dusche III
shower gel ['ʃaʊə ˌdʒel] Duschgel III
*__to shut up__ [ʃʌt‿'ʌp] die Klappe halten IV U3, 63
shy [ʃaɪ] schüchtern IV U2, 39
sick [sɪk] krank III
to be sick [biː 'sɪk] sich übergeben I
to feel sick [ˌfiːl 'sɪk] Übelkeit verspüren; sich schlecht fühlen IV U5, 103
side [saɪd] Seite II
sight [saɪt] Sehenswürdigkeit II
sightseeing ['saɪtsiːɪŋ] Besichtigungstour <IV U4, 207>
to go sightseeing [gəʊ 'saɪtsiːɪŋ] eine Besichtigungstour machen II

sign [saɪn] Schild; Zeichen III
sign language ['saɪn ˌlæŋgwɪdʒ] Gebärdensprache; Zeichensprache III
star sign ['stɑː ˌsaɪn] Sternzeichen IV U1, 14
to **sign** [saɪn] unterschreiben; unterzeichnen IV U3, 53
to sign autographs [ˌsaɪn 'ɔːtəgrɑːfs] Autogramme geben IV U3, 53
signal ['sɪgnl] Empfang; Signal; Zeichen III
signature ['sɪgnətʃə] Unterschrift <IV U2, 44>
silence ['saɪləns] Stille; Schweigen; Ruhe III
silent ['saɪlənt] stumm; schweigsam III
silk [sɪlk] Seide III
silly ['sɪli] albern II; dumm; doof III
simple ['sɪmpl] einfach III
simple past [ˌsɪmpl 'pɑːst] einfache Vergangenheit <III>
simple present [ˌsɪmpl 'preznt] Gegenwart; Präsens <III>
since [sɪns] seit; seitdem IV U4, 80
*to **sing** [sɪŋ] singen I
singer ['sɪŋə] Sänger; Sängerin I
single ['sɪŋgl] Single IV U5, 97
single ticket ['sɪŋgl ˌtɪkɪt] einfache Fahrkarte III
*to **sink** [sɪŋk] untergehen; sinken III
siren ['saɪrən] Sirene; Martinshorn <IV U1, 19>
sister ['sɪstə] Schwester I
site [saɪt] Seite *(im Internet)* IV U4, 80
construction site [kən'strʌkʃn ˌsaɪt] Baustelle IV U1, 15
situation [ˌsɪtju'eɪʃn] Situation II
six [sɪks] sechs I
sixteen [ˌsɪk'stiːn] sechzehn I
sixty ['sɪksti] sechzig I
size [saɪz] Größe II
skateboard ['skeɪtbɔːd] Skateboard III
to **ski** [skiː] Ski fahren II
skiing ['skiːɪŋ] Skifahren III
to **skim** [skɪm] überfliegen <III>
skirt [skɜːt] Rock I
skyline ['skaɪlaɪn] Skyline IV U1, 12
skyscraper ['skaɪskreɪpə] Wolkenkratzer IV U1, 14
slave [sleɪv] Sklave; Sklavin IV U4, 86
slavery ['sleɪvri] Sklaverei <IV U3, 138>
sled [sled] Schlitten <IV U1, 30>
sleep [sliːp] Schlaf III
*to **sleep** [sliːp] schlafen I
sleepover ['sliːpˌəʊvə] Übernachtung I
slept [slept] simple past, past participle von *to sleep* II
sliced bread [ˌslaɪst 'bred] in Scheiben geschnittenes Brot III
slogan ['sləʊgən] Slogan; Werbespruch IV U4, 77
slow [sləʊ] langsam III
small [smɔːl] klein III
small talk ['smɔːl ˌtɔːk] Smalltalk <IV U3, 55>
smart [smɑːt] schlau; klug; intelligent III
smartphone ['smɑːtˌfəʊn] Smartphone IV U4, 80
smell [smel] Geruch; Gestank; Duft IV U3, 62
*to **smell** [smel] riechen III
smelt [smelt] simple past, past participle von *to smell* III
to **smile** [smaɪl] lächeln <IV U1, 188>
smoke [sməʊk] Rauch III
smoothie ['smuːði] Smoothie <IV U3, 72>
smuggler ['smʌglə] Schmuggler; Schmugglerin II
smurf [smɜːf] Schlumpf I
snack [snæk] Snack; Imbiss I
snake [sneɪk] Schlange I
snow [snəʊ] Schnee IV U1, 14
so [səʊ] deshalb; also I; so II
so much [ˌsəʊ 'mʌtʃ] so sehr III
soap [səʊp] Seife III
social ['səʊʃl] sozial; gesellschaftlich <IV U1, 134>
social media [ˌsəʊʃl 'miːdiə] soziale Medien IV U4, 80
society [sə'saɪəti] Gesellschaft IV U5, 100
sock [sɒk] Socke I
sofa ['səʊfə] Sofa II
software ['sɒftweə] Software II
sold [səʊld] simple past, past participle von *to sell* III
soldier ['səʊldʒə] Soldat; Soldatin III
solid ['sɒlɪd] fest III
solution [sə'luːʃn] Lösung IV U5, 98
to **solve** [sɒlv] lösen I
some [sʌm] einige; etwas I
someone ['sʌmwʌn] jemand IV U2, 38
something ['sʌmθɪŋ] etwas I
sometimes ['sʌmtaɪmz] manchmal II
son [sʌn] Sohn III
song [sɒŋ] Lied <I>
soon [suːn] bald II
as soon as [əz 'suːn‿əz] sobald IV U4, 89
See you soon! [ˌsiː juː 'suːn] Bis bald! I
sore [sɔː] schmerzhaft; wund II
sore throat [ˌsɔː 'θrəʊt] Halsschmerzen II
Sorry. ['sɒri] Tut mir leid.; Entschuldigung. I
to be sorry [biː 'sɒri] leidtun III
to feel sorry [ˌfiːl 'sɒri fə] Mitleid haben mit; bedauern III
to say sorry [ˌseɪ 'sɒri] sich entschuldigen II
sort [sɔːt] Sorte; Art II
to **sort** [sɔːt] sortieren IV U2, 38
sound [saʊnd] Ton; Laut; Geräusch III
to **sound** [saʊnd] klingen II
soup [suːp] Suppe II
sweet and **sour** [ˌswiːt‿ən 'saʊə] süßsauer <IV U5, 213>
source [sɔːs] Quelle <IV U1, 27>
south [saʊθ] Süden III
south of ['saʊθ‿əv] südlich von IV ZI, 9
in the south of [ˌɪn ðə 'saʊθ‿əv] im Süden von III
southern ['sʌðən] südlich IV U5, 96
Southerner ['sʌðənə] Südstaatler; Südstaatlerin IV U5, 97
souvenir [ˌsuːvn'ɪə] Souvenir; Andenken III

souvenir shop ['su:vnɪə ˌʃɒp] Souvenirladen III
soy bean ['sɔɪ ˌbi:n] Sojabohne IV ZI, 9
spaghetti [spə'geti] Spaghetti II
Spanish ['spænɪʃ] spanisch; Spanisch; aus Spanien IV U5, 98
*to **speak** [spi:k] sprechen III
speaker ['spi:kə] Redner; Rednerin; Sprecher; Sprecherin <IV U3, 138>
speaking ['spi:kɪŋ] Sprechen <I>
speaking skills ['spi:kɪŋ ˌskɪlz] Fertigkeit Sprechen <I>
spear [spɪə] Speer <IV U2, 136>
special ['speʃl] besonders; speziell I
special effect [ˌspeʃl ɪ'fekt] Spezialeffekt <IV U4, 140>
special offer [ˌspeʃl‿'ɒfə] Sonderangebot III
with special needs [wɪθ ˌspeʃl 'ni:dz] mit Behinderung; mit besonderen Bedürfnissen III
spectacular [spek'tækjələ] spektakulär IV U4, 77
speech [spi:tʃ] Sprache; Rede III
direct speech [dɪˌrekt 'spi:tʃ] direkte Rede <IV U5, 110>
farewell speech [feə'wel spi:tʃ] Abschiedsrede II
speech bubble ['spi:tʃ ˌbʌbl] Sprechblase <III>
speech impaired ['spi:tʃ ɪmˌpeərd] sprachbehindert IV U5, 102
*to **spell** [spel] buchstabieren I
spelling ['spelɪŋ] Rechtschreibung I
*to **spend** [spend] ausgeben *(Geld)*; verbringen *(Zeit)* II
spent [spent] simple past, past participle von *to spend* II
spice [spaɪs] Gewürz II
spider ['spaɪdə] Spinne III
spoke [spəʊk] simple past von *to speak* III
spoken ['spəʊkn] past participle von *to speak* III
spoon [spu:n] Löffel II
sport [spɔ:t] Sport I; Sportart III
sports shop ['spɔ:ts ˌʃɒp] Sportgeschäft I
sporting event ['spɔ:tɪŋ ɪˌvent] Sportereignis; Sportveranstaltung <IV U2, 50>
to **sprain** [spreɪn] verstauchen; verrenken III
spring roll [ˌsprɪŋ 'rəʊl] Frühlingsrolle II
square [skweə] Platz II
square mile (= sq. mi.) [ˌskweə 'maɪl] Quadratmeile IV ZI, 8
stadium ['steɪdiəm] Stadion II
stage [steɪdʒ] Bühne II
stall [stɔ:l] Stand; Bude <IV U5, 110>
food stall ['fu:d ˌstɔ:l] Essensstand II
market stall ['mɑ:kɪt ˌstɔ:l] Marktstand; Marktbude <IV U2, 195>
stallholder ['stɔ:lˌhəʊldə] Standinhaber; Standinhaberin II
stamp [stæmp] Briefmarke III
*to **stand** [stænd] stehen II
standup paddleboarding ['stændʌp ˌpædlbɔ:dɪŋ] Stehpaddeln <IV U3, 72>
star [stɑ:] Star I; Stern III
star sign ['stɑ: ˌsaɪn] Sternzeichen IV U1, 14
start [stɑ:t] Start; Anfang III
to **start** [stɑ:t] anfangen; beginnen; starten II; gründen III
to start a band [ˌstɑ:t‿ə 'bænd] eine Band gründen II
starting point ['stɑ:tɪŋ ˌpɔɪnt] Ausgangspunkt <III>
state [steɪt] Staat; Bundesstaat; Land IV ZI, 8
state government ['steɪt ˌgʌvnmənt] Landesregierung IV U5, 98
State House *(AE)* ['steɪt ˌhaʊs] Regierungsgebäude IV U5, 98
statement ['steɪtmənt] Aussage; Behauptung <IV U3, 201>
station ['steɪʃn] Haltestelle; Station; Bahnhof III
statistical [stə'tɪstɪkl] statistisch <IV U1, 26>
statistics *(no pl)* [stə'tɪstɪks] Statistik IV U1, 22
status ['steɪtəs] Status IV U4, 81
to **stay** [steɪ] übernachten; bleiben II
*to **steal** [sti:l] stehlen IV U2, 38
steam engine ['sti:m‿endʒɪn] Dampfmaschine III
paddle **steamer** ['pædl ˌsti:mə] Raddampfer <IV U5, 142>
steel [sti:l] Stahl III
step [step] Schritt III; Stufe II
stereotype ['steriəʊtaɪp] Stereotyp; Klischee <IV U2, 42>
sticker ['stɪkə] Aufkleber II
sticky note [ˌstɪki 'nəʊt] Haftnotizzettel <IV U3, 65>
still [stɪl] dennoch III
to **stir** [stɜ:] rühren; umrühren II
stocks [stɒks] Pranger III
stole [stəʊl] simple past von *to steal* IV U2, 38
stolen ['stəʊlən] past participle von *to steal* IV U2, 38
stomach ['stʌmək] Magen; Bauch II
stomach ache ['stʌmək ˌeɪk] Bauchweh; Bauchschmerzen II
stone [stəʊn] Stein III
stood [stʊd] simple past, past participle von *to stand* II
stop [stɒp] Haltestelle; Halt III
bus stop ['bʌs ˌstɒp] Bushaltestelle II
one stop [ˌwʌn 'stɒp] einmal Umsteigen <IV U3, 66>
to **stop** [stɒp] aufhören I
store *(AE)* [stɔ:] Laden; Geschäft IV U2, 33
department store [dɪ'pɑ:tmənt ˌstɔ:] Kaufhaus II
to **store** [stɔ:] aufbewahren; lagern <IV U1, 30>
storm [stɔ:m] Sturm I
story ['stɔ:ri] Geschichte I
feature story ['fi:tʃə ˌstɔ:ri] Leitartikel; Sonderbericht <IV U5, 110>
mystery story ['mɪstri ˌstɔ:ri] Krimi (= Kriminalgeschichte); Detektivgeschichte IV U3, 53

story *(AE)* ['stɔ:ri] Stock; Stockwerk; Etage IV U1, 14
straight [streɪt] gerade <IV U2, 47>
straight ahead [ˌstreɪt ə'hed] geradeaus <IV U1, 187>
straight on [streɪt‿'ɒn] geradeaus I
hair **straightener** ['heə ˌstreɪtnə] Haarglätter IV U3, 59
strange [streɪndʒ] merkwürdig; seltsam II
straw [strɔ:] Trinkhalm II
strawberry ['strɔ:bri] Erdbeere II
stream [stri:m] Bach II; <IV U2, 136>
street [stri:t] Straße III
street gang ['stri:t ˌgæŋ] Straßengang <IV U1, 134>
stress [stres] Stress IV U3, 57
strict [strɪkt] streng; strikt IV U2, 34
striking ['straɪkɪŋ] bemerkenswert; auffallend III
strong [strɒŋ] stark III
structure ['strʌktʃə] Struktur; Aufbau <III>
to **structure** ['strʌktʃə] strukturieren; gliedern <IV U2, 46>
*to be **stuck** [bi: 'stʌk] feststecken; nicht weg können I
*to get **stuck** [ˌget 'stʌk] stecken bleiben IV U3, 54
student ['stju:dnt] Schüler; Schülerin I
studio ['stju:diəʊ] Studio IV U4, 75
TV studio [ˌti:'vi: ˌstju:diəʊ] Fernsehstudio II
study hall period ['stʌdi hɔ:l ˌpɪəriəd] Freistunde IV U2, 34
study skills [ˌstʌdi 'skɪlz] Fertigkeit Lern- und Arbeitstechniken <I>
to **study** ['stʌdi] studieren; lernen IV U2, 34
stunt [stʌnt] Stunt <IV U2, 50>
style [staɪl] Stil III
subject ['sʌbdʒɪkt] Schulfach I
submarine [ˌsʌbmr'i:n] U-Boot I
to **subscribe** [səb'skraɪb] abonnieren IV U4, 81
subtotal ['sʌbˌtəʊtl] Zwischensumme <IV U3, 66>
suburb ['sʌbɜ:b] Vorort IV U1, 15
subway *(AE)* ['sʌbweɪ] U-Bahn IV U1, 14
to **succeed** (in) [sək'si:d (ɪn)] Erfolg haben (mit/bei); nachfolgen IV U1, 19
success [sək'ses] Erfolg III
successful [sək'sesfl] erfolgreich IV U1, 18
such [sʌtʃ] solch IV U2, 38
suddenly ['sʌdnli] plötzlich; auf einmal II
suggestion [sə'dʒestʃn] Vorschlag; Anregung <IV U3, 72>
to **suit** [su:t] stehen; passen II
suitable ['su:təbl] geeignet; passend <IV U2, 51>
suitcase ['su:tkeɪs] Koffer II
to **sum up** [ˌsʌm‿'ʌp] zusammenfassen IV U3, 73
to **summarise** ['sʌmraɪz] zusammenfassen <IV U3, 73>
summary ['sʌmri] Zusammenfassung <III>
summer ['sʌmə] Sommer II
sun [sʌn] Sonne III
to **sunbathe** ['sʌnbeɪð] sonnenbaden II
Sunday ['sʌndeɪ] Sonntag I
sunglasses *(pl)* ['sʌnˌglɑ:sɪz] Sonnenbrille II
sunk [sʌŋk] past participle von *to sink* III
sunny ['sʌni] sonnig I
superhero ['su:pəˌhɪərəʊ] *(sg)*, **superheroes** ['su:pəˌhɪərəʊz] *(pl)* Superheld IV U3, 61
supermarket ['su:pəˌmɑ:kɪt] Supermarkt II
supplies *(pl)* [sə'plaɪz] Vorräte <IV U1, 30>
support [sə'pɔ:t] Unterstützung; Hilfe IV U1, 19
supporter [sə'pɔ:tə] Anhänger; Anhängerin; Fan <IV U2, 50>
sure [ʃʊə] sicher II
to make sure [ˌmeɪk 'ʃɔ:] sich versichern IV U1, 14
sure of oneself ['ʃʊər‿əv ˌwʌnself] selbstsicher III
to **surf** [sɜ:f] surfen; wellenreiten II
to surf the internet [ˌsɜ:f ði 'ɪntənet] im Internet surfen II
surfer ['sɜ:fə] Wellenreiter; Wellenreiterin; Surfer; Surferin IV ZI, 9
surfing ['sɜ:fɪŋ] Wellenreiten; Surfen IV U4, 74
surprise [sə'praɪz] Überraschung I
surprised [sə'praɪzd] überrascht II
survey ['sɜ:veɪ] Umfrage II
to **survive** [sə'vaɪv] überleben III
sushi ['su:ʃi] Sushi IV U5, 99
swam [swæm] simple past von *to swim* II
swamp [swɒmp] Sumpf IV ZI, 9
sweatshirt ['swetʃɜ:t] Sweatshirt I
*to **sweep** [swi:p] fegen II
sweet [swi:t] Süßigkeit; Bonbon I
sweet [swi:t] süß III
sweet and sour [ˌswi:t‿ən 'saʊə] süßsauer <IV U5, 213>
swept [swept] simple past, past participle von *to sweep* II
*to **swim** [swɪm] schwimmen II
swimmer ['swɪmə] Schwimmer; Schwimmerin IV U4, 79
*to go **swimming** [ˌgəʊ 'swɪmɪŋ] schwimmen gehen I
swimming pool ['swɪmɪŋ ˌpu:l] Schwimmbad I
Swiss [swɪs] schweizerisch; aus der Schweiz; Schweizer; Schweizerin IV U4, 84
sword [sɔ:d] Schwert III
swum [swʌm] past participle von *to swim* II
symbol ['sɪmbl] Symbol IV U1, 13
Syrian ['sɪriən] syrisch; aus Syrien; Syrer; Syrerin <IV U5, 213>
system ['sɪstəm] System IV U5, 107

T

table ['teɪbl] Tisch I; Tabelle <III>
table tennis ['teɪbl ˌtenɪs] Tischtennis II

tablespoon ['teɪblspu:n] Esslöffel II
tablet ['tæblət] Tablette II; Tablet IV U4, 80
tactic ['tæktɪk] Taktik; Vorgehensweise III
take [teɪk] Aufnahme <III>
*to **take** [teɪk] nehmen; mitnehmen; bringen; mitbringen; hinbringen II; dauern III
to take a break [ˌteɪk‿ə 'breɪk] Pause machen II
to take a photo [ˌteɪk‿ə 'fəʊtəʊ] ein Foto machen I
to take a test [ˌteɪk‿ə 'test] eine Prüfung machen <IV U2, 44>
to take a trip [ˌteɪk‿ə 'trɪp] eine Fahrt machen III
to take care of sb [ˌteɪk 'keər‿əv] sich um jmdn. kümmern; für jmdn. sorgen IV U2, 41
to take notes [ˌteɪk 'nəʊts] sich Notizen machen I
to take off [ˌteɪk‿'ɒf] ausziehen III
to take out [ˌteɪk‿'aʊt] herausnehmen I
to take part (in) [ˌteɪk 'pɑ:t] teilnehmen (an) III
to take place [ˌteɪk 'pleɪs] stattfinden <IV U4, 140>
to take sth seriously [ˌteɪk 'sɪəriəsli] etw. ernst nehmen IV U1, 18
to take the dog for a walk [ˌteɪk ðə dɒg fɔ:r‿ə 'wɔ:k] den Hund ausführen I
to take turns [ˌteɪk 'tɜ:nz] sich abwechseln <II>
to take up [ˌteɪk‿'ʌp] einnehmen *(Platz)* <IV U1, 27>
takeaway ['teɪkəweɪ] Essen zum Mitnehmen II
taken ['teɪkn] past participle von *to take* II
talent show ['tælənt ˌʃəʊ] Talentwettbewerb I
What's your **talent**? [wɒts jɔ: 'tælənt] Was ist dein Talent? I
talented ['tæləntɪd] talentiert III
talk [tɔ:k] Vortrag; Rede <III>
to give a talk [ˌgɪv‿ə 'tɔ:k] einen Vortrag halten <III>
small talk ['smɔ:l ˌtɔ:k] Smalltalk <IV U3, 55>
talk show ['tɔ:k ˌʃəʊ] Talkshow <IV U3, 68>
to **talk** (to) [tɔ:k] sprechen (mit); reden (mit) I
to talk about ['tɔ:k‿əˌbaʊt] sprechen über II
tall [tɔ:l] groß; hoch II
task [tɑ:sk] Aufgabe; Auftrag <I>
to **taste** [teɪst] schmecken <IV U3, 72>
tasty ['teɪsti] lecker; schmackhaft III
tax [tæks] Steuer <IV U3, 66>
taxi ['tæksi] Taxi II
tea [ti:] Tee; (frühes) Abendessen I
teacher ['ti:tʃə] Lehrer; Lehrerin I
team [ti:m] Team; Gruppe I
teamwork ['ti:mwɜ:k] Teamwork II
to **tease** [ti:z] hänseln; sticheln; reizen IV U2, 38
teaspoon ['ti:spu:n] Teelöffel II
Design **Technology** (DT) [dɪˌzaɪn tek'nɒlədʒi, ˌdi:'ti:] Technik I
teen [ti:n] Jugend-; Teenager; Jugendliche; Jugendlicher II
teenage ['ti:neɪdʒ] jugendlich IV U3, 54
teenager ['ti:nˌeɪdʒə] Teenager; Jugendliche; Jugendlicher III
telephone ['telɪfəʊn] Telefon III
telephone box ['telɪfəʊn ˌbɒks] Telefonzelle II
*to **tell** [tel] erzählen; sagen I
ten [ten] zehn I
tennis ['tenɪs] Tennis I
tent [tent] Zelt III
tepee ['ti:pi:] Tipi <IV U2, 136>
terrible ['terəbl] schrecklich; furchtbar IV U2, 32
territory ['terɪtri] Gebiet; Revier; Territorium <IV U5, 142>
test [test] Test; Klassenarbeit; Prüfung IV U3, 61
to take a test [ˌteɪk‿ə 'test] eine Prüfung machen <IV U2, 44>
to **test** [test] testen; prüfen II
text [tekst] Text II
text message ['tekst ˌmesɪdʒ] Textnachricht (SMS) I
to **text** [tekst] texten; eine SMS schreiben II
texter ['tekstə] SMS-Schreiber; SMS-Schreiberin II
than [ðæn] als II
Thank you. ['θæŋk ju] Danke. I
thankful ['θæŋkfl] dankbar IV U3, 54
Thanks. [θæŋks] Danke. I
Thanks so much. [ˌθæŋk‿səʊ 'mʌtʃ] Vielen Dank.; Herzlichen Dank. IV U4, 94
Thanksgiving [ˌθæŋks'gɪvɪŋ] Erntedankfest IV U3, 53
that [ðæt] das I; dass III
after that [ˌɑ:ftə 'ðæt] danach I
that's £2.24 [ðæts ˌtu: paʊndz twenti'fɔ:] das macht 2 Pfund und 24 Pence I
the [ðə] der; die; das I
the same [ðə 'seɪm] derselbe; gleich II
theater *(AE)* ['θɪətə] Theater IV U1, 13
movie theater *(AE)* ['mu:vi ˌθi:ətə] Kino IV U5, 106
theatre ['θɪətə] Theater II
their [ðeə] ihr I
theirs [ðeəz] ihre III
them [ðem] sie II
theme park ['θi:m ˌpɑ:k] Freizeitpark I
themselves [ðəm'selvz] selber; sie selbst; sich selbst; selbst III
then [ðen] dann; danach I; damals III
there [ðeə] da; dort I
down there [ˌdaʊn 'ðeə] dahin; da unten IV U5, 98
over there [ˌəʊvə 'ðeə] da drüben; dort drüben II
there are [ðeər‿'ɑ:] da sind; es gibt I
there is (= there's) [ðeə‿'ɪz] da ist; es gibt I
these [ði:z] diese II
they [ðeɪ] sie *(Pl.)* I
thing [θɪŋ] Sache; Ding II

*to **think** [θɪŋk] denken I
to think of ['θɪŋk‿əv] sich ausdenken; sich etwas einfallen lassen <III>
third [θɜ:d] dritte I
thirsty ['θɜ:sti] durstig II
thirteen [θɜ:'ti:n] dreizehn I
thirty ['θɜ:ti] dreißig I
this [ðɪs] das; dies I
like this [laɪk 'ðɪs] so; auf diese Weise III
this way [ðɪs 'weɪ] in diese Richtung II
those [ðəʊz] jene II
thought [θɔ:t] Gedanke IV U3, 62
thought [θɔ:t] simple past, past participle von *to think* II
a/one **thousand** [ə/wʌn 'θaʊznd] eintausend; tausend II
three [θri:] drei I
threw [θru:] simple past von *to throw* IV U2, 38
throat [θrəʊt] Hals II
sore throat [ˌsɔ: 'θrəʊt] Halsschmerzen II
through [θru:] durch II
*to **throw** [θrəʊ] werfen IV U2, 38
thrown [θrəʊn] past participle von *to throw* IV U2, 38
Thursday ['θɜ:zdeɪ] Donnerstag I
ticket ['tɪkɪt] Karte II; Fahrschein; Eintrittskarte III
return ticket [rɪ'tɜ:n ˌtɪkɪt] Hin- und Rückfahrkarte III
single ticket ['sɪŋgl ˌtɪkɪt] einfache Fahrkarte III
to **tidy (up)** [ˌtaɪdi 'ʌp] aufräumen; in Ordnung bringen II
to **tie** [taɪ] binden; zubinden; fesseln IV U3, 62
tiger ['taɪgə] Tiger I
tight [taɪt] eng; fest II
time [taɪm] Zeit; Uhrzeit I; Mal III
free time [ˌfri: 'taɪm] Freizeit I
on time [ɒn 'taɪm] pünktlich III
opening times ['əʊpənɪŋ ˌtaɪmz] Öffnungszeiten IV U5, 105
time travel ['taɪm ˌtrævl] Zeitreise III
time zone ['taɪm ˌzəʊn] Zeitzone IV ZI, 8
the first time [ðə ˌfɜ:st 'taɪm] das erste Mal I
timeline ['taɪmlaɪn] Zeitlinie <IV U4, 87>
timetable ['taɪmˌteɪbl] Stundenplan I; Fahrplan III
tin [tɪn] Dose; Büchse; Mülleimer IV U3, 63
tiny ['taɪni] klein; winzig III
tip [tɪp] Tipp III; Ratschlag <I>
language tip [ˌlæŋgwɪdʒ 'tɪp] Grammatikhinweis <I>
tired [taɪəd] müde I
tissue ['tɪʃu:] Taschentuch III
title ['taɪtl] Titel; Überschrift <II>
job title ['dʒɒb ˌtaɪtl] Stellenbezeichnung; Berufsbezeichnung IV U2, 38
to [tu:] in; nach; zu; vor *(bei Uhrzeitangaben)* I; bis II
today [tə'deɪ] heute I
together [tə'geðə] zusammen; gemeinsam I
told [təʊld] simple past von *to tell* I
to **tolerate** ['tɒlreɪt] tolerieren; dulden IV U5, 98
tomato *(sg)* [tə'ma:təʊ], **tomatoes** *(pl)* [tə'ma:təʊz] Tomate II
tomorrow [tə'mɒrəʊ] morgen II
tongue twister ['tʌŋ ˌtwɪstə] Zungenbrecher <III>
tonne [tʌn] Tonne II
too [tu:] auch I; zu II
too much [ˌtu: 'mʌtʃ] zu sehr II
took [tʊk] simple past von *to take* II
tool [tu:l] Werkzeug II
tooth *(sg)* [tu:θ], **teeth** *(pl)* [ti:θ] Zahn III
toothbrush ['tu:θbrʌʃ] Zahnbürste III
toothpaste ['tu:θpeɪst] Zahnpasta III
toothpick ['tu:θpɪk] Zahnstocher II
top [tɒp] Top; Oberteil II; Spitze; oberer Teil; oberes Ende IV U1, 13
topic ['tɒpɪk] Thema IV U2, 51
torch [tɔ:tʃ] Taschenlampe I
torn [tɔ:n] zerrissen; aufgerissen IV U4, 83
tornado [tɔ:'neɪdəʊ] Tornado; Wirbelsturm IV U2, 32
total ['təʊtl] Summe <IV U3, 66>
total ['təʊtl] Gesamt-; gesamt IV ZI, 8
*to keep in **touch** [ˌki:p ɪn 'tʌtʃ] in Verbindung bleiben II
touchdown ['tʌtʃdaʊn] Touchdown <IV U2, 50>
tough [tʌf] hart III
tour [tʊə] Tour; Fahrt; Reise IV U4, 76
guided tour ['gaɪdɪd ˌtɔ:] Führung <IV U1, 13>
tourist ['tʊərɪst] Tourist; Touristin I
Tourist Information Centre [ˌtʊərɪst‿ɪnfə'meɪʃn ˌsentə] Touristeninformation I
in **tow** [ɪn 'təʊ] im Schlepptau IV U2, 42
towards [tə'wɔ:dz] in Richtung; auf … zu IV U3, 62
towel ['taʊəl] Handtuch III
tower ['taʊə] Turm II
clock tower ['klɒk ˌtaʊə] Uhrenturm II
town [taʊn] Stadt I
toy [tɔɪ] Spielzeug III
cuddly toy ['kʌdli ˌtɔɪ] Kuscheltier III
track [træk] Strecke IV U5, 102
railway track ['reɪlweɪ ˌtræk] Gleis IV U3, 64
tractor ['træktə] Traktor I
trader ['treɪdə] Händler; Händlerin <IV U2, 136>
tradition [trə'dɪʃn] Tradition III
traffic ['træfɪk] Verkehr III
traffic jam ['træfɪk ˌdʒæm] Stau IV U1, 14
tragic ['trædʒɪk] tragisch <IV U2, 136>
trail [treɪl] Wanderweg; Spur IV U5, 102
train [treɪn] Zug I
to go by (train) [ˌgəʊ baɪ ('treɪn)] mit (dem Zug) fahren I

trainer ['treɪnə] Turnschuh I; Trainer; Trainerin IV U5, 103
training ['treɪnɪŋ] Training III
tram [træm] Straßenbahn III
transcontinental [ˌtrænsˌkɒntɪ'nentl] transkontinental *(über den Kontinent hinweg)* IV U4, 86
transfer [træns'fɜ:] Transport; Transfer IV U5, 102
to **translate** [trænz'leɪt] übersetzen IV U5, 102
transparency [træn'spærnsi] Folie <IV U2, 51>
transport ['trænspɔ:t] Transport <IV U1, 30>
public transport [ˌpʌblɪk 'trænspɔ:t] öffentliche Verkehrsmittel III
to **transport** [træn'spɔ:t] transportieren; befördern <IV U1, 30>
travel ['trævl] (das) Reisen <IV U1, 30>
time travel ['taɪm ˌtrævl] Zeitreise III
to **travel** ['trævl] reisen II; fahren III
tray [treɪ] Tablett II
treasure ['treʒə] Schatz II
tree [tri:] Baum I
tree house ['tri: ˌhaʊs] Baumhaus I
trend [trend] Trend; Entwicklung; Richtung IV U4, 83
trending ['trendɪŋ] trendsetzend IV U4, 81
trendy ['trendi] trendy; modisch IV U4, 81
tribe [traɪb] Stamm; Volksstamm <IV U1, 24>
trick [trɪk] Trick; Streich I; Kunststück III
Trick or treat! [ˌtrɪk‿ə 'tri:t] Süßes, sonst gibt's Saures! I
trip [trɪp] Ausflug I; Trip; Fahrt; Reise III
boat trip ['bəʊt ˌtrɪp] Bootsfahrt; Schiffsfahrt II
field trip ['fi:ld ˌtrɪp] Schulausflug <IV U2, 46>
outgoing trip [ˌaʊtgəʊɪŋ 'trɪp] Hinfahrt <IV U3, 66>
return trip [ˌrɪtɜ:n 'trɪp] Rückfahrt <IV U3, 66>
round trip [ˌraʊnd 'trɪp] Hin- und Rückflug; Hin- und Rückfahrt <IV U3, 66>
to take a trip [ˌteɪk‿ə 'trɪp] eine Fahrt machen III
trouble ['trʌbl] Schwierigkeiten; Problem; Ärger III
trousers *(pl)* ['traʊzəz] Hose I
truck [trʌk] Wagen; Karre III; Truck; Lastwagen <IV U1, 30>
true [tru:] wahr II; treu IV U2, 34
to **trust** [trʌst] vertrauen IV U5, 109
to **try** [traɪ] ausprobieren III
to try on [ˌtraɪ 'ɒn] anprobieren II
to try out [ˌtraɪ‿'aʊt] ausprobieren III
T-shirt ['ti:ʃɜ:t] T-Shirt I
tube [tju:b] Schlauch; Rohr III
Tuesday ['tju:zdeɪ] Dienstag I
on Tuesday [ˌɒn 'tju:zdeɪ] am Dienstag I
tuna ['tju:nə] Thunfisch II
tunnel ['tʌnl] Tunnel III
(wind) **turbine** [(wɪnd) 'tɜ:baɪn] Windrad III
turkey ['tɜ:ki] Truthahn; Pute IV U3, 53
Turkish ['tɜ:kɪʃ] türkisch; Türkisch; aus der Türkei IV U5, 99
turn [tɜ:n] Drehung IV U5, 102
to take turns [ˌteɪk 'tɜ:nz] sich abwechseln <II>
to wait one's turn [ˌweɪt wʌnz 'tɜ:n] warten, bis man an der Reihe ist <IV U5, 110>
to **turn** [tɜ:n] abbiegen III
to turn left (into ...) [ˌtɜ:n 'left] (nach) links abbiegen I
to turn on [ˌtɜ:n‿'ɒn] einschalten IV U3, 64
to turn right (into ...) [ˌtɜ:n 'raɪt] rechts abbiegen I
tutor ['tju:tə] Klassenlehrer; Klassenlehrerin I
tutor group ['tju:tə ˌgru:p] Klasse I
tutorial [tju:'tɔ:riəl] Anleitung; Tutorial IV U4, 80
TV [ˌti:'vi:] Fernseher I
on TV [ɒn ˌti:'vi:] im Fernsehen IV U1, 13
TV show [ˌti:'vi: ˌʃəʊ] Fernsehsendung II
TV studio [ˌti:'vi: ˌstju:diəʊ] Fernsehstudio II
to watch TV [ˌwɒtʃ ti:'vi:] fernsehen I
twelve [twelv] zwölf I
twenty ['twenti] zwanzig I
twenty-one [ˌtwenti'wʌn] einundzwanzig I
to **twist** [twɪst] verdrehen; verzerren II
two [tu:] zwei I
type [taɪp] Sorte; Typ; Art III
to **type** [taɪp] tippen <III>
tyre [taɪə] Reifen III

U

umbrella [ʌm'brelə] Regenschirm II
umpire ['ʌmpaɪə] Schiedsrichter; Schiedsrichterin <III>
unappealing [ˌʌnə'pi:lɪŋ] uninteressant IV U4, 77
uncle ['ʌŋkl] Onkel II
uncomfortable [ʌn'kʌmftəbl] unbequem; unangenehm II
under ['ʌndə] unter I
underground ['ʌndəgraʊnd] U-Bahn II
underlined [ˌʌndə'laɪnd] unterstrichen <III>
*to **understand** [ˌʌndə'stænd] verstehen II
understood [ˌʌndə'stʊd] simple past, past participle von *to understand* II
unemployment *(no pl)* [ˌʌnɪm'plɔɪmənt] Arbeitslosigkeit <IV U2, 137>
unfair [ʌn'feə] unfair III
unfashionable [ʌn'fæʃnəbl] unmodisch II
to **unfriend** [ʌn'frend] entfreunden *(jmdn. von seiner Freundesliste streichen)* IV U4, 81

unfriendly [ʌn'frendli] unfreundlich III
unhappy [ʌn'hæpi] unglücklich II
uniform ['ju:nɪfɔ:m] Uniform I
unit ['ju:nɪt] Lektion; Kapitel <I>
unmotivated [ˌʌn'məʊtɪveɪtɪd] unmotiviert IV U2, 39
until [ʌn'tɪl] bis I
unusual [ʌn'ju:ʒl] ungewöhnlich; außergewöhnlich IV U4, 77
up [ʌp] hinauf; oben II
to pick **up** [ˌpɪk‿'ʌp] abholen IV U2, 43
to put **up** [ˌpʊt‿'ʌp] aufstellen; errichten IV U3, 64
to show **up** [ˌʃəʊ‿'ʌp] auftauchen; erscheinen IV U2, 42
to shut **up** [ˌʃʌt‿'ʌp] die Klappe halten IV U3, 63
to wash **up** [ˌwɒʃ‿'ʌp] abwaschen; abspülen <IV U2, 195>
to **update** ['ʌpdeɪt] updaten; auf den neuesten Stand bringen IV U4, 81
updated [ʌp'deɪtɪd] aktualisiert <IV U1, 30>
to **upload** ['ʌpləʊd] ins Internet stellen; hochladen II
upper ['ʌpə] obere III
us [ʌs] uns I
US [ˌju:'es] US-amerikanisch IV U1, 18
to **use** [ju:z] benutzen; verwenden II
to get **used** to (sth) [ˌget 'ju:zd tə] sich an (etw.) gewöhnen IV U1, 18
used to (+ infinitive) ['ju:st tə] pflegte(n) zu; tat(en) früher IV U3, 54
used to (live) ['ju:st tə] (wohnte) früher III
useful ['ju:sfl] nützlich; hilfreich III
usually ['ju:ʒli] normalerweise; gewöhnlich II

V

vacation *(AE)* [və'keɪʃn] Ferien; Urlaub IV U5, 104
vacuum cleaner ['vækju:m ˌkli:nə] Staubsauger IV U3, 59
valid ['vælɪd] gültig III
van [væn] Lieferwagen; Transporter III
variety [və'raɪəti] Auswahl <IV U3, 72>
veganism *(no pl)* ['vi:gənɪzm] Veganismus IV U4, 83
vegetable (veg) ['vedʒtəbl] Gemüse II
vegetarian [ˌvedʒɪ'teəriən] Vegetarier; Vegetarierin I
veggie bean cake [ˌvedʒi 'bi:n keɪk] vegetarisches Bohnengericht II
version ['vɜ:ʃn] Version <IV U1, 135>
very ['veri] sehr I
vet [vet] Tierarzt; Tierärztin II
Victorian era [vɪkˌtɔ:riən 'ɪərə] viktorianisches Zeitalter III
video ['vɪdiəʊ] Video IV U3, 54
video chat ['vɪdiəʊ ˌtʃæt] Video-Chat III
Vietnamese [ˌvjetnə'mi:z] vietnamesisch; Vietnamesisch; aus Vietnam; Vietnamese; Vietnamesin <IV U5, 213>
view [vju:] Aussicht; Sicht; Ausblick; Blick IV U1, 14
viewing ['vju:ɪŋ] Hör-/Sehverstehen <I>
viewing skills ['vju:ɪŋ ˌskɪlz] Fertigkeit Hör-/Sehverstehen <I>
the **Vikings** [ðə 'vaɪkɪŋz] die Wikinger III
village ['vɪlɪdʒ] Dorf III
visa ['vi:zə] Visum; Einreisebewilligung IV U1, 19
to **visit** ['vɪzɪt] besuchen II
visitor ['vɪzɪtə] Besucher; Besucherin II
voice [vɔɪs] Stimme III
volleyball ['vɒlibɔ:l] Volleyball II
volunteer [ˌvɒlən'tɪə] Freiwilliger; Freiwillige; ehrenamtlicher Helfer; ehrenamtliche Helferin III
to **vote** for ['vəʊt fə] abstimmen über; wählen IV U2, 33
voyage ['vɔɪɪdʒ] Reise; Fahrt III

W

wage [weɪdʒ] Lohn IV U2, 38
wagon ['wægən] Waggon; Planwagen IV U4, 85
to **wait** [weɪt] warten II
to **wait** for [weɪt 'fɔ:] warten auf II
to **wait** one's turn [ˌweɪt wʌnz 'tɜ:n] warten, bis man an der Reihe ist <IV U5, 110>
waiter ['weɪtə] Kellner II
waitress ['weɪtrəs] Kellnerin; Bedienung IV U4, 89
*to **wake** up [ˌweɪk‿'ʌp] aufwachen II
walk [wɔ:k] Spaziergang III
to go for a **walk** [ˌgəʊ fər‿ə 'wɔ:k] spazieren gehen I
night **walk** ['naɪt wɔ:k] Nachtwanderung I
a five minute **walk** [ə 'faɪv mɪnɪt ˌwɔ:k] fünf Minuten zu Fuß III
to take the dog for a **walk** [ˌteɪk ðə dɒg fɔ:r‿ə 'wɔ:k] den Hund ausführen I
to **walk** [wɔ:k] gehen; laufen I
dog **walker** ['dɒg ˌwɔ:kə] Hundeausführer; Hundeausführerin IV U2, 41
walking ['wɔ:kɪŋ] Wandern III
wall [wɔ:l] Mauer; Wand II
to **want** (to) ['wɒnt] wollen I
war [wɔ:] Krieg <IV U1, 188>
Civil **War** [ˌsɪvl 'wɔ:] Bürgerkrieg <IV U3, 138>
wardrobe ['wɔ:drəʊb] Kleiderschrank I
warm [wɔ:m] warm I
was [wɒz] simple past von *to be* I
to **wash** [wɒʃ] (sich) waschen; spülen III
to **wash** up [ˌwɒʃ‿'ʌp] abwaschen; abspülen <IV U2, 195>
*to do the **washing** up [ˌdu: ðə 'wɒʃɪŋ‿ʌp] abspülen II
waste [weɪst] Abfall <IV U1, 30>
to **watch** [wɒtʃ] anschauen I; aufpassen auf; zuschauen; beobachten II
to **watch** TV [ˌwɒtʃ ti:'vi:] fernsehen I

p pen • b bed • t ten • d dad • k cat • g grey • tʃ chair • dʒ joke • f fan • v very • θ three • ð the

bird watching ['bɜːd ˌwɒtʃɪŋ] Vogelbeobachtung III
water ['wɔːtə] Wasser III
mineral **water** ['mɪnrl ˌwɔːtə] Mineralwasser III
water level ['wɔːtə ˌlevl] Wasserpegel; Wasserstand <IV U5, 142>
wave [weɪv] Welle IV ZI, 9
to wave [weɪv] winken II
way [weɪ] Weg; Art und Weise III
way in [ˌweɪ 'ɪn] Einstieg <I>
way to go ['weɪ tə ˌgəʊ] super II
asking the **way** [ˌɑːskɪŋ ðə 'weɪ] nach dem Weg fragen I
No **way**! [ˌnəʊ 'weɪ] Auf keinen Fall!; Was?!; Echt?! III
this **way** [ðɪs 'weɪ] in diese Richtung II
we [wiː; wi] wir I
weak [wiːk] schwach III
wealth [welθ] Reichtum III
*to **wear** [weə] tragen I
weather ['weðə] Wetter I
web [web] Spinnennetz; Netz III
website ['websaɪt] Website II
wedding ['wedɪŋ] Hochzeit II
Wednesday ['wenzdeɪ] Mittwoch I
week [wiːk] Woche I
on **weekdays** [ɒn 'wiːkdeɪz] unter der Woche; an Werktagen III
weekend ['wiːkend] Wochenende I
at the **weekend** [ət ðə ˌwiːk'end] am Wochenende I
weekly ['wiːkli] wöchentlich III
to **weigh** [weɪ] wiegen II
weight [weɪt] Gewicht <IV U1, 31>
to **welcome** ['welkəm] willkommen heißen IV U4, 80
welcome (to) ['welkəm tʊ] willkommen (bei/in) I
You're **welcome**. [jɔː 'welkəm] Gern geschehen. I
well [wel] na ja I; gut II
Well done! [ˌwel 'dʌn] Gut gemacht! I
Well, look ... [wel 'lʊk] Na ja, schau mal ... nach. I

Welsh [welʃ] walisisch; Walisisch; Waliser; Waliserin III
went [went] simple past von *to go* I
were [wɜː] simple past von *to be* I
west [west] Westen III
west of ['west‿əv] westlich von IV ZI, 9
western ['westən] Western *(Filmart)* <IV U4, 140>
country and **western** music [ˌkʌntri ənd 'westən ˌmjuːzɪk] Countrymusik <IV U5, 143>
wet [wet] nass I
what [wɒt] was I; welche II; wie III
What about you? [ˌwɒt‿əbaʊt 'juː] Und du? II
What have you been up to? [ˌwɒt‿əv juː biːn 'ʌp tə] Was hast du (in letzter Zeit) gemacht?; Wie läuft's bei dir? IV U3, 55
What time is it? [ˌwɒt 'taɪm‿ɪz‿ɪt] Wie spät ist es?; Wie viel Uhr ist es? I
What to ... ['wɒt tə] Was man ... II
What's up? [ˌwɒts‿'ʌp] Wie geht's? IV U3, 54
What's wrong? [ˌwɒts 'rɒŋ] Was ist los?; Was stimmt nicht? II
What's your name? [ˌwɒts jə 'neɪm] Wie heißt du? I
wheel [wiːl] Rad III
big **wheel** [ˌbɪg 'wiːl] Riesenrad II
wheelchair ['wiːltʃeə] Rollstuhl III
when [wen] wann I; wenn; als II
where [weə] wo; wohin; woher I
Where are you from? [ˌweər‿ə ju 'frɒm] Woher kommst du? I
wherever [weə'revə] wo(hin) auch immer; egal wo(hin); überall wo(hin) III
which [wɪtʃ] welche II; die; der; dem; den; das III
while [waɪl] während II
to whisper ['wɪspə] flüstern <IV U5, 104>
white [waɪt] weiß I
who [huː] wer I; die; welche II; der; dem; den III

whom [huːm] wem; wen IV U3, 58
whose [huːz] dessen; deren III
why [waɪ] warum II
the **wild** [ðə 'waɪld] Wildnis; freie Wildbahn IV U5, 102
wildlife ['waɪldlaɪf] Tierwelt *(in freier Wildbahn)* IV U5, 102
will [wɪl] werden II
*to **win** [wɪn] gewinnen; siegen I
wind [wɪnd] Wind I
wind farm ['wɪnd fɑːm] Windpark III
window ['wɪndəʊ] Fenster I
windy ['wɪndi] windig I
winner ['wɪnə] Gewinner; Gewinnerin I
winter ['wɪntə] Winter I
wish [wɪʃ] Wunsch <III>
Best **wishes**, [ˌbest 'wɪʃɪz] Mit den besten Wünschen, I
to **wish** [wɪʃ] wünschen III
witch [wɪtʃ] Hexe I
with [wɪð] mit I
with special needs [wɪθ ˌspeʃl 'niːdz] mit Behinderung; mit besonderen Bedürfnissen III
within [wɪ'ðɪn] innerhalb <IV U2, 136>
without [wɪ'ðaʊt] ohne III
woke up [ˌwəʊk‿'ʌp] simple past von *to wake up* II
woman *(sg)* ['wʊmən], **women** *(pl)* ['wɪmɪn] Frau II
won [wʌn] past participle von *to win* II
won't (= will not) [wəʊnt] nicht werden II
wonderful ['wʌndəfl] wunderbar III
wood [wʊd] Holz III; Wald II
wool [wʊl] Wolle I
word [wɜːd] Wort <I>
linking **word** [ˌlɪŋkɪŋ 'wɜːd] Verbindungswort <IV U3, 73>
wore [wɔː] simple past von *to wear* I
work [wɜːk] Arbeit I
to **work** [wɜːk] arbeiten I
worker ['wɜːkə] Arbeiter; Arbeiterin II
working hours *(pl)* ['wɜːkɪŋ ˌaʊəz] Arbeitszeit IV U2, 39

workshop ['wɜ:kʃɒp] Workshop II
acting workshop ['æktɪŋ ˌwɜ:kʃɒp] Schauspielworkshop II
world [wɜ:ld] Welt II
in the world [ɪn ðə 'wɜ:ld] auf der Welt II
world-class ['wɜ:ldˌklɑ:s] weltklasse <IV U1, 134>
worried ['wʌrid] beunruhigt; besorgt II
to **worry** ['wʌri] sich Sorgen machen I
worst [wɜ:st] schlimmste; schlechteste III
would [wʊd] würde(n) II
would like [wʊd 'laɪk] würde(n) gern; hätte(n) gern II
I wouldn't like (to) … [aɪ 'wʊdnt laɪk (tə)] ich möchte nicht …; ich würde nicht gerne … I
Would you like (to)…? [ˌwʊd jə 'laɪk (tə)] Möchtest du? I
wrap [ræp] Wrap II
wrist [rɪst] Handgelenk IV U3, 63
*to **write** [raɪt] schreiben I
writer ['raɪtə] Schriftsteller; Schriftstellerin II; Verfasser; Verfasserin; Autor; Autorin III
writing ['raɪtɪŋ] Schreiben <I>
written ['rɪtn] past participle von *to write* <IV U3, 72>; schriftlich <IV U2, 44>
wrong [rɒŋ] falsch I
wrote [rəʊt] simple past von *to write* II

Y

year [jɪə] Jahr; Jahrgangsstufe; Klasse I
year-old [ˌjɪər‿'əʊld] jährig; Jahre alt IV U2, 38
to **yell** [jel] brüllen; laut schreien <IV U2, 50>
yellow ['jeləʊ] gelb I
yes [jes] ja I
yesterday ['jestədeɪ] gestern I
yet [jet] schon II
not … yet [nɒt … 'jet] noch nicht II
yogurt ['jɒgət] Joghurt II
you [ju:] du; Sie; ihr; dich; euch; dir; Ihnen I
Would you like (to)…? [ˌwʊd jə 'laɪk (tə)] Möchtest du? I
You're right. [jɔ:‿'raɪt] Du hast recht. I
You're welcome. [jɔ: 'welkəm] Gern geschehen. I
young [jʌŋ] jung II
your [jɔ:] dein; euer I
Your turn. [jɔ: 'tɜ:n] Du bist dran. <I>
yours [jɔ:z] deine; eure; Ihre II
yourself [jɔ:'self] dich selbst II
yourselves [jɔ:'selvz] selber; ihr/euch/Sie/sich (selbst) III
youth *(no pl)* [ju:θ] Jugend-; Jugend III

Z

zebra ['zebrə] Zebra I
zero ['zɪərəʊ] null I
zip line ['zɪp ˌlaɪn] Seilrutsche III
ZIP Code ['zɪp kəʊd] Postleitzahl <IV U2, 44>
time **zone** ['taɪm ˌzəʊn] Zeitzone IV ZI, 8
zoo [zu:] Zoo; Tierpark I
at the zoo [ət ðə 'zu:] im Zoo I
zookeeper ['zu:ˌki:pə] Tierpfleger; Tierpflegerin I
to **zoom in** ['zu:m‿ɪn] heranzoomen <I>

Boys' names

Al [æl] IV U5, 105
Alaqua ['ælækwə] <IV U2, 137>
Chris [krɪs] IV U3, 62
CJ ['si:ˌdʒeɪ] IV U2, 45
Daniel ['dænjəl] IV U4, 76
David ['deɪvɪd] IV U1, 14
Derek ['derɪk] IV U4, 81
Edward ['edwəd] IV U4, 85
Ethan ['i:θn] IV U5, 102
Finn [fɪn] IV U3, 72
Gordie ['gɔ:di] IV U3, 62
Henry ['henri] IV U1, 17
Jacob ['dʒeɪkəb] IV U3, 54
José [həʊ'zeɪ] IV U1, 18
Matt [mæt] IV U5, 102
Matteo [mə'tɪəʊ] <IV U4, 88>
Michael ['maɪkl] IV U2, 38
Pablo ['pɑbləʊ] IV U1, 20
Ramon [rə'mɒn] <IV U4, 88>
Robert ['rɒbət] IV U3, 54
Ronan ['rəʊnən] IV U1, 25
Roy [rɔɪ] IV U2, 45
Teddy ['tedi] IV U3, 63
Vern [vɜ:n] IV U3, 63
Warren ['wɒrn] IV U2, 33
Wesley ['wezli] IV U1, 25

Girls' names

Amy ['eɪmi] <IV U2, 44>
Angela ['ændʒlə] IV U1, 19
Anna ['ænə] IV U5, 98
Becky ['beki] IV U4, 78
Brenda ['brendə] IV U3, 54
Caitlin ['keɪtlɪn] <IV U2, 44>
Claudette [klɔ:'det] IV U5, 106
Emma ['emə] <IV U3, 72>
Jennifer ['dʒenɪfə] IV U3, 58
Jessica ['dʒesɪkə] IV U1, 25
Julia ['dʒu:liə] IV U3, 54
Lily ['lɪli] IV U3, 54
Linda ['lɪndə] IV U1, 17
Lisa ['li:sə] IV U1, 17
Marie [mə'ri:] IV U2, 39
Nancy ['nænsi] IV U1, 17
Pam [pæm] <IV U3, 72>
Ruth [ru:θ] IV U3, 58
Sandy ['sændi] IV U4, 78
Stacey ['steɪsi] IV U2, 39
Susan ['su:zn] IV U1, 17

Surnames

Beeman ['bi:mən] IV U3, 64
Blanco ['blæŋkəʊ] IV U1, 18
Colvin ['kɒlvɪn] IV U5, 106
Lachance ['læʃɑ:ns] IV U3, 63
Lane [leɪn] IV U5, 105

Singh [sɪŋ] IV U1, 14
Sutter ['sʌtə] IV U4, 84
Warner ['wɔ:nə] <IV U3, 72>
Williams ['wɪljəmz] IV U5, 98

Place names

Africa ['æfrɪkə] Afrika I
Alabama (AL) [ælə'bæma] *Bundesstaat in den USA* IV ZI, 9
Alaska [ə'læskə] Alaska IV ZI, 8
America [ə'merɪkə] Amerika II
Arkansas (AR) ['ɑ:kənsɔ:] *Fluss und Bundesstaat in den USA* <IV U2, 136>
Asia ['eɪʒə] Asien IV U4, 74
Atlantic [ət'læntɪk] Atlantik IV U2, 34
Australia [ɒs'treɪliə] Australien I
Bishop ['bɪʃəp] *Ortsname* IV U4, 76
Bodie ['bəʊdi] *Ortsname* IV U4, 86
Boston ['bɒstən] *Stadt in den USA* III
The **British Isles** [ðə ˌbrɪtɪʃ 'aɪlz] die Britischen Inseln III
the **Bronx** [ðə 'brɒŋks] *Stadtteil von NYC* IV U1, 12
Brooklyn ['brʊklɪn] *Stadtteil von NYC* IV U1, 12
California (CA) [ˌkælɪ'fɔ:niə] Kalifornien IV ZI, 9
Canada ['kænədə] Kanada III
Castle Rock [ˌkɑ:sl 'rɒk] *Stadt in den USA* IV U3, 63
Central Valley [ˌsentrl 'væli] *Tal in Kalifornien* <IV U4, 88>
Chicago [ʃɪ'kɑ:gəʊ] *Stadt in den USA* <IV U2, 44>
China ['tʃaɪnə] China IV U1, 23
Coloma [kə'ləʊmə] *Ortsname* IV U4, 84
Colorado (CO) [ˌkɒlər'ɑ:dəʊ] *Bundesstaat in den USA* IV ZI, 10
Cuba ['kju:bə] Kuba IV U1, 18
Daytona [deɪ'təʊnə] *Stadt in den USA* IV U5, 102
Del Mar [ˌdel 'mɑ:] *Ortsname* <IV U4, 77>
Denmark ['denmɑ:k] Dänemark III
Doheny [də'hi:ni] *Strand in Kalifornien* <IV U4, 77>

The **Dominican Republic** [ðə dəˌmɪnɪkn rɪ'pʌblɪk] Dominikanische Republik IV U1, 23
Eastern Europe ['i:stn ˌjʊərəp] Osteuropa IV U1, 23
England ['ɪŋglənd] England I
Europe ['jʊərəp] Europa II
Florida (FL) ['flɒrɪdə] *Bundesstaat in den USA* IV U5, 96
Florida Keys ['flɒrɪdə ˌki:z] *Inselkette in den USA* IV U5, 143
France [frɑ:ns] Frankreich III
Georgia (GA) ['dʒɔ:dʒə] *Bundesstaat in den USA* IV U5, 103
Germany ['dʒɜ:məni] Deutschland I
Great Britain [ˌgreɪt 'brɪtn] Großbritannien III
Greece [gri:s] Griechenland IV U1, 23
Harlow ['hɑ:ləʊ] *Stadt in den USA* IV U3, 64
Hawaii [hə'waɪi:] *Inselkette im Pazifischen Ozean* IV ZI, 9
Huntsville ['hʌntsvɪl] *Ort in den USA* IV ZI, 10
Illinois (IL) [ˌɪlɪ'nɔɪ] *Bundesstaat in den USA* <IV U2, 44>
India ['ɪndiə] Indien I
Indiana (IN) [ˌɪndi'ænə] *Bundesstaat in den USA* IV ZI, 10
Italy ['ɪtəli] Italien II
Jamaica [dʒə'meɪkə] Jamaika II
Japan [dʒə'pæn] Japan <IV U4, 90>
Kentucky (KY) [ken'tʌki] *Bundesstaat in den USA* IV ZI, 10
LA (Los Angeles) [ˌel'eɪ (lɒs‿'ændʒɪli:z)] *Stadt in den USA* IV U3, 52
Las Vegas [ˌlæs 'veɪgəs] *Großstadt in den USA* IV ZI, 10
Little Italy [ˌlɪtl 'ɪtli] *Stadtteil von NYC* IV U1, 25
London ['lʌndən] *Hauptstadt von England* I
Louisiana (LA) [luˌi:zi'ænə] *Bundesstaat in den USA* IV ZI, 9
Maine (ME) [meɪn] *Bundesstaat in den USA* IV U3, 53

Manhattan [mæn'hætn] *Stadtteil von NYC* IV U1, 12
Massachusetts [ˌmæsə'tʃu:sɪts] *Bundesstaat in den USA* <IV U3, 66>
Mexico ['meksɪkəʊ] Mexiko IV U1, 19
Miami [maɪ'æmi] *Stadt in den USA* IV U3, 54
The **Midwest** [ˌðə 'mɪdwest] der Mittlere Westen IV ZI, 9
Mississippi (MS) [ˌmɪsɪ'sɪpi] *Bundesstaat in den USA* IV ZI, 9
Montgomery [mɑ:nt'gʌmri] *Stadt in den USA* IV U5, 106
Narrabeen ['nærəbi:n] *Strand in Australien* <IV U4, 77>
Nashville ['næʃvɪl] *Ort in den USA* IV U5, 97
Nevada (NV) [nə'vɑ:də] *Bundesstaat in den USA* IV ZI, 10
New England [ˌnju:‿'ɪŋglənd] Neuengland IV ZI, 8
New Mexico (NM) [nju: 'meksɪkəʊ] *Bundesstaat in den USA* IV ZI, 10
New Orleans [ˌnju:‿ɔ:'liənz] *Stadt in den USA* IV U5, 97
New York City (NYC) [ˌnju: jɔ:k 'sɪti] *Großstadt in den USA* IV U1, 12
North America [ˌnɔ:θ‿ə'merɪkə] Nordamerika IV ZI, 8
North Carolina (NC) [ˌnɔ:θ kær'laɪnə] *Bundestaat in den USA* IV U5, 101
North Dakota (ND) [ˌnɔ:θ də'kəʊtə] *Bundesstaat in den USA* IV ZI, 10
Northern Ireland [ˌnɔ:ðn‿'aɪələnd] Nordirland III
Norway ['nɔ:weɪ] Norwegen III
Oklahoma (OK) [ˌəʊklə'həʊmə] *Bundesstaat in den USA* <IV U2, 137>
Panama [ˌpænə'mɑ:] *Ortsname* IV U4, 85
Park Ridge ['pɑ:k ˌrɪdʒ] *Ortsname* <IV U2, 44>
Pennsylvania (PA) [ˌpensɪl'veɪniə] *Bundesstaat in den USA* IV ZI, 10
Philadelphia [ˌfɪlə'delfiə] *Stadt in den USA* <IV U3, 66>
The **Philippines** [ˌðə 'fɪlɪpi:nz] die Philippinen <IV U1, 21>

Pittsburgh ['pɪtsbɜːg] *Stadt in den USA* IV U3, 53
Poland ['pəʊlənd] Polen II
Queens [kwiːnz] *Stadtteil von NYC* IV U1, 12
Raleigh ['rɑːli] *Ort in den USA* IV U5, 101
The **Republic of Ireland** [ðə rɪˌpʌblɪk‿əv‿'aɪələnd] Irland III
Russia ['rʌʃə] Russland IV U1, 23
Sacramento [ˌsækrə'mentəʊ] *Ortsname* IV U4, 84
San Francisco [ˌsæn frən'sɪskəʊ] *Stadt in den USA* IV U4, 74
Santa Cruz [ˌsæntə 'kruːz] *Stadt in den USA* <IV U4, 77>
Scandinavia [ˌskændɪ'neɪviə] Skandinavien IV U1, 23
Scotland ['skɒtlənd] Schottland II
Seattle [si'ætl] *Großstadt in den USA* IV ZI, 10
Siberia [saɪ'bɪəriə] Sibirien <IV U2, 136>
Snowdonia [snəʊ'dəʊniə] *Nationalpark in Nordwales* III
South Carolina (SC) [ˌsaʊθ kær'laɪnə] *Bundesstaat in den USA* IV U5, 98
South Dakota (SD) [ˌsaʊθ də'kəʊtə] *Bundesstaat in den USA* IV U2, 34
Spain [speɪn] Spanien II
Staten Island [ˌstætn‿'aɪlənd] *Stadtteil von NYC* IV U1, 12
Trestles ['treslz] *Strand in Kalifornien* <IV U4, 77>
Turkey ['tɜːki] Türkei II
The **United Kingdom** [ðə juːˌnaɪtɪd 'kɪŋdəm] Vereinigtes Königreich von Großbritannien und Nordirland III
USA (United States of America) [ˌjuːes'eɪ (juːˌnaɪtɪd ˌsteɪts‿əv ə'merɪkə)] USA (Vereinigte Staaten von Amerika) III
Vietnam [ˌvjet'næm] Vietnam IV U1, 23
Wales [weɪlz] Wales III
Washington (WA) ['wɒʃɪŋtən] *Bundesstaat in den USA* IV ZI, 10
Washington, D.C. [ˌwɒʃɪŋtən ˌdiː'siː] *Hauptstadt der USA* IV ZI, 8
West Africa [ˌwest 'æfrɪkə] Westafrika IV U5, 98

Other names

Academy Award [əˌkædəmi‿ə'wɔːd] *Filmpreis* <IV U4, 140>
American Dream [əˌmerɪkən 'driːm] der amerikanische Traum IV U1, 18
The **Appalachian Mountains** [ðə ˌæpəleɪʃən 'maʊntɪnz] Die Appalachen IV ZI, 8
Avatar [ˌævə'tɑː] *Filmtitel* <IV U4, 140>
Batman ['bætmæn] *Filmtitel* <IV U1, 135>
Baxendale Road ['bæksndeɪl ˌrəʊd] *Straßenname* <IV U2, 44>
bento ['bentəʊ] *Kästchen für Speisen* <IV U4, 90>
Bird Highway [ˌbɜːd 'haɪweɪ] *Straßenname* <IV U2, 44>
Bollywood ['bɒliwʊd] *indische Filmindustrie: Bombay + Hollywood* II
Broadway ['brɔːdweɪ] *Straße in NYC* IV U1, 14
Brooklyn Bridge [ˌbrʊklɪn 'brɪdʒ] *Brücke in NYC* IV U1, 16
California Star [ˌkælɪfɔːniə‿'stɑː] *Name einer Zeitung* IV U4, 84
Carbine Street [ˌkɑːbaɪn 'striːt] *Straßenname* IV U3, 62
Central Park [ˌsentrl 'pɑːk] *Park in NYC* IV U1, 14
Chief Ten Bears [ˌtʃiːf 'ten beəz] Häuptling Zehn Bären <IV U2, 136>
Chinatown ['tʃaɪnətaʊn] *chinesisches Stadtviertel* IV U4, 74
Colorado River [ˌkɒlərɑːdəʊ 'rɪvə] *Fluss in den USA* IV ZI, 8
Christopher **Columbus** [ˌkrɪstəfə kə'lʌmbəs] *Personenname* <IV U2, 136>
Columbus Day [kəˌlʌmbəs 'deɪ] *Feiertag in den USA* <IV U3, 139>
The **Confederate Flag** [ðə kən'fedrət ˌflæg] Konföderiertenflagge IV U5, 98
cookie ['kʊki] *Spitzname* <IV U4, 90>
Declaration of Independence [ˌdekləreɪʃn‿əv‿ɪndɪ'pendəns] Unabhängigkeitserklärung IV ZI, 10
Denali [də'nɑːli] *höchster Berg in Nordamerika (neuer Name)* IV ZI, 8
Department of Homeland Security [dɪˌpɑːtmənt‿əv ˌhəʊmlænd sɪ'kjʊərəti] Heimatschutzbehörde IV U1, 23
Steve **Ditko** [ˌstiːv 'dɪtkəʊ] *Künstler* <IV U1, 135>
Ellis Island [ˌelɪs‿'aɪlənd] *Insel vor NYC* IV U1, 20
Empire State Building [ˌempaɪə steɪt 'bɪldɪŋ] *Gebäude in NYC* IV U1, 14
Empire State of Mind (Part II) Broken Down [ˌempaɪə ˌsteɪt‿əv 'maɪnd (pɑːt 'tuː) ˌbrəʊkn 'daʊn] *Liedname* <IV U1, 19>
European Union [ˌjʊərəpiːən 'juːnjən] Europäische Union III
The **Everglades** [ði 'evəgleɪdz] *Nationalpark in den USA* IV U5, 102
Family History Center [ˌfæmli 'hɪstri ˌsentə] Familiengeschichtezentrum IV U1, 22
Fifth Avenue [ˌfɪfθ‿'ævənjuː] *Straße in NYC* <IV U1, 134>
First World War ['fɜːst ˌwɜːld ˌwɔː] Erster Weltkrieg <IV U2, 136>
Fort Knox [ˌfɔːt 'nɒks] *Lager für die Goldreserven des Schatzamtes der USA* IV ZI, 10
Fruit4U [ˌfruːtfə'juː] *Firmenname* <IV U2, 39>
Mahatma **Gandhi** [məˌhɑːtmə 'gændi] *Personenname* IV U5, 107
Gold Rush ['gəʊld ˌrʌʃ] Goldrausch in Kalifornien IV U4, 75
The **Golden Gate Bridge** [ðə gəʊldn ˌgeɪt 'brɪdʒ] *berühmte Brücke in San Francisco* IV U4, 74

V

Gone with the Wind [ˌgɒn wɪð ðə ˈwɪnd] Vom Winde verweht <IV U4, 140>
Gotham City [ˌgɒθəm ˈsɪti] *fiktiver Ort im Film Batman* <IV U1, 135>
Grand Canyon [ˌgrænd ˈkænjən] *Sehenswürdigkeit in den USA* IV U4, 76
Grand Central Station [ˌgrænd sentrl ˈsteɪʃn] *Hauptbahnhof in NYC* IV U1, 14
The **Great Plains** [ðə ˌgreɪt ˈpleɪnz] *Flachland in den USA* <IV U2, 136>
Gulf Coast [ˈgʌlf ˌkəʊst] Golfküste IV U5, 96
The **Hobbit** [ðə ˈhɒbɪt] Der Hobbit <IV U4, 140>
Hollywood [ˈhɒliwʊd] *Zentrum der amerikanischen Filmindustrie (in Los Angeles)* II
Huarache [ˌhuːəˈrɑːtʃə] *Name einer Schuhfirma* <IV U4, 77>
Hurricane Katrina [ˌhʌrɪkən kəˈtriːnə] *Name eines Wirbelsturms* <IV U5, 108>
Independence Day [ˌɪndɪˈpendəns ˌdeɪ] amerikanischer Unabhängigkeitstag <IV U3, 139>
Indy 500 [ˌɪndi faɪvˈhʌndred] *Name eines Autorennens* IV ZI, 10
Iron Man [ˈaɪən ˌmæn] *Filmtitel* <IV U1, 135>
Jaws [dʒɔːz] Der weiße Hai <IV U4, 140>
Jurassic World [dʒʊˈræsɪk ˌwɜːld] *Filmtitel* <IV U4, 140>
Martin Luther **King** [ˌmɑːtɪn ˌluːθə ˈkɪŋ] *Personenname* IV U5, 107
Jack **Kirby** [ˌdʒæk ˈkɜːbi] *Künstler* <IV U1, 135>
Ku Klux Klan [ˌkuː klʌks ˈklæn] *ein rassistischer Geheimbund in den Südstaaten der USA* IV U5, 107
Stan **Lee** [ˌstæn ˈliː] *Schriftsteller* <IV U1, 135>
Lexington Avenue [ˈleksɪŋtn ˌævənjuː] *Straße in NYC* IV U1, 14

Abraham **Lincoln** [ˌeɪbrəhæm ˈlɪŋkən] *16. Präsident der USA (1861–1865)* <IV U3, 138>
Long Island [ˌlɒŋ‿ˈaɪlənd] *Teilort von NYC* <IV U1, 135>
Mardi Gras [ˌmɑːdi ˈgrɑː] Faschingsdienstag IV U5, 98
Martin Luther King Day [ˌmɑːtɪn ˌluːθə ˌkɪŋ ˈdeɪ] *Feiertag in den USA zu Ehren Martin Luther Kings* <IV U3, 138>
Tim **McGraw** [ˌtɪm məˈgrɔː] *Liedtitel* IV U5, 97
Memorial Day [məˌmɔːriəl ˈdeɪ] *Feiertag in den USA* <IV U3, 138>
Mesa Verde [ˌmeɪsə ˈvɜːdi] *US-Nationalpark* IV ZI, 10
Mississippi River [ˌmɪsɪsɪpi ˈrɪvə] *Fluss in den USA* IV ZI, 8
Missouri River [mɪˌzʊəri ˈrɪvə] *Fluss in den USA* IV ZI, 8
Mt. McKinley [ˌmaʊnt məˈkɪnli] *höchster Berg in Nordamerika (alter Name)* IV ZI, 8
NASCAR (National Association for Stock Car Racing) [ˈnæzkɑː] *amerikanischer Motorsportverband* IV U5, 102
Niagara Falls [naɪˌægrə ˈfɔːlz] Niagarafälle IV U3, 52
One World Trade Center [ˌwʌn ˈwɜːld ˌtreɪd ˌsentə] *Gebäude in NYC* IV U1, 12
Oscar [ˈɒskə] *Filmpreis* <IV U4, 140>
Pacific Ocean [pəˌsɪfɪk‿ˈəʊʃn] Pazifischer Ozean IV ZI, 9
Rosa **Parks** [ˌrəʊzə ˈpɑːks] *amerikanische Bürgerrechtlerin* IV U5, 107
PNC Plaza [ˌpiːensiː ˈplɑːzə] *Name eines Wolkenkratzers* IV U5, 101
President's Day [ˌprezɪdnts ˈdeɪ] *Feiertag in den USA* <IV U3, 138>
Sir Walter **Raleigh** [sɜː ˌwɒltə ˈrɔːli] *englischer Schriftsteller* IV U5, 101
Rio Grande [ˌriːəʊˈgrænd] *Fluss in den USA* <IV U2, 136>
River Thames [ˌrɪvə ˈtemz] *Fluss in London* II

the **Rockies** (= the Rocky Mountains) [ðə ˈrɒkiz] *Gebirge in Nordamerika* <IV U4, 89>
Rocky Mountains [ˌrɒki ˈmaʊntɪnz] *Gebirge in Nordamerika* IV ZI, 9
Sherlock [ˈʃɜːlɒk] *Tiername* I
Silicon Valley [ˌsɪlɪkən ˈvæli] *Ort, wo viele Computerfirmen ihren Sitz haben* IV U4, 75
Silverley [ˌsɪlvəˈli] *Firmenname* <IV U5, 109>
Sitting Bull [ˌsɪtɪŋ ˈbʊl] *Name des Häuptlings eines Indianerstammes* IV ZI, 10
Sydney **Smith** [ˌsɪdni ˈsmɪθ] *Personenname* IV U5, 107
Snow White and the Seven Dwarfs [ˌsnəʊ waɪt‿ən ðə ˌsevn ˈdwɔːfs] Schneewittchen und die sieben Zwerge <IV U4, 140>
Space Needle [ˈspeɪs ˌniːdl] *Sehenswürdigkeit in Seattle* IV ZI, 10
Star Wars [ˈstɑː ˌwɔːz] Krieg der Sterne <IV U4, 140>
Statue of Liberty [ˌstætʃuː‿əv ˈlɪbəti] *Freiheitsstatue in NYC* IV U1, 13
Joseph **Strauss** [ˌdʒəʊzɪf ˈstraʊs] *Architekt* IV U4, 75
Super Bowl [ˈsuːpə bəʊl] *Meisterschaftsendspiel des NFL* <IV U2, 50>
Surfin' USA [ˈsɜːfɪn ˌjuːesˈeɪ] *Liedtitel* <IV U4, 77>
Taylor **Swift** [ˌteɪlə ˈswɪft] *Personenname* IV U5, 97
Times Square [ˈtaɪm‿ˌskweə] *Platz in NYC* IV U1, 14
US Space & Rocket Center [juːˌes ˌspeɪs‿ən ˈrɒkɪt ˌsentə] *Raumfahrtmuseum in den USA* IV ZI, 10
Ventura County Line [venˌtʊərə ˌkaʊnti ˈlaɪn] *Name einer Bahnlinie* <IV U4, 77>
Very Large Array [ˌveri lɑːdʒ‿əˈreɪ] *Radioteleskop in den USA* IV ZI, 10
Walk of Fame [ˌwɔːk‿əv ˈfeɪm] *Straße in Hollywood mit Sternen für bekannte Leute* IV U4, 75

Wall Street ['wɔːl ˌstriːt] *Straße in NYC* IV U1, 14

George **Washington** [ˌdʒɔːdʒ 'wɒʃɪŋtən] *1. Präsident der USA (1789–1797)* <IV U3, 138>

The **Wizard of Oz** [ðə ˌwɪzəd‿əv 'ɒz] Der Zauberer von Oz <IV U4, 140>

World Wide Web [ˌwɜːld waɪd 'web] *ein über das Internet abrufbares System* IV U4, 80

Yosemite [jəʊ'semɪti] *Nationalpark in den USA* IV U4, 76

Malala **Yousafzai** [ˌməlælæ 'juːsæfzaɪ] *Personenname* IV U5, 107

A

abbiegen to turn III
abdecken to cover IV U3, 58
Abend evening I
Abendessen dinner II
(frühes) **Abendessen** tea I
abends in the evenings III
Abenteuer adventure III
aber but I
abfahren leave II
Abfall rubbish II
abholen to pick up IV U2, 43
Abholung pick-up IV U5, 102
ablehnen to reject IV U5, 99; to refuse IV U5, 107
abonnieren to subscribe IV U4, 81
den Tisch **abräumen** to clear the table II
abschaffen to abolish IV U5, 107
abschicken *(einen Brief)* to post III
Abschieds- leaving II
Abschiedsrede farewell speech II
absichtlich on purpose II
absolut absolutely IV U3, 59
abspülen to do the washing up II
abstimmen über to vote for IV U2, 33
Abteilung department II
acht eight I
Achterbahn roller coaster II
achtzehn eighteen I
achtzig eighty I
Ackerbau farming IV U4, 84
Ackerboden farmland IV U2, 32
Ackerland farmland IV U2, 32
Action action IV U5, 107
Adapter adaptor III
Adresse address II
Affe monkey I
Afrikaner African IV U5, 97
Afrikanerin African IV U5, 97
afrikanisch African IV U5, 97
Afroamerikaner African American IV U5, 96
afroamerikanisch African-American IV U5, 101
Aktenkoffer briefcase III
Aktentasche briefcase III
Aktivität activity I
nicht mehr **aktuell** out of fashion IV U4, 81
akzeptieren to accept IV U5, 99
albern silly II
Alkohol alcohol *(no pl)* IV U3, 58
alle all I; everyone II; every III; everybody IV U3, 53
Allee avenue IV U1, 14
Allergie allergy II
allergisch gegen allergic to II
alles everything II
  alles klar all right II
allgemein in general IV U3, 73
Alligator alligator IV ZI, 9
Alphabet alphabet I
als than; as II; when II
  als Nächstes next II
also so I
alt old I
Alter age I
Altglascontainer bottle bank II
altmodisch out of fashion IV U4, 81
Aluminium aluminium III
am on; at I
  am Wochenende at the weekend I
  am Dienstag on Tuesday I
Amerikaner American IV ZI, 9
Amerikanerin American IV ZI, 9
Amerikanisch American IV ZI, 9
amerikanisch American IV ZI, 9
amisch amish IV U3, 58
die **Amischen** the Amish IV U3, 53
Ampel lights IV U1, 14
an on; at I
  an Bord on board III
Ananas pineapple III
anbauen to produce IV U1, 13; to grow IV U3, 58
Anblick look IV U1, 14
Andenken souvenir III
andere other I; others II
  ein anderer another II
  anderer Meinung sein to disagree II
(sich) **ändern** to change III
  seine Meinung ändern to change one's mind III
anerkennen to appreciate IV U5, 99
Anfang start; beginning III
anfangen to start II
Anfrage request IV U4, 81
anführen to lead IV U3, 58
Anführer leader III
Anführerin leader III
Angeln fishing IV U5, 104
angenehm comfortable II
angezogen (wie) dressed III
angreifen to attack IV U2, 42
Angriff attack IV U1, 12
Angst haben to be afraid II; to be scared III
ängstlich afraid II
Anhänger follower IV U4, 81
Anhängerin follower IV U4, 81
anhören to listen (to) I
ankommen to arrive II
Ankündigung announcement II
anlegen to put on III
Anleitung tutorial IV U4, 80
anmalen to paint IV U4, 75
Anmeldeformular entry form II
annehmen to guess IV U3, 59; to accept IV U5, 99
Annonce ad(vert) (= advertisement) IV U2, 38
Anordnung layout IV U4, 77
anprobieren to try on II
Anruf call III
anrufen to call II; to phone I
Anrufer caller III
Anruferin caller III
anschauen to watch; to look at I; to have a look II
sich **anschließen** to join III
Anspitzer pencil sharpener I
morgendliche **Ansprache** morning message IV U2, 34
ansprechend appealing IV U4, 77
anstelle von instead IV U4, 80
anstoßen to hit III
Antwort answer I
antworten to answer I
Anzeige ad(vert) (= advertisement) IV U2, 38
anziehen to put on III

sich anziehen to get dressed II
Apfel apple I
April April I
Arbeit work I; job II
arbeiten to work I
Arbeiter worker II
Arbeiterin worker II
Arbeitskollege co-worker IV U2, 38
Arbeitskollegin co-worker IV U2, 38
Arbeitszeit working hours *(pl)* IV U2, 39
Architekt architect IV U4, 75
Architektin architect IV U4, 75
Archiv archive II
Areal area IV ZI, 9
Ärger trouble III
Arm arm III
arm poor IV U1, 18
Armee army III
armselig miserable III
Armut poverty IV U1, 23
Art sort II; type III
Art und Weise way III
Arzt doctor II
Ärztin doctor II
atmen to breathe III
Attacke attack IV U1, 12
auch too I; also III
auch nicht not ... either III
auf on; at I
auf der Welt in the world II
auf diese Weise like this III
auf einmal suddenly II
Auf keinen Fall! No way! III
Auf Wiedersehen. Goodbye. I
auf ... zu towards IV U3, 62
aufbewahren to keep IV U2, 34
auffallend striking III
Aufführung show IV U5, 102
Aufgabe job II
aufgeben to give up IV U4, 84
aufgeben *(einen Brief)* to post III
aufgeregt excited; nervous II
aufgerissen torn IV U4, 83
aufheben to pick up III
jmdn. **aufheitern** to cheer sb up III
aufhören to stop I; to finish II; to end IV U2, 34
Aufkleber sticker II
aufkrempeln to roll up IV U3, 62
Auflage edition IV U4, 84
aufmachen to open I
jmdn. **aufmuntern** to cheer sb up III
aufpassen to look after II
aufpassen auf to watch II
aufräumen to tidy (up) II
aufregend exciting I
Aufregung excitement IV U4, 86
aufrollen to roll up IV U3, 62
aufstehen to get up I
aufstellen to put up IV U3, 64
auftauchen to show up IV U2, 42
aufwachen to wake up II
aufwachsen to grow up III
Aufzug elevator *(AE)* IV U1, 13
Auge eye II
Augenblick moment II
August August I
im August in August I
aus from I
aus dem Weg gehen to avoid IV U3, 62
Ausbildung education IV U2, 38
Ausblick view IV U1, 14
auschecken to check out III
Auseinandersetzung argument II
ausfallen to fail IV U1, 19
Ausflug trip I
den Hund **ausführen** to take the dog for a walk I
Ausgabe edition IV U4, 84
ausgeben *(Geld)* to spend II
ein **ausgefüllter** Tag a busy day I
ausgehen *(Ware)* to run out of III
ausländisch foreign IV U1, 18
ausleihen to borrow II
ausprobieren to try; to try out III
ausruhen to rest II
Ausrüstung equipment III
Ausschnitt clip IV U4, 80
aussehen to look II
außer except III
außergewöhnlich unusual IV U4, 77
außerhalb outside IV U2, 38
außerhalb des Lehrplans extracurricular IV U2, 34
Außerirdische alien I
Außerirdischer alien I
äußerst extremely IV U4, 80
außerunterrichtlich *(Zusatzangebot)* extracurricular IV U2, 34
Aussicht view IV U1, 14
Aussichtspunkt lookout point II
aussteigen to get off II
Austausch exchange IV U2, 34
Ausverkauf sale II
Auswahl choice IV U5, 102
auswählen to choose II
auswandern to emigrate IV U1, 18
ausweichen to avoid IV U3, 62
Ausweis ID III; pass IV U2, 34
Auswirkung impact IV U4, 80
Auto car I
Autofahrt drive III
Autogramm autograph IV U3, 53
Autogramme geben to sign autographs IV U3, 53
Automat machine II
Autor writer III
Autorin writer III

B

Babysitter babysitter IV U2, 41
Babysitterin babysitter IV U2, 41
Bach stream II
Bäcker baker III
Bäckerei baker's III
Bäckerin baker III
Bad(ezimmer) bathroom I; bathroom (AE) IV U2, 34
Bahnhof station I
bald soon II
Ball ball II
Banane banana I
Band band II
Bank bench III
Baseball baseball IV U1, 13
Basketball basketball II
Bauarbeiter builder II
Bauarbeiterin builder II
Bauch stomach II
Bauchschmerzen stomach ache II
Bauchweh stomach ache II

bauen to build II
Bauer farmer I
Bäuerin farmer I
Bauernhof farm I
Baum tree I
Baumhaus tree house I
Baumwolle cotton III
beängstigend scary I
beantworten to answer I
bedauern to feel sorry III; to regret IV U3, 58
bedecken to cover IV U3, 58
bedeuten to mean III
bedeutend major IV ZI, 8; powerful IV U1, 22
sich **bedienen** to help oneself III
Bedienung waitress IV U4, 89
Bedingung condition IV U1, 22
mit besonderen **Bedürfnissen** with special needs III
sich **beeilen** to hurry; to rush III
beeindrucken to impress III
beeindruckend powerful IV U1, 22
beeinflussen to influence IV U4, 80
beenden to finish II; to end IV U2, 34
sich **befassen** mit to deal (with) IV U3, 73
befolgen to follow III
befragen to interview I
Befrager interviewer IV U1, 18
Befragerin interviewer IV U1, 18
Befragung interview II
befreunden *(jmdn. zu seiner Freundesliste hinzufügen)* to friend IV U4, 81
begeistert excited II
Beginn beginning III
beginnen to start II
begnadigen to pardon IV U3, 53
Begnadigung pardon IV U3, 67
behalten to keep IV U2, 34
mit **Behinderung** with special needs III
bei at I
bei Bewusstsein awake III
Bein leg II
beinahe almost III
Beispiel example IV U1, 18
zum Beispiel for example IV U2, 34
bekannt familiar IV U2, 34
Bekleidungsvorschriften dress code IV U2, 36
bekommen to get I
bekräftigen to confirm IV U4, 84
beliebt popular III
bemerken to notice IV U2, 42
bemerkenswert striking III
benennen to name IV ZI, 9
benutzen to use II
beobachten to watch II
bequem comfortable II
bereit ready I
bereits already II
Berg mountain III; hill IV U4, 74
Bergarbeiter miner III
Bergarbeiterin miner III
bergen to save III
Bergwerk mine III
Bericht report IV U4, 84
berichten (über) to report (on) IV U2, 33
Beruf job II; career IV U1, 18
Berufsbezeichnung job title IV U2, 38
berühmt famous I
berühmte Person celebrity IV U5, 97
Besatzung crew III
beschäftigt busy I
beschreiben to describe IV U3, 73
eine **Besichtigungstour** machen to go sightseeing II
besiedeln to settle IV U4, 75
besitzen to have I; to own II
mit **besonderen** Bedürfnissen with special needs III
besonders special I
besorgt worried II
Besorgungen machen to do the shopping II
bestätigen to confirm IV U4, 84
bestbezahlt best-paid IV U5, 97
beste best II
besteigen to climb III
bestellen to order II
die **besten** the best II
besuchen to visit II
Besucher visitor II
Besucherin visitor II
betreiben to run III
betreten to enter IV U3, 54
betrunken drunk IV U3, 63
Bett bed I
ins Bett gehen to go to bed I
Bettdecke blanket IV U3, 62
beunruhigt worried II
Bevölkerung population IV ZI, 8
bevor before II
(sich) **bewegen** to move III
Bewegung move III
beweisen to prove IV U4, 84
sich **bewerben** (für/um) to apply (for) IV U2, 38
bewerten to rate III
Bewohner inhabitant III
Bewohnerin inhabitant III
bei **Bewusstsein** awake III
Bezahlautomat payment machine II
bezahlen to pay II
Bezirk borough IV U1, 12
bezweifeln to doubt IV U3, 59
Bibliothek library III
Bild picture I
Bildung education IV U2, 38
billig cheap II
binden to tie IV U3, 62
Biologie Biology I
bis until I; to II
Bis bald! See you!; See you soon! I
bis (spätestens) by III
bis zu before II
ein **bisschen** a little; a bit II
bitte please I
Bitte schön. Here you are. I
blau blue I
bleiben to stay II
etw. bleiben lassen to give sth a miss III
in Verbindung bleiben to keep in touch II
Bleistift pencil I
Blick look; view IV U1, 14
Blog blog II
bloß only III
Blume flower III

Bluse blouse I
bluten to bleed III
Boden ground III
Bonbon sweet I
Bonus bonus IV U2, 39
Boot boat II
Bootsfahrt boat trip II
an **Bord** on board III
böse angry II; bad; naughty III
Boss boss II
Boulevard avenue IV U1, 14
Bowlen bowling IV U3, 58
Box box I
braten to fry IV U5, 98
Bratwurst sausage II
Brauch custom IV U5, 97
brauchen to need II
  nicht brauchen needn't I
braun brown I
brechen to break II
brennen to burn III
Brief letter III
Briefmarke stamp III
bringen to bring II
britisch British II
Broschüre brochure III; booklet IV U5, 102
Brot bread II
  belegtes Brot sandwich I
Brotlaib loaf III
Brücke bridge II
Bruder brother I
Buch book I
buchen to book IV U4, 76
Bücherei library III
Büchse tin IV U3, 63
Buchstabe letter III
buchstabieren to spell I
Bucht bay IV U4, 85
Büfett buffet III
Bühne stage II
Bundesstaat state IV ZI, 8
bunt colourful II
Burg castle II
Bürgerrechte civil rights *(pl)* IV U5, 96
Büro office II
Bus bus I
  im Bus on the bus II
Bushaltestelle bus stop II
Butter butter I

C

Café café I
Cafeteria cafeteria I
Camp camp II
campen gehen to go camping II
Camping camping III
Campingplatz campsite III
Campus campus IV U2, 35
Center centre III; center *(AE)* IV U1, 13
Chance chance II; opportunity IV U1, 18
chatten to chat II
Cheerleader *(Mädchen, das in einer Gruppe eine Sportmannschaft anfeuert)* cheerleader IV U2, 34
Chef boss II
Chefin boss II
Chefkoch head chef II
Chili chilli II
chillen to chill out IV U4, 76
Chinese Chinese IV U5, 99
Chinesich Chinese IV U5, 99
Chinesin Chinese IV U5, 99
chinesisch Chinese IV U5, 99
christlich Christian IV U3, 53
circa about II
Clip clip IV U4, 80
Cola coke I
College college IV U1, 19
Comic(heft) comic II
Computer computer I
Computerspiel computer game I
Courage courage IV U5, 107
Cousin cousin II
Cousine cousin II
Crew crew III
Curry curry II
Cyber-Mobbing cyberbullying IV U4, 80

D

da there I
  da drüben over there II
  da unten down there IV U5, 98
da because I
Dach roof II
Dachboden attic I
dahin down there IV U5, 98
damals then III
Dampfmaschine steam engine III
danach then; after that I; after III
Herzlichen **Dank**. Thanks so much. IV U4, 94
Vielen **Dank**. Thanks so much. IV U4, 94
dankbar thankful IV U3, 54
Danke. Thanks.; Thank you. I
dann then I
das the I; this; that I; which III
dass that III
Datei file II
Datum date I
dauern to take III
Decke blanket IV U3, 62
decken to lay II
dein your I
deine yours II
dem who; which III
Demonstration protest IV U5, 96
den who; which III
denken to think I
Denkmal monument II
dennoch still III
der the I; who; which III
deren whose III
derselbe the same II
Desaster disaster III
deshalb so I
Design design IV U4, 77
dessen whose III
Detail detail IV U5, 102
Detektivgeschichte mystery story IV U3, 53
deutlich clear IV U4, 77
Deutsch German I
deutsch German III
Deutschland Germany I
Dezember December I
dich you I
  dich selbst yourself II
die the I; who II; which III

Diele hall IV U2, 34
Dienst service III
Dienstag Tuesday I
am Dienstag on Tuesday I
dies this I
diese these II
Ding thing II
dir you I
Diskriminierung discrimination IV U5, 96
Distanz distance IV ZI, 9
Dollar *(amer. Währungseinheit)* dollar IV ZI, 8
Donnerstag Thursday I
doof silly III
Dorf village III
dort there I
dort drüben over there II
Dose tin IV U3, 63
eine Dose ... a can of I
Dr. *(Anrede)* Dr III
Drama drama III
drängeln to push III
Draufgänger daredevil IV U3, 53
Draufgängerin daredevil IV U3, 53
draußen halten to keep out III
draußen outside III
dreckig dirty I
Drehort location III
Drehung turn IV U5, 102
drei three I
dreißig thirty I
dreizehn thirteen I
drinnen inside IV U1, 25
dritte third I
Dschungel jungle IV U5, 102
du you I
Dudelsack bagpipes *(pl)* III
Duft smell IV U3, 62
dulden to tolerate IV U5, 98
dumm silly III
dunkel dark I
Dunkelheit the dark III
durch through II
Durcheinander mess I
Durchsage announcement II
durchschnittlich average IV U3, 58
dürfen may II; to be allowed to IV U2, 33; to be able to IV U2, 34
nicht dürfen mustn't III
nicht/nie dürfen must not/never III
durstig thirsty II
Dusche shower III
Duschgel shower gel III

E

echt real II; really II
Echt?! No way! III
Ecke corner III
Edition edition IV U4, 84
Es ist **egal**. It doesn't matter. II
egal wo(hin) wherever III
Ehemaligentreffen Homecoming *(AE)* IV U2, 33
Ehemann husband IV U3, 54
Ehre honor *(AE)* IV U1, 25
ehrenamtliche Helferin volunteer III
ehrenamtlicher Helfer volunteer III
ehrlich honestly IV U3, 63
Ei egg II
eifersüchtig jealous II
eigene own II
eigentlich actually III
Eigentümer landlord II
eilen to rush III
ein a; an I
ein bisschen a bit II
ein paar a few III
ein wenig a bit II
einander each other III
einchecken to check in III
eindeutig clear IV U4, 77
eindringen (in) to invade III
eine a; an I
einfach easy I; plain II; simple III
einfache Fahrkarte single ticket III
Einfluss impact IV U4, 80; influence IV U5, 98
einflussreich important III
einfügen to paste II
einführen to introduce IV U5, 98
eingängig catchy IV U4, 77
Eingangstor gateway IV U1, 12
einholen to catch up with IV U3, 62
einhundert a/one hundred I
einige some I; few III; a number of IV U5, 98
Einkäufe machen to do the shopping II
Einkaufen shopping I
einkaufen gehen to go shopping II
Einkaufszentrum shopping centre I
Einkaufszettel shopping list I
einladen to invite I
Einladung invitation I
einleiten to introduce IV U5, 98
einmal once IV U1, 25
auf einmal suddenly II
noch einmal again; once more II
einmarschieren (in) to invade III
einpacken to pack; to pack up II
einprägsam catchy IV U4, 77
Einreisebewilligung visa IV U1, 19
eins one I
einsam lonely III
einschalten to turn on IV U3, 64
einschlafen to fall asleep III
einsetzen to put in I
einst once IV U1, 25
Einstellung attitude IV U4, 89
einstufen to rate III
Eintrag entry IV U4, 86
eintreten to enter IV U3, 54
Eintrittskarte ticket III
nicht **einverstanden** sein to disagree II
Einwanderer immigrant IV U1, 13
Einwanderin immigrant IV U1, 13
einwandern to immigrate IV U1, 18
Einwohner inhabitant III; population IV ZI, 8
Einwohnerin inhabitant III
Einwohnerzahl population IV ZI, 8
Einzelheit detail IV U5, 102
einzige only II
Eis ice cream II
Eisberg iceberg III
Eiscreme ice cream II
Eisenbahn railway IV U4, 86
eiskalt freezing IV U3, 54
Elefant elephant I

elegant chic I
elektrisch electric IV U3, 59
Elektrizität electricity III
elend miserable III
elf eleven I
Eltern parents *(pl)* II
E-Mail e-mail II
emigrieren to emigrate IV U1, 18
Empfang signal III
Ende end II; ending III
am Ende at the back IV U5, 106
oberes Ende top IV U1, 13
enden to finish II; to end IV U2, 34
endlich at last II
eng tight II
die **Engländer** the English III
Englisch English I
Entdeckung discovery IV U4, 84
entfernt away II
Entfernung distance IV ZI, 9
entfliehen to escape IV U1, 23
entfreunden *(jmdn. von seiner Freundesliste streichen)* to unfriend IV U4, 81
entkommen to escape IV U1, 23
entlang along I; down III
(sich) **entscheiden** to decide III
Entscheidung decision IV U1, 18
entschuldigen to pardon IV U3, 53
sich entschuldigen to say sorry II
Entschuldigung pardon IV U3, 67
Entschuldigung. Sorry.; Excuse me. I
sich **entspannen** to chill out IV U4, 76
entspannt relaxed IV U4, 74
entwickeln to develop IV U4, 75
Entwicklung trend IV U4, 83
Enzyklopädie encyclopedia IV U4, 86
er he I
er selbst himself III
erbrechen to puke IV U3, 62
Erdbeere strawberry II
Erdboden ground III
Erdkunde Geography I
Erdnussbutter peanut butter III
Ereignis event IV U1, 13
etwas **erfahren** über to learn about sth III
Erfahrung experience IV U5, 109
erfinden to invent III
Erfinder inventor III
Erfinderin inventor III
Erfindung invention III
Erfolg success III
Erfolg haben (mit/bei) to succeed (in) IV U1, 19
erfolgreich successful IV U1, 18
erforschen to explore II
Ergebnis result II
ergreifen to grab III
sich **erinnern** (an) to remember II
erklären to explain III
erkunden to explore II
erlauben to allow IV U4, 84
Ermordung killing IV U5, 98
ernst serious III
etw. ernst nehmen to take sth seriously IV U1, 18
Im Ernst? Are you serious? III
Erntedankfest Thanksgiving IV U3, 53
erraten to guess II
erreichen to reach IV U3, 63
errichten to put up IV U3, 64
erscheinen to show up IV U2, 42
erschöpft exhausted III
erschrecken to scare II; to jump III
erschrocken sein to be scared III
ersetzen to replace IV U1, 12
erst only III
erstaunlich amazing III
erste first I
erste Stunde *(in der Schule)* homeroom IV U2, 45
das erste Mal the first time I
als **Erstes** first I
Erwachsene adult III
Erwachsener adult III
erwarten to expect III
erzählen to tell I
Erzähler narrator I
Erzählerin narrator I
erzeugen to produce IV U1, 13
Erziehung education IV U2, 38
es it I
es gibt there is (= there's); there are I
Essen food I; meal II
Essen zum Mitnehmen takeaway II
essen to eat I
Essensstand food stall II
Esslöffel tablespoon II
Esszimmer dining room I
Etage story *(AE)* IV U1, 14
etwa about II
etwas something; some I
euch you I
euer your I
eure yours II
Euro *(Währung)* euro III
Europäisch European IV U2, 32
europäisch European IV U2, 32
ewig forever II
exakt exact III
Exemplar copy IV U5, 97
existieren to be around IV U4, 80
Experte expert IV U4, 77
Expertin expert IV U4, 77
explodieren to explode III
Explosion explosion III
exzellent excellent IV U5, 102

F

Fabel fable III
Fabrik factory III
(zu etw.) **fähig** sein to be able to (do sth) IV U2, 34
Fahne flag II
fahren to go I; to ride II; to travel III; to drive IV U2, 33
gegen etw. fahren to hit III
mit (dem Zug) fahren to go by (train) I
Fahrer driver III
Fahrerin driver III
einfache **Fahrkarte** single ticket III
Fahrplan timetable III; schedule *(AE)* IV U2, 32
Fahrpreis fare III
Fahrrad bike I
Fahrschein ticket III
Fahrt drive; trip; voyage; journey III; ride IV U1, 14; tour IV U4, 76

eine Fahrt machen to take a trip III
Fakt fact II
fallen to fall I; to fall (over) III
falsch wrong I
Faltblatt flyer II
Familie family I
Fan fan I
Fantasie fantasy II
Fantasieausflug fantasy trip I
fantastisch fantastic II
Fantasy fantasy II
Farbe colour I; color *(AE)* IV ZI, 8
Fasching carnival I
Fass barrel IV U3, 53
fast almost III
faszinierend fascinating IV U4, 77
faul lazy IV U2, 39
Februar February I
Federmäppchen pencil case I
Feedback feedback IV U2, 39
fegen to sweep II
fehlschlagen to fail IV U1, 19
Feier party I; celebration IV U3, 52
feiern to celebrate I
Feind enemy III
Feindin enemy III
Feld field IV ZI, 9
Fels rock III
Fenster window I
Ferien holiday II; vacation *(AE)* IV U5, 104
in der **Ferne** in the distance IV U1, 15
fernsehen to watch TV I
Fernseher TV I
Fernsehsendung TV show II
Fernsehstudio TV studio II
fertig ready I
sich fertig machen to get ready IV U3, 54
fertigstellen to finish II; to complete IV U5, 101
fesseln to tie IV U3, 62
fest tight II; solid III
festhalten to hold III
festnehmen to arrest IV U5, 107
feststecken to be stuck I
Feuer fire II
Feuerwehrauto fire engine II
Fieber fever IV U4, 84
Film film; movie I
Filzstift felt-tip I
finden to find I
Finger finger III
Fingerabdruck fingerprint II
Firma company II
Fisch fish I
Pommes mit Fisch fish and chips I
Fischen fishing IV U5, 104
fit fit III
Fitnessraum gymnasium III
flach flat IV U2, 32
Fläche area IV ZI, 9
Flagge flag II
Flamingo flamingo I
eine **Flasche** ... a bottle of I
Fledermaus bat I
Fleisch meat I
fleißig hard-working IV U2, 39
fliegen to fly II
fliehen to escape IV U1, 23
fließend fluent III
Flohmarkt jumble sale II
flüchten to escape IV U1, 23
Flug flight IV U3, 52
Flughafen airport II
Flugzeug plane II
Flur corridor III; hall IV U2, 34
Fluss river I
flüssig fluent III
Flyer flyer II
folgen to follow III
Follower follower IV U4, 81
Followerin follower IV U4, 81
Fön hairdryer III
in **Form** fit III
Foto photo I
ein Foto machen to take a photo I
Frage question I
fragen to ask I
Frankreich France III
die **Franzosen** the French IV U5, 98
Französisch French I
Frau woman II
Frau *(Anrede)* Mrs; Ms I
frech cheeky; naughty III
freie Wildbahn the wild IV U5, 102
die **freie** Natur the outdoors IV U5, 96
im **Freien** outside III
freigeben to release IV U5, 97
Freiheit freedom *(no pl)* IV U1, 23
Freiland- free range II
Freiluft- outdoor III
freisetzen to release IV U5, 97
Freistunde study hall period IV U2, 34
Freitag Friday I
Freiwillige volunteer III
Freiwilliger volunteer III
Freizeit free time I
Freizeitpark theme park I
fremd foreign IV U1, 18
Freude fun I
Freund friend I
Freund *(in einer Paarbeziehung)* boyfriend IV U3, 54
Freundin friend I
Freundin *(in einer Paarbeziehung)* girlfriend IV U2, 38
freundlich friendly III
Freundschaften schließen to make friends I
Frieden peace III
friedlich peaceful IV U5, 96
frieren to freeze; to get cold III
Frisbeescheibe frisbee I
frisch fresh II
Friseur hairdresser II
Friseurin hairdresser II
frittieren to fry IV U5, 98
froh happy I; glad IV U3, 54
Frucht fruit I
früh early III
(wohnte) früher used to (live) III
tat(en) früher to used to (+ infinitive) IV U3, 54
Frühlingsrolle spring roll II
Frühstück breakfast I
frühstücken to have breakfast I
Frühstückspension bed and breakfast (B & B) III
(sich) **fühlen** to feel II
sich schlecht fühlen to feel sick IV U5, 103
führen to run III; to lead IV U3, 58

Führer leader III
Führerin leader III
Füller pen I
fünf five I
fünfzehn fifteen I
fünfzig fifty I
für for I
für immer forever II
furchtbar awful I; horrible; dreadful III; terrible IV U2, 32
sich **fürchten** to be afraid II
Fuß foot I
zu Fuß gehen to go on foot I
Fußball football I
Fußgelenk ankle II
Fußknöchel ankle II
füttern to feed I

G

Gabel fork II
Gang corridor III
ganz quite III
den ganzen Tag all day III
Garten garden I
Gas gas III
Gasse alley IV U2, 32
Gast guest III
Gastfamilie host family IV U2, 34
Gasthaus pub III
Gebärdensprache sign language III
Gebäude building II
geben to give I; to be around IV U4, 80
Autogramme geben to sign autographs IV U3, 53
jmdm. das Gefühl geben, etw. zu sein to make sb feel like sth III
es gibt there is (= there's); there are I
Gebiet area IV ZI, 9; grounds *(pl)* IV U1, 13
geboren werden to be born III
(in der Pfanne) **gebraten** fried II
Geburtstag birthday I
Alles Gute zum Geburtstag! Happy birthday! I
Gedanke thought IV U3, 62
Gedicht poem III
geduldig patient III
gefährlich dangerous III
Gefängnis prison II
gefrieren to freeze III
gefrierend freezing IV U3, 54
jmdm. das **Gefühl** geben, etw. zu sein to make sb feel like sth III
gegen against; around III
gegen etw. fahren to hit III
Gegend area IV ZI, 9; region IV U5, 97
sich **gegenseitig** each other III
gegenüber opposite I
geheim secret II
Geheimnis mystery I; secret II
gehen to go; to walk I
gehen mit to go out with IV U3, 58
gehen um to be about III
aus dem Weg gehen to avoid IV U3, 62
campen gehen to go camping II
ins Bett gehen to go to bed I
spazieren gehen to go for a walk I
über die Grenze gehen to cross the border IV U1, 19
zu Fuß gehen to go on foot I
gehören (zu) to belong (to) IV U1, 14
gehörlos deaf III
Geist ghost II
Gel gel III
Gelände grounds *(pl)* IV U1, 13
gelangweilt bored IV U3, 57
gelassen relaxed IV U4, 74
gelb yellow I
Geld money I
Geldschein note II
Gelegenheit chance II; opportunity IV U1, 18
Gemeinde community IV U1, 18
gemeinsam together I
Gemeinschaft community IV U1, 18
Gemüse vegetable (veg) II
Obst- und **Gemüseladen** greengrocer's III
gemustert patterned II
gemütlich cosy III
genau exact III; right IV U2, 42; exactly IV U3, 59
generell in general IV U3, 73
genießen to enjoy III
genug enough III
genügend enough III
Geografie Geography I
gerade right now III; right IV U2, 42
geradeaus straight on I; right ahead IV U1, 15
Gerät device IV U3, 58
Geräusch noise I; sound III
Gerede gossip IV U3, 58
Gericht dish II; court IV U5, 107
Gerichtsverhandlung court case IV U5, 107
gern haben to like I
Gern geschehen. You're welcome. I
ich würde gerne ... I'd like (to) ... (= I would like to) I
Geruch smell IV U3, 62
gesamt total IV ZI, 8
Gesamt- total IV ZI, 8
Geschäft shop I; store *(AE)* IV U2, 33
Geschäftsführer manager IV U2, 38
Geschäftsführerin manager IV U2, 38
Geschäftsmann businessman IV U4, 84
geschehen to happen II
Geschenk present I
Geschichte History; story I; history III
Geschoss bullet IV U3, 63
Gesellschaft company II; society IV U5, 100
Gesetz law IV U5, 96
Gesicht face I
Gestaltung design IV U4, 77
Gestank smell IV U3, 62
gestatten to allow IV U4, 84
gestern yesterday I
Getränk drink II
Getreide corn IV ZI, 9
getrennt segregated; separate IV U5, 106
gewinnen to win I
Gewinner winner I
Gewinnerin winner I
sich an (etw.) **gewöhnen** to get used to (sth) IV U1, 18
gewöhnlich usually II

Gewürz spice II
Gips cast III
Giraffe giraffe I
Gitarre guitar III
Gitter grid IV U5, 101
glänzen to shine IV ZI, 8
Glas glass II; jar III
glauben to believe II
gläubig religious IV U1, 23
gleich the same II; right away IV U4, 80
jetzt gleich right now III
gleichmäßig regular IV U4, 89
Gleis railway track IV U3, 64
Glocke bell II
viel Glück good luck II
glücklich happy I
Glückstag lucky day II
Glückwunsch! Congratulations! II
Glühbirne light bulb III
Gold gold III
Gold- gold III; golden IV U4, 75
golden gold III; golden IV U4, 75
Goldrausch gold rush IV U4, 84
Grab grave III
Grad degree IV U5, 102
grau grey I
greifen to grab III
Grenze border IV U1, 19
über die Grenze gehen to cross the border IV U1, 19
die Grenze überschreiten to cross the border IV U1, 19
Griechisch Greek IV U5, 99
griechisch Greek IV U5, 99
Grill barbecue I
grinsen to grin IV U3, 64
groß high; big I; tall; large II
großartig great I; fantastic II
Größe size II
Großeltern grandparents *(pl)* II
Großmutter grandmother II
Großstadt city II
Großvater grandfather II
großzügig generous IV U2, 39
grün green I
Grund reason III
Gründe angeben to give reasons III
Gründe nennen to give reasons III
Grundbesitzer landowner IV U4, 84
Grundbesitzerin landowner IV U4, 84
gründen to start III; to found IV U5, 98
Gruppe group; team I
gruselig scary I; creepy IV U3, 53
Grüße ... von mir. Say hi to ... I
gültig valid III
Gummi rubber III
Gürtel belt IV U3, 62
gut good I; fine II; well II; nice III
Gut gemacht! Well done! I
gut sein in to be good at I
Guten Morgen. Good morning. II
gut sein bei to be good at I

H

Haar hair III
Haarbürste hairbrush III
Haare hair III
sich die Haare schneiden lassen to have a haircut II
Haargel hair gel III
Haarglätter hair straightener IV U3, 59
Haarschnitt haircut II
haben to have I
Angst haben to be scared III
Mitleid haben mit to feel sorry III
hast du have you got II
hätte(n) gern would like II
Du hast recht. You're right. I
Hafen harbour II; harbor *(AE)* IV U1, 22
Hafer oat III
Haferbrei porridge III
Hai shark I
halb half III
halb (drei) half past (two) I
eine halbe Million half a million III
Halbtags- part-time IV U2, 38
(die) Hälfte half IV U4, 80
Hallen- indoor III
Hallo. Hello.; Hi. I
Hals throat II
Halsband collar I
Halsschmerzen sore throat II
Halt stop III
halten to keep II; to hold III
die Klappe halten to shut up IV U3, 63
Haltestelle stop II
Haltung attitude IV U4, 89
Hamburger burger II
Hand hand III
handeln von to be about III
Handgelenk wrist IV U3, 63
Handlung action IV U5, 107
Handtuch towel III
Handy mobile (phone) I
hängen to hang II
hänseln to tease IV U2, 38
hart hard II; tough III
hassen to hate III
häufig often I
Haupt- major IV ZI, 8
Hauptgericht main course II
hauptsächlich mostly IV U3, 58
Hauptstadt capital (city) III
Hauptverkehrszeit rush hour IV U1, 14
Haus house I
zu Hause at home; around the house I
Hausaufgabe(n) machen to do homework I
Häuschen cottage III
Hausmeister caretaker I
Hausmeisterin caretaker I
Haustier pet I
Heer army III
Heft book I; booklet IV U5, 102
Heim home I
Heimweh haben to be homesick III
heiraten to get married II
heiß hot I
heißen to be called II
willkommen heißen to welcome IV U4, 80
Held hero III
helfen to help I
Helfer helper IV U4, 89

Helferin helper IV U4, 89
Helikopter helicopter IV U4, 79
hell bright IV ZI, 8
Helm helmet I
Hemd shirt II
heraus out II
herausfallen aus to fall out of IV U2, 42
herausfinden to find; to find out I
herausgeben to release IV U5, 97
herauskommen to get out III
herausnehmen to take out I
Herberge hostel III
Herbst fall *(AE)* IV ZI, 8
hereinkommen to get in I; to enter IV U3, 54
hergestellt sein aus to be made of III
Herr *(Anrede)* Mr I
herrlich lovely II
herstellen to produce IV U1, 13
herum around III
herumkommen to get around III
sich **herumtreiben** (mit) to hang out (with) IV U3, 58
herunter down III
herunterladen to download II
hervorkommen to come out II
hervorragend excellent IV U5, 102
Herzlichen Dank. Thanks so much. IV U4, 94
heute today I
heutzutage now II
Hexe witch I
hier here I
hiesig local III
Highschool *(weiterführende Schule, Oberstufe)* high school IV U1, 18
Hightech- high-tech IV U4, 75
Hilfe help II; support IV U1, 19
hilfreich useful III; helpful IV U2, 38
hilfsbereit cooperative; helpful IV U2, 38
Himbeere raspberry III
Hin- und Rückfahrkarte return ticket III
hinauf up II
hinbringen to take II
in … **hinein** inside II
hineingehen to enter IV U3, 54
hineingelangen to get into IV U1, 14
hineinkommen to get into IV U1, 14
hinfallen to fall I; to fall (over) III
zu … **hinfügen** to bookmark II
hinnehmen to accept IV U5, 99
hinten at the back IV U5, 106
  im hinteren Teil at the back IV U5, 106
hinter behind II
Hinter- back IV U3, 62
Hintergrund background III
  im Hintergrund in the background III
hinüber across IV U3, 54
hinunter down III
Hinweis clue I
hinzufügen to add II
Hip-Hop *(Musik)* hip hop III
historisch historic IV U5, 98
Hitze heat IV U5, 102
Hobby hobby III
hoch high I; tall II
hochladen to upload II
Hochzeit wedding II
hoffen to hope II
Hoffnung hope IV U1, 13
hoffnungsvoll hopeful III
höflich polite II
Höhe height II
Höhle cave II
Holz wood III
hören to listen (to); to hear I
Hose trousers *(pl)* I
  kurze Hose shorts *(pl)* I
Hot Dog *(Würstchen im Brötchen)* hot dog IV U1, 14
Hotel hotel II
Hotelfachschule catering college II
hübsch beautiful I; pretty; lovely II
Hubschrauber helicopter IV U4, 79
Hügel hill IV U4, 74
Huhn chicken I
Hühnchen chicken II
Hund dog I
Hundeausführer dog walker IV U2, 41
Hundeausführerin dog walker IV U2, 41
Hundekeks dog biscuit II
hundert a/one hundred I
hungrig hungry I
husten to cough III
Hut hat II
hüten to look after II

I

ich I; me I
  ich möchte … I'd like (to) … (= I would like to) I
  ich würde gerne … I'd like (to) … (= I would like to) I
  ich würde lieber I'd rather III
  ich würde nicht gerne … I wouldn't like (to) … I
Idee idea I
ihm him I
ihn him I
Ihnen you I
ihr you; her; their I; its III
ihre hers II; theirs III
Ihre yours II
im in I
  im August in August I
  im Bus on the bus II
  Im Ernst? Are you serious? III
  im Fernsehen on TV IV U1, 13
  im Freien outside III
  im Schlepptau in tow IV U2, 42
  im Süden von in the south of III
Imbiss snack I
immer always I
  für immer forever II
Immigrant immigrant IV U1, 13
Immigrantin immigrant IV U1, 13
Immigration immigration IV U1, 22
immigrieren to immigrate IV U1, 18
in in; to; at I; inside III
  in … hinein inside II
  in der Ferne in the distance IV U1, 15
  in der Mitte von in the centre of III
  in der Schule at school I
  in der Unterzahl outnumbered IV U5, 102
  in Form fit III

in Ordnung fine; all right II
in Richtung towards IV U3, 62
Indien India I
indisch Indian II
Industrie industry III
industrielle Revolution Industrial Revolution III
Informatik IT (Information Technology) I
Information information desk II
informativ informative IV U4, 77
Ingenieur engineer II
Ingenieurin engineer II
Inhalt content III
innen inside IV U1, 25
innen in inside III
Innen- indoor III
im **Innern** inside III
Insekt insect III
Insel island II
Institut college IV U1, 19
intelligent clever II; smart; intelligent III
interessant interesting I
sich **interessieren** für to be interested in III
interessiert sein an to be interested in III
Internet internet II
im Internet surfen to surf the internet II
ins Internet stellen to upload II
Internettagebuch blog II
Interview interview II
interviewen to interview I
Interviewer interviewer IV U1, 18
Interviewerin interviewer IV U1, 18
irgendein any II
irgendetwas anything II
irgendwelche any II
Irisch Irish III
irisch Irish III
Italiener Italian IV U5, 99
Italienerin Italian IV U5, 99
Italienisch Italian IV U5, 99
italienisch Italian IV U5, 99

J

ja yes I
Jacke coat I; jacket II
Jäger chaser IV U2, 33; hunter IV U4, 85
Jägerin chaser IV U2, 33; hunter IV U4, 85
Jahr year I
Jahre alt year-old IV U2, 38
Jahrgangsstufe year I
Jahrhundert century III
jährig year-old IV U2, 38
jamaikanisch Jamaican II
jämmerlich miserable III
Januar January I
Japaner Japanese IV U5, 99
Japanerin Japanese IV U5, 99
Japanisch Japanese IV U5, 99
japanisch Japanese IV U5, 99
Jeans jeans *(pl)* I
jede every I
jedenfalls anyway IV U1, 14
jeder everyone I; everybody IV U3, 53
jedoch however III
jemals ever II
jemand someone IV U2, 38
jene those II
jetzt now I
jetzt gleich right now III
Job job II
Joghurt yogurt II
Journalismus journalism IV U2, 34
Journalistik journalism IV U2, 34
Jugend youth *(no pl)* III
Jugend- teen II; youth *(no pl)* III
jugendlich teenage IV U3, 54
Jugendliche teen II; teenager III
Jugendlicher teen II; teenager III
Jugendzentrum activity centre III
Juli July I
jung young II
Junge boy I
Juni June I
Juror judge II
Jurorin judge II
Juwelierladen jeweller's III

K

Käfig cage I
kalt cold I
Kamel camel III
Kamm comb III
Kampf battle; fight III
kämpfen to fight III
Kanarienvogel canary III
Kanone cannon II
Kanonenkugel cannon ball II
Kanufahren canoeing I
Kapitän captain I
Kapitänin captain I
Kappe cap I
kaputt machen to break II
Karneval carnival I
Karotte carrot II
Karre truck III
Karriere career IV U1, 18
Karte ticket; card II
Kartoffel potato II
Kartoffelbrei mashed potatoes II
Kartoffelchip crisp I
Karton cardboard III
Käse cheese I
Käsekuchen cheesecake II
Katastrophe disaster III
Katholik Catholic III
Katholikin Catholic III
katholisch Catholic III
Katze cat I
kaufen to buy I
Kaufhaus department store II
Kaugummi chewing gum I
kaum little IV U1, 22
kein no I; not ... any II
Keks biscuit II
Kellner waiter II
Kellnerin waitress IV U4, 89
kennen lernen to meet I; to get to know II
Kerze candle I
Ketchup ketchup II
sieben **Kilogramm** täglich 7 kilograms a day I
40 **Kilometer** pro Stunde 40 kilometres an hour I

Kilt kilt III
Kind kid II
Kinder children *(pl)* II
Kinderzimmer bedroom I
Kino cinema I; movie theater *(AE)* IV U5, 106
Kirche church II
Kiste box I
die **Klappe** halten to shut up IV U3, 63
klar clear IV U4, 77
alles klar all right II
Klasse year; tutor group I; class III; grade *(AE)* IV U2, 32
Klassenarbeit test IV U3, 61
Klassenlehrer tutor I
Klassenlehrerin tutor I
Klassenzimmer classroom I
Klatsch gossip IV U3, 58
Klebstoff glue I
Kleeblatt shamrock III
Kleid dress II
Kleider *(Pl.)* clothes *(pl)* I
Kleiderordnung dress code IV U2, 36
Kleiderschrank wardrobe I
Kleidung clothes *(pl)* I; outfit III
klein little II; tiny; small III
Kletter- climbing IV U4, 78
Klettern rock climbing I
klettern to climb III
klicken to click I
klingeln to ring II
klingen to sound II
Kloß dumpling II
Klub club II
Klubhaus clubhouse IV U3, 62
klug clever II; smart; intelligent III
Kneipe pub III
Knie knee III
Knoblauch garlic II
knuddelig cuddly III
Koch chef II
Kochbanane plantain II
kochen to cook II
Köchin chef II
Koffer suitcase II
Kohl cabbage II
Kohle coal III
Kombination combination II
komisch funny I
kommen to come I
Kommentar comment IV U4, 82
kommunizieren to communicate IV U4, 80
Komödie comedy III
Konfitüre jam III
König king III
Königin queen III
königlich royal II
Konkurrenz competition IV U2, 34
können can I; may II; to be able to IV U2, 34
nicht können can't I; cannot III
nicht weg können to be stuck I
konnte could III
Ich konnte nicht anders als ... I couldn't help but ... III
könnte could III
Kontakt contact IV U3, 58
Konto account IV U4, 80
Kontrolle check IV U1, 22
kontrollieren to check III
(sich) **konzentrieren** to concentrate IV U3, 58
Konzert concert II
kooperativ cooperative IV U2, 38
Kopf head II
Kopfsalat lettuce II
Kopfschmerzen headache II
kopfüber head first III
Kopfweh headache II
Kopie copy II
kopieren to copy II
Korbball netball I
Korn corn IV ZI, 9
Körper body III
Körperlotion body lotion III
korrekt right I
Korridor corridor III; hall IV U2, 34
kosten to cost III
... kostet 99 Pence ... is 99p I
kostenlos free III
köstlich delicious II
Kostüm costume; fancy dress I
krank ill II; sick III
Krankenhaus hospital I
Krankenpfleger nurse II
Krankenschwester nurse II
Krankenwagen ambulance III
Krankheit disease IV U1, 22
Kraut cabbage II
Kreis circle III
kreischen to scream IV U3, 63
Kricket cricket II
Krimi (= Kriminalgeschichte) mystery story IV U3, 53
Kritik review III
Krokodil crocodile I
Kubaner Cuban IV U1, 21
Kubanerin Cuban IV U1, 21
kubanisch Cuban IV U1, 21
Küche kitchen I
Kuchen cake I; pie II
Kugel bullet IV U3, 63
Kuh cow III
kühl cool I
kühlen to cool III
Kühlschrank fridge III
Kultur culture IV U5, 97
sich **kümmern** (um) to care (for) III
sich um jmdn. kümmern to take care of sb IV U2, 41
Kumpel buddy *(infml)* IV U2, 45
Kunde customer III
Kundin customer III
Kunst Art I
Künstler artist III
Künstlerin artist III
Kunststoff plastic III
Kunststück trick III
Kuppel dome II
Kurs course III; class IV U2, 34
kurz short II
kurze Hose shorts *(pl)* I
kurz shortly III
Kurzfilm clip IV U4, 80
Kuscheltier cuddly toy III
Kuss kiss II
Küste coast III
an der Küste on the coast III

L

Lachen laugh IV U3, 63
lachen to laugh II

Ladegerät charger III
Laden shop I; store *(AE)* IV U2, 33
Tante-Emma-Laden corner shop I
Lage location III
Lager camp II
Lamm lamb II
Lampe lamp I
Land country I; land II; countryside III; state IV ZI, 8
landen to land IV U3, 54
Landesregierung state government IV U5, 98
Landkarte map I
ländliche Gegend country I
Landschaft countryside III; landscape IV ZI, 9
Landwirt farmer I
Landwirtin farmer I
Landwirtschaft farming IV U4, 84
Landwirtschaftsflächen farmland IV U2, 32
lang long I
langsam slow III
langweilig boring I; dull IV U4, 77
Lasagne lasagne II
lassen leave II
etw. bleiben lassen to give sth a miss III
lass(t) uns let's (= let us) I
Laufbahn career IV U1, 18
laufen to run; to walk I
Wie läuft's? How's it going? IV U3, 54
Laut sound III
laut noisy; loud III
läuten to ring II
Layout layout IV U4, 77
Leben life I; lifetime IV U4, 76
leben to live I
Lebensart lifestyle IV U4, 74
Lebensmittel food I; groceries *(pl)* IV U4, 89
Lebenszeit lifetime IV U4, 76
lecker nice; tasty III
Leder leather III
legen to put II
Lehrer teacher I; instructor III
Lehrerin teacher I; instructor III
Leiche body IV U3, 62
leicht easy I
Tut mir **leid.** Sorry. I
leidtun to be sorry III
leihen to lend II
leise quiet III
leiten to run III
Leiter ladder I
lernen to learn II; to study IV U2, 34
kennen lernen to meet I; to get to know II
lesen to read I
Leser reader IV U1, 21
Leserin reader IV U1, 21
letzte last I
leuchtend bright IV ZI, 8
Leute people I; guys II
Lexikon encyclopedia IV U4, 86
Licht light IV U1, 13
Liebe(r) ..., *(Anrede in Briefen)* Dear ..., I
lieben to love I
ich würde **lieber** I'd rather III
Liebesgeschichte romance III
Lieblings- favourite I; favorite *(AE)* IV U4, 80
Lieferwagen van III
liegen to rest II
Lifestyle lifestyle IV U4, 74
Lift elevator *(AE)* IV U1, 13
lila purple I
Limonade lemonade II
Lineal ruler I
Linie line III
links on the left I; left III
auf der linken Seite on the left I
Liste list II
LKW-Fahrer lorry driver II
LKW-Fahrerin lorry driver II
Loch hole I
locker relaxed IV U4, 74; loose II
Löffel spoon II
Lohn wage IV U2, 38
lokal local III
lose loose II
lösen to solve I
loslassen to release IV U5, 97
Lösung solution IV U5, 98
Löwe lion I
Luft air IV U1, 22
Luftballon balloon I
Lunchpaket packed lunch II
lustig funny I

M

machen to do; to make I
ein Foto machen to take a photo I
Hausaufgabe(n) machen to do homework I
kaputt machen to break II
sich Notizen machen to take notes I
Mach dir nichts draus. Never mind. II
Macht nichts. Never mind. II
mächtig powerful IV U1, 22
Mädchen girl I
Magen stomach II
Magie magic II
Mahlzeit meal II
Mai May I
Mais corn IV ZI, 9
Make-up make-up IV U3, 58
Mal time III
das erste Mal the first time I
malen to paint IV U4, 75
Mama mum I; mama II
Mammutbaum redwood (tree) IV U4, 74
Manager manager IV U2, 38
Managerin manager IV U2, 38
manchmal sometimes II
Mann man I
Mannschaft crew III
Märchen fable III
Marke brand III
Markt market II
Marmelade jam III
März March I
Maschine machine II
Mathe Maths I; Math *(AE)* IV U2, 34
Mathematik Maths; Math *(AE)* IV U2, 34
Matsch mud I
matt dull IV U4, 77

Mauer wall II
Maus mouse I
Mayonnaise mayonnaise II
meckern to nag III
soziale **Medien** social media IV U4, 80
Medikamente medicine III
Medizin medicine III
Meer sea I; ocean IV ZI, 9
am Meer at the seaside I
Meerschweinchen guinea pig II
Mehl flour IV U5, 98
in Mehl wenden to cover in flour IV U5, 98
mehr more II
mehrere a number of IV U5, 98
Mehrheit majority IV U1, 22
Mehrzahl majority IV U1, 22
meiden to avoid IV U3, 62
Meile mile II
mein my I
meine mine II
meinen to mean III
Meinung opinion III
seine Meinung ändern to change one's mind III
anderer Meinung sein to disagree II
meistens mostly IV U3, 58
eine **Menge** a lot of I
jede **Menge** lots of I; lots III
Mensa cafeteria I
Mensch person II
Menschenmenge crowd II
sich **merken** to remember II
merkwürdig funny I; strange II
Messer knife II
Metall metal III
Meter metre I
Metzgerei butcher's III
mich me I
Miete rent II
Mikrowelle microwave II
Milch milk II
Milchmischgetränk milkshake III
Milchshake milkshake III
mild mild I
Milliarde billion IV U1, 13
Million million III
eine halbe Million half a million III
Minderheit minority IV U1, 23
Mindest- minimum IV U2, 38
mindestens at least IV U3, 64
Mineralwasser mineral water III
minimal minimum IV U2, 38
Minimum minimum IV U2, 38
Minute minute II
mir me I
mischen to mix IV U5, 98
mit with I
mit besonderen Bedürfnissen with special needs III
Mit den besten Wünschen, Best wishes, I
mitbringen to bring II
Mitleid haben mit to feel sorry III
Mittagessen lunch I; dinner II
Mittagspause lunchtime I
Mittagszeit lunchtime I
Mitte centre; middle III; center *(AE)* IV U1, 13
in der Mitte in the middle III
in der Mitte von in the centre of III
Mitternacht midnight III
Mittwoch Wednesday I
mixen to mix IV U5, 98
Mode fashion *(no pl)* IV U3, 58
modern modern I
modisch fashionable II; trendy IV U4, 81
mögen to like I; to enjoy III
gern mögen to love I
nicht mögen to hate III; to dislike IV U4, 81
ich möchte nicht … I wouldn't like (to) … I
ich möchte … I'd like (to) … (= I would like to) I
Möchtest du? Would you like (to)…? I
Möglichkeit chance II
Moment moment II
in dem Moment als right IV U2, 42
Monat month I
monatlich monthly III
Monster monster III
Montag Monday I
Mörder murderer III
Mörderin murderer III
Morgen morning I
Guten Morgen. Good morning. II
morgen tomorrow II
morgendliche Ansprache morning message IV U2, 34
Moschee mosque II
motiviert motivated IV U1, 18
Motor engine IV U3, 54
Motorrad motorbike I
Moussaka moussaka II
müde tired I
Müll rubbish II
Mülleimer tin IV U3, 63
multikulturell multicultural IV U5, 98
Mund mouth II
Münze coin III
Münzgeld change II
Münztelefon pay phone III
Museum museum II
Musik music I
Musik- musical III
musikalisch musical III
Musikgruppe band II
Müsli cereal III
Muslim Muslim I
Muslimin Muslim I
müssen must I; to have to II
nicht müssen needn't I
Mut courage IV U5, 107
mutig brave III
Mutter mother I
Mutti mum I
Mütze cap I

N

na ja well I
Na ja, schau mal … nach. Well, look … I
nach to; after I
nach *(bei Uhrzeitangaben)* past I
Nachbar neighbour III
Nachbarin neighbour III
nachfolgen to succeed (in) IV U1, 19
Nachmittag afternoon I

am Nachmittag in the afternoon I
nachmittags p.m. II
Nachricht message II
Nachricht(en) news II
nachschauen to look I
Nachsitzen detention IV U2, 35
Nachspeise dessert; pudding II
nachsprechen to say I
nächste next I
als **Nächstes** next II
Nacht night I
Nachtwanderung night walk I
Nagel nail III
Nagelschere nail scissors III
nah near III
in der **Nähe** von near I; close III
nahe close III
Name name I
Nase nose I
die Nase voll haben (von) to be fed up (with) III
nass wet I
national national III
National- national III
Natur nature III
die freie **Natur** the outdoors IV U5, 96
natürlich of course II
Naturwissenschaft Science I
neben next to I
neblig foggy IV U4, 75
nehmen to take II
etw. ernst nehmen to take sth seriously IV U1, 18
neidisch jealous II
nein no I
nennen to say I
genannt werden to be called II
nervös nervous II
nett nice I; friendly III
Nett, dich kennen zu lernen. Nice to meet you. I
Netz web III; net IV U4, 75
neu new I
auf den neuesten Stand bringen to update IV U4, 81
Neuigkeit(en) news II
neun nine I
neunzehn nineteen I
neunzig ninety I
nicht not I
auch nicht not … either III
nicht dürfen mustn't III
nicht einverstanden sein to disagree II
nicht können can't I; cannot III
nicht mehr not … any more III
nicht mögen to hate III; to dislike IV U4, 81
nicht wahr? isn't it? II
nicht werden won't (= will not) II
Nichte niece III
nichts nothing IV U5, 99
nie never I
sich **niederlassen** to settle IV U4, 75
niedlich cute II
niedrig low II
niemals never I
niemand no one I; nobody III
nirgendwo nowhere IV U2, 34
nirgendwohin nowhere IV U2, 34
noch even II
noch ein another II
noch einmal again II; once more II
noch nicht not … yet II
Norden north III
nördlich von north of IV ZI, 9
Nordwesten northwest III
nordwestlich northwest of III
nörgeln to nag III
normal regular IV U4, 89
normalerweise usually II
Normanne Norman III
die **Normannen** the Normans III
Normannin Norman III
Notdienst emergency service III
Note grade *(AE)* IV U2, 32
Notfall emergency III
sich **Notizen** machen to take notes I
Notruf emergency call III
November November I
Nudelauflauf pasta bake II
Nudeln pasta II
null zero I
null *(bei Uhrzeiten und Telefonnummern)* oh I
Nummer number I
nun now I
nur just II; only III
Nuss nut I
nützlich useful III; helpful IV U2, 38

O

oben up II
obere upper III
oberer Teil top IV U1, 13
oberes Ende top IV U1, 13
Oberteil top II
Obst fruit I
Obst- und Gemüseladen greengrocer's III
oder or I
Ofenkartoffel jacket potato II
öffentliche Verkehrsmittel public transport III
öffnen to open I
Öffnungszeiten opening times IV U5, 105
oft often I
ohne without III
Ohr ear II
okay OK I
Oktober October I
Öl oil IV U5, 98
Oma grandma II
Onkel uncle II
online online II
online stellen to post IV U4, 80
Opa grandad III
Operation operation III
optimistisch optimistic III
Orange orange I
orange orange I
Orchester orchestra III
Ordinalzahl ordinal number I
in **Ordnung** fine; all right II
in Ordnung bringen to tidy (up) II
organisieren to organize II
Ort place I
örtlich local III
Osten east III
Ostern Easter IV U3, 56
östlich von east of IV ZI, 9
Outdoor- outdoor III

Outfit outfit III
Ozean ocean IV ZI, 9

P

Paar pair IV U2, 41
ein Paar a pair of II
ein **paar** a few III
packen to pack; to pack up II
eine **Packung** ... a packet of I
Paella paella IV U5, 99
Paket package IV U5, 102
panisch werden to panic II
Papa dad I
Papier paper III
Papiere papers IV U1, 19
Pappe cardboard III
Parade parade III
Paradies paradise IV ZI, 9
Parfüm perfume III
Park park I
Parkplatz parking lot *(AE)* IV U1, 15
Partner partner III
Partnerin partner III
Party party I
Pass pass IV U2, 34
Passagier passenger II
Passagierin passenger II
passen to suit; to fit II
passieren to happen II
Pasta pasta II
Pastete pasty; pie II
Patient patient II
Patientin patient II
Pause break IV U2, 39
in der Pause at break I
Pause machen to take a break II
Pausenhof playground I
peinlich embarrassing IV U2, 42
Pekannuss pecan IV U3, 67
Pence *(brit. Währungseinheit)* pence I
perfekt perfect IV ZI, 9
Person person II
berühmte Person celebrity IV U5, 97
Personalausweis ID III
persönlich personal III
Pfannkuchen pancake II
Pfeffer pepper II
Pferd horse I
Pfirsich peach I
Pflanze plant III
Pflaster plaster III
pflegte(n) zu to used to (+ infinitive) IV U3, 54
Pfund *(brit. Währungseinheit)* pound I
das macht 2 Pfund und 24 Pence that's £2.24 I
Picknick picnic I
Pick-up pick-up IV U5, 102
Pilot pilot IV U4, 79
Pilotin pilot IV U4, 79
Pinguin penguin I
pink pink I
Pirat pirate I
Piratin pirate I
Pirogge pierogi II
Pizza pizza I
Plan plan II
planen to plan II
Plantage plantation IV U5, 97
Planwagen wagon IV U4, 85
Plastik plastic III
platt flat IV U2, 32
Platz place I; square II; seat IV U5, 102
plaudern to chat II
plötzlich suddenly II
Podcast podcast IV U4, 94
politisch political IV U1, 23
Polizei police III
Polizeibeamter police officer I
Polizeibeamtin police officer I
polnisch Polish IV U5, 99
Polnisch Polish IV U5, 99
Pommes chips *(pl)* I
Pommes mit Fisch fish and chips I
Popcorn popcorn I
positiv positive III
Postamt post office I
Poster poster I
Postkarte postcard I
praktisch practical IV U4, 89
Praline chocolate IV U3, 54
Prämie bonus IV U2, 39
Pranger stocks III
Präsentation presentation IV U2, 51
präsentieren to present I
Preis prize; price II
Prise pinch II
pro Stück each II
Problem problem I; trouble III
produzieren to produce IV U1, 13
Projekt project III
Prominente celebrity IV U5, 97
Prominenter celebrity IV U5, 97
Propellerboot airboat IV U5, 102
Prospekt brochure III
Protest protest IV U5, 96
Protestant Protestant III
Protestantin Protestant III
protestantisch Protestant III
Prozent percent (%) IV U1, 23
prüfen to test II
Prüfung test IV U3, 61
prügeln to beat IV U3, 62
Pudding pudding II
pünktlich on time III
Pute turkey IV U3, 53
putzen to clean I

Q

Quadratmeile square mile (= sq. mi.) IV ZI, 8
quer durch across IV U3, 54
Quittung receipt II

R

Rad wheel III
Radfahren cycling III
Radiergummi eraser I
Radio radio III
Rafting rafting III
rappen to rap II
Rapper rapper III
Rapperin rapper III
Rasierapparat razor IV U3, 59
Rasierer razor IV U3, 59
Rassentrennung segregation IV U5, 106
Rassismus racism IV U5, 98
rasten to rest II

Raster grid IV U5, 101
Rat advice III
raten to guess II
Ratschlag advice III
Rätsel mystery I
Rauch smoke III
Raum room I
(Taschen-)Rechner calculator I
Rechnung bill III
Recht right; law IV U5, 96
recht haben to be right II
Du hast recht. You're right. I
rechthaberisch bossy IV U2, 39
rechts on the right I; right III
auf der rechten Seite on the right I
Rechtschreibung spelling I
Rechtsfall court case IV U5, 107
Rede speech III
reden (mit) to talk (to) I
Regal shelf I
Regalbrett shelf I
Regel rule III
regelmäßig regular IV U4, 89
Regenbogen rainbow III
Regenmantel raincoat III
Regenschirm umbrella II
Regierung government IV U5, 96
Regierungsgebäude State House *(AE)* IV U5, 98
Region region IV U5, 97
Regisseur director II
Regisseurin director II
regnen to rain I
reich rich III
reichen to pass II
Reichtum wealth III
Reifen tyre III
in die richtige Reihenfolge bringen to put in the right order I
Reis rice II
Reise trip; voyage; journey III; tour IV U4, 76
reisen to travel II
Reiten horse riding I
reiten to ride II
reizen to tease IV U2, 38
Religionsunterricht RE (Religious Education) I
religiös religious IV U1, 23
Rennen race I
rennen to run I
reparieren to repair III
Reporter reporter III
Reporterin reporter III
Republik republic III
Requisit prop III
Reservat reservation IV U2, 32
reservieren to make a reservation III; to book IV U4, 76
Reservierung reservation IV U4, 76
respektieren to respect IV U4, 89
der Rest the rest IV U1, 22
Restaurant restaurant II
retten to save III
Rettungsboot lifeboat III
Rettungsdienst emergency service III
Rezept recipe II
richtig right I; real II
das Richtige tun to do the right thing III
Richtung direction IV U2, 33; trend IV U4, 83
in Richtung towards IV U3, 62
in diese Richtung this way II
riechen to smell III
Riese giant III
Riesen- giant IV U4, 74
riesengroß huge III
Riesenrad big wheel II
riesig huge III; giant IV U4, 74
Rindfleisch beef II
Ring circle III
Ritt ride IV U1, 14
Ritter knight III
Rock skirt I
Rohr tube III
Rolle part II; role IV U5, 107
Rollstuhl wheelchair III
Rolltreppe escalator II
die Römer the Romans III
rosa pink I
Rose rose IV ZI, 8
rot red I
Hin- und Rückfahrkarte return ticket III
Rückmeldung feedback IV U2, 39
Rucksack backpack IV U3, 62
Ruf call III
rufen to call; to shout II
Rugby rugby III
Ruhe silence III
ruhig quiet III
Rührei scrambled egg II
rühren to stir II
ruinieren to ruin II
rumhängen (mit) to hang out (with) IV U3, 58
Russe Russian IV U5, 99
Russin Russian IV U5, 99
Russisch Russian IV U5, 99
russisch Russian IV U5, 99
Rüstung armour III

S

Sache thing II
Sack bag I
Saft juice II
sagen to say; to tell I
Salat salad II
Salz salt II
sammeln to collect I
(sich) sammeln to gather IV U3, 64
Samstag Saturday I
samstags on Saturdays I
Sand sand II
Sandwich sandwich I
Sänger singer I
Sängerin singer I
sauber clean III
sauber machen to clean I
sauer sein to be fed up (with) III
Saxofon saxophone I
eine Schachtel ... a box of I
(es ist) schade it's a pity IV U3, 63
Schaf sheep I
Schal scarf II
Schälchen bowl II
Schale bowl II
Schatz treasure II
schätzen to guess IV U3, 59; to appreciate IV U5, 99
Schau show IV U5, 102

schauen to look I
Schauspielen acting III
Schauspieler actor II
Schauspielerei acting III
Schauspielerin actor II
Schauspielworkshop acting workshop II
scheinen to shine IV ZI, 8; to seem IV U3, 64
Schere scissors *(pl)* III
schick chic I
schicken to send I
schieben to push I
schießen (auf) to shoot (at) IV U3, 63
Schiff ship I
Schiffsbauer ship builder III
Schiffsbauerin ship builder III
Schiffsfahrt boat trip II
Schild sign III
Schinken ham II
Schlacht battle III
Schlaf sleep III
schlafen to sleep I; to be asleep III
Schlafzimmer bedroom I
schlagen to hit II; to beat IV U3, 62
Schlagzeile headline IV U4, 77
Schlamm mud I
Schlange snake I
schlau clever II; smart III
Schlauch tube III
schlecht ill II; bad III
sich schlecht fühlen to feel sick IV U5, 103
schlechteste worst III
schleifen to drag IV U5, 107
schleppen to drag IV U5, 107
im **Schlepptau** in tow IV U2, 42
schlicht plain II
schließen to close I
Schließfach locker IV U2, 34
schließlich in the end; finally II
schlimm bad III
schlimmste worst III
Schloss castle II
Schlumpf smurf I
Schluss end II; ending III
zum Schluss in the end; finally II
Schlussfolgerung conclusion III
Schlussverkauf sale II
schmackhaft tasty III
schmerzhaft sore II
Schminke make-up IV U3, 58
Schmuck jewellery II
Schmuggler smuggler II
Schmugglerin smuggler II
schmutzig dirty I
Schnäppchen bargain II
schnappen to grab III
Schnee snow IV U1, 14
schneiden to cut III
sich die Haare schneiden lassen to have a haircut II
schnell fast II; quickly II; quick III
der/die/das schnellste the fastest I
Schokolade chocolate I
eine Tafel Schokolade a bar of chocolate I
schon already; yet II
Schon gut. Never mind. II
schön nice; beautiful I; fine; lovely II
Schotte Scot III
Schottenrock kilt III
Schottin Scot III
schottisch Scottish III
Schrank cupboard III
schrecklich awful I; horrible III; terrible IV U2, 32
Schrei shout I
schreiben to write I
eine SMS schreiben to text II
Schreibtisch desk IV U3, 62
schreien to shout II; to scream IV U3, 63
Schriftsteller writer II
Schriftstellerin writer II
Schritt step III
schubsen to push III
schüchtern shy IV U2, 39
Schuh shoe II
Schule school I
in der Schule at school I
Schüler student I
Schülerin student I
Schulfach subject I
Schulgelände campus IV U2, 35
Schulhof playground I
Schulleiter principal *(AE)* IV U2, 34
Schulleiterin principal *(AE)* IV U2, 34
Schulstunde lesson I
Schüssel bowl II
Schusswaffe gun IV U3, 62
schützen to protect III
schwach weak III
schwarz black I
Schweigen silence III
schweigsam silent III
Schweinefleisch pork II
Schweizer Swiss IV U4, 84
Schweizerin Swiss IV U4, 84
schweizerisch Swiss IV U4, 84
schwer heavy; hard II
schwerhörig deaf III
Schwert sword III
Schwester sister I
schwierig difficult; hard II
Schwierigkeiten trouble III
Schwimmbad swimming pool I
schwimmen to swim II
schwimmen gehen to go swimming I
Schwimmer swimmer IV U4, 79
Schwimmerin swimmer IV U4, 79
Science-Fiction science fiction I
Scone *(eine Art süßes Brötchen)* scone II
sechs six I
sechzehn sixteen I
sechzig sixty I
See lake III
sehen to see I; to look II
Sehenswürdigkeit sight II
sehr very I; extremely IV U4, 80
so sehr so much III
zu sehr too much II
Seide silk III
Seife soap III
Seil rope I
Seilrutsche zip line III
sein to be I
sein his I; its III
seit for IV U4, 80; since IV U4, 80
seitdem since IV U4, 80
Seite side II

Seite *(im Internet)* site IV U4, 80
Sekunde second II
selber myself; ourselves; yourselves; themselves III
selbst myself; self III
dich selbst yourself II
ihr/euch/Sie/sich (selbst) yourselves III
sie selbst herself; themselves III
selbstbewusst confident III
selbstsicher confident; sure of oneself III
selbstsüchtig selfish IV U2, 39
selbstverständlich of course II
Selfie *(Schnappschuss von sich selbst)* selfie IV U4, 83
seltsam strange II
senden to send I
Senf mustard II
separat separate IV U5, 106
September September I
servieren to serve IV U2, 33
Serviette napkin II
setzen to put II
Setz dich. Have a seat. IV U3, 54
Setzen Sie sich. Have a seat. IV U3, 54
Shampoo shampoo III
Shirt shirt II
Shorts shorts *(pl)* I
Show show IV U5, 102
sich each other; self III
sich gegenseitig each other III
sicher sure II; safe III
Sicherheit safety IV U4, 75
Sicherheitsnetz safety net IV U4, 75
Sicht look; view IV U1, 14
Sie you I
sie she I; them II
sie *(Pl.)* they I
sieben seven I
siebzehn seventeen I
siebzig seventy I
Siedler settler IV U2, 32
Siedlerin settler IV U2, 32
siegen to win I
Signal signal III
singen to sing I
Single single IV U5, 97
sinken to sink III
sinnlos pointless IV U4, 77
Sitte custom IV U5, 97
Situation situation II
Sitzbank bench III
Sitzplatz seat IV U5, 102
Skateboard skateboard III
Ski fahren to ski II
Skifahren skiing III
Sklave slave IV U4, 86
Sklavin slave IV U4, 86
Skyline skyline IV U1, 12
Slogan slogan IV U4, 77
Smartphone smartphone IV U4, 80
SMS message II
eine SMS schreiben to text II
SMS-Schreiber texter II
SMS-Schreiberin texter II
Snack snack I
so like that I; so II; like this III
so sehr so much III
so ... wie as ... as II
sobald as soon as IV U4, 89
Socke sock I
soeben just II
Sofa sofa II
sofort right now III; right away IV U4, 80
Software software II
sogar even II
Sohn son III
Sojabohne soy bean IV ZI, 9
solch such IV U2, 38
Soldat soldier III
Soldatin soldier III
sollte should III
Sommer summer II
Sonderangebot special offer III
Sonne sun III
sonnenbaden to sunbathe II
Sonnenbrille sunglasses *(pl)* II
sonnig sunny I
Sonntag Sunday I
sich **Sorgen** machen to worry I
für jmdn. **sorgen** to take care of sb IV U2, 41
Sorte sort II; type III
sortieren to sort IV U2, 38
Soße sauce II
Souvenir souvenir III
Souvenirladen souvenir shop III
sowieso anyway IV U1, 14
soziale Medien social media IV U4, 80
Spaghetti spaghetti II
spanisch Spanish IV U5, 98
Spanisch Spanish IV U5, 98
spannend exciting I
sparen to save IV U1, 22
Spaß fun I
zum Spaß for fun III
(zu) **spät** late II
später later I; after III
spazieren gehen to go for a walk I
Spaziergang walk III
speichern to save II
Speise dish II
Speisekarte menu II
spektakulär spectacular IV U4, 77
sperren to ban IV U5, 99
speziell special I
Spiegel mirror III
Spiel game I
spielen to play I; to act II
Spieler player II; gamer II
Spielerin player II; gamer II
Spielfeld court III
Spielkarte card II
Spielplatz playground I
Spielzeug toy III
Spind locker IV U2, 34
Spinne spider III
Spinnennetz web III
Spitze top IV U1, 13
spitze awesome IV U2, 34
Spitzname nickname IV U4, 75
Sport sport I
Sportart sport III
Sportgeschäft sports shop I
Sportunterricht PE (Physical Education) I
sprachbehindert speech impaired IV U5, 102
Sprache language II; speech III
sprechen to say I; to speak III

sprechen (mit) to talk (to) I
sprechen über to talk about II
springen to jump IV U3, 63
Spritze injection III
spülen to wash III
Spülmaschine dishwasher IV U3, 59
Spur clue I; trail IV U5, 102
Staat state IV ZI, 8
Staatsangehörige citizen IV U1, 18
Staatsangehöriger citizen IV U1, 18
Staatsbürger citizen IV U1, 18
Staatsbürgerin citizen IV U1, 18
Stadion stadium II
Stadt town I; city II
Stadtmitte city centre III
Stadtplan map I
Stadtteil borough IV U1, 12
Stadtzentrum city centre III
Stahl steel III
Stand cart IV U1, 14
auf den neuesten Stand bringen to update IV U4, 81
Standinhaber stallholder II
Standinhaberin stallholder II
Star star I
stark heavy II; powerful IV U1, 22
Start start III
starten to start II
Statistik statistics *(no pl)* IV U1, 22
stattdessen instead IV U4, 80
Status status IV U4, 81
Stau traffic jam IV U1, 14
staubsaugen to hoover II
Staubsauger vacuum cleaner IV U3, 59
stecken bleiben to get stuck IV U3, 54
stehen to suit; to stand II
stehlen to steal IV U2, 38
steigen to climb III
Stein rock; stone III
Stelle place I
stellen to put II
online stellen to post IV U4, 80
Stellenbezeichnung job title IV U2, 38
sterben to die III
Stern star III
sticheln to tease IV U2, 38
Stiefel boot II
Stift pen I
Stil style III
still quiet III
Stille silence III
Stimme voice III
stimmt's? isn't it? II
Stock story *(AE)* IV U1, 14
Stockwerk floor II; story *(AE)* IV U1, 14
stolz (auf) **proud** (of) III
(sich) **stoßen** to hit III
strahlend bright IV ZI, 8
Strand beach I
den Strand nach Strandgut absuchen to go beach combing II
Straße road I; street III
Straßenbahn tram III
Straßenbauarbeiten roadwork *(AE)* IV U1, 14
Strecke track IV U5, 102
Streich trick I
streichen to paint IV U4, 75
Streit argument II; fight III
(sich) **streiten** to fight III
streng strict IV U2, 34
Stress stress IV U3, 57
strikt strict IV U2, 34
Strom electricity III
Stück piece II
pro Stück each II
studieren to study IV U2, 34
Studio studio IV U4, 75
Stufe step II
Stuhl chair I
stumm silent III
Stunde period IV U2, 34
erste Stunde *(in der Schule)* homeroom IV U2, 45
40 Kilometer pro Stunde 40 kilometres an hour I
Stundenplan timetable I; schedule *(AE)* IV U2, 32
Sturm storm I
stürzen to rush III
suchen to look for I
Süden south III
im Süden von in the south of III
südlich southern IV U5, 96
südlich von south of IV ZI, 9
Südstaatler Southerner IV U5, 97
Südstaatlerin Southerner IV U5, 97
Sumpf swamp IV ZI, 9
super cool I; way to go II; awesome IV U2, 34
Superheld superhero IV U3, 61
Supermarkt supermarket II
Suppe soup II
Surfen surfing IV U4, 74
surfen to surf II
im Internet surfen to surf the internet II
Surfer surfer IV ZI, 9
Surferin surfer IV ZI, 9
Sushi sushi IV U5, 99
süß cute II; sweet III
Süßigkeit sweet I
Sweatshirt sweatshirt I
Symbol symbol IV U1, 13
System system IV U5, 107
Szene scene II

T

Tablet tablet IV U4, 80
Tablett tray II
Tablette tablet II
Tafel board I
eine Tafel Schokolade a bar of chocolate I
Tag day I
ein ausgefüllter Tag a busy day I
eines Tages one day III
den ganzen Tag all day III
Tagebuch diary I
täglich daily III
vier Stunden täglich four hours a day I
Taktik tactic III
talentiert talented III
Talentwettbewerb talent show I
Tante aunt II
Tanz- dancing IV U2, 43
Tanzen dancing IV U2, 43
tanzen to dance I
Tänzer dancer I
Tänzerin dancer I
tapfer brave III

Tapferkeit courage IV U5, 107
Tasche bag I
Taschengeld allowance *(AE)* IV U2, 38
Taschenlampe torch I
Taschentuch tissue III
Tasse cup II
tat(en) früher used to (+ infinitive) IV U3, 54
Tätigkeit job II
tatkräftig energetic IV U4, 89
Tatsache fact II
tatsächlich actually III
taub deaf III
tausend a/one thousand II
Taxi taxi II
Team team I
Teamwork teamwork II
Technik Design Technology (DT) I
Techniker engineer II
Technikerin engineer II
Tee tea I
Teelöffel teaspoon II
Teenager teen II; teenager III
Teil part II
oberer Teil top IV U1, 13
teilen to share III
teilnehmen (an) to take part (in) III
Telefon phone II; telephone III
ans Telefon gehen to answer the phone III
Telefonanruf phone call I
telefonieren to phone I
Telefonnummer phone number III
Telefonzelle telephone box II
Teller plate II
Tennis tennis I
Teppich carpet I
Test test IV U3, 61
testen to test II
teuer expensive II
Text lines *(pl)*; text II
texten to text II
Textnachricht (SMS) text message I
Theater theatre; drama II
Theaterstück play II
Thema topic IV U2, 51
Thunfisch tuna II
Tier animal I
Tierarzt vet II
Tierärztin vet II
Tierhandlung pet shop III
Tierheim animal rescue shelter I
Tierpark zoo I
Tierpfleger zookeeper I
Tierpflegerin zookeeper I
Tierwelt *(in freier Wildbahn)* wildlife IV U5, 102
Tiger tiger I
Tipp tip III
Tisch table I
den Tisch decken to lay the table II
Tischler carpenter II
Tischlerin carpenter II
Tischtennis table tennis II
Tochter daughter I
tod- deadly III
tödlich deadly III
Toilette bathroom (AE) IV U2, 34
tolerieren to tolerate IV U5, 98
toll great; brilliant I; amazing III
Tomate tomato II
Ton sound III
Tonne tonne II; barrel IV U3, 53
Top top II
Topf pot III
Tor gateway IV U1, 12
Tornado tornado IV U2, 32
tot dead III
töten to kill III
Tötung killing IV U5, 98
Tour tour IV U4, 76
Tourist tourist I
Touristin tourist I
Touristeninformation Tourist Information Centre I
Tradition tradition III
tragen to wear I; to carry III
Trainer trainer IV U5, 103
Trainerin trainer IV U5, 103
trainieren to practise III
Training practice I; training III
Traktor tractor I
Transfer transfer IV U5, 102
transkontinental *(über den Kontinent hinweg)* transcontinental IV U4, 86
Transport transfer IV U5, 102
Transporter van III
Tratsch gossip IV U3, 58
Traum dream II
träumen to dream III
traurig sad; down III
treffen to hit II
sich treffen (mit) to hang out (with) IV U3, 58
(sich) treffen to meet II
treiben to drive IV U2, 33
Trend trend IV U4, 83
trendsetzend trending IV U4, 81
trendy trendy IV U4, 81
Trennung segregation IV U5, 106
treu true IV U2, 34
Treue allegiance IV U2, 34
Treueeid pledge of allegiance IV U2, 34
Trick trick I
trinken to drink II
Trinkhalm straw II
Trip trip III
trocken dry III
Trommel- drumming III
trotzdem anyway IV U1, 14
Truthahn turkey IV U3, 53
Tschüss! Bye!; See you! I
T-Shirt T-shirt I
Tuch scarf II
tun to do; to make I
Tut mir leid. Sorry. I
Tunnel tunnel III
Tür door II
Türkei Turkey II
Türkisch Turkish IV U5, 99
türkisch Turkish IV U5, 99
Türklingel doorbell IV U3, 54
Turm tower II
Turnhalle gym(nasium) IV U2, 42
Turnier competition III
turnieren to joust III
Turnierzweikampf jousting III
Turnschuh trainer I
Tüte bag I
eine Tüte ... a packet of I
Tutorial tutorial IV U4, 80
Typ type III

U

U-Bahn underground II; subway *(AE)* IV U1, 14
U-Boot submarine I
Übelkeit verspüren to feel sick IV U5, 103
übelnehmen to resent IV U5, 99
üben to practise III
über about II; across IV U3, 54; over IV U1, 12
über die Grenze gehen to cross the border IV U1, 19
überall wo(hin) wherever III
überfüllt crowded IV U1, 22
sich **übergeben** to be sick I; to puke IV U3, 62
überleben to survive III
überlegen to guess II
übernachten to stay II
Übernachtung sleepover I
überprüfen to check III
überqueren to cross III
überrascht surprised II
Überraschung surprise I
die Grenze **überschreiten** to cross the border IV U1, 19
Überschrift headline IV U4, 77
übersetzen to translate IV U5, 102
überzeugt convinced IV U3, 59
üblich regular IV U4, 89
Übung practice I
Übungsheft exercise book I
Uhr clock II
Uhr *(Zeitangabe bei vollen Stunden)* o'clock I
Uhrenturm clock tower II
Uhrzeit time I
um at I
um … herum around IV U1, 14
umfallen to fall (over) III
Umfrage survey II
umher around III
umrühren to stir II
umsteigen to change III
umziehen to move (house) II
Umzug parade III
Unabhängigkeit independence IV U1, 13; freedom *(no pl)* IV U1, 23
unangenehm uncomfortable II
unbequem uncomfortable II
und and I
unfair unfair III
Unfall accident III
unfreundlich unfriendly III
ungefähr about II
ungefähr um around III
ungefährlich safe III
Ungeheuer monster III
ungewöhnlich unusual IV U4, 77
unglaublich amazing III
Unglück disaster III
unglücklich unhappy II
unhöflich rude IV U2, 39
Uniform uniform I
uninteressant unappealing IV U4, 77
unmodisch unfashionable II
unmöglich impossible III
unmotiviert unmotivated IV U2, 39
Unordnung mess I
uns us I
unschuldig innocent IV U3, 63
unser our I
unsere ours III
da **unten** down there IV U5, 98
unter under I
unterbrechen to interrupt IV U4, 94
untere lower III
untergehen to sink III
Unterhaltsgeld allowance *(AE)* IV U2, 38
Unterlagen papers IV U1, 19
Unterricht lesson I; class III
Unterrichtsstunde class; period IV U2, 34
unterschreiben to sign IV U3, 53
Unterstützung support IV U1, 19
unterwegs out and about I
in der **Unterzahl** outnumbered IV U5, 102
unterzeichnen to sign IV U3, 53
unverschämt rude IV U2, 39
updaten to update IV U4, 81
Ureinwohner Amerikas Native American IV U2, 32
Ureinwohnerin Amerikas Native American IV U2, 32
Urgroßeltern great-grandparents IV U1, 25
Urlaub holiday II; vacation *(AE)* IV U5, 104
Uropa great-great-grandad I
US-amerikanisch US IV U1, 18

V

Vanillesauce custard II
Vater father I
Vati dad I
Veganismus veganism *(no pl)* IV U4, 83
Vegetarier vegetarian I
Vegetarierin vegetarian I
Ventilator fan IV U3, 59
sich mit jmdm. **verabreden** to ask sb out IV U2, 42
Verabredung date IV U2, 42
veraltet outdated IV U4, 81
verändern to change III
verängstigt scared I
Veranstaltung event IV U1, 13
verantwortlich responsible IV U2, 38
verantwortungsvoll responsible IV U2, 38
verärgert angry II; annoyed III
Verband bandage III
verbannen to ban IV U5, 99
verbessern to correct I
verbieten to ban IV U5, 99
verbinden to connect III; to link IV U5, 107
in **Verbindung** bleiben to keep in touch II
verboten forbidden IV U3, 58
verbrennen to burn III
verbringen *(Zeit)* to spend II
verdienen to earn IV U2, 38
verdrehen to twist II
Verein club II
Vereinsheim clubhouse IV U3, 62
Verfasser writer III
Verfasserin writer III
Verfolger chaser IV U2, 33

Verfolgerin chaser IV U2, 33
Vergangenheit past III
vergessen to forget I
vergleichen to compare I
vergrößern to increase IV U4, 84
verhaften to arrest IV U5, 107
Verhalten behavior *(AE)* IV U2, 38
verkaufen to sell III
Verkäufer shop assistant II; assistant III; sales associate *(AE)* IV U2, 38
Verkäuferin shop assistant II; assistant III; sales associate *(AE)* IV U2, 38
Verkehr traffic III
öffentliche **Verkehrsmittel** public transport III
verkleidet (als) dressed III
Verkleidung fancy dress I
verlassen leave II
verlässlich reliable IV U5, 109
verlegen embarrassed II
verletzen to hurt II
sich **verlieben** (in) to fall in love (with) III
verlieren to lose II
vermeiden to avoid IV U3, 62
vermischen to mix IV U5, 98
vermissen to miss II
Vermittlung operator III
vermuten to guess IV U3, 59
vernünftig intelligent III
veröffentlichen to release IV U5, 97
verprügeln to beat IV U3, 62
verrenken to sprain III
verrückt crazy I
jmdn. verrückt machen to drive sb crazy III
versagen (in/bei) to fail (at) IV U1, 19
verschieden separate IV U5, 106
verschwinden to disappear IV U3, 62
sich **versichern** to make sure IV U1, 14
Versprechen pledge IV U2, 34
versprechen to promise IV U2, 34
sich **verständigen** to communicate IV U4, 80
verstauchen to sprain III
(sich) **verstecken** to hide III
verstehen to understand II; to get III; to know IV U5, 103
etw. verstehen to get sth IV U5, 102
Versuch experiment II
vertrauen to trust IV U5, 109
vertrauenswürdig reliable IV U5, 109
vertraut familiar IV U2, 34
verübeln to resent IV U5, 99
verursachen to produce IV U1, 13; to cause IV U4, 86
vervollständigen to complete I; to finish II
verwenden to use II
verwirrt confused III
verzeihen to pardon IV U3, 53
Verzeihung pardon IV U3, 67
verzerren to twist II
auf etw. **verzichten** to give sth a miss III
Vesper packed lunch II
Video video IV U3, 54
Video-Chat video chat III
viel much; lots of; a lot of I; lots III; a lot of III
viele many II
wie viele how many II
Vielen Dank. Thanks so much. IV U4, 94
vielleicht may II; maybe II
vier four I
vierte fourth I
Viertel nach quarter past I
Viertel vor quarter to I
vierzehn fourteen I
vierzig forty I
viktorianisches Zeitalter Victorian era III
violett purple I
Visum visa IV U1, 19
Vogel bird III
Vogelbeobachtung bird watching III
voll full IV U5, 106
Volleyball volleyball II
völlig quite III; absolutely IV U3, 59
vollkommen perfect IV ZI, 9
von from I; by II
ein Foto von a photo of I
von ... weg off IV U5, 107
vor ago II; before IV U3, 61
vor *(bei Uhrzeitangaben)* to I
vorbei (an) past III
vorbereiten to prepare III
sich vorbereiten to get ready IV U3, 54
Vordergrund foreground III
im Vordergrund in the foreground III
Vorgehensweise tactic III
vorhaben to be up to III
vorher before II
vorhersagen to foretell III
Vormittag morning I
vormittags a.m. II
Vorrichtung device IV U3, 58
vorsichtig sein to be careful II
Vorsingen audition II
Vorspielen audition II
Vorsprechen audition II
vorstellen to introduce IV U5, 98
Vorstellungsgespräch interview IV U2, 38
Vortanzen audition II
Vortrag presentation IV U2, 51
vorziehen to prefer II

W

wach awake III
wachsen to grow IV U3, 58
Wagen truck III
Waggon wagon IV U4, 85
Wahl choice IV U5, 102
wählen to choose II; to vote for IV U2, 33
Wahlfach elective IV U2, 34
Wahnsinnsspaß blast IV U2, 34
wahr true II
während while II; during III
wahrnehmen to notice IV U2, 42
wahrscheinlich probably III
Währung currency IV ZI, 8
Wahrzeichen landmark IV U1, 14
Wald wood II; forest IV U3, 52
Waliser Welsh III
Waliserin Welsh III
walisisch Welsh III

Walisisch Welsh III
Wand wall II
Wandern hiking; walking III
wandern to hike II
Wanderweg trail IV U5, 102
Wandgemälde mural III
wann when I
warm warm I
warten to wait II
warten auf to wait for II
Warteschlange queue II
warum why II
was what I
Was?! No way! III
Was hast du (in letzter Zeit) gemacht? What have you been up to? IV U3, 55
Was ist los? What's wrong? II
Was man ... What to ... II
Was stimmt nicht? What's wrong? II
Waschbär raccoon I
(sich) **waschen** to wash III
Wasser water III
Website website II
Wechselgeld change II
wechseln to change II
Wecker alarm clock I
Weg way III; alley IV U2, 32
aus dem Weg gehen to avoid IV U3, 62
nach dem Weg fragen asking the way I
weg away II
nicht weg können to be stuck I
wegen because of III
weglaufen to run away III
weh tun to hurt II
Weide field IV ZI, 9
sich **weigern** to refuse IV U5, 107
Weihnachten Christmas I
Weihnachtstheaterstück pantomime II
weil because I
auf diese **Weise** like this III
weiß white I
Ich **weiß** (es) nicht! I don't know! I
Weißkopfseeadler bald eagle IV ZI, 8
weit far III
weitergehen to keep going IV U4, 85
weitermachen to keep going IV U4, 85
welche which; what; who II
Welle wave IV ZI, 9
Wellenreiten surfing IV U4, 74
wellenreiten to surf II
Wellenreiter surfer IV ZI, 9
Wellenreiterin surfer IV ZI, 9
Welt world II
auf der Welt in the world II
wem whom IV U3, 58
wen whom IV U3, 58
in Mehl **wenden** to cover in flour IV U5, 98
wenig little IV U1, 22
ein wenig a bit II
wenige a few III; few IV U1, 23
weniger less III
wenigstens at least IV U3, 64
wenn when; if II
wer who I
Werbespot ad(vert) (= advertisement) IV U2, 38
Werbespruch slogan IV U4, 77
werden will; to become II
nicht werden won't (= will not) II
werfen to throw IV U2, 38
Werft shipyard III
Werk factory III
an **Werktagen** on weekdays III
Werkzeug tool II
Westen west III
westlich von west of IV ZI, 9
Wettbewerb competition III
Wetter weather I
Wettrennen race I
wichtig important III; major IV ZI, 8
wie how I; as II; like II; what III
wie viele how many II
Wie alt bist du? How old are you? I
Wie bitte? Pardon? I
Wie geht es dir? How are you? I
Wie geht's? What's up?; How's it going? IV U3, 54
Wie geht's dir? How are you doing? IV U3, 55
Wie heißt du? What's your name? I
Wie läuft's? How's it going? IV U3, 54
Wie läuft's bei dir? What have you been up to? IV U3, 55
Wie man ... How to ... II
Wie spät ist es? What time is it? I
Wie viel (kostet/kosten) ...? How much (is/are) ...? I
Wie viel Uhr ist es? What time is it? I
so ... wie as ... as II
wieder again II
wiederholen to repeat III
Auf **Wiedersehen**. Goodbye. I
wiegen to weigh II
Wiese field IV ZI, 9
die **Wikinger** the Vikings III
freie **Wildbahn** the wild IV U5, 102
Wildnis the wild IV U5, 102
willkommen (bei/in) welcome (to) I
willkommen heißen to welcome IV U4, 80
Wind wind I
windig windy I
Windpark wind farm III
Windrad (wind) turbine III
winken to wave II
Winter winter I
winzig tiny III
wir we I
Wirbelsturm tornado IV U2, 32
wirklich real II; actually III; really IV U3, 58
Wirklich? Really? I
wirr confused III
Wissenschaft Science I
Witz joke I
witzig funny I
wo where I
wo(hin) auch immer wherever III
Woche week I
unter der Woche on weekdays III
Wochenende weekend I
am Wochenende at the weekend I
wöchentlich weekly III
woher where I

Woher kommst du? Where are you from? I
wohin where I
wohnen to live I
Wohnung flat I
Wohnwagen caravan III
Wohnzimmer living room I
Wolke cloud IV U2, 33
Wolkenkratzer skyscraper IV U1, 14
wolkig cloudy I
Wolldecke blanket IV U3, 62
Wolle wool I
wollen to want (to) I
Workshop workshop II
Wrap wrap II
wund sore II
Mit den besten **Wünschen**, Best wishes, I
wünschen to wish III
würde(n) would II
würde(n) gern would like II
ich würde gerne … I'd like (to) … (= I would like to) I
ich würde nicht gerne … I wouldn't like (to) … I
würdigen to appreciate IV U5, 99
Wurst sausage II
wütend angry II; furious III

Z

Zahl number I
zählen to count IV U5, 105
Zahn tooth III
Zahnbürste toothbrush III
Zahnpasta toothpaste III
Zahnstocher toothpick II
Zauberei magic II
Zebra zebra I
zehn ten I
Zeichen sign; signal III
Zeichensprache sign language III
zeichnen to draw II
zeigen to show II
Zeit time I
viktorianisches **Zeitalter** Victorian era III
Zeitpunkt date I
Zeitreise time travel III
Zeitschrift magazine I
Zeitschriftenladen newsagent's III
Zeitungsausträger paperboy IV U2, 41
Zeitungsausträgerin papergirl IV U2, 41
Zeitzone time zone IV ZI, 8
Zelt tent II
Zelten camping III
Zeltplatz campsite III
Zentimeter (cm) centimetre (cm) I
Zentrum centre III; center *(AE)* IV U1, 13
zerrissen torn IV U4, 83
zerstören to ruin II
Ziege goat III
ziehen to pull I; to grow IV U3, 58; to drag IV U5, 107
ziemlich quite III; pretty IV U3, 58
Zimmer room I
Zimmerdecke ceiling IV U1, 14
Zimmerin carpenter II
Zimmermann carpenter II
Zitrone lemon II
Zoo zoo I
im Zoo at the zoo I
zornig angry II
zu to I; too II
auf … zu towards IV U3, 62
zu Hause back home II
zu sehr too much II
zubereiten to prepare III
zubinden to tie IV U3, 62
züchten to grow IV U3, 58
zuerst first I
Zug train I
mit (dem Zug) fahren to go by (train) I
Zuhause home I
zuhören to listen (to) I
Zukunft future IV U1, 18
zukünftig future IV U1, 22
zum Schluss finally II
zum Spaß for fun III
zumachen to close I
zunehmen to increase IV U4, 84
zuordnen to match I
zurück back III
zurückgeben to return IV U1, 23
zurückkehren to return IV U1, 23
zurückweisen to reject IV U5, 99
zurückzahlen to pay back II
zusammen together I; everyone II
zusammenfassen to sum up IV U3, 73
zusammenrollen to roll up IV U3, 62
zusammenzucken to jump III
Zusatz- extra II
zusätzlich extra II
zuschauen to watch II
Zustand condition IV U1, 22
zustimmen to agree II
Zutat ingredient II
zuverlässig reliable IV U5, 109
zuvor before II
Zuwanderung immigration IV U1, 22
zwanzig twenty I
zwei two I
zweite second I
zweitens second IV U2, 51
Zwiebel onion II
zwingen to force IV U5, 96
zwischen between II
zwölf twelve I

Lösungen Extra practice

Seite 28

1 Find the words.

1. subway
2. rush hour
3. skyline
4. roadwork
5. traffic lights
6. traffic jam

2 Match the phrases with the pictures and present the places.

1. Buy a sandwhich and a drink and walk in the park.
2. Take the subway downtown.
3. Enjoy the view of the Empire State Building.
4. Try the best hot dogs in Manhattan.
5. Go for a walk in Central Park.
6. Finish the day with a Broadway show.

Seite 29

3 Answer the questions.

1. Yes, he did. He answered lots of questions.
2. No, he didn't. He came when he was ten years old.
3. No, he didn't. He arrived with his mother and sisters.
4. Yes, they did. They didn't speak English.
5. No, they didn't. They had a small shop.
6. No, he didn't. He started his career when he was fifteen.
7. Yes, he did. He became a football star in high school.

4 Put the verbs in the past perfect.

1. I became a taxi driver in new York after I hadn't found a job in my town.
2. Before that I had been a bus driver.
3. After a passenger had left my taxi, I found her bag with $10,00.
4. Once it smelled funny. A passenger hadn't finished his fish burger.
5. A passenger was late for his plane because he had forgotten his passport.
6. A movie star got out in a traffic jam because I hadn't known who he was.
7. We arrived after the show had started.

5 Complete the questions with the verbs in the past perfect.

1. Had you been to New York before we went together?
2. Had she wanted to see a Broadway show before I invited her?
3. What sights had you visited before we met?
4. Had they taken the subway before you met them?
5. Had he gone to a baseball game before he went to the USA?
6. How much coffee had you drunk before I saw you?
7. Where had they decided to go before Beth got sick?

6 What are the questions?

1. Where did the immigrants arrive?
2. When did most immigrants come?
3. What did the people first see?
4. Where did poor immigrants travel?
5. Why were they sick?
6. Who did the doctors send back?

Seite 48

1 Find the right word.

1. locker(s)
2. principal
3. grade(s)
4. schedule
5. study hall
6. History class

2 Complete last year's school rules. Use (not) be allowed to and (not) be able to.

1. Steve wasn't allowed to leave early when he finished his homework.
2. Teachers are allowed to give detentions.
3. Jackie, you aren't allowed to bring your skateboard to school.
4. Students aren't allowed to eat during classes.
5. Mr. Grant is able to speak German. Talk to him if you need help.
6. Students are able to use computers in class when the teacher says its OK.
7. Matt and Ramon aren't able to work together. They always fight. Don't put them together.
8. Kayla isn't able to listen very well. She needs the teachers' help.

3 Ask and answer Sue's questions.

1. Sue: Did you have to wear a uniform?
   Kate: No, I didn't. I just had to wear nice clothes.
2. Sue: Did you have to arrive early?
   Kate: Yes, did. I had to be there at 7:30.
3. Sue: Did you have to take extra classes?
   Kate: Yes, I did. I had to take American History.
4. Sue: Did you have to get a hall pass?
   Kate: No, I didn't. I just had to ask the teacher.
5. Sue: Where did you have to go after lunch?
   Kate: I always had to go to the library.
6. Sue: What did your parents have to do?
   Kate: My parents had to agree.

4 Put in the right words.

This summer Susan has found a job (1). It's in a restaurant which needs summer help (2). It's her job to serve (3) ice cream. She has five co-workers (4), and they are all very friendly. The customers (5) are usually happy too when the sun is shining. Susan works hard and is friendly to everyone. She doesn't want to lose her job (6)!

Seite 49

5 Match the photos with the adjectives.

1. unmotivated
2. responsible
3. lazy
4. helpful
5. busy
6. hard-working

6 Complete what a manager tells his workers.

1. John, if you always leave early, you will get a bad report card.
2. Louise, if you don't talk to the customers, they will think that you aren't polite.
3. Carol, if you wear that short skirt again, I will send you home.
4. George, if you work with a partner, it will be easier to carry the heavy boxes.
5. José, if you don't have your card with you, you will get into trouble.
6. Laura, if you want to get a bonus, you will have to work harder.
7. Janet, if you need extra holidays, we will talk about it later.
8. Michael, if you don't follow the rules, you won't be here for a long time.

7 Complete the dialogues with one or ones.

1. A: Those flowers are beautiful.
   B: Which ones?
   A: The yellow ones.
2. A: I know a better store.
   B: Which one?
   A: The one just opposite.
3. A: Are those CDs cheaper?
   B: Which ones?
   A: The ones on the small table.
4. A: Have you got a credit card?
   B: I don't need one. I've got $50.
5. A: Do you know that girl?
   B: Which one?
   A: The one with the red top.

Seite 70

1 Choose the most polite answer.

1. a; 2. b; 3. a; 4. a; 5. b; 6. b

2 Ask questions.

a)

1. Did you arrive yesterday?
2. Do you always drive there?
3. Will you go home tomorrow?
4. Did you make the pumkin pie this morning?
5. Did you move here two months ago?
6. Will you come for Thanksgiving again next year?

b)

1. Do your children often help you in the kitchen?
2. Did you cook everything yesterday evening?
3. Do you always enjoy cooking?
4. Do you usually invite the same people?
5. Will you come to tea with us next weekend?

3 Complete the questions with where, what, when, who, why and choose the right answer.

1. Where are you flying to?
   c) To Portland, Maine.
2. Who will you stay with there?
   b) I'll stay with grandpa.
3. Where does he live?
   a) He lives on a farm.
4. What time will you get there?
   a) I'll arrive late.
5. When did you visit him the last time?
   c) Last Thanksgiving, I think.
6. Why do you like it there?
   b) Because I can often go to the beach.

Seite 71

4 Which of the devices (1–6) do the people need?

1. 3 washing machine
2. 6 headphones
3. 1 microwave
4. 5 cell phone
5. 4 hairdryer
6. 2 fridge

5 What did the two girls say? Make sentences with If I ....

Rachel (Amish):

1. If I had electricity at home, I would iron all my clothes.
2. If I owned a TV, evenings would not be so boring.
3. If I didn't live in the Amish community, I would still go to church on Sundays.

Maisie (high school student):

4. If I didn't have a cell phone, I would talk more to my friends.
5. If I didn't go to school by car, I would walk and be more fit.
6. If I didn't always make meals in the microwave, I would cook better food.
7. If I didn't hang out with my friends so much on the weekends, I would help Mum at home.

6 Make the questions and answer them.

1. A: What would you do if you lived in an Amish community for a day?
   B: If I lived in an Amish community, I would miss my phone.
2. A: What would you do if you went to the Northeast of America?
   B: If I went to the Northeast of America, I would visit Niagara Falls.
3. A: What would you do if you lived thousands of kilometres away from your family?
   B: If I lived thousands of kilometres away from my family, I would call them every day.
4. A: What would you do if you had only one day in America?
   B: If I had only one day in America, I would take a tour of New York City.
5. A: What would you do if you found a gun?
   B: If I found a gun, I would call the police.
6. A: What would you do if your friend was unhappy?
   B: If my friend was unhappy, I would tell him a joke.

Seite 92

1 Read these sentences from ads. Fill in the missing adjectives.

1. We have an informative brochure with lots of tips for you.
2. You will find the Grand Canyon fascinating.
3. What makes California so special? Come and find out!
4. Our trips are never boring.
5. We promise you'll have a great time!
6. There are lots of interesting activities for families.
7. Come to the show. It's so funny, so you will laugh a lot.

2 Describe the ad.

1. headline
2. slogan
3. layout
4. message

3 Simple present or present progressive?

The Brown family lives (1) in Chicago. They always go (2) to California in the summer. At the moment they are renting (3) a house in San Fransisco. Their daughter is there, but their son Bruce is not travelling (4) with them this time because he is skiing (5) in Canada. Mr Brown usually goes (6) shopping for the family, and he is doing (7) that now. But sometimes he doesn't understand (8) what people say because many people speak (9) Spanish in California. So he is learning (10) Spanish durng this trip.

Seite 93

4 Complete the sentences with an adjective or an adverb.

1. My American friend Olivia get excited easily.
2. And she often talks excitedly about her home.
3. She enjoys telling lots of funny jokes.
4. But sometimes Olivia has a bad day. Then she misses California and feels sad.
5. She had a good life there. She liked the beautiful beaches.
6. She is a good surfer, and she can swim very fast.
7. She lived there happily, but her friend didn't feel well in Berlin.

5 Find the opposites.
1. in fashion – out of fashion
2. trendy – outdated
3. make a friend request – unfriend
4. share – keep
5. funny – serious

6 Make sentences with the present perfect and use for or since.
1. California has become more and more important since the Gold Rush.
2. Silicon Valley has been the home of high-tech industry since the 1990s.
3. We have lived here since 2014.
4. I have followed the best trends here for years.
5. I haven't watched TV for two weeks because I prefer online videos.
6. Todays's teenagers have known the internet since they were little.
7. For a number of years people have bought more phones than computers.

7 Complete the dialogue with the present perfect or the simple past.
1. A: Have you seen my new smartphone yet? I bought it last week.
2. B: Yes, you showed it to me yesterday afternoon.
3. A: But what did you think of it? You haven't told me.
4. B: Well, I took some cool photos with it yesterday. But I have always preferred having a bigger one.
5. A: Really? I didn't choose a big one because my bag was too small. I have had the phone for about a week, but I haven't learned half the things I can do with it yet.
6. B: Have you tried e-books yet? I haven't bought a paper book since last year. I have already read lots of e-books on my phone.

Seite 112

1 Find the country.
1. India
2. France
3. Africa
4. Scotland
5. Italy
6. Spain

2 How does New Orleans get ready for Mardi Gras? Make sentences in the simple present passive.
1. Fantastic costumes are made.
2. Special food is cooked.
3. A small plastic baby is put in some cakes.
4. Lots of parties are celebrated before Mardi Gras.
5. The faces of the guests aren't seen.
6. Small presents are bought to throw at the crowds.

3 Choose was or were.
1. New homes were built with their help.
2. The workers weren't tolerated by some people.
3. The smell of their food wasn't liked by others.
4. But many other people disliked that their jobs were taken away.
5. The new immigrants were accepted as part of the multicultural society.
6. These different opinions were accepted by the city government.
7. It was decided to find solutions quickly.

Seite 113

4 Make passive sentences in the simple past about New Orleans.
1. New Orleans was founded in 1718 by the French.
2. French houses were built in the city centre.
3. In 1763 the city was given to Spain.
4. At the end of the 18th century the French houses were lost in two terrible fires.
5. New houses were built by Spanish people.
6. The state was sold to to the United States.
7. In the 20th century cheap houses were rented by many artists.

5 Put the sentences in each of the dialogues in the correct order.
1. C; A; D; B
2. A; D; B; C

6 Report what the people say at an alligator farm.
1. Sarah says (that) she plans to see and do everything on the farm.
2. Luke says (that) he loves the boat trips.
3. Carol asks if she will get wet on the boat trip.
4. Alice asks if a boat trip costs extra.
5. Sophie and Ken say (that) they find the guides very friendly and helpful.
6. Jeff says he doesn't think (that) the cages are very clean.
7. Angela asks if she can hold a baby alligator.

7 Report what a girl told you yesterday about life in Florida.

1. She said (that) they played outside from January to December.
2. She said (that) she didn't need a winter coat.
3. She said (that) she often went to an outdoor movie.
4. She said (that) her parents took her to Disney World every year.
5. She said (that) they learned to swim before they could walk.
6. She said (that) they never had to drive in the snow.
7. She said (that) she wore flip flops every day.

Lösungen Mediation

1. It said that the United States is free (from Great Britain).
2. President …
3. November
4. political, religious, economic reasons
5. Africans; people from Africa
6. New Hampshire, Massachusetts, Rhode Island, Connecticut, New York, New Jersey, Pennsylvania, Delaware, Maryland, Virginia, North Carolina, South Carolina, Georgia
7. Cherokee, Navajo, Sioux, Chippewa, Choctaw, Pueblo, Apache, Iroquois, Creek, Blackfeet, Seminole, Cheyenne, Arawak, Shawnee, Mohegan, Huron, Oneida, Lakota, Crow, Teton, Hopi, Inuit
8. Pacific (Ocean)
9. because there are 50 states
10. New Year's Day, Martin Luther King, Jr. Day, Presidents' Day, Memorial Day, Independence Day, Labor Day, Columbus Day, Veterans Day, Thanksgiving, Christmas

Lösungen Grammatik

TEST YOURSELF

G1
1. had
2. liked
3. did not / didn't take
4. did … do
5. Were
6. was not / wasn't

G2
1. had left
2. had not / hadn't done
3. had … started
4. had … done
5. had lived
6. had not / hadn't seen

G3
1. could not / couldn't / was not / wasn't allowed to
2. had to
3. could / was able to / was allowed to
4. did not / didn't have to
5. could / were allowed to
6. could not / couldn't / was not able to / wasn't able to

G4
1. need; will / 'll help
2. do not / don't phone; will / 'll be
3. does not / doesn't come; will / 'll lose
4. will not / won't find; does not / doesn't look
5. will / 'll talk; meet
6. will not / won't sleep; read

G5
1. ones
2. one
3. ones
4. ones
5. one
6. one

G6
1. aren't you?
2. isn't it?
3. weren't you?
4. don't you?
5. didn't you?
6. does he?

G7
1. Do
2. does
3. will
4. Did
5. –
6. did

G8
1. visited; would be
2. had; would not / wouldn't meet
3. was / were; would like
4. would … miss; did not / didn't come
5. would not / wouldn't worry; lived
6. would be; did not / didn't phone

G9
1. goes
2. is not / isn't surfing
3. Are … listening
4. do not / don't like
5. do … do
6. meet

G10
1. fast; slowly
2. well; easily
3. pretty
4. good; hard
5. heavily
6. unhappy

G11
1. has … met
2. have not / haven't seen
3. has … not called / hasn't … called
4. Have … forgotten
5. have not / haven't been
6. Have … watched

G12
1. was introduced
2. is made
3. are not / aren't cooked
4. were founded
5. is celebrated
6. was not / wasn't built

G13
1. Anna says (that) they prefer the Everglades.
2. She says (that) she wants to go on a boat tour.
3. She says (that) she doesn't like all those crowds.
4. She says (that) she doesn't want to feed the alligators.
5. She asks Ethan if he knows Florida.
6. She asks Ethan what he thinks.

G14
1. Al Lane said (that) he often worked with the alligators.
2. He said (that) some tourists didn't like alligators.
3. He said (that) they fed the animals at 10 o'clock.
4. He said (that) it was too late to feed the alligators.
5. He said (that) he didn't speak German.
6. He said (that) the visitors loved the warm weather.

Bildquellennachweis

Cover.1 Getty Images (Photolibrary/Nick Daly), München; **Cover.2** Getty Images (The Image Bank), München; **2.1** Getty Images (Photolibrary/Maremagnum), München; **3.1** Alamy Stock Photo (World History Archive), Abingdon, Oxon; **3.2** plainpicture GmbH & Co. KG (Michael Runkel), Hamburg; **4.1** Getty Images (Lonely Planet/jean pierre lescourret), München; **5.1** Getty Images (Stockbyte), München; **5.2** Getty Images (Daniel Zuchnik), München; **8.7** Getty Images RF (The Image Bank), München; **8.6** Getty Images (Corbis), München; **8.3** Getty Images (Perspectives), München; **8.4** Getty Images (First Light), München; **8.8** plainpicture GmbH & Co. KG (Ableimages/David Harrigan), Hamburg; **8.5** Getty Images (National Geographic Magazines), München; **8.1** Getty Images (Iconica), München; **8.2** Getty Images (E+/Ron Thomas), München; **8.9** plainpicture GmbH & Co. KG (Aurora Photos/Josh Miller), Hamburg; **10.6** Getty Images (The Image Bank), München; **10.3** Getty Images (Bettmann), München; **10.11** Getty Images (Lonely Planet), München; **10.12** Getty Images (Lonely Planet), München; **10.13** Getty Images (Universal Images Group), München; **10.1** Getty Images (DigitalGlobe), München; **10.2** Getty Images (The Image Bank), München; **10.9** Getty Images (Tim Fitzharris), München; **10.15** Getty Images (Photodisc), München; **10.16** Getty Images (Alan Copson), München; **10.17** Getty Images (David Sucsy), München; **10.14** Getty Images (Science Source), München; **10.4** plainpicture GmbH & Co. KG (Fancy Images/Whisson/Jordan), Hamburg; **10.7** plainpicture GmbH & Co. KG (Image Source/Gu), Hamburg; **10.8** Getty Images (Corbis Documentary), München; **10.18** Getty Images (Cameron Davidson), München; **10.5** By John Dunlap, text by Thomas Jefferson et al. - http://lcweb2.loc.gov/cgi-bin/ampage?collId=rbc3&fileName=rbc0001_2004pe76546page.db, Public Domain, https://commons.wikimedia.org/w/index.php?curid=33408334; **10.10** By Orlando Scott Goff, Bismarck, Dakota Territory - Heritage Auctions, Public Domain, https://commons.wikimedia.org/w/index.php?curid=27530348; **12.1** Getty Images (Photolibrary/Maremagnum), München; **12.2** plainpicture GmbH & Co. KG (Gine Seitz), Hamburg; **13.1** Avenue Images GmbH (ponton), Hamburg; **13.3** Getty Images (Moment/© 2014 Noppon Umnajwannaphan), München; **13.2** Getty Images (Lonely Planet/Michael Marquand), München; **14.2** Alamy Stock Photo (Etcheverry Images), Abingdon, Oxon; **14.1** Thinkstock (LUNAMARINA), München; **19** Song: Empire State of Mind, Text: CARTER, SHAWN/HUNTE, ANGELA/KEYES, BERT/Keys, Alicia/Robinson, Sylvia/SEWELL, JANET ANDREA/SHUCKBURGH, ALEXANDER WILLIAM, Verlag: Carter Boys Music / EMI April Music / Foray Music / Gambi Music Inc / Global Talent Publishing / J Sewell Publishing / Lellow Productions Inc / Masani El Shabazz EMI Music Publishing Germany GmbH, Berlin / Rolf Budde Musikverlag GmbH, Berlin / Neue Welt Musikverlag GmbH, Hamburg; **19.1** Corbis (PT Images/Tetra Images), Berlin; **19.2** plainpicture GmbH & Co. KG (Kniel Synnatzschke), Hamburg; **22.1** Alamy Stock Photo (The Print Collector), Abingdon, Oxon; **25.1** shutterstock (Vacclav), New York, NY; **25.3** Thinkstock (stu99), München; **25.2** Alamy Stock Photo (Michael Dwyer), Abingdon, Oxon; **25.4** Thinkstock (iStockphoto), München; **26.1** Getty Images (Lonely Planet/jean pierre lescourret), München; **27.1** Reis, Axel, Oberderdingen; **28.1** Thinkstock (william87), München; **28.2** Thinkstock (Medioimages/Photodisc), München; **28.5** Thinkstock (kasto80), München; **28.6** Thinkstock (eyfoto), München; **28.4** Thinkstock (RobertCrum), München; **28.3** Thinkstock (Digital Vision), München; **30.3** Thinkstock (mlharing), München; **30.1** Getty Images (First Light), München; **30.2** Getty Images (Gallo Images), München; **32.2** Alamy Stock Photo (World History Archive), Abingdon, Oxon; **32.1** Thinkstock (welcomia), München; **33.3** Getty Images (J. Meric), München; **33.1** Thinkstock (IPGGutenbergUKLtd), München; **33.2** Alamy Stock Photo (Martin Shields), Abingdon, Oxon; **34.5** Getty Images, München; **34.1** Thinkstock (LivingImages), München; **34.3** Alamy Stock Photo (Marjorie Kamys Cotera/Bob Daemmrich Photography /), Abingdon, Oxon; **34.4** Getty Images (Universal Images Group), München; **34.5** Alamy Stock Photo (Bob Daemmrich), Abingdon, Oxon; **34.2** plainpicture GmbH & Co. KG (Fancy Images/Hero), Hamburg; **35** Song: Cool Kids, Text: Dzwonek, Jesiah/Sierota, Graham/Sierota, Jamie/Sierota, Jefery/Sierota, Noah/Sierota Sydney, Verlag: Echosmith Songs/WB Music Corp./Jeffery David Songs/Upcast Music D/A/CH Neue Welt Musikverlag GmbH, Hamburg/Roba Music Verlag GmbH, Hamburg, Reach Music Publishing, Burbank CA; **35.1** Getty Images (The Image Bank), München; **35.2** Getty Images (E+/Pamela Moore), München; **35.3** Alamy Stock Photo (Marjorie Kamys Cotera/Bob Daemmrich Photography), Abingdon, Oxon; **35.5** Getty Images (Fuse), München; **36.5** Thinkstock (Antonius_), München; **36.6** Thinkstock (Ramsey), München; **36.3** Thinkstock (xantuanx), München; **36.2** Thinkstock (Jupiterimages), München; **36.1** Thinkstock (Wylius), München; **36.4** Thinkstock (WestLight), München; **37.1** plainpicture GmbH & Co. KG (Fancy Images/Hero), Hamburg; **41.1** Thinkstock (Creatas), München; **45.1** JDM Productions Inc, New York; **47.1** Getty Images (E+/Steve Debenport), München; **48.1** Thinkstock (Stewart Cohen/Pam Ostrow), München; **49.1** Thinkstock (MaksimVasic), München; **49.3** Thinkstock (Jupiterimages), München; **49.5** Thinkstock (Monkey Business Images), München; **49.6** Thinkstock (Stockbyte), München; **49.4** Thinkstock (Jupiterimages), München; **49.2** Thinkstock (Chelnok), München; **50.1** Thinkstock (Mike Watson Images), München; **50.2** Thinkstock (Enterline Design Services LLC), München; **50.3** plainpicture GmbH & Co. KG (Image Source), Hamburg; **52.1** plainpicture GmbH & Co. KG (Michael Runkel), Hamburg; **52.2** Getty Images (Corbis), München; **53.1** plainpicture GmbH & Co. KG (NaturePL/Edwin Giesbers), Hamburg; **53.2** Getty Images (Aurora), München; **53.3** f1 online digitale Bildagentur, Frankfurt; **56.1** Getty Images (Thomas M. Barwick INC), München; **58.2** Thinkstock (Flying Colours Ltd), München; **58.1** Alamy Stock Photo (brt PHOTO), Abingdon, Oxon; **59.5** shutterstock (Zorandim), New York, NY; **59.4** MEV Verlag GmbH, Augsburg; **59.3** shutterstock (Maxx-Studio), New York, NY; **59.2** Thinkstock (Oleksiy Mark), München; **59.1** iStockphoto (RF/Sascha Burkard), Calgary, Alberta; **61.1** Getty Images (Taxi/Troy Aossey), München; **62** From: The body, Stephen King, retold by Robin Waterfield; **62.1** Ullstein Bild GmbH (United Archives / KPA), Berlin; **63.1** Ullstein Bild GmbH (United Archives), Berlin; **67.3** JDM Productions Inc, New York; **67.4** JDM Productions Inc, New York; **67.1** JDM Productions Inc, New York; **67.2** JDM Productions Inc, New York; **71.5** shutterstock (Maxx-Studio), New York, NY; **71.6** Avenue Images GmbH (stock disc), Hamburg; **71.2** Thinkstock (iStockphoto), München; **71.1** iStockphoto (RF/Sascha Burkard), Calgary, Alberta; **71.4** shutterstock (Rafa Irusta), New York, NY; **71.3** shutterstock (Adisa), New York, NY; **74.1** shutterstock (mariakraynova), New York, NY; **74.2** plainpicture GmbH & Co. KG (Cl2/Joel Bear Studios),

Hamburg; **75.3** Getty Images (Lonely Planet/jean pierre lescourret), München; **75.1** Getty Images (E+/Johnny Greig), I **75.2** Getty Images (Kiyoshi Ota/Bloomberg), München; **76.5** Getty Images (Blend Images), München; **76.2** Thinkstock München; **76.3** Thinkstock (somchaij), München; **76.4** Alamy Stock Photo (Russ Bishop), Abingdon, Oxon; **76.1** shutters (bikeriderlondon), New York, NY; **77** Song: Surfin' U.S.A., Text: Brian Wilson, Verlag: ARC Music Corp. Good Tunes Music **77.1** Ullstein Bild GmbH (Rolf Schulten), Berlin; **79.3** Beutel, Ulrike, Stuttgart; **79.1** Reis, Axel, Oberderdingen; **79.2** Beute Stuttgart; **79.4** Beutel, Ulrike, Stuttgart; **80.1** Getty Images (Hero Images), München; **81.1** Getty Images (South_agency), München; **83.1** Thinkstock (McIninch), München; **85.1** Alamy Stock Photo (Granger Historical Picture Archive), Abingdon, **86.1** Alamy Stock Photo (Russ Bishop), Abingdon, Oxon; **87.1** Getty Images (E+/Steve Debenport), München; **88.1** Alamy Sto Photo (nik wheeler), Abingdon, Oxon; **89.1** JDM Productions Inc, New York; **91.1** Thinkstock (littlewormy), München; **92.1** Gett Images (Blend Images), München; **92.2** Thinkstock (Gunnar Pippel), München; **93.1** iStockphoto (clu), Calgary, Alberta; **94.2** Re Axel, Oberderdingen; **94.1** Reis, Axel, Oberderdingen; **96.2** Alamy Stock Photo (World History Archive), Abingdon, Oxon; **96.1** Ge Images (Stockbyte), München; **97.1** Getty Images (Hulton Archive/The Print Collector), München; **97.2** Getty Images (Blend Images), München; **97.3** Getty Images (2013 Kevin Mazur), München; **98.1** shutterstock (Michael Rosebrock), New York, NY; **98.2** Thinkstock (emarto), München; **99.7** Thinkstock (silviacrisman), München; **99.1** Klett-Archiv-RF-HF, Stuttgart; **99.3** Klett-Archiv-RF-HF, Stuttgart; **99.5** Geoatlas, Hendaye; **99.2** Klett-Archiv-RF-HF, Stuttgart; **99.4** Geoatlas, Hendaye; **99.6** Thinkstock (Monkey Business Images), München; **99.8** Thinkstock (bubu45), München; **102.2** Getty Images (Stocktrek Images), München; **102.1** Getty Images (Jon Feingersh Photography 2011), München; **104.1** Getty Images (kristian sekulic), München; **106.1** laif (Richard Harbus/Polaris), Köln; **106.2** Picture-Alliance (Everett Collection), Frankfurt; **108.1** Getty Images (Sean Gardner), München; **109.3** February Films, London; **109.4** JDM Productions Inc, New York; **109.2** JDM Productions Inc, New York; **109.1** JDM Productions Inc, New York; **112.3** Getty Images (Tribune News Service), München; **112.1** Getty Images (Erika Goldring), München; **112.6** Getty Images (Mario Tama), München; **112.2** Getty Images (Mario Tama), München; **112.5** Getty Images (Jonathan Bachman), München; **119.5** Getty Images (Fuse), München; **119.3** Alamy Stock Photo (Marjorie Kamys Cotera/Bob Daemmrich Photography), Abingdon, Oxon; **119.4** Alamy Stock Photo (Jane Campbell), Abingdon, Oxon; **119.1** Getty Images (The Image Bank), München; **119.2** Getty Images (E+/Pamela Moore), München; **125.1** iStockphoto (RF/Sascha Burkard), Calgary, Alberta; **125.3** shutterstock (Maxx-Studio), New York, NY; **125.4** MEV Verlag GmbH, Augsburg; **125.5** shutterstock (Zorandim), New York, NY; **125.2** Thinkstock (Oleksiy Mark), München; **126.1** Getty Images (Taxi/Troy Aossey), München; **129.1** Getty Images (Hero Images), München; **131.2** Klett-Archiv-RF-HF, Stuttgart; **131.3** Klett-Archiv-RF-HF, Stuttgart; **131.1** Klett-Archiv-RF-HF, Stuttgart; **131.4** Geoatlas, Hendaye; **131.5** Geoatlas, Hendaye; **134.6** Getty Images (WireImage), München; **134.5** Alamy Stock Photo (PYMCA), Abingdon, Oxon; **134.4** Getty Images (Hulton Archive), München; **134.3** Getty Images (Michael Ochs Archives), München; **134.2** Corbis (Owaki - Kulla), Berlin; **134.1** Getty Images (The Image Bank), München; **135.1** Corbis (Bo Zaunders), Berlin; **135.2** Getty Images (Daniel Zuchnik), München; **136.3** Getty Images (Dorling Kindersley RF), München; **136.2** 08.09.16 mü: Bild ist NICHT gemeinfrei! Muss bei der Kansas Historical Society lizenziert werden: Bildnummer 00373021_high.tif in MDB; **136.1** Getty Images (The Image Bank), München; **137.1** Getty Images (The Image Bank), München; **138.1** Getty Images RF (The Image Bank), München; **138.4** Thinkstock (JoeGough), München; **138.3** Getty Images (National Geographic Magazines), München; **138.2** Getty Images (Popperfoto), München; **139.3** iStockphoto (circlePS), Calgary, Alberta; **139.2** Getty Images (De Agostini Picture Library), München; **139.1** Getty Images (M_a_y_a), München; **140.1** Getty Images RF (The Image Bank), München; **140.4** Getty Images (Jemal Countess), München; **140.3** Getty Images (Kevin Winter), München; **140.2** Getty Images (Corbis Documentary), München; **141.1** Getty Images (Albert L. Ortega), München; **141.2** Getty Images (DreamPictures), München; **142.1** Getty Images RF (The Image Bank), München; **142.3** Getty Images (Corbis Documentary), München; **142.2** Getty Images (Lonely Planet), München; **143.2** Getty Images (Corbis Documentary), München; **143.1** Getty Images (Photographer's Choice), München; **144.4** Getty Images (Jiji Press / AFP), München; **144.3** Getty Images (Lonely Planet), München; **144.2** Getty Images (Photolibrary), München; **144.1** Getty Images (Spencer Sutton), München; **145.1** Getty Images (Gary S. Chapman), München; **147.1** Getty Images (Blend Images), München; **148.1** The Absolutely True Diary of a Part-Time Indian, Author: Sherman Alexie, Illustrator: Ellen Forney, Andersen Press.; **148** The Absolutely True Diary of a Part-Time Indian, Sherman Alexie, Andersen Press; **149.1** The Absolutely True Diary of a Part-Time Indian, Author: Sherman Alexie, Illustrator: Ellen Forney, Andersen Press.; **150.2** The Absolutely True Diary of a Part-Time Indian, Author: Sherman Alexie, Illustrator: Ellen Forney, Andersen Press.; **150.1** The Absolutely True Diary of a Part-Time Indian, Author: Sherman Alexie, Illustrator: Ellen Forney, Andersen Press.; **187.9** Fotolia.com (naughtynut), New York; **187.8** Fotolia.com (blondsteve), New York; **187.7** iStockphoto (Dominic Burke RF), Calgary, Alberta; **187.6** Fotolia.com (thorabeti), New York; **187.5** Fotolia.com (Pavel Losevsky), New York; **187.4** iStockphoto (Marcel Pfost), Calgary, Alberta; **187.3** Fotolia.com (axeldrosta), New York; **187.2** iStockphoto (Michael Utech), Calgary, Alberta; **187.1** iStockphoto (stockcam), Calgary, Alberta; **188.3** Bananastock, Watlington / Oxon; **188.2** Das Fotoarchiv RF (RF), Essen; **188.1** Thinkstock (Owat Tasai), München; **194.11** iStockphoto (Alejandro Rivera), Calgary, Alberta; **194.10** Klett-Archiv (Weccard), Stuttgart; **194.9** Avenue Images GmbH (StockDisc), Hamburg; **194.8** shutterstock (igor.stevanovic), New York, NY; **194.7** Thinkstock (Stockbyte), München; **194.6** Avenue Images GmbH (Digital Vision), Hamburg; **194.5** Fotolia.com (Michael Shake), New York; **194.4** iStockphoto (Steve Debenport), Calgary, Alberta; **194.3** iStockphoto (herreid), Calgary, Alberta; **194.2** shutterstock (bikeriderlondon), New York, NY; **194.1** Fotosearch Stock Photography (Digital Vision), Waukesha, WI; **206.14** iStockphoto (Linda Steward), Calgary, Alberta; **206.13** Fotolia.com (Markus Mainka), New York; **206.12** iStockphoto (kodachrome25), Calgary, Alberta; **206.11** shutterstock (AXL), New York, NY; **206.10** iStockphoto (RF/Lukasz Janicki), Calgary, Alberta;

206.9 Thinkstock (iStock/Wojciech Gajda), München; **206.8** shutterstock (hadot 760), New York, NY; **206.7** Fotolia.com (Angela Jones), New York; **206.6** iStockphoto (David Mathies), Calgary, Alberta; **206.5** Fotolia.com (pondchao), New York; **206.4** shutterstock (Alex Melnick), New York, NY; **206.3** iStockphoto (Marcel Pfost), Calgary, Alberta; **206.2** Fotolia.com (Sharpshot), New York; **206.1** Fotolia.com (Achim Thomae), New York; **212.27** shutterstock (Campre83), New York, NY; **212.26** shutterstock (Various-Everythings), New York, NY; **212.25** shutterstock (Niyazz), New York, NY; **212.24** shutterstock (Steve Allen), New York, NY; **212.23** shutterstock (argus), New York, NY; **212.22** shutterstock (Anchiy), New York, NY; **212.21** shutterstock (NAN SKYBLACK), New York, NY; **212.20** shutterstock (Various-Everythings), New York, NY; **212.19** shutterstock (Various-Everythings), New York, NY; **212.18** shutterstock (Various-Everythings), New York, NY; **212.17** shutterstock (Daboost), New York, NY; **212.16** shutterstock (Niyazz), New York, NY; **212.15** shutterstock (Various-Everythings), New York, NY; **212.14** shutterstock (PhotoStockImage), New York, NY; **212.13** shutterstock (Irina Rumyantseva), New York, NY; **212.12** shutterstock (ArpornSeemaroj), New York, NY; **212.11** shutterstock (Various-Everythings), New York, NY; **212.10** shutterstock (Aleksandar Mijatovic), New York, NY; **212.9** shutterstock (Visionsi), New York, NY; **212.8** shutterstock (stockcreations), New York, NY; **212.7** shutterstock (hlphoto), New York, NY; **212.6** shutterstock (rj lerich), New York, NY; **212.5** shutterstock (Aleksandra Duda), New York, NY; **212.4** shutterstock (Troscha), New York, NY; **212.3** shutterstock (stocksolutions), New York, NY; **212.2** shutterstock (Anna Mandrikyan), New York, NY; **212.1** shutterstock (Iryna Denysova), New York, NY; **213.16** Fotolia.com (Stefano Gasparotto), New York; **213.15** Fotolia.com (Kzenon), New York; **213.14** iStockphoto (Lya_Cattel), Calgary, Alberta; **213.13** shutterstock (Kzenon), New York, NY; **213.12** Fotolia.com (Iuliia Sokolovska), New York; **213.11** shutterstock (Scott Sanders), New York, NY; **213.10** Thinkstock (Jupiterimages), München; **213.9** iStockphoto (Linda Steward), Calgary, Alberta; **213.8** shutterstock (gorillaimages), New York, NY; **213.7** Fotolia.com (Thaut Images), New York; **213.6** Fotolia.com (Robert Pernell), New York; **213.5** Fotolia.com (Sharpshot), New York; **213.4** shutterstock (AXL), New York, NY; **213.3** shutterstock (Alex Melnick), New York, NY; **213.2** Fotolia.com (pondchao), New York; **213.1** iStockphoto (Marcel Pfost), Calgary, Alberta

Textquellennachweis

S. 19: Song: Empire State of Mind, Text: CARTER, SHAWN/HUNTE, ANGELA/KEYES, BERT/Keys, Alicia/Robinson, Sylvia/SEWELL, JANET ANDREA/SHUCKBURGH, ALEXANDER WILLIAM, Verlag: Carter Boys Music / EMI April Music / Foray Music / Gambi Music Inc / Global Talent Publishing / J Sewell Publishing / Lellow Productions Inc / Masani El Shabazz EMI Music Publishing Germany GmbH, Berlin / Rolf Budde Musikverlag GmbH, Berlin / Neue Welt Musikverlag GmbH, Hamburg

S. 35: Song: Cool Kids, Text: Dzwonek, Jesiah/Sierota, Graham/Sierota, Jamie/Sierota, Jefery/Sierota, Noah/Sierota Sydney, Verlag: Echosmith Songs/WB Music Corp./Jeffery David Songs/Upcast Music D/A/CH Neue Welt Musikverlag GmbH, Hamburg/ Roba Music Verlag GmbH, Hamburg, Reach Music Publishing, Burbank CA

S. 62: From: The body, Stephen King, retold by Robin Waterfield

S. 77: Song: Surfin' U.S.A., Text: Brian Wilson, Verlag: ARC Music Corp. Good Tunes Music AG

S. 148 – 151: The Absolutely True Diary of a Part-Time Indian, Sherman Alexie, Andersen Press

Sollte es in einem Einzelfall nicht gelungen sein, den korrekten Rechteinhaber ausfindig zu machen, so werden berechtigte Ansprüche selbstverständlich im Rahmen der üblichen Regelungen abgegolten.

ALASKA
Denali
CANADA
CANADA
Seattle
Portland
WASHINGTON
OREGON
Rocky Mountains
MONTANA
NORTH DAKOTA
IDAHO
WYOMING
SOUTH DAKOTA
NEBRASKA
NEVADA
UTAH
San Francisco
Denver
CALIFORNIA
COLORADO
Las Vegas
ARIZONA
Los Angeles
Pacific Ocean
San Diego
Phoenix
NEW MEXICO
TEXAS
HAWAII
MEXICO

Great
Lakes
INNESOTA
apolis
MICHIGAN
WISCONSIN
Milwaukee
Detroit
IOWA
Chicago
ILLINOIS
INDIANA
OHIO
MISSOURI
KENTUCKY
Nashville
TENNESSEE
ARKANSAS
Mississippi
MISSIS-
SIPPI
ALABAMA
Atlanta
GEORGIA
llas
LOUISIANA
New Orleans
on
Gulf of Mexico
FLORIDA
Miami
Everglades
MAINE
NEW YORK
PENNSYLVANIA
Philadelphia
Boston
New
York
City
WEST
VIRGINIA
Washington, D.C.
VIRGINIA
NORTH CAROLINA
SOUTH
CAROLINA
Atlantic Ocean
1 VERMONT
2 NEW HAMPSHIRE
3 MASSACHUSETTS
4 CONNECTICUT
5 RHODE ISLAND
6 NEW JERSEY
7 MARYLAND
8 DELAWARE
NORTH
WEST
EAST
SOUTH
0
500
1000 km
0
500 miles